CAMBRIDGE TEXTS IN THE HISTORY OF
POLITICAL THOUGHT

CATHARINE MACAULAY
Political Writings

The writings of republican historian and political pamphleteer Catharine
Macaulay (1731–91) played a central role in debates about political reform in
the Age of Enlightenment and Revolution. A critical reader of Hume's
bestselling *History of England*, she broke new ground in historiography by
defending the regicide of Charles I and became an inspiration for many
luminaries of the American and French revolutions. While her historical and
political works engaged with thinkers from Hobbes and Locke to
Bolingbroke and Burke, she also wrote about religion, philosophy, education
and animal rights. Influencing Wollstonecraft and proto-feminism, she
argued that there were no moral differences between men and women and
that boys and girls should receive the same education. This book is the first
scholarly edition of Catharine Macaulay's published writings and includes all
her known pamphlets along with extensive selections from her longer historical and political works.

MAX SKJÖNSBERG is a Leverhulme Early Career Fellow at the University
of Cambridge and a College Research Associate at Emmanuel College. He
has previously been a lecturer in history and politics at the University of St
Andrews and the University of York, and held post-doctoral positions at the
University of Liverpool and the Institute for Advanced Studies in the
Humanities, Edinburgh. He is the author of *The Persistence of Party: Ideas
of Harmonious Discord in Eighteenth-Century Britain* (Cambridge University
Press, 2021). His research has also been published in leading journals, includ-
ing the *Historical Journal*, *Journal of the History of Ideas*, *History of Political
Thought* and *Modern Intellectual History*.

T0381598

CAMBRIDGE TEXTS IN THE HISTORY OF POLITICAL THOUGHT

General editor
QUENTIN SKINNER
Queen Mary University of London

Editorial board
MICHAEL COOK
Princeton University
HANNAH DAWSON
King's College London
ADOM GETACHEW
University of Chicago
EMMA HUNTER
University of Edinburgh
GABRIEL PAQUETTE
University of Oregon
ANDREW SARTORI
New York University
HILDE DE WEERDT
Leiden University

Cambridge Texts in the History of Political Thought is firmly established as the major student series of texts in political theory. It aims to make available all the most important texts in the history of political thought, from ancient Greece to the twentieth century, from throughout the world and from every political tradition. All the familiar classic texts are included, but the series seeks at the same time to enlarge the conventional canon through a global scope and by incorporating an extensive range of less well-known works, many of them never before available in a modern English edition, and to present the history of political thought in a comparative, international context. Where possible, the texts are published in complete and unabridged form, and translations are specially commissioned for the series. However, where appropriate, especially for non-western texts, abridged or tightly focused and thematic collections are offered instead. Each volume contains a critical introduction together with chronologies, biographical sketches, a guide to further reading and any necessary glossaries and textual apparatus. Overall, the series aims to provide the reader with an outline of the entire evolution of international political thought.

For a list of titles published in the series, please see end of book

CATHARINE MACAULAY

Political Writings

EDITED BY

MAX SKJÖNSBERG
University of Cambridge

CAMBRIDGE
UNIVERSITY PRESS

Shaftesbury Road, Cambridge CB2 8EA, United Kingdom

One Liberty Plaza, 20th Floor, New York, NY 10006, USA

477 Williamstown Road, Port Melbourne, VIC 3207, Australia

314–321, 3rd Floor, Plot 3, Splendor Forum, Jasola District Centre,
New Delhi – 110025, India

103 Penang Road, #05–06/07, Visioncrest Commercial, Singapore 238467

Cambridge University Press is part of Cambridge University Press & Assessment,
a department of the University of Cambridge.

We share the University's mission to contribute to society through the pursuit of
education, learning and research at the highest international levels of excellence.

www.cambridge.org
Information on this title: www.cambridge.org/9781009307482

DOI: 10.1017/9781009307451

First published 2023

A catalogue record for this publication is available from the British Library.

A Cataloging-in-Publication data record for this book is available from the Library of Congress.

ISBN 978-1-009-30748-2 Hardback
ISBN 978-1-009-30744-4 Paperback

To my mother

Contents

Contents

Acknowledgements

Like all scholars who publish in this series, I am deeply grateful to Quentin Skinner, and my debt is all the greater since he has given me such stellar advice on my editorial materials. I am also thankful to Julia-Anne Costet, Caroline Ashcroft, Janet Chan, Hannah Dawson, Robin Douglass, Karen Green, Signy Gutnick-Allen, Lucy Moynihan, Johan Olsthoorn and Tim Stuart-Buttle, who read earlier drafts of the manuscript, either in part or in full, and provided me with invaluable feedback and suggestions. I am also thankful to Joseph Hone, Adam Lebovitz, Blair Worden and Samuel Zeitlin for their help with specific references, to Sylvana Tomaselli for her advice and scholarship, and to Richard Bourke for enlightening conversations about the eighteenth century in general. My final thanks are due to Liz Friend-Smith, Natasha Whelan and Hilary Hammond at Cambridge University Press and the anonymous reviewers of my proposal. All the usual caveats apply.

Abbreviations

Correspondence	*The Correspondence of Catharine Macaulay*, ed. Karen Green (Oxford, 2019)
History	Catharine Macaulay, *The History of England from the Accession of James I to the Revolution* (6 vols., London, 1763–83) (vols. I–V were originally entitled *The History of England from the Accession of James I to That of the Brunswick Line*)
History since the Revolution	Catharine Macaulay, *The History of England, from the Revolution to the Present Time, in a Series of Letters to the Reverend Doctor Wilson* (Bath, 1778)
Hume's History	David Hume, *The History of England from the Invasion of Julius Caesar to the Revolution in 1688* (1754–61; 6 vols., Indianapolis, 1983, based on the 1778 ed.)
Letters on Education	Catharine Macaulay, *Letters on Education. With Observations on Religious and Metaphysical Subjects* (London, 1790)
Reflections	Edmund Burke, *Reflections on the Revolution in France, and on the Proceedings in Certain Societies in London Relative to That Event. In a Letter Intended to Have Been Sent to a Gentleman in Paris* (London, 1790)
Works	*The Works of the Late Right Honourable Henry St. John, Lord Viscount Bolingbroke*, ed. David Mallet (5 vols., London, 1754)

Introduction

> There was a Macaulay's History of England long before Lord
> Macaulay's was heard of; and in its day a famous history it was.
>
> Robert Chambers, *The Book of Days* (2 vols., 1863–4)

Catharine Macaulay (1731–91) was a remarkably influential writer in the
second half of the eighteenth century. Her fame rested mainly on her
History of England (8 vols., 1763–83). As a historian, Macaulay was a
moralist who sought to educate and inspire her contemporaries by retell-
ing the great deeds of the English revolutionaries, and reminding them
of the republican political thought of the previous century. In justifying
the regicide of Charles I, she broke new ground in historiography, and
presented a sharp contrast not only to David Hume's sceptical *History of
England* but also to establishment Whig history. While her writings are
today mainly known by specialists, they were widely read and discussed
in her day. For the political reformer James Burgh, her *History* was
simply 'incomparable'.[1] The French Revolutionaries Mirabeau and
Brissot viewed her *History* as the best in its genre. American
Revolutionary luminaries such as George Washington, Thomas
Jefferson and John Adams paid her ample compliments. As Macaulay's
reputation in her native Britain declined in the final decades of the
eighteenth century, Mary Wollstonecraft hoped that posterity would
pay her greater respect.[2] In the nineteenth century, however, the name
Macaulay in historiography became synonymous with Thomas

---

[1] James Burgh, *Political Disquisitions* (3 vols., London, 1774–5), II, p. 18.
[2] Mary Wollstonecraft, *A Vindication of the Rights of Woman* (London, 1792), p. 235.

Babington Macaulay. Even if she was not entirely forgotten in the nineteenth century, with W. E. H. Lecky dubbing her 'the ablest writer of the New Radical School',[3] scholarly interest in Macaulay was not renewed until the second half of the twentieth century. This was largely due to the republican revival among historians such as Caroline Robbins and J. G. A. Pocock on the one hand, and the history of women and feminism on the other.

Macaulay did not write a single systematic treatise on politics but a variety of texts in different genres, including history, educational and religious writings, and pamphlets. Her many writings are unified by her opposition to modern scepticism – historical, political, religious and philosophical – and her championing of the natural rights and liberties of all human beings as well as animals. Along with her advanced ideas about animal rights, her views on women, set out most fully in her *Letters on Education* (1790), may be her most significant contribution to political thought. As her writings on women and education inspired Wollstonecraft, Macaulay played a central role in the history of women's rights and feminism.

This edition aims to do justice to the range and depth of Macaulay's political writings by bringing together all her known publications on politics and history, either in part or in full. It begins with selections from her *History of England*, followed by her political pamphlets, and culminates in her writings on education and the French Revolution published in the penultimate year of her life. Macaulay's final texts brought together, accentuated and clarified many of her long-held views on what she thought was wrong with eighteenth-century society: a society that defended hierarchies of birth in the form of monarchy, aristocracy and patriarchy, while levelling all human beings by holding everyone to be equally passionate and corruptible. For the deeply religious Macaulay, the latter drift risked normalising and exonerating corruption and vice instead of inspiring honesty and virtue, and ultimately prevented human beings from achieving happiness in this life and perfection in the next. This process was further retarded by the general exclusion of animals from human considerations of justice and the mistaken notion that men and women were morally and intellectually distinct. The French Revolution, however, like the English revolution in

---

[3] W. E. H. Lecky, *A History of England in the Eighteenth Century* (1878; 8 vols., London, 1917), III, p. 414.

the seventeenth century, was a providential sign embodying what she regarded as the core teaching of Jesus Christ: the equal rights of all human beings.

The remainder of this introduction provides a sketch of Macaulay's life – including its familial and social settings, and her political networks – as well as an outline of some of her most important political and philosophical commitments, and their contexts. Additionally, each text is given its own individual introduction, which briefly sets out its specific historical and intellectual significance.

Catharine Macaulay's Life and Works

On 23 March 1731,[4] Catharine Macaulay was born as Catharine Sawbridge into a gentry family with strong mercantile and political links. She grew up on an estate in Wye, Kent, bought by her grandfather Jacob Sawbridge (1665–1748) in 1717, when he was one of the original directors of the then still successful South Sea Company. Elected as a Member of Parliament for Crickdale in 1715, Jacob Sawbridge was an opposition Whig who voted to repeal the Tory party's Occasional Conformity and Schism Acts. He was also one of only thirty-three Whigs who voted against the Septennial Act of 1716, which extended the maximum life of Parliament from three to seven years. After the South Sea Bubble in 1720 – and the fraud and corruption that accompanied the company's collapse – he was arrested and expelled from Parliament. Allowed to keep only £5,000 out of a fortune of £77,000 (equivalent to approximately £600,000 and £9 million respectively in 2017), Sawbridge was classed by the House of Commons as among the more culpable of the directors. He was allowed to keep the family home by giving it as a wedding gift to his son John, Macaulay's father. Jacob Sawbridge's experience certainly contributed to his granddaughter's loathing of modern finance. She would later seek to vindicate him in her historical writings.[5]

The first marriage of John Sawbridge (1699–1762) did not produce any children, as his wife Elizabeth (née Turner) died shortly after they were wedded in July 1727. Just over a year later he married Dorothy – heiress of wealthy London banker George Wanley – with whom he had

[4] 23 March 1730, old style.   [5] *History since the Revolution*, pp. 306–7.

xiii

two sons, John and Wanley, and two daughters, Dorothy and Catharine. Macaulay's father was an admirer of the opposition Whig William Pulteney, but this admiration turned into disgust when Pulteney became a courtier upon the fall of Sir Robert Walpole in 1742.[6] Macaulay's mother died in childbirth in 1733 at the age of twenty-two. When John Sawbridge (senior) passed away nearly thirty years later, his son John inherited a fortune and the family estate, Wanley received £3,000 (along with a further £5,000 gifted to him by his brother), while Dorothy and Catharine inherited £50 each.

With no extant memoirs or diary entries, Macaulay's earliest known correspondence dates from 1762, when she was in her early thirties. Because of the lack of evidence, we do not know exactly when she began her studies. While she was inspired by the ancients, she later admitted to being not particularly well versed in classical works. This made her all the more convinced of the importance of female education. 'It is under a full sense of the many inconveniences that I have my self struggled with that I recommend a learned education to Women,' she wrote to the editor of the *Monthly Review* after the appearance of her *Letters on Education* in 1790.[7] It is clear, however, that despite their financial setback, the Sawbridges amassed an impressive library, which is likely to have formed the basis of Macaulay's early education. From a recorded conversation she had with the classicist Elizabeth Carter (1717–1806) in 1757, we learn about Macaulay's 'interest in the Spartan laws [and] the Roman politics'. Early sources of these interests were the English translations of the *Ancient History* and *History of Rome* by the Jansenist Charles Rollin (1661–1741) and Jean Crevier (1693–1765). These popular pedagogical works analysed the mixed and balanced governments of Sparta and Rome, Sparta's equal distribution of land and its aversion to luxury, and Rome's embrace of patriotism – themes that would have a lasting influence on Macaulay's political thought.

In 1760 Catharine Sawbridge married the Scottish widower Dr George Macaulay, educated at Edinburgh and Padua. George Macaulay was related to several prominent thinkers of the Scottish Enlightenment via his sister Anne's marriage to David Gregorie, a grandson of David Gregory (1625–1720), many of whose descendants became prominent scholars at Aberdeen. George Macaulay was also a

[6] Ibid., p. 422.
[7] Macaulay to Ralph Griffiths, November 1790, in *Correspondence*, p. 290.

distant cousin of the Scottish man of letters Tobias Smollett (1721–71). More important for his wife's political journey was his connection with Thomas Hollis (1720–74). Hollis was one of the early publishers of the commonwealth canon as well as a collector of tracts and paraphernalia relating to the English republicans of the seventeenth century. He continued the publishing enterprise of John Toland (1677–1720) at the turn of the century, reprinting and disseminating works by Algernon Sidney, Edmund Ludlow, Marchamont Nedham, Henry Neville and John Locke, and Toland's *Life of Milton* – the bread and butter of Macaulay's political thought. Hollis designed a frontispiece to the third volume of Macaulay's *History of England* in 1767, which depicted Macaulay as the goddess of liberty.

George Macaulay was supportive of his wife's literary aspirations. By the mid eighteenth century many women had distinguished themselves in literature. Nevertheless, it was unusual for a woman to write history, which was one of the most widely read and politicised genres of the time, as the *Monthly Review* remarked on the appearance of the first volume of the *History* in 1763. Mary Astell's *Impartial Enquiry into the Causes of the Rebellion and Civil War* (1704) was a partial exception, but it was a pamphlet rather than a multivolume work of narrative history. A notable and more recent predecessor was her acquaintance Sarah Scott (1720–95), who published *The History of Gustavus Ericson, King of Sweden* and *The History of Mecklenburgh* in 1761 and 1762 respectively. The appearance of the first volume of Macaulay's *History of England* became a literary sensation thanks to its explosive content as well as the sex of the author.

In 1765 Macaulay gave birth to her only child, Catharine Sophia. A year later, George Macaulay died after a period of bad health, leaving all his property to his widow. As a relatively wealthy widow, she held weekly meetings with political and literary friends at her home in Berners Street, London. In the early 1770s her own health became more precarious, leading to a hiatus of ten years between the publication of the fifth and sixth volumes of the *History*, which appeared in 1771 and 1781. In the interval Macaulay published a series of pamphlets on British politics and a work of contemporary history. Macaulay and her daughter moved to Bath in 1774, to reside with widower and retired rector the Reverend Thomas Wilson (1703–84), who belonged to similar political circles. Wilson was a friend of the Presbyterian minister John Leland (1691–1766) and the addressee of Leland's two-volume *View of the*

Principal Deistical Writers (1754–5), which defended Christianity from the infamous onslaught of Henry St John, 1st Viscount Bolingbroke (1678–1751). While she approved of many of Bolingbroke's political and historical writings, Macaulay would present similar criticisms of his religious writings in her own works on religion and philosophy.

Macaulay addressed her *History of England from the Revolution to the Present Time in a Series of Letters to a Friend* (1778) to Wilson. Their relationship ended abruptly that same year, however, when Macaulay married for the second time. Her new husband was the 21-year-old Scottish ship steward William Graham (1757–1845). At this stage, Macaulay was a literary celebrity, and the fact that she was more than twice her new husband's age predictably attracted critical remarks from both male and female commentators in the public sphere. It may even have affected the sales of her works, as the *New Annual Register* pointed out in 1781 in a review of the sixth and seventh volumes of the *History*.

In any event, Macaulay's second marriage had, if anything, a positive impact on her productivity. In 1783 she published her first philosophical work, *A Treatise on the Immutability of Moral Truth*, in favour of rational religion – that is, the conviction that everyone is able to comprehend their moral and religious duties and achieve salvation – and in opposition to philosophical and religious scepticism. In the same year the eighth and final volume of her *History* also appeared. After a trip to the newly independent United States of America in 1784, where she was a guest of George Washington and other luminaries, and a second visit to France in 1785–6, Macaulay retired to Berkshire and turned her attention to writing a treatise on education. The third part of *Letters on Education* (1790) also repackaged and to an extent revised her philosophical views set out in the *Treatise*, which had been rather unkindly received. Later that same year she published her final work, a rapidly put together but well-crafted reply to Edmund Burke's *Reflections on the Revolution in France* (1790). Though well-received, her *Observations* was quickly over-shadowed by Thomas Paine's *Rights of Man* (1791). Macaulay died in June 1791, and only a year later Wollstonecraft lamented in *A Vindication of the Rights of Woman* (1792) that Macaulay's reputation was waning.[8]

---

[8] Wollstonecraft, *Vindication of the Rights of Woman*, p. 235.

Macaulay's Political Circle

Members of Macaulay's circle are frequently called 'radicals', and sometimes 'radical Whigs' (or 'Real Whigs'), but there are reasons for avoiding
these terms. 'Radical' only gained political traction in the nineteenth
century as a term for the followers of Jeremy Bentham (John Stuart
Mill's philosophical radicals). 'Whig' was a crucial contemporary term,
but its ubiquity makes it less helpful. Many parliamentary groupings
sought to claim the Whig label, and the most organised connection which
called itself Whig was an aristocratic one led by Charles Watson-
Wentworth, 2nd Marquess of Rockingham (1730–82). The Rockingham
party often co-operated with elements of Macaulay's political circle, but
while they sometimes made common cause and shared some traditions,
they were distinct and generally of different temperaments. Macaulay
differed fundamentally with the Rockingham party and its chief publicist,
Burke, on key questions, including parliamentary reform. Like Paine,
moreover, she had no attachment to the Whig label, and had no qualms
about citing and celebrating Tories and even Jacobites in her works.[9]

The members of her circle are sometimes labelled as republicans and
commonwealthmen, which were terms in use at the time, and especially
appropriate in relation to Hollis's publishing activities. They are in some
ways pertinent for Macaulay too, since they look back to the seventeenth
century and the writers and events which shaped her politics. But republicanism had a loose meaning in the eighteenth century, and it was often
used humorously, as an accusation or an insult. When used affirmatively,
it rarely entailed hostility to monarchy as such, at least before the
American and French revolutions. While Macaulay at times seems to have
taken pleasure in her reputation as 'a hater of kings',[10] it does not apply to
many others in her circle, and in her more serious moments Macaulay
accepted the institution of monarchy, though reluctantly. According to her
friend Horace Walpole, Macaulay and her brother were two chiefs of 'an
avowed though very small Republican party' in the late 1760s and early
1770s.[11] We will return to the nature of Macaulay's republicanism and her
views on liberty below.

---

[9] See, e.g., *History since the Revolution*, pp. 33, 59.
[10] Macaulay to George Simon, 17 January 1778, in *Correspondence*, p. 80.
[11] Horace Walpole, *Memoirs and Portraits*, ed. Matthew Hodgart (rev. ed., London, 1963),
     p. 209.

Macaulay's broader circle could simply be identified as reformist, a term with political and religious connotations that often but not always went together. Since the accession of George III and the onset of the American crisis in the 1760s, the Protestant Dissenters had become increasingly dissatisfied with the limitations of the Toleration Act 1689 and the fact that they remained formally barred from holding political office under the Test and Corporation Acts. In the second half of the eighteenth century, the Dissenters and their allies took the lead in calling for the reform of Britain's unequal and irregular system of parliamentary representation. There were, however, different kinds of reformers at the time. The Rockingham Whigs, under Burke's guidance, were distrustful of constitutional reform. They wanted Parliament to limit the power of the crown, but they believed that this could be most effectively done through party solidarity and later by 'economical reform' to curtail and supervise the crown's budget. This approach was insufficient for Macaulay and her circle, who usually referred to themselves as 'the Friends of Liberty', and often Patriots. The Patriot programme was effectively summarised by John Adams (1735–1826) in a letter to Macaulay describing her brother John Sawbridge's political principles: 'Shorter parliaments, a more equitable Representation, the abolition of Taxes and the Payment of the Debt, the Reduction of Placemen and Pensioners, the annihilation of Corruption, the Reformation of Luxury, Dissipation & Effeminacy, the Disbanding of the Army'.[12]

The most important person in Macaulay's political circle was her brother Sawbridge, a prominent politician in London as well as a Member of Parliament for Hythe in 1768–74 and for London between 1774 and his death in 1795. He was known for annually (and unsuccessfully) introducing a motion to repeal the Septennial Act. Macaulay repeatedly praised and promoted her brother's political conduct in her correspondence. She viewed him and herself as united and involved in 'the glorious cause of liberty and man', as she wrote after his election to Parliament in 1768.[13] By not retiring after dinner with the ladies when dining in his company, Macaulay enraged other female writers such as Elizabeth Montagu (1718–1800).

---

[12] John Adams to Macaulay, 28 December 1774, in *Correspondence*, p. 123.
[13] Macaulay to William Harris, [July 1769?], in *Correspondence*, p. 63.

In the 1760s John Wilkes (1725–97) emerged as a political figure of critical importance. Arrested for seditious libel after criticising the king's speech in 1763 in *North Briton*, and declared an outlaw in the following year, Wilkes fled to France to avoid imprisonment on these grounds and for the publication of his scandalous *Essay on Woman*, a satire of Alexander Pope's *Essay on Man*. In 1768 he was compelled to return to England due to his dire financial situation and sought election to Parliament to obtain legal immunity. The Grafton ministry expelled him from Parliament, but Wilkes was repeatedly re-elected and ejected as MP for Middlesex in a series of by-elections, all the while himself being locked up in the King's Bench prison. The whole episode led to significant unrest in London, as Wilkes's cause mustered popular support. The question of whether the House of Commons could rightfully disqualify a representative elected by the people raised constitutional questions, and commentators from many corners, from Samuel Johnson to Jean-Jacques Rousseau, voiced their opinions.

Macaulay (and her first husband) did not approve of Wilkes's womanising and his anti-Scottish propaganda (directed at the king's Scottish favourite, John Stuart, 3rd Earl of Bute), but they defended his cause. This position was similar to that of their acquaintance William Pitt the Elder (the Earl of Chatham after 1766), who is reported to have praised her *History* in Parliament. In fact, the Macaulays were close not only to Wilkes's intellectual antagonist Smollett, author of *The Briton*, but also to Charles Townshend, who served in the Bute administration. Macaulay and her brother Sawbridge were caught up in Wilkes's campaign to be reinstated as the representative of Middlesex in 1768–70. She even lent money to Wilkes to help him pay his debts when he was imprisoned, although it is apparent that she resented his profligacy. In the early 1770s Sawbridge along with the reformers John Horne Tooke and Richard Oliver separated from the Wilkeite Society of the Gentlemen Supporters of the Bill of Rights and established the rival Constitutional Society. Many of the Protestant Dissenters in the reformist camp were deeply religious and disapproved of Wilkes's philandering and indebtedness. In the general election of 1774, however, Sawbridge and Wilkes were reunited.

Macaulay inspired founding members of the Society for Constitutional Information (SCI) – perhaps especially Capel Lofft – which was set up in April 1780 and joined by her brother. This society campaigned for parliamentary reform and universal male suffrage, following John Cartwright's *Take Your Choice!* (1776). Macaulay does not seem to have been involved with the SCI and appears to have become somewhat more marginalised in the 1780s than she had been in London politics in the late 1760s and early 1770s. At the same time, Jacques-Pierre Brissot de Warville, later one of the leaders of the Girondins during the French Revolution, was in London between 1782 and 1784, and he befriended Macaulay, whose *History* he admired and would later cite in defence of the right to have Louis XVI tried. As we shall see, the outbreak of the French Revolution threw her back into contemporary political debates.

Macaulay's History *and David Hume*

Macaulay's historical enterprise was explicitly written in opposition to Hume's bestselling but highly controversial history. In terms of method, she used manuscript sources to a far greater extent than Hume, one of which Hume in fact quoted in later editions of his *History of England* (6 vols., 1754–61).[14] More importantly, Macaulay's alleged strict political approach to history has sometimes been called old-fashioned in comparison with Hume's more philosophical and social approach.[15] Notably, her historical works do not engage with contemporary discussions of the historical 'progress of women', the feminisation of manners, or the economic and intellectual advantages of a mixed-gender public culture.[16] We should note, however, that Macaulay, like Hume in his *History*, paid attention to the economic and social circumstances of political changes and ideas. Her citations of Hume's *History* are many and they are not all hostile. Like Hume, she stressed the importance of accident and contingency in the development of the spirit of liberty, which had been stumbled upon before it had been theorised. 'Liberty, in an enlarged sense, was never a general principle of action among the English,' she wrote in a Humean spirit.[17] Moreover, her analysis of the state of politics, and its absolutist

---

[14] *Hume's History*, v, p. 575.
[15] J. G. A. Pocock, 'Catharine Macaulay: Patriot Historian', in *Women Writers and the Early Modern British Political Tradition*, ed. H. Smith (Cambridge, 1998), pp. 243–58.
[16] Karen O'Brien, *Women and Enlightenment in Eighteenth-Century Britain* (Cambridge, 2009), p. 154.
[17] *History*, IV, p. 160 (note).

nature, at the accession of James I in 1603 was highly reliant on Hume, as she happily acknowledged. Nevertheless, the differences between Macaulay and Hume are key to understanding her intentions.

Hume's *History* was not intended to favour any specific party, either in his own day or in the past. However, he certainly attempted to exonerate the Stuart monarchs, villainised by Whigs, from constitutional misconduct, and he was predictably accused of Toryism and Jacobitism, in other words, of being a supporter of the exiled Stuart court. Much of the criticism of Hume's *History* had an anti-Scottish dimension, as Scotland was the native land of the Stuart dynasty and had frequently been the nerve centre of Jacobitism. Macaulay, unlike Wilkes, can hardly be accused of anti-Scottish xenophobia since both her husbands were Scottish. She also had many Scottish friends and admirers, one of them writing to her in 1769: 'I must do Scotland the justice to say that I have heard several people in it claim you . . . & that some few have even a very high opinion not only of the Stile but the Candor & Spirit of your History.'[18]

Despite a degree of mutual respect, Macaulay and Hume both acknowledged in their only known exchange of letters that they differed in 'original principles'. According to Hume, political arrangements were grounded in the acceptance of useful conventions. Any established authority that could uphold useful and indeed necessary conventions such as property rights was therefore lawful, he believed. He wrote in his letter to Macaulay that he viewed 'all kinds of subdivisions of power, from the monarchy of France to the free democracy of some Swiss Cantons, to be equally legal, if established by custom and authority'. In his letter to Macaulay, Hume repeated the notorious argument from his *History* that the first Stuart monarchs of England simply supported the strong royal government which had been left to them by Elizabeth I, and they were therefore largely blameless. Instead, it was the partisans of the cause of liberty who had disgraced their cause, noble and generous in itself, 'by their violence, and also by their cant, hypocrisy, and bigotry'.[19] Macaulay countered that even if all kinds of government were legal, they were surely 'not equally expedient'. Moreover, Hume's position made reform impossible 'since opposition to established error must needs

---

[18] David Steuart Erskine to Macaulay, 25 June 1769, in *Correspondence*, p. 48.
[19] Hume to Macaulay, 29 March 1764, in *Correspondence*, p. 38.

be opposition to authority'. She concluded her riposte by comparing the Stuart line to Caesar, recounting its cruel treatment of the Puritan Alexander Leighton (1570–1649), who had been whipped, had one of his ears cut off, his nose slit and was branded on the forehead with S. S. for 'sower of sedition'.[20]

Macaulay and Hume not only differed politically but also philosophically and religiously. Macaulay's belief in the afterlife, divine providence and immutable moral truths discoverable through reason was diametrically opposite to Hume's scepticism. By drawing attention to the religious extremism of the Parliamentarians and the monarchical bias of England's constitution, even some of Macaulay's friends such as David Steuart Erskine, 11th Earl of Buchan, believed that Hume's account of the seventeenth century was closer to the truth than Macaulay's. Indeed, she can be suspected of having shared some of the religious enthusiasm of the seventeenth-century republicans, writing that '[t]he matchless Milton has observed that no government comes nearer to this precept of Christ [of the equal rights of men] than a free Commonwealth'.[21] For Macaulay, as for many Dissenters in her wider circle, rational religion, morality and political legitimacy coincided and were mutually supportive. As she wrote about the rise of scepticism and voluntarism during the Restoration: 'in contradiction to that great oracle of history, Mr. Hume, we cannot help thinking that the cure of fanaticism, by the prevalence of licentiousness, debauchery, and irreligion, was a very great evil rather than a benefit to the kingdom'.[22]

In one key sense, Hume and Macaulay spoke past each other rather than in dialogue since Hume in his historical writings first and foremost sought to explode the Whig myth of an ancient constitution. But Macaulay had little time for this form of Whiggism. Although she sometimes spoke of the 'ancient constitution', and even of the Anglo-Saxon constitution having been corrupted by the Normans, she consistently argued for the universal rights of men – rights that were abstract rather than historical. Crucially, she was convinced that the regicide of Charles I had to be justified by Lockean natural law – that is to say, the king had to be punished as a tyrant in the name of natural justice – rather than on constitutional grounds. This frame of mind

[20] Macaulay to Hume, [April] 1764, in *Correspondence*, p. 39.
[21] *History*, III, p. 345 (note).   [22] *History*, VIII, pp. 70–1.

would put her on a collision course with one of the most famous Whigs of the second half of the eighteenth century, the Irish man of letters and parliamentarian Burke, whom she attacked directly in two pamphlets in 1770 and 1790.

Macaulay on Religion

Macaulay's belief in natural rights was intimately linked with her religious persuasion. She assumed the existence of a benevolent God in her philosophical works, in which she wrestled with the existence of evil. In short, she believed that evil and sin in the experienced world produced greater good in the afterlife in which virtue would be rewarded and wickedness punished. She regarded earthly life as a trial in which reason and experience directed human beings towards meritorious virtue and away from the passions and appetites. In this way she sought to make the existence of evil consistent with the omnipotence and infinite benevolence of God, in opposition to Bolingbroke's deism. Bolingbroke accepted the existence of God, but held that we have no reason to think that he is good or just in human terms. According to Macaulay, accepting the existence of God while doubting his traditional attributes – omnipotence, goodness and wisdom – was no better than atheism, and undercut morality. Since life could be conceived as a trial in virtue, education was necessary; habits of virtue and self-control needed to be taught and encouraged, which is what she sought to do in her *Letters on Education* (1790).

According to Bolingbroke, the example of China demonstrated that a country could be governed justly without any notion of a supreme being, as justice was based on useful conventions. Macaulay retorted that women and children had never been treated justly in China. As in her response to Hume, she argued that existing conventions could lead to abuses of power in the name of rational self-interest. Justice in its abstract or general sense was thus indispensable, and was supported by an understanding of the true nature of God. Macaulay was convinced that the rise of irreligion and scepticism threatened moral motivation, arguing that Hobbes's and Hume's undermining of the notion that human beings are morally motivated creatures who participate in God's goodness weakened beliefs that are necessary for promoting peace and prosperity, as well as salvation.

Macaulay wrote that 'the empire of religious sentiment, and the empire of reason, are the same'.[23] In a biographical sketch, Erskine speculated that it was her frequent contacts with Protestant Dissenters which made her 'prepossessed against the Principle of Monarchy'.[24] Several members of her wider circle were Unitarian ministers: Richard Price, Joseph Priestley, Theophilus Lindsay and Andrew Kippis. Hollis and her friend the Scottish reformer James Burgh, author of *Political Disquisitions* (1774–5), were also Dissenters. Though she never left the Church of England, in private correspondence she admitted her belief in Unitarianism, which was strictly speaking illegal according to England's Toleration Act as it only accepted trinitarian dissent.[25]

Too much can be made of the fact that Macaulay remained with the established church. Already in 1767, she applauded a pamphlet against the Church of England by the Presbyterian historian William Harris.[26] The same pamphlet criticised Catholicism for having 'recommended and authorized croisades, the drains of *Europe*, and the disgrace of human nature!'[27] Even though Harris viewed Protestant established churches as superior to 'Popish' ones, they were more inconsistent with the principles of Protestantism.[28] Macaulay shared this hostility to Catholicism, as was common in her circle of reformist Protestants, and indeed as in eighteenth-century Britain at large. By contrast, her antagonist Burke, with multiple familial ties with Catholics, was known as one of the foremost champions of Catholics of the time. The reformers and Dissenters at the time were not all irredeemably anti-Catholic. Priestley, for instance, included Catholics in his call for complete religious liberty, as one of Macaulay's correspondents complained.[29] Macaulay seems to have thought that this criticism of Priestley was 'very judicious'.[30] In the third volume of the *History*, she wrote damningly about the Irish massacre of 1641, on which Hume had also taken a hard

---

[23] Macaulay, *A Treatise on the Immutability of Moral Truth* (London, 1783), p. 283; *Letters on Education*, p. 265.
[24] Edinburgh University Library La. II. 588, cited in *Correspondence*, p. 41.
[25] Macaulay to Capel Lofft, 12 November 1789, in *Correspondence*, p. 285.
[26] Macaulay to William Harris, 16 December 1767, in *Correspondence*, p. 58.
[27] William Harris, *Observations on National Establishments in Religion in General* (London, 1767), pp. 28, 33–4.
[28] Ibid., p. 35.   [29] Erskine to Macaulay, 12 February 1769, in *Correspondence*, p. 46.
[30] Macaulay to Erskine, 9 June 1769, in *Correspondence*, p. 47.

line and clashed with Burke. In Hume's narrative of the late seventeenth century, Macaulay believed that he was too favourable to the 'Papists', and she was not as dismissive as he was of the reality of the Popish Plot. Indeed, she believed that it was fully rational for people to believe in such a plot given Charles II's 'conspiracy to re-establish Popery as the national religion'.[31] She also offered a partial defence of Shaftesbury and those involved in the Rye House Plot to assassinate the king, which she called the 'Protestant Plot'. Yet, elsewhere in her historical account, she was critical of the Presbyterians for not allowing a more general toleration, and she also wrote sympathetically about the sincerity of James II's Catholic faith. On balance, then, her position on Catholics may be located somewhere between Harris's and Priestley's respective views.

Liberty, Rights and Equality

J. G. A. Pocock and others have placed Macaulay in the civic humanist tradition, which valued the independence of the citizen soldier. This context can be misleading for Macaulay, however, since liberty for her was deeply connected with religion, and more specifically with freedom of conscience and moral autonomy. Pocock's description of Macaulay as 'an eighteenth-century Hannah Arendt, a woman wholly committed to the ancient ideal of active citizenship and wholly undeterred by its hyper-intense masculinity'[32] thus becomes problematic. For her, political liberty was a prerequisite for securing rights and individual liberty in the sense of moral self-determination, and not an end in itself. Importantly, Macaulay's religious views were fundamental for her views on women, as she was convinced that God had created women and men as equally sociable and moral, who can and ought to perfect themselves as moral beings. Singling out one sex for preferential treatment would thus be inconsistent with divine justice. 'Manly' and 'masculine' are terms of approbation and 'effeminacy' is linked with corruption in her *History*. For a Latinist culture, however, 'manly' and 'masculine' often implied little more than a direct translation of *virtù* – the qualities of the *vir*, the masculine man. 'Effeminacy' could afflict women and men alike,

---

[31] *History*, VII, p. 288.   [32] Pocock, 'Catharine Macaulay: Patriot Historian', p. 251.

and it was not always linked with femininity.[33] For Macaulay, it was more frequently associated with aristocracy and servitude. There would be loud echoes of Macaulay's views on women in the more famous writings of Wollstonecraft, who was an avid reader of Macaulay's writings and reviewed her *Letters on Education* favourably in the *Analytical Review*.

Macaulay followed Locke in believing that free individuals are governed by reason, and to be politically free was to be governed by laws conformable to reason and natural law. Laws that prevented the operation of reason, for instance those governing religious worship or impeding the freedom of thought and expression, were pernicious. The purpose of civil laws was to protect the basic natural rights of men and women. For Macaulay and many members of her circle, liberty and rights were often intimately linked and even conflated. Benjamin Rush, a signatory of the Declaration of Independence, called Macaulay 'a patroness of Liberty and a defendant of the rights of Mankind'.[34]

Macaulay also persistently championed the rights of animals. Though lacking in reason, animals were created by God for happiness and not for misery, and since happiness was not always attained in the earthly life, the consistency of God's benevolence meant that there must be an afterlife for animals. The capacity for reasoning implied a hierarchy of beings, and the superiority of humans was accompanied by their responsibility to care for the welfare of animals. In her *Letters on Education*, Macaulay argued that children's benevolence and sympathy would be developed if they were trained to refrain from animal cruelty, which she wanted to see punished. While she promoted vegetarianism for adults, she believed that children should eat a small amount of meat when growing, underlining the implied hierarchy of God's creatures.

The liberty Macaulay favoured was an ordered one and routinely contrasted with licentiousness. Such an ordered liberty was underpinned by equality, she argued, writing in the third volume of the *History* '[t]hat

---

[33] Samuel Johnson presented two distinct definitions in his *Dictionary* (1755): '1. Having the qualities of a woman; womanish; soft to an unmanly degree; mean submission ... 2. Lasciviousness; loose pleasure.'

[34] Rush to Macaulay, 25 November 1769, in *Correspondence*, p. 69.

invidious distinctions and privileges are so far from being instrumental to the laws, or the order, regularity, and decency of society that they must necessarily act contrary to these purposes'.[35] She complained that the 'levelling' doctrine had been misunderstood and stressed that it only threatened aristocratic privilege and not the security of property. While aware of the danger of excessive economic inequality, she certainly accepted a degree of difference in wealth, and the importance of property rights, which she thought had been infringed by the Stuart monarchs in the seventeenth century. Yet Macaulay was concerned that Englishmen had a tendency to put too much emphasis on private property, which must be subordinated to the superior value of the common good.[36]

Macaulay favoured free trade and wrote that 'there cannot be a truer political maxim than that a free commerce is the only source of opulence to a state, and that every tax laid upon trade is a very pernicious and a very heavy burthen on society'.[37] This made her a critic of key elements in Britain's economic order, not only its high taxes but also its debt financing, which she believed created both instability and inequality. She was also deeply worried about the corrupting effects of the wrong kinds of luxury. Many in Macaulay's circle were from commercial backgrounds, notably Hollis, who took an active interest in the management of his inherited fortune through the buying and selling of stocks, and who supported the Society for Promotion of Arts, Manufactures, and Commerce. In her mature views in *Letters on Education*, Macaulay stressed that the benefits that derive from the progress of civilisation, such as hygiene, are luxuries that should be promoted. There was thus a balance to be struck between puritan austerity and licentious consumption that satisfied vanity. This approach is also notable in her attitude to culture: rather than banning theatres, like Rousseau had prescribed for Geneva, she sought to promote *day-time* theatre to avoid vice. Moreover, she thought that painting and music should be directed towards improving the beauty of churches rather than private spaces.

---

[35] *History*, III, p. 116.
[36] *History*, VI, p. 211. Karen Green has shown that Macaulay's conception of property is similar to Richard Cumberland's and John Locke's; see *Catharine Macaulay's Republican Enlightenment* (New York, 2020), p. 71.
[37] *History since the Revolution*, p. 264.

The American and French Revolutions

Macaulay was well connected with revolutionaries in both France and America, having travelled to France in the 1770s and to both countries in the 1780s. She was a celebrity in America long before her visit in 1784. Having written about the imposition of ship money in the seventeenth century, her *History* became topical as a result of the American crisis, which escalated after the Stamp Act in 1765. In the 1760s Hollis and the publisher John Almon began a campaign of printing and disseminating pro-American tracts. American pamphlets such as James Otis's *Vindication of the British Colonies* (1765) supported both British reformers at home and the American cause against taxation without representation. In a similar vein, Macaulay's writings formed part of the intellectual and political skirmishes fought on both sides of the Atlantic.

Macaulay's many correspondents in America encouraged her to visit the colonies before the American War of Independence, but her health did not allow it. Her correspondence with Rush shows, however, that she was eager for her writings to be disseminated among his friends in America. She wrote to him that the 'general principles of the rights of mankind inculcated in my great work [her *History*]' were more advantageous to 'the cause of the Americans' than the pamphlet literature.[38] This interest was certainly mutual. As the standoff between Britain and the Thirteen Colonies intensified, the Italian newspaper *Notizie del mondo* wrote in December 1769: 'The American-English inhabitants of the northern part of that hemisphere have prohibited entry of all English books to their parts, except the history of Mrs. Macaulay, which is written in a very free style, and they call it the foundation of liberty.'[39]

Macaulay admired America for its simplicity. She wrote to the Quaker John Dickinson that she hoped the Americans would 'emulate that meritorious simplicity and moderation which was to be found in the happy and virtuous periods of the Greek and Roman States than the vices and Luxuries which afterwards prevailed in those illustrious Republicks to their entire ruin and which mistaken moderns miscal [*sic*] civilisation'.[40] Like Dickinson, she was not in favour of American

---

[38] Macaulay to Rush, 20 January 1769, in *Correspondence*, p. 69.

[39] Cited in Franco Venturi, *The End of the Old Regime in Europe, 1768–1776: The First Crisis* (Princeton, 1989), p. 413.

[40] Macaulay to Dickinson, 18 July 1771, in *Correspondence*, pp. 126–7.

independence, at least not immediately. Her hope was rather that the Americans would be 'the Saviours of the Liberties of the whole British Empire', as she wrote to Mercy Otis Warren.[41] But like many British reformers and oppositional figures, she is likely to have realised that separation was inevitable, at least after France formally entered the war on the American side in February 1778. Otis Warren continuously implored Macaulay to write a history of the American revolution, but this was a vain hope, and instead Otis Warren undertook the enterprise herself, as Macaulay had encouraged her to do.[42]

Although her visit to the newly independent United States of America in 1784 left Macaulay optimistic about its prospects, this would quickly change. Her closest American friends were Anti-Federalists such as Mercy Otis Warren and her husband James Warren, and along with them she expressed her uneasiness with the monarchical tendencies of the Federal Constitution, created in 1787 and gradually adopted by the states. They all regretted the Federalist proclivities of their friend John Adams. Macaulay expressed these worries in her correspondence with Washington and other American friends. According to Macaulay, the key issue for America after the revolution was the spectre of European luxury. America needed to avoid foreign dependence and should therefore prioritise domestic manufacturers producing the necessities for the comforts of life. She was convinced that '[w]hilst Agriculture continues the prime object of American industry and her riches as a Society are moderate she will enjoy domestic liberty'. As the Federalists, led by Alexander Hamilton, were aiming to turn America into 'a large commercial State', Macaulay feared that '[America's] security will be rendered precarious'. A large revenue would increase 'the power and pageantry of government', and the people would be left 'robbed and deluded', and ready to receive the 'invidious distinctions of Aristocracy'.[43]

In the introduction to the first volume of the *History*, Macaulay had complained about the fashion of travelling abroad and the risk of becoming seduced by foreign things. But when she visited France in the late

---

[41] Macaulay to Otis Warren, 11 September 1774, in *Correspondence*, p. 152.
[42] Macaulay to Otis Warren, April 1790, in *Correspondence*, p. 171. Warren published *A History of the Rise, Progress, and Termination of the American Revolution* in three volumes in 1805.
[43] Ibid.

1770s, she, like Hume, benefited from the high regard paid by the French to literary merit. She socialised with the physiocrat Anne Robert Jacques Turgot, France's first minister in 1774–6, among others, but due to the suspension of the Habeas Corpus Act she had to decline the opportunity of meeting Benjamin Franklin, who was in Paris at the time as commissioner for America.[44] Macaulay was so enthused by French society that she complained that war between Britain and France in 1778 would delay the opportunity for her to return to the country.

Macaulay was also interested in having her *History* translated into French.[45] Her friend Brissot argued for a French translation in the *Journal du Lycée de Londres*. Mirabeau the Younger (1749–91) took it upon himself to translate it and took credit for some of the work, which eventually appeared in 1791, with Brissot doubting that Mirabeau had actually completed any of the translation himself. Its introduction pointed out that there were so many parallels between the English and the French revolutions that Macaulay's work could serve as a history of both. In the preface to the third volume, Mirabeau gave Macaulay's *History* a monarchical slant, as he was concerned about the extreme direction of the French Revolution.

In 1778, after Macaulay had visited Paris for a few weeks, she claimed that 'sentiments of liberty which are ... lost in these united Kingdoms never flourished in a larger extent or with more vigorous animating force than they do at present in France'.[46] Already at this point, she stated that '[a]ll the enlightened French wish ardently to see a large empire established on a republican basis to keep the monarchies of the world in order'.[47] When the French Revolution eventually broke out, Macaulay viewed the two revolutions as connected, as she made clear in a letter to Washington.[48] She reflected that the French as well as the Americans looked to the British constitution for example. However, the closeness of France to Britain meant that the French were able to see 'the deformities of our government in their full extent <due magnitude> and they have

---

[44] Macaulay to Benjamin Franklin, 8 December 1777, in *Correspondence*, p. 206.
[45] Guy-Claude, Count of Sarsfield, to Macaulay, 16 December 1777 and 2 May 1779, in *Correspondence*, pp. 208–9.
[46] Macaulay to Erskine, 23 February 1778, in *Correspondence*, p. 54.
[47] Macaulay to Simon, 17 January 1778, in *Correspondence*, p. 80.
[48] Macaulay to Washington, 30 October 1789, in *Correspondence*, p. 274.

carefully avoided the adopting any part of the english system but the only part which is worth having vis[.] the mode of trial by jury'.[49] This meant that the French Revolution quickly became superior to the American one. She wrote to Samuel Adams that 'we look upon its [the French Revolution's] firm establishment, as an event which will necessarily bring after it the final emancipation of every other society in Europe, from those Monarchic and Aristocratic chains imposed by the violence of arms and rivetted on mankind by ignorance[,] credulity, and priestcraft'.[50] One society she believed needed to be emancipated was eighteenth-century Britain.

Macaulay and Britain

One of the most conspicuous elements of Macaulay's political writings is her criticism of Britain, which was consistent with her views on political reform, yet almost uniquely bold when she first expressed it. The theoretical merits of the British constitution and the salutary peculiarities of English society were noted by many political writers in the eighteenth century, including Montesquieu and Voltaire. Many were pessimistic, however, about the sustainability of Britain's debt-fuelled politics, notably Hume and Price, and its imperial ambitions and monopolistic companies, a line of criticism most famously formulated by Adam Smith under the heading of the 'mercantile system'. Many voices lamented parliamentary corruption in a more traditional Bolingbrokean fashion, or the decline of manners, following John Brown's bestselling *Estimate of the Manners and Principles of the Times* (2 vols., 1757–8). During the American crisis, Britain was accused of not extending its benefits to its subjects in America. But few were as exhaustive and unrelenting in their critique of Britain as Macaulay, who combined all these lines of criticism. Notably, few if any non-Jacobites targeted the Revolution Settlement before her. The *Political Register* wrote in 1770 that Macaulay 'attacks the principles and system of government of the revolution, in so strange and unaccountable manner that her best friends are astonished at it'.[51]

---

[49] Macaulay to Otis Warren, April 1790, in *Correspondence*, p. 172.
[50] Macaulay to Samuel Adams, 1 March 1791, in *Correspondence*, p. 296.
[51] *Political Register, and Impartial Review for 1770* (London, 1770), p. 363.

Even Price – who was worried about Britain's debt and wanted comprehensive religious and political reform – held Britain to be a more positive model, at least publicly. Indeed, he said that he was 'sharing in the benefits of one Revolution', with reference to 1688–9.[52] Unlike Price, Macaulay was unwilling to pay lip service to the Glorious Revolution and its legacy. Across her political writings, Macaulay boldly presented the Glorious Revolution as a revolt by the nobility, creating 'a monarchy supported by aristocracy', which was the 'very worst species of government'.[53] This was a momentous move which set the stage for bolder ideas of political reform. Macaulay emphasised that she supported universal rather than historically grounded rights, in opposition to Burke's brand of Whiggism. The 'boasted birthright of an Englishman' was 'an *arrogant* pretension', because it excluded the rest of humanity.[54] In other words, even though Macaulay wrote primarily about her country of birth and its history, her concerns and ambitions were cosmopolitan, embracing all God's creatures, even including animals, whose rights she championed in her *Treatise on the Immutability of Moral Truth* and *Letters on Education* (1790).

Eight months before her death in June 1791, Macaulay defended the French Revolution in her final publication, *Observations on the Reflections of the Right Hon. Edmund Burke on the Revolution in France* (1790). Unlike Burke, who died in 1797, she did not live to see the extremely violent phase of the French Revolution, which Burke had accurately predicted in the *Reflections*. Her earlier death meant that she did not witness the executions of her friend Brissot, her admirer Jeanne-Marie Roland, who wanted to become 'the Macaulay of [her] country',[55] and the publisher of her works in French, François-Charles Gattey, during the Reign of Terror. The bloody development of the French Revolution, and the crackdown on reformist politics which followed in its wake in Britain, may indeed go some way towards explaining the relative eclipse of Macaulay in the nineteenth century.

---

[52] Richard Price, *A Discourse on the Love of our Country, Delivered on Nov. 4, 1789, at the Meeting-House in the Old Jewry, to the Society for Commemorating the Revolution in Great Britain* (London, 1790), p. 41.

[53] *History since the Revolution*, p. 311.

[54] Macaulay, *Observations on the Reflections of the Right Hon. Edmund Burke on the Revolution in France* (1790), p. 31.

[55] *An Appeal to Impartial Posterity, by Madame Roland, Wife of the Minister of the Interior* (2nd ed., 2 vols., London, 1796), II, p. 81.

Chronology

1775	*An Address to the People of England, Scotland and Ireland on the Present Important Crisis of Affairs* published.
1775–83	American War of Independence.
1777	Macaulay visits France.
1778	*History since the Revolution* published; Catharine Macaulay marries William Graham.
1781	Sixth and seventh volumes of the *History* published.
1783	Eighth and final volume of the *History* and *A Treatise on the Immutability of Moral Truth* published.
1784	Macaulay visits America.
1785–6	Macaulay visits France.
1789	Outbreak of the French Revolution; Richard Price praises it in London on 4 November.
1790	*Letters on Education, with Observations on Religious and Metaphysical Subjects* and *Observations on the Reflections of the Right Hon. Edmund Burke on the Revolution in France* published.
1791	Catharine Macaulay dies.

Further Reading

Macaulay's Life and Writings

Students of Catharine Macaulay are especially indebted to two modern scholars: Bridget Hill and Karen Green. Bridget Hill's biography, *The Republican Virago: The Life and Times of Catharine Macaulay, Historian* (Oxford, 1992), is the starting point for anyone interested in her life. See also Bridget Hill, 'Daughter and Mother: Some New Light on Catharine Macaulay and Her Family', *British Journal for Eighteenth-Century Studies*, 22 (1999), pp. 35–49, and other essays by Hill cited below. Earlier biographical studies include L. M. Donnelly, 'The Celebrated Mrs. Macaulay', *William and Mary Quarterly*, 7 (1949), pp. 173–207. Karen Green has edited *The Correspondence of Catharine Macaulay* (Oxford, 2019) and written an essential intellectual biography, *Catharine Macaulay's Republican Enlightenment* (New York, 2020). In addition, Green has written about Macaulay in several path-breaking essays and chapters; see especially chapter eight in *A History of Women's Political Thought in Europe, 1700–1800* (Cambridge, 2014), and her entry for Macaulay in the *Stanford Encyclopedia of Philosophy*.

Macaulay's historical writings are treated in the following: Karen O'Brien, *Women and Enlightenment in Eighteenth-Century Britain* (Cambridge, 2009), ch. 4; Karen O'Brien, 'Catharine Macaulay's Histories of England: A Female Perspective on the History of Liberty', in *Women, Gender and Enlightenment*, ed. Sarah Knott and Barbara Taylor (Basingstoke, 2005); Philip Hicks, 'Catharine Macaulay's Civil War: Gender, History, and Republicanism in Georgian Britain', *Journal of British Studies*, 41 (2002), pp. 170–99; Susan Wiseman, 'Catharine

Macaulay: History, Republicanism and the Public Sphere', in *Women, Writing and the Public Sphere, 1700–1830*, ed. E. Eger, C. Grant, C. Ó Gallchoir and P. Warburton (Cambridge, 2001); Devoney Looser, *British Women Writers and the Writing of History, 1670–1820* (Baltimore, 2000), ch. 5; J. G. A. Pocock, 'Catharine Macaulay: Patriot Historian', in *Women Writers and the Early Modern British Political Tradition*, ed. H. Smith (Cambridge, 1998), pp. 243–58; Bridget Hill and Christopher Hill, 'Catharine Macaulay's History and Her Catalogue of Tracts', *The Seventeenth Century*, 8 (1993), pp. 269–85; Rolando Minuti, 'Il problema storico della libertà inglese nella cultura radicale dell'età di George III. Catharine Macaulay e la Rivoluzione puritana', *Revista istorica italiana*, 98 (1986), pp. 793–860; Lynne E. Withey, 'Catharine Macaulay and the Uses of History: Ancient Rights, Perfectionism and Propaganda', *Journal of British Studies*, 16 (1976), pp. 59–83; Vera Nünning, *A Revolution in Sentiments, Manners, and Moral Opinions: Catharine Macaulay und die politische Kultur des englischen Radikalismus* (Heidelberg, 1998). The reception of Macaulay is treated in Susan Staves, '"The Liberty of a She-Subject of England": Rights, Rhetoric and the Female Thucydides', *Cardozo Studies in Law and Literature*, 1 (1989), pp. 161–83.

Sarah Hutton has written about Macaulay's religious thought; see 'Liberty, Equality and God: The Religious Roots of Catharine Macaulay's Feminism', in *Women, Gender and Enlightenment*, ed. S. Knott and B. Taylor (Basingstoke, 2005). See also Karen Green, 'Catharine Macaulay's Enlightenment Faith and Radical Politics', *History of European Ideas*, 44 (2018), pp. 35–48. For Macaulay's philosophical writings see Karen Green, 'Liberty and Virtue in Catharine Macaulay's Enlightenment Philosophy', *Intellectual History Review*, 22 (2012), pp. 411–26; Karen Green, 'Catharine Macaulay and the Concept of "Radical Enlightenment"', *Intellectual History Review*, 31 (2021), pp. 165–80; Wendy Gunther-Canada, 'Catharine Macaulay on the Paradox of Paternal Authority in Hobbesian Politics', *Hypatia*, 21 (2006), pp. 150–73; and Karen Green and Shannon Weekes, 'Catharine Macaulay on the Will', *History of European Ideas*, 39 (2013), pp. 409–25.

For Macaulay's connections with the American Revolution and American Revolutionaries, see Kate Davies, *Catharine Macaulay and Mercy Otis Warren: The Revolutionary Atlantic and the Politics of Gender* (Oxford, 2005); Kate Davies, 'Revolutionary Correspondence:

Reading Catharine Macaulay and Mercy Otis Warren', *Women's Writing*, 13 (2006), pp. 73–97; and Carla H. Hay, 'Catharine Macaulay and the American Revolution', *The Historian*, 56 (1994), pp. 301–16. For Macaulay's reputation in eighteenth-century France, see Laurence Bongie, *David Hume: Prophet of the Counter-Revolution* (1965; Indianapolis, 1998). For her critical interpretation of the Glorious Revolution, see Bridget Hill, 'Reinterpreting the "Glorious Revolution": Catharine Macaulay and Radical Response', in *Culture and Society in the Stuart Restoration: Literature, Drama, History*, ed. Gerald MacLean (Cambridge, 1995), pp. 267–85.

The relationship between Macaulay and Mary Wollstonecraft is treated in Bridget Hill, 'The Links between Mary Wollstonecraft and Catharine Macaulay: New Evidence', *Women's History Review*, 4 (1995), pp. 177–92; Martina Reuter, 'Catharine Macaulay and Mary Wollstonecraft on the Will', in *Virtue, Liberty and Toleration: Political Ideas of European Women 1400–1800*, ed. Jacqueline Broad and Karen Green (Dordrecht, 2007); Elizabeth Frazer, 'Mary Wollstonecraft and Catharine Macaulay on Education', *Oxford Review of Education*, 37 (2011), pp. 603–17; Alan Coffee, 'Catharine Macaulay', in *The Wollstonecraftian Mind*, ed. Sandrine Bergès, Eileen Hunt Botting and Alan Coffee (Abingdon, 2019); and Karen Green, 'Catharine Macaulay's Influence on Mary Wollstonecraft', in *The Routledge Handbook of Women and Early Modern European Philosophy*, ed. Karen Detlefsen and Lisa Shapiro (Abingdon, 2020).

Connie Titone has written about Macaulay's contribution to educational theory in *Gender Equality in the Philosophy of Education: Catharine Macaulay's Forgotten Contribution* (New York, 2004) and 'Virtue, Reason, and the False Public Voice: Catharine Macaulay's Philosophy of Moral Education', *Educational Philosophy and Theory*, 41 (2009), pp. 91–108. Macaulay's contribution to republican theory has been treated in Alan Coffee, 'Catharine Macaulay's Republican Conception of Social and Political Liberty', *Political Studies*, 65 (2017), pp. 844–59.

Intellectual and Political Contexts

For eighteenth-century republicanism and the commonwealth tradition, see Rachel Hammersley, *Republicanism: An Introduction* (Cambridge, 2020), esp. chs. 4–8; Rachel Hammersley, *The English Republican Tradition and Eighteenth-Century France: Between the Ancients and the*

Moderns (Manchester, 2010) – esp. ch. 11; Gaby Mahlberg, *The English Republican Exiles in Europe during the Restoration* (Cambridge, 2020); Blair Worden, *Literature and Politics in Cromwellian England: John Milton, Andrew Marvell, Marchamont Nedham* (Oxford, 2007); J. G. A. Pocock, *The Machiavellian Moment: Florentine Political Thought and the Atlantic Republican Tradition* (Princeton, 1975); and Caroline Robbins, *The Eighteenth-Century Commonwealthman: Studies in the Transmission, Development and Circumstances of English Liberal Thought from the Restoration of Charles II until the War with the Thirteen Colonies* (Cambridge, MA, 1959). Robbins's classic *Eighteenth-Century Commonwealthman* is still useful, perhaps especially for the history of political networks. Its last chapter discusses Macaulay and her network, on which see also Caroline Robbins, 'The Strenuous Whig: Thomas Hollis of Lincoln's Inn', *William and Mary Quarterly*, 7 (1950), pp. 406–53.

For studies on women in the Enlightenment and the eighteenth-century public sphere, many of which have material on Macaulay, see Sarah Hutton, 'The Persona of the Woman Philosopher in Eighteenth-Century England: Catharine Macaulay, Mary Hays, and Elizabeth Hamilton', *Intellectual History Review*, 18 (2009), pp. 403–12; Devoney Looser, *Women Writers and Old Age in Great Britain, 1750–1850* (Baltimore, 2008) – ch. 2 on Macaulay; Devoney Looser, '"Those Historical Laurels Which Once Graced My Brow Are Now in Their Wane": Catharine Macaulay's Last Years and Legacy', *Studies in Romanticism*, 42 (2003), pp. 203–25; Sarah Knott and Barbara Taylor (eds.), *Women, Gender and Enlightenment* (Basingstoke, 2005); Philip Hicks, 'The Roman Matron in Britain: Female Political Influence and Republican Response, ca. 1750–1800', *Journal of Modern History*, 77 (2005), pp. 35–69; Elaine Chalus and Hannah Barker (eds.), *Women's History, Britain 1700–1850: An Introduction* (London and New York, 2004); Harriet Guest, *Small Change: Women, Learning, Patriotism, 1750–1810* (Chicago, 2000); Elaine Chalus and Hannah Barker (eds.), *Gender in Eighteenth-Century England: Roles, Representations and Responsibilities* (London, 1997); and Sylvia Harcstark-Myers, *The Bluestocking Circle: Women, Friendship and the Life of the Mind in Eighteenth-Century England* (Oxford, 1990).

For Macaulay's wide circle, its politics and key events and contexts, see Peter N. Miller, *Defining the Common Good: Empire, Religion and Philosophy in Eighteenth-Century Britain* (Cambridge, 1994); W. H. Bond, *Thomas Hollis of Lincoln's Inn: A Whig and His Books*

(Cambridge, 1990); John Sainsbury, *Disaffected Patriots: London Supporters of Revolutionary America, 1769–1782* (Montreal, 1987); Colin Bonwick, *English Radicals and the American Revolution* (1977); Carl Cone, *The English Jacobins: Reformers in Late 18th Century England* (1968; Abingdon, 2017); Verner W. Crane, 'The Club of Honest Whigs: Friends of Science and Liberty', *William and Mary Quarterly*, 23 (1966), pp. 210–33; Ian R. Christie, *Wilkes, Wyvill and Reform: The Parliamentary Reform Movement in Britain, 1760–1785* (London, 1962); George Rudé, *Wilkes and Liberty: A Social Study of 1763 to 1774* (Oxford, 1962); and Lucy Sutherland, *The City of London and the Opposition to Government, 1768–1774* (London, 1959).

Many of the preconceptions about English 'radicalism', the connection between the American and the French revolutions, and the Enlightenment are critically examined and forcefully challenged by J. C. D. Clark in *Thomas Paine: Britain, America, and France in the Age of Enlightenment and Revolution* (Oxford, 2018) and 'How Did the American Revolution Relate to the French? Richard Price, the Age of Revolutions, and the Enlightenment', *Modern Intellectual History*, 19 (2022), pp. 105–27. Clark's *English Society, 1660–1832* (1985; Cambridge, 2000) and *The Language of Liberty* (Cambridge, 1994) are also valuable reading for the religious politics of the period and its relation to the questions of reform and revolution. For religious thought see also Isabel Rivers, *Reason, Grace, and Sentiment: A Study of the Language of Religion and Ethics in England, 1660–1780* (Cambridge, 2 vols., 1991–2000); Knud Haakonssen (ed.), *Enlightenment and Religion: Rational Dissent in Eighteenth-Century Britain* (Cambridge, 1996); and Justin Champion, *Republican Learning: John Toland and the Crisis of Christian Culture, 1696–1722* (Manchester, 2003).

For the financial revolution and political economy, see especially P. G. M. Dickson, *The Financial Revolution in England: A Study in the Development of Public Credit, 1688–1756* (London, 1967); J. G. A. Pocock, *Virtue, Commerce, and History* (Cambridge, 1983); John Brewer, *The Sinews of Power: War, Money, and the English State, 1688–1783* (London, 1989); Istvan Hont, *Jealousy of Trade: International Competition and the Nation-State in Historical Perspective* (Cambridge, MA, 2005); Carl Wennerlind, *Casualties of Credit: The English Financial Revolution, 1620–1720* (Cambridge, MA, 2011); and Helen J. Paul, *The South Sea Bubble: An Economic History of Its Origins and Consequences* (New York, 2011).

I treat Bolingbroke's political thought, Hume's *History of England* and Burke's writings on politics and party, including Macaulay's 1770 response to Burke, in *The Persistence of Party: Ideas of Harmonious Discord in Eighteenth-Century Britain* (Cambridge, 2021). For Bolingbroke (and other important writers for Macaulay such as Swift), see Isaac Kramnick, *Bolingbroke and His Circle: The Politics of Nostalgia in the Age of Walpole* (1968; Ithaca, 1992). See Richard Bourke, *Empire and Revolution: The Political Life of Edmund Burke* (Princeton, 2015) for the best treatment of Burke's political thought and its contexts. For Hume see James Harris, *Hume: An Intellectual Biography* (Cambridge, 2015) and Duncan Forbes, *Hume's Philosophical Politics* (Cambridge, 1975), both of which also provide useful introductions to eighteenth-century historiography. For this topic see also Ben Dew, *Commerce, Finance and Statecraft: Histories of England, 1600–1780* (Manchester, 2018); Karen O'Brien, *Narratives of Enlightenment: Cosmopolitan History from Voltaire to Gibbon* (Oxford, 1997); Philip Hicks, *Neoclassical History and English Culture: From Clarendon to Hume* (Basingstoke, 1996); and Mark Towsey, *Reading History in Britain and America, c. 1750 – c. 1840* (Cambridge, 2019).

Editorial Conventions

Eighteenth-century spelling in the texts has been kept in general, as have inconsistencies in spelling. However, blatant typos, misprints and a small number of grammatical errors have been corrected. All additions to the text have been marked by square brackets, including original pagination and errata provided by Macaulay. Macaulay's own footnotes are indicated by Roman numerals and editorial footnotes in Arabic numerals. I have formatted book titles in italics in Macaulay's footnotes for clarity. Quotation marks have been standardised when appropriate. Marginal text which only reproduces material in the text or repeats dates has been removed, but references to sources and authors in the margins have been kept, as have dates when needed, and enclosed by interpolation marks: i.e. ^interpolated text^.

Selections from *The History of England* (1763–83)

Introduction to the Text

Macaulay's *History of England* treats the period from the accession of James I in 1603 to the Glorious Revolution which removed his grandson James II from power in 1688–9. It was published in eight volumes between 1763 and 1783. The first volume is dated 1763, the second 1765, the third 1767, the fourth 1768, the fifth 1771, the sixth and seventh 1781 and the eighth 1783. The first five volumes appeared in three editions, and the last three in only one edition. The present selections are drawn from the first editions of all the volumes. During the long gap between volumes five and six, Macaulay wrote political pamphlets and one volume of contemporary history. The title of the first five volumes – *The History of England from the Accession of James I to That of the Brunswick Line* – indicates that the narrative was originally meant to continue until the Hanoverian succession in 1714. Instead, she treated this part of the history in her separate *History since the Revolution* (see below). For volumes six, seven and eight, the title was changed to *The History of England from the Accession of James I to the Revolution*. The present edition includes selections from Macaulay's introductions and prefaces emphasising her intentions, some of the analytic chapters that place her narrative in larger social and intellectual contexts, her engagement with political ideas such as those of the Levellers, key set pieces including Charles I's execution and Algernon Sidney's trial, and the conclusion to the entire work.

The political orientation of the *History* was evident from the start. The preface to the first volume was followed by 'Address to Liberty' by the Scottish poet and playwright James Thomson (1700–48), who had belonged to the literary opposition to Robert Walpole's 'Court Whigs' earlier in the eighteenth century. While she defended the regicide of Charles I, unlike her friend Hollis she was not an admirer of Oliver Cromwell, whom she believed 'deprived his country of a full and equal system of Liberty, at the very instant of fruition' (v, p. [213]). With her *History*, Macaulay wanted to show that even though the triumph of liberty in the seventeenth century was short-lived, its achievements were vast and worthy of emulation. The English revolution was principally a revolution in political theory, which had resulted in '[t]he works of Nevil, Sydney, and Harrington ... which excel[led] even the antient classics on the science of policy' (v, p. [383]). One of the conspicuous aspects of Macaulay's *History* is indeed that it is a history of political arguments, with reference to specific works and pamphlets, to a far greater extent than any other history of England written in the same period.

Macaulay's *History* quickly became a sensation on both sides of the Atlantic, and eventually also in France. Most reviews were serious and generous, even if some were bewildered by her sex and the boldness of her arguments. In any case, the work quickly earned Macaulay a reputation as a formidable historian, if a controversial one. John Adams described how his countrymen were smitten by her *History* along with the works of John Trenchard and Thomas Gordon, as well as those of Macaulay's friend James Burgh, in the run up to the American Revolution. However, having originally been complimentary about the *History* in his correspondence with Macaulay, Adams later presented his own political writings as written against 'the erroneous opinions of government' propagated by Macaulay, Paine, Burgh and Turgot, probably with reference to their anti-aristocratic biases.[1]

Horace Walpole was initially ecstatic about the work, calling it 'the most sensible, unaffected and best history of England that we have had yet'.[2] Later, however, he remarked that its weakness was that Macaulay seemed to have thought that 'men have acted from no views but those of establishing a despotism or republic'.[3] In other words, she imputed everything to political motivations and left little room for the influence

---

[1] Adams to Price, 20 May 1789, in *The Works of John Adams* (10 vols., Boston, 1856), IX, p. 558.
[2] *The Letters of Horace Walpole*, ed. Peter Cunningham (9 vols., London, 1886), IV, p. 157.
[3] Horace Walpole, *Memoirs and Portraits*, ed. Matthew Hodgart (rev. ed., London, 1963), p. 189.

of passions, weaknesses, errors, prejudices and chance. Though this criticism was exaggerated, it is true that Macaulay intended to celebrate the heroic deeds of specific individuals. This is notable in her vindication of the character of Algernon Sidney, who was executed in 1683 for plotting against the king. She defended Sidney at a time when new evidence emerged from the French archives, presented by the Scottish historian Sir John Dalrymple in 1773 in the second volume of his *Memoirs of Great Britain and Ireland*. This evidence had shown that Sidney may have been offered and even taken money from the French court earlier in his career. Rather than disputing the evidence, Macaulay argued that if Sidney had taken the money it would not have been corruption since he would have done so in order to advance the cause of liberty. In this context, Macaulay attacked moral scepticism under the heading of modern 'levelling', that is to say, the notion that all human beings were equally corruptible and governed by their passions – ideas she associated with Hume.

The conclusion to the final volume of Macaulay's *History* must be read in the context of the movement for parliamentary reform in the 1780s. This cause was for a few years championed by William Pitt the Younger in Parliament, and outside by Christopher Wyvill and the Yorkshire Association Movement, as well as by Macaulay's brother and friends in the Society for Constitutional Information. Conspicuous here is Macaulay's indictment of the legacy of the Glorious Revolution, which she believed, in a Bolingbrokean manner, had opened the floodgates to corruption. Though Macaulay is primarily known as an anti-monarchical republican, she may at one point have hoped, like her friends Hollis and Burgh, that the accession of George III would bring an end to corruption and partisanship. This is suggested by her reference to Bolingbroke's *Idea of a Patriot King* (1738). Her positive citations from and allusions to Bolingbroke in the *History* show that she distinguished between his political writings, which were fundamental for her political circle, and his sceptical religious and philosophical writings, which she despised.

Selections from *The History of England* (1763–83)

[vii] Introduction.

Though the rectitude of my intention has hitherto been, and, I trust in God! ever will be, my support, in the laborious task of delineating the political history of this country, yet I think it incumbent on me to give the public my reasons for undertaking a subject which has been already treated of by several ingenious and learned men. From my early youth I have read with delight those histories that exhibit Liberty in its most exalted state, the annals of the Roman and the Greek republics. Studies like these excite that natural love of freedom which lies latent in the breast of every rational being, till it is nipped by the frost of prejudice, or blasted by the influence of vice.

The effect which almost constantly attends such reading operated on my inclinations in the strongest manner, and Liberty became the object of a secondary worship in my delighted imagination. A mind thus disposed can never see through the medium held up by party-writers; or incline to that extreme of candour which, by colouring the enormous vices, and [viii] magnifying the petty virtues, of wicked men, confound together in one undistinguished groupe, the exalted patriots that have illustriously figured in this country, with those time-serving placemen who have sacrificed the most essential interests of the public to the baseness of their private affections.

The societies of the modern ages of the world are not constituted with powers to bring to an impartial tribunal men trusted in the higher offices of the state. Fame is the only reward which, in the present times, true virtue hath to hope; and the only punishment which the guilty great have to apprehend, is eternal infamy. The weight of punishment ought ever to be determined by the importance of the consequences which attend the crime: In this ballance the vices of men in public characters can admit of no alleviation. A good citizen is a credit to his country, and merits the approbation of every virtuous man. Patriots who have sacrificed their tender affections, their properties, their lives, to the interest of society, deserve a tribute of praise unmixed with any alloy. With regret do I accuse my country of inattention to the most exalted of their benefactors: Whilst they enjoy privileges unpossessed by other nations, they have lost a just sense of the merit of the men by whose virtues these privileges were attained; men that, with the hazard and even the loss of their lives, attacked the [ix] formidable pretensions of the Stewart family, and set up the banners of liberty against a tyranny which had been established for a series of more than one hundred and fifty years; and this by the exertion of faculties, which, if compared with the barren produce of modern times, appear more than human. Neglect is not the only crime committed against these sacred characters. Party prejudice, and the more detestable principle of private interest, have painted the memoirs of past times in so false a light, that it is with difficulty we can trace features, which, if justly described, would exalt the worthies of this country beyond the fame of any set of men, which the annals of other nations can at any one period produce.

To do justice therefore to the memory of our illustrious ancestors to the utmost extent of my small abilities, still having an eye to public liberty, the standard by which I have endeavoured to measure the virtue of those characters that are treated of in this history, is the principal motive that induced me to undertake this intricate part of the English history. If the execution is deficient, the intention must be allowed to be meritorious; and if the goodness of my head may justly be questioned, my heart will stand the test of the most critical examination. In this country, where luxury has made a great progress, it is not to be supposed that the people of fortune will fathom the depth of politics, [x] or examine the voluminous collections in which can only be found a faithful representation of the important transactions of past ages. It is the business of an historian to digest these, and to give a true and accurate sense of them to the public. I have ever looked upon a supposed knowledge of facts seen in the false mirror of misrepresentation as one of the great banes of this country. Individuals may err, but the public judgment is infallible. They only want a just information of facts to make a proper comment. Labour, to attain truth, integrity to set it in its full light, are indispensible duties in an historian. I can affirm that I am not wanting in those duties. The invidious censures which may ensue from striking into a path of literature rarely trodden by my sex, will not permit a selfish consideration to keep me mute in the cause of liberty and virtue, whilst the doctrine of slavery finds so many interested writers to defend it by fraud and sophistry, in opposition to the common reason of mankind and the experience of every age. Absurd as are the principles, and notions, on which the doctrine of arbitrary power is established, there have been ever in this country found many to adopt it. The vulgar are at all times liable to be deceived, and this nation has ever produced a number of bad citizens, who, prone to be corrupted, have been the ready tools of wicked ministers and the zealous partizans, in a cause big with the ruin of the state, and the destruction of that felicity which the in-[xi]dividuals of this country have for some years enjoyed. It is justly remarked by an able writer, 'That there may be a faction for the crown as well as against it, and conspiracies against freedom as well as against prerogative.'[1] Whosoever attempts to remove the limitations necessary to render monarchy consistent with liberty, are rebels in the worst sense; rebels to the laws of their country, the law of nature, the law of reason, and the law of God. Can there be such men? was I to put the question to my own heart, it would answer, that it was impossible there should be such. But the annals of this country have a shameful tale to tell, that such a faction has ever existed in this state, from the earliest period of our present constitution.

This faction has not only prevented the establishing any regular system to preserve or improve our liberties; but lie at this time in wait for the first opportunity that the imperfections of this government may give them, to destroy those rights, which have been purchased by the toil and blood of the most exalted individuals that ever adorned humanity. To shew the causes of so great a malignancy it will be necessary to observe, that there are in every society a number of men to whom tyranny is in some measure profitable; men devoid of every virtue and qualification requisite to rise in a free state. The emoluments and favours they gain for supporting tyranny, are the only means by which they can obtain [xii] distinctions, which in every equal government are the

---

[1] Bolingbroke, *Remarks on the History of England* (1730), in *Works*, I, p. 438.

rewards of public service. The selfish affections of these men, exalted above worthier citizens, fancy a recompense in this exaltation ample enough for the sacrifice of their liberty. To avoid the censures of injured posterity, their children are brought up in the doctrine of a necessary servitude, and are taught to regard the champions of liberty as the disturbers of the peace of mankind. Hence is produced a numerous class of men, who having been educated in the principles of slavery, become the deluded instruments of all the villainous purposes of mean ambition.

Some there are, who envying the reputation which illustrious characters have acquired, bend their endeavours to destroy the genuine notions of virtue and public utility, on which the fame of great men is built. Others, whose affections are of so base an alloy, that they envy the independency which every individual of this country may enjoy, and would willingly forfeit that natural privilege to superior tyrants, provided they might have the power of domineering over the lower class of people. Others again, who having drudged through what is called a regular education, with much learning or rather reading, but without judgment to have acquired any real knowledge, become a magazine of other men's conceits, and commence the disciples of the first doctrine which accident flings in their way. [xiii] These scholars, in the pursuit of science, lose the distinctions of common sense, and are as obstinately fixed in the prejudices of the authors with whom they have conversed, as if these prejudices were the produce of their own imaginations. Hence proceed those opposite opinions among the speculative part of mankind in regard to popular and monarchical privileges. All men can acquire the jargon of terms, but the depth of science is only to be attained by genius. The greater proportion of ignorance there may be in a disputant, the more reluctant he is to give way to reasoning that contradicts the borrowed opinions which he has taken in the gross; he looks with a sovereign contempt on his antagonist, not because he can confute his arguments, but because his arguments contradict the tenets that have been laid down by Hobbs,[2] and other writers of that stamp. Unequal to the combat, he skirmishes at a distance, wilfully converses in generals, and never enters into those particulars which may investigate the subject. Men like these,

---

[2] Thomas Hobbes (1588–1679).

without the desire of attaining truth, wrangle but for victory; and if they have sense enough to see their mistakes, they never have candor enough to acknowledge them.

The general education of the English youth is not adapted to cherish those generous sentiments of independency, which is the only charac-teristic of a real gentleman. The business of the public schools is nothing [xiv] more than to teach the rudiments of grammar, and a certain degree of perfection in the Latin and Greek tongues. Whilst the languages of these once illustrious nations are the objects of attention, the divine precepts which they taught and practised are totally neglected. From the circle of these barren studies, the school-boy is transplanted into the university. Here he is supposed to be initiated in every branch of knowledge which distinguishes the man of education from the ignorant herd; but here, as I am told and have great reason to believe, are taught doctrines little calculated to form patriots to support and defend the privileges of the subject in this limited monarchy. 'In these seats of education', says an ingenious author, 'instead of being formed to love their country and constitution, the laws and liberties of it, they are rather disposed to love arbitrary government, and to become slaves to absolute monarchy. A change of interest, provocation, or some other consider-ation, may set them right as to the public; but they have no inward principle of love to their country and of public liberty; so that they are easily brought to like slavery, if they may be made the tools for managing it.'[3] The study of history is little cultivated in these seminaries, and not at all those fundamental principles of the English constitution on which our ancestors founded a system of government, in which the liberty of the subject is as absolutely instituted as the dignity of the sovereign.[i] [xv] Yet the knowledge of these fundamental principles are as necessary to understand this system of government, as the knowledge of them was necessary to construct it.

---

[i] I take this opportunity of mentioning the late excellent institution in the university of Oxford; of a profession of the common law of England; which, if carried on with the same ability and spirit that Dr. Blackstone has begun it, must be productive of the greatest public utility. [William Blackstone (1723–80) became the first incumbent of the Vinerian Professorship of English Law at Oxford in 1758. In this position, Blackstone gave his famous lectures on the common law, which were published between 1765 and 1770 as *Commentaries on the Laws of England*.]

[3] Gilbert Burnet, *History of His Own Time* (6 vols., London, 1725–34), VI, p. 1281.

The form of the constitution may be preserved, when the spirit of it is lost;[4] and nothing is more likely to happen, whilst those persons who are constituted to maintain it, are ignorant of those fundamental principles, on which the barriers, that defend civil liberty from prerogative, are founded. Prejudiced with a love of slavery, or at least ignorant of the advantages of liberty, the last part of the education of the men of fortune in this country, is what is called the tour of Europe, that is a residence for two or three years in the countries of France and Italy. This is the finishing stroke that renders them useless to all the good purposes of preserving the birth-right of an Englishman. Without being able to distinguish the different natures of different governments, their advantages, their disadvantages; without being able to comprehend how infinitely they affect the interest and happiness of individuals, they grow charmed with every thing that is foreign, are caught with the gaudy tinsel of a superb [xvi] court, the frolic levity of unreflecting slaves, and thus deceived by appearances, are rivetted in a taste for servitude.

These are the causes which occasion the irrational inclinations of many of the English people in regard to government: and would to God that these, tho' very important in themselves, were the only ones that liberty had to fear. In forming of this government a latent evil crept into the vitals of the state, and hath in the course of time poisoned every part of the constitution. Corruption, that undermining mischief, hath sapped the foundation of a fabric, whose building was cemented with the blood of our best citizens. The growing evil hath spread far and wide, tainted the minds of men with such an incurable degeneracy, that the virtue of our forefathers is become the ridicule of every modern politician.

It is become an established maxim, that corruption is a necessary engine of government.[5] There are some amongst us who have not been

---

[4] 'But tho we have preserved the armour, we have lost the spirit, of our constitution'. Bolingbroke, *Letter on the Spirit of Patriotism* (1736), in *Works*, III, p. 18. Distinguishing between the form and the spirit of the constitution was also a central theme in Bolingbroke's *Dissertation upon Parties* (1733–4).

[5] Hume advanced a defence of corruption in the technical eighteenth-century sense of the term, that is to say, executive influence over the legislature, in 'Of the Independency of Parliament' (1741), which he repeated in the final volume of his *History*; see *Hume's History*, VI, p. 532. Soame Jenyns had also, in his *Free Enquiry into the Nature and Origin of Evil* (1757), argued that a decrease in absolute power necessitated corruption in order to govern people successfully, since they were naturally and incurably wicked. Hume's argument had been directed against Bolingbroke, who wrote against 'Court Whig' writers such as James Pitt and William Arnall whom he contended were prepared to argue 'that

ashamed to say, that it is proper for the other parts of the legislature to depend on the monarch by corruption. How opposite this is to the genius and spirit of our constitution, is too apparent to need a proof. That the consequences of it are already severely felt in this country, our debts and heavy taxes fatally demonstrate. How destructive it is to [xvii] every virtue that preserves society, or dignifies human nature, is as apparent. This is a sad but certain truth, that corruption is so general amongst us that it has dissolved the sacred bonds of mutual trust. By the influence of bribery, every man in these days has a triple temptation to sin against his country: The emoluments of favour; the fear of being laughed at for his honesty; of being abandoned by his associates, and left single to stand the insults of a victorious faction.

If I have digressed from the subject I set out with, which was to inform the public of my intention in writing this history, they will, I hope, excuse a warmth which national evils have excited in a breast zealous in the cause of Liberty, and attached with a fervent devotion to the civil rights of my country. There remains nothing now but to assure my readers that I shall finish this morsel of history, to the accession of the Brunswick Line,[6] with the same indefatigable industry that I have executed this small part of it: and having nothing so much in view as the investigation of truth, shall pursue it with an integrity that, I think, cannot justly be called in question by the most invidious inquisitors.

[xviii] The inaccuracies of stile which may be found in this composition, will, I hope, find favour from the candour of the public; and the defects of a female historian, in these points, not weighed in the ballance of severe criticism.

[270] Chap. IX. ^Ann. 1625^

State of the civil and ecclesiastical government of England at the accession of the Stewart family. Causes of the change of government that took place during the administration of the Stewart family. State of the finances. State of trade during the reign of King James.

corruption serves to oil the wheels of government, and to render the administration more smooth and easy'. See *Dissertation upon Parties* (1733–4), in *Works*, II, p. 139.
[6] The Hanoverian succession in 1714. In the event, however, the *History* concluded with the Glorious Revolution.

To enable the reader to form just notions on the interesting transactions that brighten the following period of the English story, it may not be improper to enter into a detail of the state of the kingdom in regard to government at the accession of the Scottish line.[7] It must be owned, that it was in many respects very arbitrary, and that the liberties of the subject were neither accurately defined, nor apparently defended. The ecclesiastical faction that broke out in this kingdom during the administration of the Tudors had enabled that family to make pernicious encroachments on the legal rights of the subjects, stipulated by Magna Charta;[8] time had given strength to these usurpations, and oppo-[271]sition in the people to the will of the sovereign was unauthorized by examples of modern date. The universal simplicity of manners that subsisted during the early periods of the English history, and continued till the latter end of the sixteenth century, rendered the wiles of power less intricate; but at the same time it occasioned in the people an aptness to put a dangerous confidence in their princes: Thus, when the violence of Henry VIII had wrested the ecclesiastical jurisdiction over this country from the Roman pontiff,[9] the people readily submitted to the crown of England's being vested with that large addition of prerogative; and regal authority attained without difficulty the supreme power in all affairs relative to the government of the church, and the conscience of the subject.

Though the English people had long groaned under the oppressive tyranny of the see of Rome, yet this in latter years had become more moderate in its effects: Many statutes had been made to defend the people against the inordinate claims of this spiritual prince; and by these statutes individuals were in a great measure protected both in their persons and property: But when the same pretensions were united to the coercive power of civil magistracy, it appeared with all its former terrors, and became in reality the comprehensive engine of regal

---

[7] When Elizabeth I died childless, the Union of Crowns in 1603 saw the accession of James VI of Scotland to the throne of England as James I.

[8] Royal Charter of rights agreed to by King John in 1215. It was first drafted by Archbishop of Canterbury Stephen Langton to make peace between the king and a group of rebellious barons, and promised the protection of church rights, the exclusion of the barons from illegal imprisonment, and limitations on feudal payments to the crown. It became famous in the seventeenth century as a foundational document guaranteeing the liberty of Englishmen.

[9] Henry VIII, who reigned from 1509 until his death in 1547, enlisted England in the Reformation. The Act of Supremacy 1534 named Henry VIII and his successors as the head of the national church, replacing the pope.

despotism. This disadvantageous change could not but be severely felt in the most early periods of its establishment, though the resentment had been suppressed by the zeal which at that time prevailed for reforming the doctrine of the church, and for emancipating the nation from foreign jurisdiction. This zeal [272] was not subsided when the reformers met with a severe check by the succession of Mary,[10] that bigoted papist, who restored to the pope his authority, and reinstated the catholics in the administration. The severities the protestants suffered under this government erased from their minds every impression of evil less dreadful than that of a general and merciless persecution. Thus, when Elizabeth, who professed their principles and faith, possessed the regal dignity, they unanimously agreed to arm her with full powers to suppress opposition, and the high-commission court was re-erected in the very beginning of her reign. This was the supreme ecclesiastical tribunal, and was immediately under the direction of the crown. ^Hume^[11] A conformity of religion was exacted through the whole kingdom, and every refusal of the ceremonies then established was liable to be chastized by this court with deprivation, fines, confiscation, and imprisonment. Any word or writing that tended towards schism or sedition was punishable by the high-commissioners, or any three of them; they were the judges what expressions had that tendency. These inquisitors were not limited to proceed by legal information; rumour, suspicion, were sufficient grounds. To the party cited before them they administred an oath, by which they were bound to answer any question that should be propounded to them; this oath could not be evaded by any pretext, and a refusal incurred the punishment of imprisonment. The power of the star-chamber,[12] in civil matters, was as arbitrary as that of the high-commission court in ecclesiastical: Its authority was carried to this height by Henry VII the first of the Tudor line.[13] Nor was arbitrary judicature

---

[10] Mary I, who reigned between 1553 and her death in 1558, restored Catholicism in England. The re-establishment of Catholicism was reversed by her half-sister and successor Elizabeth I.

[11] *Hume's History*, v, pp. 124–5. See also IV, pp. 207–9.

[12] The Star Chamber was an English court at the royal Palace of Westminster, which was active from the late fifteenth century to the middle of the seventeenth century. It comprised privy counsellors and common-law judges, and supplemented the judicial activities of the common-law and equity courts. In 1641 the Long Parliament, led by John Pym and outraged by the treatment of religious Dissenters, abolished the Star Chamber.

[13] Henry VII reigned from 1485 until his death in 1509.

the only ensign of despotism that was attached [273] to the monarchy of England: The dispensing power, the power of imprisonment, of exacting forced loans and benevolence, of pressing and quartering soldiers, of erecting monopolies, had been all exercised in their turns by the several sovereigns that preceded the accession of the Stewart family.[ii] No wonder, therefore, that James united his darling idea of government to circumstances that appeared so entirely conformable to it. This appearance proved a deceitful one. Parliaments, viz. a right in the people of assembling by representatives, to assist at the making of new laws, the abolishing old ones, or to give an assent or negative to extraordinary levies of money, a precious privilege, which the people had yet preserved from the ruins of the Gothic constitution, had in it many latent resources to preserve liberty which had given way, though not entirely yielded, to the encroachments of successful tyranny.

When James took possession of the reins of government, the opportunity to exert its rights with redoubled [274] vigour was approaching; those circumstances that proved favourable to the criminal ambition of the Tudors were either feeble, or no longer existed; the apprehension of suffering religious persecution was converted into the dread of sinking into civil slavery: The protestants beheld with the utmost regret themselves and posterity subject to a power which they had raised for the purpose of crushing their enemies; the lights which men had obtained from a disquisition into theological tenets, and the doctrine of ecclesiastical subjection, had enabled them to judge more rationally of the nature and end of civil subordination. Passive obedience to princes, that notion which, through the darker ages of the world, had been efficaciously inculcated into the minds of the subject, began to be treated with

---

[ii] So extensive was the authority of the monarchy at the accession of James, that Elizabeth had appointed commissioners for the inspection of prisons, with full discretionary powers to adjust all differences between prisoners and their creditors, to compound debts, and give liberty to such debtors as they found honest, and incapable of making full payment. This commission James renewed in the fifteenth year of his reign. *Hume['s History*, v, p. 128].

We find also another extraordinary act of power exercised by this king: On the erecting a new wall at his palace at Theobalds, a commission was given to a certain number of domestics to press into his service as many workmen as should be sufficient to complete the work in a short time, and to seize by force bricks, carts, tools, and every necessary material. [Thomas] *Rymer's Foedera* [(20 vols., London, 1704–35), xvii, pp. 302–3].

a scepticism that produced an entire revolution in the opinions of the intelligent. Elizabeth saw and felt this change; had life and empire continued, she would undoubtedly have sustained the mortification of beholding an entire alteration in the conduct of the Commons, who had hitherto servilely complied with her imperious will. The shortsighted James was unable to account for the inconsistence he found between the theoretical and practical government of England; whilst the servility of the nobles confirmed him in the idea that he was in actual possession of a despotic power, the determined opposition of the Commons prevented him from bringing that idea to reality; a small degree of accuracy would have reconciled the seeming contradiction. Even in that early period it might have been discerned that noble principles had taken deep root in the minds of the English people, that the progress of more enlightened reason [275] would bring these to perfection, and the harvest of such fruit must infallibly produce an important change in the manner and constitution of the government.

The revolution in the Low Countries[14] did not a little contribute to hasten such a disposition: The hearts of the English were fired with sympathetic virtue, at the example of that brave and resolute people, happily emerged from a state of servitude to a state of flourishing freedom. The revival of letters co-operated with these causes to effect an alteration in the modes of thinking of the English nation. Those models of human glory, the histories of Greece and Rome, excited all to admire, the virtuous to a desire of imitation; and, whilst the composition of the antients delighted the taste, their science and precepts enlarged the mind, corrected the judgment, and improved the heart; whilst the theory of ancient politics became the study of the judicious learned, the recent success of the Dutch stimulated them with desire, and even distant hopes of putting that theory into practice. It must be acknowledged that these exalted schemes were not universally adopted; they were entirely confined to the men of letters, and of these to the most virtuous kind: But the simplicity of manners that preceded this age, and that eager appetite for learning which accompanied its revival, occasioned their number to be extensive, when compared to the productions

---

[14] The Dutch Revolt (1566–1648) was the insurrection in the Low Countries against the rule of the Habsburg dynasty. As a result, the northern provinces adopted Calvinism and Republicanism, and the southern provinces became entirely Catholic.

of modern times. It cannot be imagined that that stiff opposition which appeared in all the parliaments throughout this reign was directed by leaders that would have been satisfied with a temporary redress of grievances, or rather that would not have made [276] use of all the advantages that offered to have enlarged to the utmost the system of liberty. The completion of this was left to the more successful heroes of the following period, notwithstanding it had made a greater progress in this reign than was apparent; and the weak and absurd administration and conduct of the Stewart family ripened the execution of schemes which might more successfully have taken place, when time, with literature, had entirely dispelled that cloud of gross superstition which had long involved the European world. The continual complaints which the Commons in parliament preferred to James on the enormities that proceeded from the arbitrary system of judicature that subsisted at his accession, in some measure checked that tyrannical use of it which had been practised by Elizabeth. It has been mentioned by an ingenious historian, with an intention to do credit to this monarch, that the punishments inflicted by the high-commissioners during his reign were infinitely less in number, and those more mild, than they had been under the administration of Elizabeth.[15] Deprivations, fines, confiscation, and imprisonment, were judgments that then continually issued from this court: Deprivation was the highest punishment inflicted in the time of her successor.

A long suspension from warlike exercises, though baneful to a luxurious state, was, to the people of England, an advantageous circumstance. A foreign war might have diverted them from an attention to domestic evils; and their manners were not at this time so effeminate as to endanger an attachment to an inglorious inactivity; idleness, servility, and their concomitant [277] vices, were, in these happy days, only to be found among the servants and followers of the court. Candour, valour, integrity, a spirit of independence, and every other masculine virtue, were possessed in a high degree by the Commons of England, viz. of the male sex; whilst chastity, modesty, and industry, were the general characteristics of the females. Peace also was favourable to commerce; it is acknowledged by all historians that trade increased much in this

---

[15] *Hume's History*, v, p. 125.

reign. The vigorous measures of the parliament heightened this circumstance by freeing it from several monopolies, an imposition with which it had been much fettered by Elizabeth.

^Hume^[16] It was in James's reign that English colonies began to flourish in America. A board of trade was erected by this king to examine the efficacy of expedients that were proposed for the advantage of commerce. Agriculture, which was formerly imperfect in England, a most useful employment, rendered illustrious by the virtue of its followers,[iii] received great improvement in this time, and the nation began to be more independant on foreign produce for their daily sustenance.

James's yearly revenue was 450,000 l.; the subsidies were granted him by the Commons and the clergy, money paid him by the States and the king of France,[iv] with the sums he raised by extraordinary and [278] illegal methods, amounted in the whole to 2,193,374 l., which, divided into twenty-two equal portions, and added to his ordinary revenue, make an annual income of nearly 550,000 l.,[v] a trifling sum when compared to the modern expences of government:[vi] But the inhabitants of this island were then free from the incumbrance, danger, and charge of a standing army. The only burthen which the subjects bore was the supplying the luxury, parade, and prodigality of the court; and this was obtained from them by methods fraudulent and violent, disallowed by the legal forms of the constitution. They were defended from the evil of being oppressively taxed, under the pretence of public utility, by the indefatigable diligence and sturdy opposition of their representatives in parliament, the guardians of the common weal.

[iii] The practice of husbandry, even to manual labour, was exercised by every rank of the Roman people, in the virtuous times of that illustrious republic.

[iv] The sum of 60,000 l. due from Henry IV to Elizabeth.

[v] To this account of the revenue must be added tonnage and poundage [see note 69, below]: The sum that this tax brought in has never yet been calculated; the encrease of trade, and the exorbitant impositions that were laid on merchandize in this reign, made it very considerable.

[vi] The difference of the valuation of money may be thought an objection to the comparison; but, according to Mr. Hume's account of the prices that several of the necessaries of life bore in these days, the difference is not so very great as has been generally imagined. [See *Hume's History*, v, pp. 138–40.]

[16] Ibid., pp. 146–9.

[VOL. 4 (1768)]

[Ch. V, 355, note on the term 'Leveller']

This is a hackneyed term of reproach flung out on all occasions by the adversary against the partisans of Liberty; both with a view to throw ridicule on their system, as visionary and impracticable, and to engage the selfish affections of men in the cause of arbitrary and unequal dominion. The levelling plan, according to the insinuations of these scoffers, never was, nor ever can be adopted by men who have accurate notions of a state of nature, or who are well informed in the science of government and the laws of society; for though the justice and wisdom of God has given equal and impartial privileges to the species in general, yet the difference which exists in the judgment, understanding, sagacity, genius, and industry of individuals, creates superiority and inferiority of character, and produces a state of dependance from man to man. To preserve that natural subordination established by God himself, and to keep that accumulation of property and influence which the different qualities of men occasion, from producing tyranny, and infringing the general rights of the species, lies the whole art of true and just policy. All political distinctions which are personal, however wisely and impartially distributed, are mischievous in their nature, because they give weight instead of ballance to the preponding scale: but hereditary privileges are the mere establishments of selfishness, and attended with the most destructive consequences; since, necessarily counteracting the laws of Providence, the vicious and foolish bear rule over the wise and virtuous, the system of nature is not regulated but overturned, and those are preposterously placed at the head of society, whose qualities often entitle them to no other than the most inferior station in it.

[Ch. VI, 410] ^The King's trial, execution, and character.^

On the twentieth of January, the commissioners proceeded in state from the Painted Chamber to Westminster-Hall. Colonel Humphry[17] carried

---

[17] It is unclear who this refers to. Humphrey Edwards was a colonel, but he may not have been present at the execution. This part of the narrative, with the names and their spelling, is adapted from the translation of the fourth volume of Isaac de Larrey, *Histoire d'Angleterre, d'Écosse et d'Irlande* (4 vols., 1707–12), published as *The History of the Reign of King Charles I* (2 vols., London, 1716), II, pp. 362–3.

the sword before the president, serjeant Dendy[18] the mace, and twenty gentlemen (commanded by colonel Fox[19]) attended as his guard of partizans. The royal prisoner, who, for the purpose of his trial, had been removed from Windsor to St. James's, was by a strong guard of musqueteers conveyed by water to West-[411]minster Hall. A chair of crimson velvet was prepared for him within the bar, and thirty officers and gentlemen waited with halberts behind it. The solicitor of the Commons, in his charge against the King, represented, That Charles Stewart, being admitted King of England, and entrusted with a limited power, had, with the wicked design to erect an unlimited and tyrannical government, traitorously and maliciously levied war against the people and their representatives: That, on the behalf of the people, he did, for this treasonable breach of trust, impeach him as a tyrant, a traitor, a murderer, and a public and implacable enemy to the commonwealth.

On the conclusion of the charge, the King demanded by what authority he was brought before that court?[vii] He told the commissioners to remember he was their King, their lawful King, and to beware of the sins with which they were going to stain themselves and the land. He was answered by the president, that he was tried in the name and authority of the parliament assembled, and the good people of England. Charles objected, That both King and house of Lords were necessary to constitute a parliament: He had a trust, he said, committed to him by God, by old and lawful descent; and he would not betray it to answer to a new and unlawful authority: He again bade the commissioners remember he was their [412] hereditary sovereign; and that the whole authority of the state, when free and united, was not entitled to try him, who derived his dignity from the supreme majesty of heaven: That, admitting those extravagant principles which place the origin of power in the people, the court could plead no authority delegated by the people, unless the consent of every individual, down to the meanest, the most ignorant

---

[vii] Ludlow says, That the King interrupted the clerk whilst he was reading, and exclaimed, 'I am not entrusted by my people; they are mine by inheritance.' [*Memoirs of Edmund*] *Ludlow* [(1698; London, 1751)], p. 107.

[18] Edward Dendy (bap. 1613–74).

[19] Colonel John 'Tinker' Fox (1610–50), Parliamentarian soldier, who was wrongly rumoured to be one of Charles I's executioners.

peasant, had been previously asked and obtained:[viii] There was no jurisdiction on earth could try a King: The authority of obedience to Kings was clearly warranted and strictly commanded both in the Old and New Testaments: This, if denied, he was ready instantly to prove; 'Where the word of a King was there was power, and who might say unto him, what dost thou?' He owned, he said, he was entrusted; a sacred trust had been committed to him by God, the liberties of his people, which he would not betray by recognizing a power founded on violence and usurpation: He had taken arms, and frequently exposed his life, in defence of public liberty, in defence of the constitution, in defence of the fundamental laws of the kingdom, and was now willing to seal with his blood those precious rights for which he had so long in vain contended. To the King's extravagant assertion, that he had taken up arms to defend the liberty of the constitution, and that he now pleaded for the rights and freedom of all his subjects, the president [413] returned, 'How great a friend, Sir, you have been to the laws and liberties of the people, let all England and the world judge: Your actions have sufficiently declared it, and your meaning has been written in bloody characters throughout the kingdom.' The court was reminded by the prisoner, that the laws of England determined the King could do no wrong; however, he was able, he said, by the most satisfactory reasons, to justify his conduct; but must forego the apology of his innocence, lest, by ratifying an authority no better founded than that of robbers and pirates, he should be justly branded as the betrayer, instead of applauded as the martyr, of the constitution.

Three several days the King was produced before the court, and as often urged to answer to his charge. The fourth, on his constantly persisting to decline its jurisdiction, the commissioners, after having examined witnesses,[ix] by whom it was proved that the King had [414]

[viii] This argument is mere sophistry; since the sense of the people, in their collective capacity, never can come to any determined conclusive point, unless the sense of the majority is binding to the whole. [John Locke, *Two Treatises of Government* (London, 1764), p. 280.]

[ix] One of these witnesses gave an evidence of the King's want of sincerity in his last treaty with the parliament, at Newport, in the Isle of Wight. The witness, Henry Goode, deposed, That having access to and discourse with the King at Newport, he told him, that, since his majesty had justified the parliament's taking up arms, he did not question but the Presbyterian party would stick close to him; that to this the King had replied, he would have all his old friends know, that, though for the present he was contented to give the parliament leave to call their own war what they pleased, yet he neither did then, nor

appeared in arms against his people, proceeded to pronounce sentence against him. Before the passing sentence, Charles earnestly desired to be admitted to a conference with the two houses: he had something to propose, he said, which he was sure would be for the welfare of the kingdom and the liberty of the Subject. It was supposed that he intended to offer to resign the crown to his son; and some of the commissioners pressed that he might be heard. This was not the opinion of the majority; and the commissioners returning from the court of Wards, where they had adjourned to consult on the King's proposal, acquainted the prisoner, that his request was considered as a delay of justice. The president passed sentence of death, by severing the head from the body; and all the members of the court stood up in token of approbation.

An example of justice, from which they had ever regarded their rank to be totally exempt, awakened in every sovereign prince a sense of horror and indignation; whilst political reasons, of a different nature, inclined them to endeavor to prevent the change of government in England. The French court was now sincere in their interposition for favor to the King; and the Dutch employed very earnest intercessions for the preservation of his life. All solicitations were found vain. The Scots fruitlesly exclaimed [415] and protested; the prince wrote an ineffectual letter to the army, and the queen to the parliament. Three days only were allowed the King between his sentence and his execution.[x] This interval he passed in reading and devotion; and preserved, from the time when his intended fate was known to him, to his last moment, a perfect tranquillity and composure; nor can his bitterest enemies deny, that in

should decline the justice of his own cause. Moreover, upon the deponent's saying his majesty's business was much retarded through want of commissions, the King made answer, That being upon a treaty, he would not dishonor himself; but if the deponent would go over to the prince his son, who had full authority from him, he or any for him should receive whatever commissions they should desire. *Rushworth*, vol. VII. p. 1413. [The seventh volume of Sir John Rushworth's *Historical Collections* (7 vols., 1659–1701) refers to *Historical Collections: The Fourth and Last Part* (2 vols., 1701).]

[x] Clement Walker, a petulant writer of the Presbyterian party, in his *History of Independency* [(1648–9)], has propagated the following calumny on the parliament and army: That they lodged the King in an apartment at Whitehall, so near the destined place of execution, that his retirement and even rest were disturbed with the noise of the workmen employed in framing the scaffold; whereas, in fact, the King remained at St. James's till the very morning of his execution, when he walked across the Park, and from thence was carried in a coach to Whitehall. [*Anarchia Anglicana: or, the History of Independency. The second Part Being a Continuation of Relations and Observations Historicall and Politique upon This Present Parliament, Begun anno 16. Caroli Primi* (London, 1649), p. 110.]

his conduct, under the dreadful apprehension of a violent death were united the magnanimity of heroism and the patience of martyrdom.

To mark to the gaping multitude the triumph of popular justice over royal rank, the scaffold for execution was erected before the palace at Whitehall; care was taken that it should be sufficiently surrounded with soldiers, to prevent disorder or interruption; and the King, finding himself shut out from the hearing of the people, addressed a speech to colonel Tomlinson,[20] the commander of the guard, in which he attempted to justify his innocence in the war he had levied, termed it defensive, accused the parliament of having first enlisted forces,[xi] and averred that he had [416] no other object in his military operations than to preserve entire that authority which had been transmitted to him by his ancestors; insisted on a perfect innocence towards his people; observed, that the unjust sentence now inflicted on him was an equitable return for that which he had suffered to be inflicted on Strafford;[21] forgave his enemies; and exhorted the people to return to the paths of obedience, and submit to the government of their lawful sovereign, his son and successor. Bishop Juxon,[22] whose attendance (though a cold inanimate speaker, and very incapable of raising the thoughts beyond their natural bounds) the King had very particularly and earnestly desired,[xii] remembered his master, that the people would expect him to make some declaration on the point of religion: On this the King very earnestly protested, that he had ever lived, and now died in the religion of the church of England. Whilst he was preparing for execution, the

---

[xi] See, on this subject, vol. III. of this *History*, p. 273, & *seq.*

[xii] Ludlow tells the following anecdote of this bishop: When the doctor was acquainted with the King's condition and desires, he, being altogether unprepared for such a work, broke out into these expressions; 'God save me! what a trick is this that I should have no more warning, and I have nothing ready!' But recollecting himself a little, he put on his scarf and his other furniture, and went to the King; where, having read the Common-Prayer and one of his old sermons, he administered the sacrament to him, not forgetting to use the words of the confession set down in the Liturgy, inviting all those who truly repent to make their confession before the congregation then gathered together, though there was no one present but the King and himself. [*Memoirs of Edmund*] *Ludlow*, p. 109.

[20] Matthew Thomlinson (1617–81), colonel in the New Model Army.

[21] Charles I had reluctantly signed the death warrant of his supporter Thomas Wentworth, 1st Earl of Strafford (1593–1641), in 1641 to placate Parliament, which had condemned Strafford to death.

[22] William Juxon (1582–1663), bishop of London from 1633 to 1646 and archbishop of Canterbury from 1660 until his death.

24

bishop poured out a few insipid lifeless exhortations: To these the King returned, 'I go from a corruptible to an incorruptible [417] crown, where no disturbance can have place.' ^Jan. 30. [1649]^ Then laying his head upon the block, the executioner (whose face was concealed in a vizor) severed it with one stroke from the body: an assistant (in the like disguise) held it up to the spectators, streaming with blood, and, after the usual manner observed in similar executions, cried aloud, 'This is the head of a traitor.'

Thus, by a fate unparalleled in the annals of princes, terminated the unfortunate life and turbulent reign of Charles Stewart; a monarch whose principles, conduct, fortune, and death, by powerfully engaging the opposite affections attending the different views and different interests of men, have given rise to bitter and irreconcileable contest. Regarded as the martyr to church[xiii] and state, the patron of the clergy, the support of the nobility, we behold him, in the representations of a considerable party, adorned with every flower of panegyrick: By the bigots of a different persuasion, his memory, notwithstanding the tribute he paid to his crimes, is held in the highest detestation. The partizans of Liberty applaud his fate; the liberal and humane condemn and pity him: To a mind softened by habits of amusement, and intoxi-[418]cated with ideas of self-importance, the transition from royal pomp to a prison, from easy, gay, and luxurious life to a premature and violent death by the hands of an executioner, are punishments so sharp and touching, that, in the suffering prince, we are apt to overlook the designing tyrant, to dwell on his hardships, and forget his crimes. Compassion is the constant attendant of liberal minds; and the commiseration of Charles's singular and unfortunate fate, but for the interests of truth and the violence of his partizans, would have inclined all such to have thrown the mantle of oblivion over the dark parts of his character, and only to have remembered that he bore his sufferings in a manner which would have done honor to the best cause. From such indulgence the ill-fated Charles is necessarily excluded: History is called upon to scrutinize with exactness

---

[xiii] The opinion of Charles's dying a martyr to the church is grounded on his refusing to give satisfaction, on this article, in his last treaty with the parliament; but, if there is any credence to be given to Lilly, the King would have signed the propositions in the form sent down to him, had he not been diverted from it by the lord Say [William Fiennes, 1st Viscount Saye and Sele (1582–1662)], on the hopes that the parliament would conclude with him upon earlier terms. *Lilly* [*Mr. William Lilly's True History of King James the First, and King Charles the First* (London, 1715)], p. 72, & *seq.*

his principles, conduct, and character; since, from the false colorings which by designing men have been thrown on these, and the rancor with which his opponents have been falsely aspersed, have been deduced consequences destructive to the security and welfare of man, and highly injurious to the reputation of patriot citizens.

In the character of Charles, as represented by his panegyrists, we find the qualities of temperance, chastity, regularity, piety, equity, humanity, dignity, condescension, and equanimity; some have gone so far as to allow him integrity;[23] and many writers, who condemn his political principles, give him the title of a moral man. In the comparison of this repre-[419]sentation with Charles's conduct, accurately and justly described, it is discernible that vices of the worst tendency, when shaded by a formal and plausible carriage, when concordant to the interests of a faction and the prejudices of the vulgar, assume the appearances of, and are imposed on the credulous world as, virtues of the first rank. – Passion for power was Charles's predominant vice; idolatry to his regal preroga-tives his governing principle:[xiv] The interests of his crown legitimated every measure, and sanctified in his eye the widest deviation from moral rule. His religion was to this a secondary and subordinate affection: The prelates of the church of England paid him an impious flattery; they inculcated a slavish dependance on the regal authority; the corruptions in their ecclesiastical discipline fostered superstition; superstition secured their influence over the people; and on these grounds, and to these ends, they kept an interest in the King's heart, which continued to the last period of his life.[xv] If Charles had an higher [420] estimation of the faith

---

[xiv] The History of Coins affords an anecdote which shews Charles's affections towards prerogative and popular rights: In the years 1601, 2, 3, 4, and 5, there were several coins stricken in Scotland by James the First, bearing on their reverse the motto, '*Salus populi suprema lex esto* [i.e. the safety of the people is the supreme law].' In the first year of Charles's government, he altered on his coins the just sentiment of this motto, to '*Salus reipublicae suprema lex esto* [i.e. the safety of the state, or literally the public thing, is the supreme law].'

[xv] In the British Museum, N° 122, there is a MS. letter from the King to his queen, dated from Newcastle, 1646, wherein he tells her, That whoever gave her the advice that he should submit to take the damned covenant, was a fool or knave, that it was the child of rebellion, and breathed nothing but treason; that if episcopacy was to be introduced by the covenant he would not take it, for he was as much bound in conscience to do no act for the destruction of monarchy as to resist heresy. In a letter of the seventeenth of October, from the same place, the King, in answer to the queen's pressing importunity

---

[23] *Hume's History*, v, p. 543.

in which he had been educated than of Popery, it was because the principles of Popery acknowledged a superior allegiance to their spiritual than their temporal prince; but regarding that superstition to be more favorable to the interests of monarchy, he preferred it to the religion of any differing sect, and publicly avowed his wish, that [421] there never had been a schism in the church. ^Birch's Enquiry, p. 297.^24 Neither gratitude,[xvi] clemency, humanity,[xvii] equity, nor

(by [Sir William] Davenant [(1606–68)]) for his agreeing to the establishment of Presbyterian government, says, That such an establishment would make him but a titular King; that a flower of the crown, given away by an act of parliament, is not recoverable; that if the supremacy in Church affairs was not a flower of the crown, he knew not what was; that the difference between episcopal and Presbyterian government was one of the least of his disputes with the parliament, who, under the pretence of a thorough reformation, did intend to take away all the ecclesiastical power of government from the crown; that they would introduce a doctrine which taught rebellion to be lawful, That the supreme power is in the people, to whom kings were accountable. In a letter of the twentieth of November, the King tells the queen, That unless religion was preserved, the militia (being not, as in France and other kingdoms, a formed powerful strength) would be of little use to the crown; that if the pulpits had not obedience, which would never be if Presbyterian government was absolutely established, the King would have but small comfort of the militia; that for his three years concession of Presbyterian government, he never heard that any right was yielded so long as the claim was kept up, which was clearly done by the article of a debate by divines how the church should be governed, the determination being still free to him and the two houses, on which if his conscience was wronged, he could blame nothing but his own want of courage. In the end of this letter the King says, He is confident that he shall in a short time be recalled with much honor, and that his friends would see he had neither a foolish nor a peevish conscience. *British Museum*, MS. 6988. [This correspondence is now in British Library Add MS 28857, and is printed in *Charles I in 1646: Letters of King Charles the First to Queen Henrietta Maria*, ed. John Bruce (London, 1856), pp. 84–6.]

[xvi] The favors which Charles's fortunes occasioned him to receive from his subjects, he regarded only as obligations of duty to their prince; and any failure, either through motives of conscience or regard to personal safety or interest, in the lengths he exacted of them, cancelled the merits of former services. Of all the nobility and gentry slain in his service, the only individuals whose premature death, it is observed, he gave any public testimony of regretting, were Sir Charles Lucas [(1613–48)] and Sir George Lisle [(1615–48)], when his mind was softened by long adversity.

[xvii] Notwithstanding Clarendon's [i.e. Edward Hyde, 1st Earl of Clarendon (1609–74), author of *The History of the Rebellion* (3 vols., 1702–3)] extravagant encomium on the King for these virtues, the severe punishments he inflicted on several individuals, by the court of Star-Chamber, shew an extreme rigor in regard to offenders who opposed his government and opinions. – Ludlow and other writers aver, That the prisoners of war, in places immediately under his command, were treated with inhuman cruelty; and

24 Thomas Birch, *An Inquiry into the Share which King Charles I Had in the Transactions of the Earl of Glamorgan, Afterwards Marquis of Worcester, for Bringing Over a Body of Irish Rebels to Assist that King in the Years 1645 and 1646* (London, 1747), pp. 247–8.

generosity,^{xviii} have place in the fair part of Charles's character. Of the virtues of temperance, fortitude, and [422] personal bravery, he was undeniably possessed. His manners partook of the dissipation, and his conversation of the indecency of a court.^{xix} His chastity has been called in question by an author of the highest repute;^{xx} and were it allowed, it was tainted by an excess of uxoriousness, which gave it the properties and the consequences of vice. The want of integrity is manifest in every part of his conduct; which, whether the corruption of his judgment or heart, lost him fair opportunities of reinstatement in the throne, and was the vice for which, above all others, he paid the tribute of his life. His intellectual powers were naturally good, and so improved by a continued exercise, that, though in the beginning of his reign he spoke with difficulty and hesitation, towards the close of his life he discovered in his writings purity of language and dignity of style, in his debates

there are some traits of history which shew an indifference, or rather hardness of heart, to the sufferings of others. One, which is to be met with in the Strafford Papers, mentions the King's laughing at the relation of an officer's having lost part of his cheek in an engagement: this anecdote happened in the beginning of his reign. The same Papers make mention of a great unfeelingness, or rather harshness, in the King's behavior to his servant Cottington, on the melancholy occasion of his wife's death. [*The Earl of Strafforde's Letters and Dispatches* (2 vols., London, 1739), I, p. 214.] Lilly, the astrologer, who knew the King well, and who was sometimes consulted on his future fortunes, says, That in the times of war he was seldom seen to be sorrowful for the slaughter of his people or his soldiers. *Lilly's Observations on the Life and Death of King Charles*, ed. 1715, p. 13.

^{xviii} The innovation of laws committed to his trust, with several mean as well as unjust acts, testify this. In particular, in the commencement of his reign, he dispensed by proclamation with the legal obligation his subjects lay under to buy the honor of knighthood; and then levied fines upon them for non-performance.

^{xix} Before the commencement of the civil wars, plays, and every kind of dissipation which the times afforded, reigned in the King's court. Milton, in his masterly *Defence, &c.* against Salmasius [i.e. *Defensio pro Populo Anglicano*, or *Defence of the People of England* (1651)], taxes the King with amorous indecencies committed in public; and, notwithstanding the contrary has been so strongly asserted by Clarendon, there are two passages in the Sydney Papers which demonstrate that the conversation of the court, and even of Charles himself, was not only indelicate but lewd. [Arthur Collins, *Letters and Memorials of State, in the Reigns of Queen Mary, Queen Elizabeth, King James, King Charles the First, Part of the Reign of King Charles the Second, and Oliver's Usurpation. Written and Collected by Sir Henry Sydney, Knight of the Garter* (2 vols., London, 1746).]

^{xx} Milton, in his *Defence, &c.* gives shrewd intimations that the King was defective in the point of chastity. Lilly says of him, That he honored the virtuous, and was very shy and choice in wandering in irregular paths; that when he did, it was with much cautiousness and secrecy; that he never prostituted his affections but to those of exquisite persons or parts. The same author asserts that Charles had one or two natural [i.e. illegitimate] children. *Lilly*, [*True History of King James the First, and King Charles the First,*] p. 11.

elocution and quickness of conception. The high opinion he [423] entertained of regal dignity occasioned him to observe a stateliness and imperiousness of manner, which, to the rational and intelligent, was unamiable and offensive; by the weak and the formal, it was mistaken for dignity.[xxi] In the exercise of horsemanship he excelled; had a good taste, and even skill in several of the polite arts; but, though a proficient in some branches of literature, was no encourager of useful learning, and only patronized adepts in the jargon of [424] the divine right and utility of kings and bishops. His understanding in this point was so depraved by the prejudices of his education, the flattery of priests, and the affections of his heart, that he would never endure conversation which tended to inculcate the principles of equal rights in men; and notwithstanding that the particularity of his situation enforced his attention to doctrines of this kind, he went out of the world with the same fond prejudices with which he had been fostered in his nursery, and cajoled in the zenith of his power.[xxii]

[xxi] In the King's palaces different rooms were allotted to the different ranks of the nobility and gentry; and orders were hung up in every apartment, forbidding all persons below a certain quality to enter. The observance of these ridiculous distinctions was exacted with such rigor, that Sir Henry Vane the younger [(bap. 1613–62)], having intruded himself into an apartment allotted to a superior rank, was so suddenly, whilst in discourse, surprised with the King's appearance, that, not having opportunity to retire unperceived, he hid himself behind a large carpet, which hung before a sideboard cupboard: in this situation he was discovered by the King, who, with an unmanly insolence, struck him with his cane. Even in Charles's days of humiliation, he struck colonel [Edward] Whaley [(c. 1607–75)] for the omission of some ceremony, or fancied disrespect; and when Sir Thomas Fairfax [(1612–71)] (who proved one of the principal actors in his overthrow) presented him on his knees a petition, the King, who knew the contents would be disagreeable to him, turned haughtily away, with a motion as sudden that the petitioner was hurt by his horse's feet, and had like to have been trampled to death. With manners so insolent and provoking, the King's general carriage was stiff and formal, to a degree which carried the appearance of high contempt, to his inferiors. Clarendon spends many pages in panegyrising the King on the article of his stateliness; sets forth the glories of Solomon's court as an example for all princes to follow; and observes, That its pompous ceremonies struck the queen of Sheba with the high idea she is said to have conceived of Solomon's wisdom: This, though a very natural sentiment in a female princess, is a little out of character in the mouth of a moralist, a philosopher, and an historian [Thomas] Carte's [*History of the*] *Life of* [*James Duke of*] *Ormond* [*from His Birth in 1610, to His Death in 1688* (3 vols., London, 1735–6)], vol. I. p. 356, & *seq.* Clarendon's *History* [*of the Rebellion* (3 vols., Oxford, 1702–4), II, p. 300].

[xxii] In apology for Charles's government, it has been often advanced, that the same tyrannical principles prevailed equally in those of all his predecessors, and in particular in the government of that favorite sovereign queen Elizabeth; that Charles only

Charles was of a middle stature; his body strong, healthy, and justly proportioned; his face was regular, handsome, and well complexioned; and his aspect melancholy, yet not unpleasing. His surviving [425] issue were three sons and three daughters.[xxiii] He was executed in the forty-ninth year of his age, and buried, by the appointment of the parliament, at Windsor, decently, yet without pomp. The duke of Richmond,[25] the marquis of Hertford,[26] the earls of Southampton[27] and Lindsay,[28] at their express desire, were permitted to pay the last duty to their master, but were denied (by colonel Whitchcot,[29] the governor of Windsor-Castle) the use of the burial service, according to the book of Common-Prayer.[xxiv]

endeavored to preserve the rights he found in the crown; and that the usurpation began on the side of the Commons. In contradiction to this assertion, it is to be observed, that Charles, by offering to bring things back to the course preserved in church and state during Elizabeth's government, acknowledged he had innovated both. Were it granted, that the Commons made the first attack on the established encroachments of the crown, was that supposed right to be defended by any mean? Charles's situation, and consequently his political conduct, differed widely from that of Elizabeth and the rest of his fortunate predecessors: in the peaceful possession of their tyranny, they ruled a willing people, and preserved the forms of the constitution. The opposition with which Charles encountered engaged him in breach of faith, in civil war, and other criminal transactions; whilst his inflexible tenacity, with the steady opposition of the Commons, must, had he prevailed, have destroyed every principle of Liberty in the constitution.

[xxiii] Charles prince of Wales, born in 1630; James duke of York, in 1633; Henry duke of Glocester, in 1641; Mary princess of Orange, born in 1631; Elizabeth, in 1635; and Henrietta, in 1644.

[xxiv] Of the voluminous works published in Charles's name, his letters and messages to the parliament, during his strict confinement in the Isle of Wight, are known to be his, with several letters written to the queen and others. Whether he was the author of the *Eikon Basilike [the Pourtraicture of His Sacred Majestie in his Solitudes and Sufferings* (London, 1649)], a work said to be composed by him in the decline of his fortunes, has been a matter highly contested. The stile of this composition has great similarity to the King's; the professions to be found in it, though contrary to the whole tenor of his conduct, he had often publicly made; many of the sentiments are his own, and others he had always assumed; yet the proofs, brought by Toland to evince that this work was not the King's, lord Clarendon's total silence on so important a point, and the testimony of the duke of

[25] James Stewart, 1st Duke of Richmond, 4th Duke of Lennox (1612–55), and a third cousin of Charles I. The four lords mentioned by Macaulay in this context assumed responsibility for Charles I's actions before the Commons and petitioned to be executed in his place.

[26] William Seymour, 1st Marquess of Hertford from 1641, and 2nd Duke of Somerset in 1660 (1588–1660).

[27] Thomas Wriothesley, 4th Earl of Southampton (1607–67).

[28] Montagu Bertie, 2nd Earl of Lindsey (1608–66).

[29] Colonel Christopher Whichcote, active in 1642–59.

A question whether the people, in any case, have a right to depose and punish their sovereign, became, [426] on the death of Charles, the subject of earnest debate, and was pursued by the high-church and prerogative party with the utmost violence and acrimony. The sufferings of the royal martyr, for so the deceased monarch was termed, were compared to those of Christ the Redeemer: In the comparison, the hard-ships of the King's case (on account of his rank) were ridiculously and impiously preferred; and the crucifiers of their God, by churchmen and their adherents, were regarded with an inferior detestation to the murderers of their King.[xxv] The corrupt doctrines which [427] had been

York, as related by Burnet, have more than equal weight against the arguments of the royalists. [Part II of John Toland, *Amyntor: Or, A Defence of Milton's Life* (London, 1699) was entitled 'A compleat history of the book intituled *Icon basilike*, proving Dr. Gauden, and not King Charles the First, to be the author of it.'] There is a letter said to be written by Charles, during his last treaty with the parliament, and addressed to the prince of Wales, which Burnet, by the same testimony, hints to be spurious: Though tinctured with Charles's prejudices, it is full of moral sentiments; and were it not for the King's insincere conduct with the parliament in regard to Ireland, at the very time it was supposed to be written, would argue his reformation in the point of integrity. [Burnet, *History of His Own Time*, I, pp. 76–7.]

[xxv] [Edward] Symmons's [*A True*] *Parallel* [*Betwixt the Sufferings of our Saviour and our Soveraign*], published in 1648. Various sermons; in particular one preached by the bishop of Down [i.e. Henry Leslie (1580–1661)], before Charles the Second, in the year 1649, printed at Breda, and reprinted at London in 1720; one preached on February 4, 1648, entitled 'The Devilish Conspiracy, &c.' [by John Warner (1581–1666), Bishop of Rochester] and another by Dr. Binks [i.e. William Binckes (1652/3–1712), proctor for the diocese of Lichfield and Coventry], preached on the thirtieth of January, before the lower house of Convocation, in 1701, and censured by the house of Lords, as a just scandal and offence to all Christian people. – The following passages, out of the bishop of Down's sermon, are given as specimens of the doctrines and opinions of high-church divines; viz. 'The person now murdered was not the Lord of glory, but a glorious lord, Christ's own vicar, his lieutenant and vicegerent here on earth; and therefore, by all laws divine and human, he was privileged from any punishment which could be inflicted by men. Albeit he was an inferior to Christ, as man is to God, yet was his privilege of inviolability far more clear than was Christ's; for Christ was not a temporal prince, his kingdom was not of this world, and therefore when he vouchsafed to come into the world, and to become the son of man, he did subject himself to the law; but our gracious sovereign was well known to be a temporal prince, a free monarch, and their undoubted sovereign, to whom they did all owe and had sworn allegiance. The parliament is the great council, and hath acted all and more against their lord and sovereign than the other did against Christ: the proceedings against our sovereign were more illegal, and in many things more cruel. The true religion delivered unto us in scripture, and professed in the true, ancient, and Catholic church, doth teach us to honor and obey the King, as God's minister set over us; and that the injuries of kings, though ever so great, are to be endured by their subjects, who have no other remedy, and are to use no other arms against their King, than to pray unto God for him,

taught by the clergy were currently broached as standards of political and divine truths; and the utmost depravity of human reason appeared in the contest. Monarchy was represented as a form of government of God's immediate appointment; kings his sacred vicegerents, whom to resist was impious, to depose was damnable, to punish was atrociously criminal beyond the hope of mercy; nor could the utmost height of depravity in the nature, or wickedness in the conduct of a monarch, excuse, in any degree, such an act of jurisdiction in revolted subjects. Systems, on the principles of fate and necessity, were written to support the doctrines of slavery: A paternal and legislative power in kings was attempted to be proved by succession from Adam; of whom it was absurdly asserted, that he was by God invested with the absolute power of life and death.[xxvi]

[428] As the scriptures were wrested to authorize the doctrines of the adversary, so the partizans of Liberty, ^Goodwin's Defence of the Honorable Sentence^[30] from the same source, argued, That the death of a bloodshedder was required by the Lord, who by his word cautions against the respect of persons, or the exempting individuals from judgment on account of their authority; that men of all ranks and orders were included in this command; and, in case of the deficiency of the magistrate, were bound to see it fulfilled. ^The Resolver, &c. quarto, ed. 1648^[31] On the rule of policy, they observed, That the constitution of a King did not

who hath the hearts of kings in his hand, and may turn them when he thinks fit.' [Leslie, *The Martyrdome of King Charles, or His Conformity with Christ in His Sufferings* (The Hague, 1649), pp. 12, 25, 23.]
The following passage, in a letter from general Digby [George Digby, 2nd Earl of Bristol (bap. 1612–77)] to the marquis of Ormond, shews that the impious nonsense preached in these and successive times, to the end of queen Anne's reign, were not only to be found in the doctrines of the high-church clergy, but had taken deep root in the opinions of their followers. 'From the creation to the accursed day of this damnable murther, nothing parallel to it was ever heard of. Even the crucifying our Blessed Savior, if we consider him only in his human nature, did nothing equal this; his kingdom not being of this world; and he, though unjustly condemned, yet judged at a lawful tribunal.' *State Letters*. Carte [i.e. Thomas Carte, *An History of the Life of James Duke of Ormonde* (3 vols., London, 1735)], vol. III. p. 607.

[xxvi] These nonsensical opinions are fully confuted in two masterly performances of Locke and Sydney [i.e. in *Two Treatises of Government* and *Discourses concerning Government*, respectively].

[30] John Goodwin, *Hybristodikai. The Obstructours of Justice. Or a Defence of the Honourable Sentence Passed Upon the Late King, by the High Court of Justice* (London, 1649).
[31] *The Resolver, or, a Short Word, to the Large Question of the Times* (1648 [i.e. 1649]). This anonymous tract is signed 'N.T'.

take away that lawful defence against force and injury allowed by the law of nature: That even the civil laws which were imperial, declared, that we are not to obey a prince ruling above the limits of the power entrusted to him; for the commonwealth, by constituting a King, doth not rob or deprive itself of the power of its own preservation: ^Sydney's Discourses on Government, quarto ed. 1763^32 That God having given the world to no one man, nor declared how it should be divided, left it to the will of man: ^Milton's Tenure of Kings and Magistrates^33 That government and magistracy, whether supreme or subordinate, was a mere human ordinance: That the laws of every nation were the measure of magistratical power: ^Goodwin's Defence^ That Kings, the servants of the state, when they degenerated into tyrants, forfeited their right to government: That where there is a covenant and oath, there must be coactive power to enforce it: ^Milton's Defence, &c. against Salmasius^34 That the oaths of allegiance were to be understood as conditionally binding, according to the observance of the oaths kings made to their people: And that neither the laws of God nor nature were against the people's laying aside Kings and kingly government, and the adopting more conve-[429]nient forms. ^[Milton,] Tenure of Kings and Magistrates^ To the opposition of the Presbyterians, it was objected, That he whom they had exclaimed against in their pulpits as a tyrant, as an enemy to God and saints, as laden with all the innocent blood spilt in the three kingdoms; that he whom they had devoted to perdition, with exhortation to curse, in the name of God, all those who did not make war against him; was without penitence or alteration in his first principles, a lawful magistrate, a sovereign lord, the Lord's anointed, his person sacred, though they had formally denied him his office, and every where resisted his power, but where it survived in their own faction. To their arguments of indefeasible right it was returned, that though a derivative power was committed in trust from the people to Kings and magistrates, yet it remained fundamentally in its source: That to say a King had as good a right to his crown and dignity as another man to his inheritance, was to make the subject no better than his slave; yet, even on the supposition of hereditary right, there were crimes for which hereditary right was justly forfeitable: That to say a King was accountable to none but God, was neither founded on command, precept, nor reason;

[32] *Discourses concerning Government by Algernon Sydney with His Letters, Trial, Apology and Some Memoirs of His Life*, ed. Thomas Hollis (London, 1763).

[33] John Milton, *The Tenure of Kings and Magistrates* (London, 1649).

[34] See note xix, above

that it was the overthrow of all law, and the destruction of good policy: That the authority of the scripture, in the example of the Israelites, established the right of chusing and changing government: That God himself had given the preference to a republic, as a more perfect form than a monarchy, and more suitable to the conditions of mankind; ^Defence against Salmasius^35 and that Christ bore testimony against the [430] absolute authority of the Gentile governors:[xxvii] ^Milton's Tenure^ That to resist, depose, and kill weak and wicked princes, had been in part the conduct of the Reformed, and the favorite doctrine of Calvinistical divines:[xxviii] That, even in the case in question, the King, by being deprived of his office, had been in a manner deposed by both the Scotch and English Presbyterians: That to war upon a King, that his instruments might be brought to condign punishment, to inflict sufferance on the instruments, and not only to spare but defend and honor the author, was the absurdest piece of justice to be called Christian, and of reason to be called human, which ever yet entered the heads of men of reverence and learning.

The positions to be found in these arguments, That government is the ordinance of man; that, being the mere creature of human invention, it may be changed [431] or altered according to the dictates of experience, and the better judgment of men; that it was instituted for the protection of the people, for the end of securing not overthrowing the rights of nature; that it is a trust either formally admitted, or supposed; and that magistracy is consequently accountable;[xxix] will meet with little

[xxvii] 'Absolute monarchy' (says Locke, that deep and accurate reasoner, on the principles of government and subjection) 'is inconsistent with civil society, and therefore no form of civil government. Where men have no standing rule to appeal to on earth, they are still in a state of nature, and under all the inconveniencies of it; but with this woeful difference to the subject of an absolute prince, that as, in an ordinary state of nature, he is at liberty to judge of, and maintain his right under such government, as if degraded from the common state of rational creatures, he is denied that privilege, and so exposed to all the miseries which a man has to fear from one, who, being in the unrestrained state of nature, is yet corrupted with flattery, and armed with power.' *Locke on Civil Government* [i.e. Locke, *Two Treatises of Government*], *oct. ed* [(London)] 1764 [pp. 272–5].

[xxviii] Zuinglius [i.e. Huldrych Zwingli], [John] Calvin, [Martin] Bucer, Peter Martyr, [Anthony] Gilby, Christopher Goodwin, John Knox.

[xxix] 'Who', says Locke, 'shall be judge whether his trustee or deputy acts well, and according to the trust reposed in him, but he who deputes him, and must, by having deputed him, have still power to discard him when he fails in his trust? If this be reason in particular cases of private men, why should it be otherwise in cases of the greatest moment, where the welfare of millions is concerned?' *Locke on Civil Government* [p. 414].

35 See note xix, above.

34

contradiction in a country enlightened with the unobstructed ray of rational learning. Systems of slavery, condemned to oblivion by general neglect, are no where to be found but among the lumber of a university; nor, till the light of letters are again extinct, will another Filmer[36] arise, to dispute the equal justice of God, and the natural freedom of mankind.

On general grounds it must be indisputably acknowledged, that the partizans of Liberty gained a complete triumph over the adversary; on the particular circumstances of the case in question it must be allowed, they discovered error and fallacy. 'The absence of twice so many members,' says Goodwin (on the argument that the parliament, by whose authority the high court of justice was erected, was no true parliament), 'as were detained from the house by force doth not at all maim its legitimacy, nor disable its legal authority, in respect of any parliamentary end [432] or purpose whatsoever. The detainment of some of their members from them by force doth not alter the case, in respect of nulling the authority or parliamentary power of those who did sit, especially they not consenting or being accessary to such their detainment. Suppose some of their members, employed by them in carrying messages or petitions to the King, during the time of the wars, had been forcibly detained by him, would such a restraint laid upon them by the King have dissolved the parliamentary authority of the house?'[37] No, it would not; but if the house had been garbled of all those members who were engaged in an opposite interest to the King, and none but his creatures permitted to sit, it certainly would: assertions like these, without argument, disgrace the cause they were intended to defend. A parliament under any undue influence or force can do no constitutional act; and it is to be disputed whether, in a free capacity, the joint powers of both houses reach to the warring with or dethroning their King:[xxx] The oaths of supremacy and allegiance,[xxxi] every form of law, are against it. Sovereignty [433] and

---

[xxx] The question here is not, What is fit and convenient? but, What the forms of the constitution prescribe? Not, Whether the King, who, on abuse of power, can only be dispossessed of it by state convulsions and civil contention, ought to be vested with sovereignty, or the house of Commons, supposed to be the free elected representative of the people, whose members, on a breach of trust, can at stated periods be dispossessed of their authority, without violence, or the infringement of the forms of the constitution?

[xxxi] When the Commons declared themselves the supreme authority of the nation, they abolished the oaths of supremacy and allegiance to the King.

[36] Sir Robert Filmer (1588–1653), whose best-known work *Patriarcha* was published posthumously in 1680.

[37] Goodwin, *Hybristodikai*, p. 35.

jurisdiction over sovereignty is a contradiction in terms;[xxxii] and in all the addresses of the two houses to the monarch, far from assuming superior or equal stations in the legislature, they acknowledge a subordinate inferiority.[xxxiii]

To attempt the defence of that eminent act of justice, the King's death, on the narrow bottom of constitutional forms, is to betray the cause of Liberty, and confound both truth and reason. When a sovereign, by enlarging the limits of that power with which he is vested for the protection of the people, weakens the authority of laws, and consequently the security of the subject; when he acts in opposition to the just ends for which government was instituted, and from a protector of the commonwealth becomes an enemy; when, by breach of trust and non-performance of obligations, the good purposes of his institution are inverted; his trust and right to government from that period are forfeited,[xxxiv] the tie of al-[434]legiance is dissolved, and the law and the constitution being rendered incapable of affording the subject protection, he is no longer bound by their forms or dictates, and may justly, by the right of self-preservation, take every probable mean to secure himself from the lawless power and enterprizes of the tyrant.[xxxv] It is on these grounds the parliament are to be defended in the war they made on the King: It is on these grounds the army, as they profess in several declarations, supported their pretensions; not as servants to the dictates of a master, but as fellow-citizens in support of equal Liberty. The parliament, as watchmen for the commonwealth, were to represent to

---

[xxxii] On the side of the cavalier faction were, in general, the forms of law; on the side of their opponents, magnanimity, justice, sense, and reason.

[xxxiii] In the style of some very late addresses, of the collective and representative bodies, can hardly be discerned the characters of a free people.

[xxxiv] 'All power,' says Locke, 'is given with trust for the attaining an end; being limited by that end, whenever that end is manifestly neglected or opposed, the trust must necessarily be forfeited, and the power devolve into the hands of those who gave it; who may place it anew, where they shall think best for their safety and security.' *Locke,* [*Two Treatises of Government,*] p. 82.

[xxxv] 'Where the body of the people,' says Locke, 'or any single man, is deprived of their right, or is under the exercise of a power without right, and have no appeal on earth, then they have a liberty to appeal to heaven, whenever they judge the cause of sufficient moment; and therefore, though the people cannot be judge, so as to have, by the constitution of that society, any superior power to determine and give effective sentence in the case, yet they have, by a law antecedent and paramount to all positive laws of men, reserved that ultimate determination to themselves which belongs to all mankind, where there lies no appeal on earth; viz. To judge whether they have just cause to make their appeal to Heaven.' *Locke,* [*Two Treatises of Government,*] p. 347.

the people their danger: The parliament, as elected by the people for the purposes of guarding the Liberties of the constitution, though not formally invested with the power of opposing by the force of arms a tyrannical headstrong prince, yet this power being, by the nature of their office, rationally implied, it was a duty binding in conscience and in honor: The parliament, by the advantages which the possession of part of the authority of the government [435] gave them, were entitled to lead in the undertaken war against the encroachments of power; but not, as masters of the community, to mould the constitution at their pleasure, and gain to themselves the sole benefits of the conquest: The parliament, on the principles of self-defence, on the principles of equity and reason, without respect to constitutional forms, had a right to oppose the tyrant to the utmost; so, upon the same principles, had the collective body of the people; so, upon the same principles, had any party or individual of the people. Exclude this position, and all governments are equal tyrannies; the destroyers, not the preservers of the rights of nature.

Never any prince who sat on the English throne had made greater innovations in the government than Charles; never any prince had laid deeper schemes against the freedom of the constitution; never any prince, even to the last period of his life, had manifested in his conduct less title to farther trust. The parliament, the majority of whom were Calvinists, against the sense of their fellow-associates, the army, who had borne the danger, the burthen, and heat of the day, neglecting or rather betraying the cause of equal Liberty, on the presence of which they had began the contention, attempted by a coalition with the King to establish their own authority over, and coerce their religion upon, the people. The army, who had fought for Freedom, not for a change of tyranny, on the same grounds of equity on which the first quarrel was began, opposed their measures, and overpowered their authority – Against the objection, That [436] on these positions all government must be unstable, that good and just, as well as bad and tyrannical, would be liable to be shaken by the interested views and giddy enterprizes of a faction, it is to be observed, that these objections, though common, are weak and designing; the fears of the frail, the ignorant, and the wicked: Government never can stand on better, never on firmer, never on equitable grounds, than on its good behavior. Just government will be felt, its advantages will be seen, its security will be fixed in the hearts of its subjects, not to be shaken by the fantastic or selfish ends of individuals. The experience of all times shews, that the people are with difficulty moved to assert their rights, even against the most obvious, the most oppressive tyrannies.

[VOL. 5 (1771), CH. 1]

[6] ^Ann. 1649; Discontent and revolt of the Levellers.^

It was not the formidable factions of Cavalier and Presbyterian alone whose enmity the English Parliament had at this time to dread. The truest friends to Liberty of their own party were disgusted with the oligarchical form into which they had modelled the government, and the undivided authority they had assumed to [7] themselves. A petition, with articles for the settlement of the nation on a new plan, had been sent up to the Commons from the general, lord Fairfax,[38] and the council of officers, immediately after that assembly had determined to proceed against the King's life. ^Parl. Hist. vol. XVIII^[39] They demanded, the sovereign authority to be lodged in a representative assembly, composed of four hundred persons, biennially elected by counties, cities, and boroughs, more equally proportioned with electors than the present distribution; that all the natives or denizens of England, being not persons who received alms, or servants receiving wages, should have the privilege of an elective voice; and that no member of a council of state, nor any officer of any salary forces in the army or garrisons, nor any treasurer or receiver of public money, should, while such, be capable of election in the representative.

These, with some proper limitations of the sovereign power, cautions against the King's party having voices in the election of the first and second representative, and proposals relative to the establishment of religious liberty, were the heads of the petition sent up by the army to the Commons. It was styled, 'The Agreement of the People;' and was to the same purport as a former agreement of the party called Levellers.[40] The Parliament were not only silent concerning any intention of dissolving their body (though their power, according to the propositions of the

---

[38] Thomas Fairfax, 3rd Lord Fairfax of Cameron (1612–71).

[39] *The Parliamentary or Constitutional History of England* (24 vols., London, 1751–61), XVIII, pp. 516–36.

[40] The earlier Leveller pamphlet refers to *An Agreement of the People: For a Firme and Present Peace, upon Grounds of Common Right* (London, 1647).

army, was to have terminated on the last day of April 1649), but treated
with a high tone of authority those of the party who ventured to shew
discontent [8] at their proceedings.[xxxvi] A conduct so ill suited to the

[xxxvi] One Lockier suffered death; and for a petition in which the party had demanded
reformation in point of lawful toleration, in point of religion, the equal administration
of law to persons of all conditions, the abolishment of tythes, and other articles of the
same nature, the petitioners (being troopers) were tried by a court-martial, and on
several of them was inflicted the punishment of riding the wooden horse. This
severity was so far from intimidating the party, that a petition, in which they
complained of the arbitrary influence of three or four military grandees over the
supreme authority of the nation; and in which they demanded that the government
should cease an illegal prosecution they had commenced against [John] Lilbourn
[commonly spelled as Lilburne (1614–57)] and three other leaders of the party, for
a pamphlet they had published, called England's Second Chains [i.e. *Englands New
Chains Discovered*, published in two parts in 1649], was signed by ten thousand
persons, and seconded by a female petition of the same tendency [*To the Supream
Authority of This Nation, the Commons Assembled in Parliament: The Humble Petition of
Divers Wel-Affected Women Inhabiting the Cities of London, Westminster, the Borough of
Southwark, Hamblets, and Places adjacent* (London, 1649)]. These movements of the
party not having the effect to intimidate the government into milder or juster
measures, Lilbourn and his three associates, though under confinement, had the
courage to print a narrative of all that passed between them and the council of state,
with a new model of government, entitled, *An Agreement of the Free People of England*
[(London, 1649)]. It was a better model than any which had been yet offered to the
public; and as it directs the reformation of all the grievances which the people of
England then labored under, and which to this very day they do with equal weight
sustain, I shall give abstracts of the most important articles. Parliaments were to be
annual, instead of biennial, and the members not capable of re-election till after the
intervention of one representative. The executive powers of government, during the
adjournments of Parliament, were to be exercised by committees of Parliament,
instead of a council of state. The exercise of the supreme power, with the limitations
established by the Petition of Right [1628], was to be bound in all religious matters,
touching the rights of conscience. They were not empowered to impress or constrain
any person to military service, either by sea or land; 'Every man's conscience', says the
Agreement, 'being to be satisfied in the justness of that cause wherein he hazards his
own life, or may destroy another's.' [(p. 5)] They were not empowered to give
judgment on person or estate, in any case where the laws were silent, or to punish
any person for refusing to answer questions against himself in criminal cases. They
were not empowered to continue or make any law to prevent any person or persons
from trading in foreign states. They were not empowered to continue excise or
customs upon any sort of food, wares, or commodities longer than four months after
the beginning of the first representative; 'Being both of them', says the Agreement,
'burthensome and oppressive on trade, and expensive in the receipt.' [(p. 6)] They
were not empowered to make or continue any law whereby the real and personal estate
of any subject should be exempted from the payment of their debts, or to imprison the
person of any man for debt; 'It being,' says the Agreement, 'both unchristian in itself,
and no advantage to the creditors.' [(p. 6)] They were not empowered to continue or
make any law for taking away the life of the subject, except for the crime of murder,
for heinous offences destructive to human society, or for endeavoring by force to

independant spirit of the Levellers, provoked them to [9] assemble at Burford, to the number of five thousand; but though this body were for the most part soldiers [10] and veterans, yet, deceived by a promise from Cromwell[41] of a delay of hostilities, they were unexpectedly attacked by a superior number of troops, under the command of Reynolds,[42] and entirely defeated[.][xxxvii]

[380] Chap. XI. *Dissertation.*

The change in government and opinion which took their rise in the beginning of James's reign, and, by gradual elevation, rose to the highest pitch of national liberty and national glory, and from thence, by the apparent general consent of the people, sunk back to a former state of monarchical tyranny, are instances so unexampled in all history, that an enquiry into those causes which produced such singular effects is well worth the attention of the intelligent reader.

It has been already observed, in the first volume of this History, that, from the revival of letters, the minds of the English nation began to be so

<hr />

destroy the Agreement. In capital offences, recompence was to be made to the party damnified, as well out of the estate of the malefactor as by loss of life. They were not empowered to impose ministers on the people, but to give free liberty to the parishioners of every parish to choose such as themselves should approve, provided none to be chosen but such as were capable of electing representatives. They were not empowered to impose any public officer upon any counties, hundreds, cities, towns, or boroughs; but those subjects who were capable of electing representatives were to choose all their public officers yearly. They were not empowered to continue or constitute any proceedings in law longer than six months to the final determination of any cause. The laws and proceedings in law were to be in no other language than English; nor was any person to be hindered from pleading his own cause, or the making use of whom he pleased to plead for him. No persons were to be exempted from the ordinary course of legal proceedings by virtue of any tenure, grant, charter, patent, degree, or birth, of any place of residence, refuge, or privilege of parliament; and to demonstrate beyond contradiction, that the party were not tainted with any principles of levelling but those which support the rights of Nature and equal government, the Agreement concludes with an injunction, That it should not be in the power of the representative to level mens estates, destroy property, or make all things common. Divers citizens of London, and the inhabitants of the county of Essex, presented two ineffectual petitions to Parliament, in favor of the authors of this Agreement. *Parl. Hist.* vol. xix. p. 49, & *feq.* p. 110, & *feq.*

xxxvii The insurrection of the Levellers was regarded in so formidable a light by the Parliament, that Fairfax and Cromwell were both at the head of the party which was sent against them.

41 Oliver Cromwell (1559–1658).   42 John Reynolds (1625–57).

far enlightened from the dark superstition of former ages, as, at the latter end of Elizabeth's reign, to bear with impatience the galling yoke of civil and ecclesiastical power, which had been united in the sovereigns of the Tudor line.

This was the disposition of the people; but such disposition, without adequate means of redress, arising from a pre-existing cause, could have produced no effect but that of vexation of spirit and re-[381]luctant bondage; for, by the system of government imposed by William the Norman tyrant,[43] all but the great landholders, who held their estates from father to son, by feodal intail, were in a state of abject and impassable vassalage, excluded from any voice in the legislature, or property in the soil. It was in the opposition to the weak and arbitrary administration of Henry the Third,[44] and to secure the earl of Leicester[45] and his party from the power of the crown and the great barons, that summonses were sent to the sheriffs of the counties, to elect and return two knights for each shire, two citizens for each city, two burgesses for each borough, and two barons for each cinqueport,[xxxviii] to represent the commons or community at large;[xxxix] and to weaken a power which had often proved fatal to his predecessors, and with the laudable intention of encouraging trade and commerce, the crafty policy of the first Henry of the Tudor line[46] passed an act in which he parted with a useless prerogative, and gave leave to those barons, or great landholders, who should attend him in his wars, to alienate their lands, to sell, to mortgage, or dispose of the same without paying for fines or licenses of alienation. The barons, whose estates had been exhausted by the long wars between the houses of York [382] and Lancaster,[47] and, by an extravagance, dissipation, and idleness which ever attends hereditary fortune, assented to this law as an act of favor and grace, which proved the great *Magna Charta* of the Commons of

---

[xxxviii] The lesser barons, who held their estates by re-grants from the crown of escheated lands, had not the privilege of a seat in parliament, but were summoned at the pleasure of the King. *Guthrie* [*A General History of England* (4 vols., 1744–51), I, p. 781].

[xxxix] In the parliament immediately preceding this, there was an attempt to give a voice in the legislature to the Commons, by an election of twelve individuals to represent the community at large. *Guthrie* [ibid.]

[43] William I, reigned from 1066 to 1087. [44] Henry III, reigned from 1216 to 1272.
[45] Simon de Montfort, 6th Earl of Leicester (*c.* 1205–65). [46] i.e. Henry VII.
[47] The Wars of the Roses (1455–85).

England. The barrier was now thrown down between them and the nobles in matters of landed property. Industry and commerce had enabled them to make the full advantages of their new privilege, by large purchases from the needy barons; and the prodigality of this order soon occasioned the money to return back to the old channel; so that, in the next reign, the balance of power against the crown visibly leaned towards the Commons, and encreased to an height which would have been formidable to the prerogative, had not the opposition of Popish and Protestant faith divided this body amongst themselves, and given opportunity to the crown, with the assistance of the now-dependant nobles, to poize in its favor the balance of religious factions. But, even with this advantage, it required all the policy of an artful woman (and in qualities of cunning the sex are supposed to excel) to keep the Commons in a subordination agreeable to the notions of prerogative which prevailed in the court of Elizabeth.

James, at the same time that he disgusted the pride of the nobility, by a profuse and indiscriminate grant of the privileges possessed by their order, bullied the Commons; whose power he was so little able to circumscribe, that the many triumphs they gained over his necessities gave them the full knowledge of their weight and importance; a knowledge which proved [383] very fatal to his successor, who, with as little ability as his father to poize factions, and conceal from the people the high pretensions and real weakness of the crown, had an obstinacy which, happily for James, was incompatible with the timidity of his nature.

The appetite for Liberty which had been occasioned by an high cultivation of their mental faculties, was, in the people of England, every day encreasing, with the means to procure that invaluable blessing. An entire change took place in their manners, from the immediate commencement of Charles's government, to what in general had existed during the preceding reigns: From a servile respect to the unjust pretensions of political privilege, from an abject submission to the dictates of church and state, from a supine tranquility under the most oppressive grievances, from a state of politic lethargy, the Commons almost suddenly roused to a spirit of free enquiry and high independence, and opposed, with unremitting ardor, that civil and ecclesiastical power to which they had hitherto paid an almost-implicit obedience. But notwithstanding this general change in the temper and manner of the times, as the English are a people not easily roused to action, it is a doubtful question, whether, to use the expression of the keenest writer in the

Republican age,^{xl} they would have broken so suddenly from the twofold cord of the law and gospel,[48] if Charles had not preposterously quarrelled with his Scotch subjects, at a time when he was trampling on [384] the established and antient rights of a people whose wishes and views were extended beyond any of the privileges enjoyed by their ancestors. But this extreme oversight in Charles, who, because he had for some time silenced the laws, imagined he had entirely subdued the spirit of opposition, by the assistance of the Scotch nation, gave reality to those schemes of government which had long been the ardent wish of the generous part of the English. The Peers, who, since their degradation, had been much insulted by the crown, and were subject to the jurisdiction of the Star-Chamber, the High-Commission, and all the tyrannical courts which had been established by the Tudors and by the First Charles, could not be brought to support that king in his contest with the Commons, till the powers of democracy had risen too high for their united force; and the particular state of Europe, as it prevented any interposition from foreign powers, was in this contest between the crown and the people very favorable for the cause of Liberty, which, in a short time, completely triumphed over and annihilated that form of government, from the spirit of which the English had, during the space of more than five hundred years, suffered evils and insults which degrade the nobleness of the human species to an inferiority to the brute.

It was just after the battle of Worcester[49] that the nation was arrived at the meridian of its glory and the crisis of its fate: All iniquitous distinction, all opposition to the powers of democracy, were totally annihilated and subdued; the government of the [377, *sic*[50]] country was in the hands of illustrious patriots, and wise legislators; the glory, the welfare, the true interest of the empire was their only care; the public money was no longer lavished on the worthless dependants of a court; no taxes were levied on the people but what were necessary to effect the purposes of the greatest national good; and such was the economy of the Parliament, that at this time, whilst they kept a superior naval force to any which the preceding sovereigns had maintained, with a land-army of eighty thousand men,

---

^{xl} Marchamont Nedham [(1620–78)].

[48] Nedham, *The Excellencie of a Free State*, ed. R. Barron (1656; London, 1767), p. 51.

[49] On 3 September 1651.

[50] The pagination in the original is inaccurate for the remainder of this chapter and volume.

partly militia and partly regulars, the public assessments in Scotland, Ireland, and England did not exceed one million a-year.[xli]

A government thus carried on on the true principles of public interest, with the advantages peculiar to the island of Great-Britain, could not but be formidable to foreign states. They felt the present strength, and trembled at the growing power of England, which bid fair to be the second mistress of the world. The great success of the Parliament's arms, with the other happy effects of their government, had to appearance totally subdued domestic opposition. The rage of party had in a great measure subsided, and the jarring factions were calmed into so general [378, *sic*] an obedience, that the king of Scots, when he invaded England, was joined by a very inconsiderable number, either of the Cavaliers[51] or Presbyterians, whilst the Parliament was with alacrity assisted by the whole force of the nation.[52]

Such being the promising aspect of the times, it is not surprising that the Commonwealth's-Men should imagine that a people who had tasted the sweets of Liberty, the benefit of equal laws, the numberless advantages of just government, after being harassed for so many years with the oppressions of king, nobles, and churchmen, would never again willingly return to their old state of vassalage; but as the true love of Liberty is founded in virtue, the Parliament were indefatigable in their endeavors to reform to a state of possible perfection the manners of the people. They have been ridiculed for a preciseness in this article; but the design was certainly laudable, and, during their short reign, attended with the happiest effects; effects which would have subsisted to this day, if they had had sufficient caution to have balanced the power of Cromwell with an equal military command in the hands of the brave and honest Ludlow,[53] till time and opportunity had enabled them totally to destroy

---

[xli] The whole taxes on the nation, the customs, excise, and additional assessments, did not amount to above two millions a-year; which, though a sum higher than the legal revenue of preceding sovereigns, was trifling, if we consider the very large naval and land force which it was necessary to maintain to secure the country from foreign and domestic foes, till the Commonwealth could be established on a permanent footing. *Hume's Hist. of Gr. Brit.* Vol. II. [(London, 1757)] p. 121, & *seq.* [*Hume's History*, VI, p. 146.]

[51] i.e. the royalist supporters of Charles I.
[52] In the summer of 1651 Charles II of Scotland and the Scottish officer David Leslie, 1st Lord Newark (*c.* 1600–82), marched south in an unsuccessful attempt to rally supporters in England.
[53] Edmund Ludlow (*c.* 1617–92).

an influence, which, from the first establishment of the Commonwealth, had threatened its existence.

It has been fully related in the preceding pages of this History, how Cromwell, assisted by a few wrong-headed fanatics, by the corrupt part of the army, by the lawyers, who were enraged at the [379, *sic*] Parliament for an intention to reform the law, and by the clergy, who were as angry at as laudable an intention to take away the burthen of tythes, and provide for their body in a manner better calculated to maintain that harmony which ought to subsist among the different members of the ministry, and between the ministry and the laity, seized the government out of the hands of the Parliament, re-subjected the nation to the yoke of an individual, and again involved it in discord, faction, and their attendant evils, tumults, conspiracies, and general discontent.

The state of the quarrel on the usurpation of Cromwell from being general became particular: It was no longer the people of England against the pretensions of the Stewart family; the contest for power lay between the family of the Stewarts and the family of the Cromwells, and the success of either pretender must be equally attended with the misery and slavery of the people. Encouraged by this important alteration in the circumstances of the contest, and the general ill humor of the public, the Cavaliers again entered into conspiracies to place their idol in the usurped seat of empire. The Presbyterians, who had been cajoled by Cromwell for the purposes of his ambition, resumed their hopes of becoming the sole dictators to the consciences of their fellow-citizens, and now caballed with the government, and now with the Cavaliers, to destroy that liberty of conscience which had so long been the object of their envy and detestation. The sectaries, who had been united to a man in the support of the Republic, were now divided, as [380, *sic*] interest or principle swayed. The weak fanatics whom he could deceive, and the corrupt individuals whom he could bribe, supported the power and pretensions of the usurper; the honest and sensible avowed an inflexible opposition. Those illustrious patriots, whose wise and virtuous conduct had raised the glory and the felicity of the nation to an unrivalled height, deserted the helm of government, which they could no longer hold with consistence to principle or former dignity. The interest of the nation was no farther considered than as it was united to the particular interest of Cromwell. The people again sustained the mortification of paying their money to support the parade of a court, and to gratify the dependants and flatterers of an individual. The opposition which these renewed grievances and the different interests of parties occasioned, rendered an high degree of oppression necessary to maintain the government of the usurper; and that oppression naturally produced in the people a general desire to return to the milder tyranny of the antient establishment. Morals, the great support of Liberty, declined under the government of Cromwell; the religion of the court degenerated into the impious fanaticism of the High Church party; these self-deceivers, instructed by Cromwell, imagined, or pretended to imagine, that their particular interests were inseparable to the interests and the will of the Deity: By their profane jargon, they poisoned those religious principles in the people which had been so sedulously cultivated by the parliament; and the great encouragement which the most dissolute of the old Com-[381, *sic*]monwealth-party, as being the proper tools to execute the purposes of the tyrant, met with, the excitement to pride and vanity, that great bane of true virtue and national felicity, which the ostentation of a court ever produces, infected the morals of the army and the whole nation.

From this state of misery and corruption, into which it was again fallen, England had a pleasing prospect of deliverance, by the death of the usurper and the restoration of the power of the Parliament; but Cromwell's reign, though short, was sufficiently long to make a perpetual entail of those evils his wicked ambition had occasioned; the corruption of the major part of the army, and the restless ambition of the military leaders, which had been highly excited by the successful example of Cromwell, prevented the honest endeavors of the parliament, to settle the government on the true principles of justice and equity, from taking any effect. The passions of hope, despair, fear, and revenge, affected the tranquility of the public, and rendered the desire of a settlement on any terms general. This impatience of the people, united to the restless prejudices of the Cavaliers, and the peevishness of the Presbyterians, who, misled by interested leaders, obviously hazarded the entire ruin of the just interests of their party, to revenge themselves on those who had prevented their putting into execution their favorite system of religious despotism, produced that shameful, that singular instance of sacrificing all those principles of Liberty and justice which had been established by the [382, *sic*] successful contest of the people with the crown, of voluntarily giving up all the advantages which had been gained by a long and bloody war, of not only admitting an expelled family into the power of their ancestors without limitation or conditions, but in receiving as a favor, from a poor, forlorn, and exiled individual, those necessary stipulations for the general security of the public, which, according to the lowest principle of Freedom, ought to have been established by the authority of its representatives.

Thus, in a fit of passion and despair, the nation plunged themselves headlong into a state of hopeless servitude; for every other revolution in government had been attended with the prospect of relief. Thus they prostituted the exalted honor and interest of their country not only to be trampled on by domestic foes, but exposed it to the scorn and derision of foreign states; and thus the mighty efforts which had been made in their favor by their illustrious countrymen were not only rendered useless, but served to complete the triumph and exalt the powers of tyranny; a tyranny which, in its consequences, for a long time obscured the lustre of the brightest age that ever adorned the page of history. That obscurity is now, in some measure, happily dispelled: Time and experience have abated the violence, and confined to narrower compass the generality of those prejudices which prevailed after the restoration. The praise due to the illustrious champions of the public cause, many of whom paid the tribute of their lives and properties for the services they endea-[383, *sic*]vored to render their country, is a theme of delight among the few enlightened citizens; nor are their memories, with inferior characters, some weak bigots excepted, branded with the ungrateful, the harsh terms, of 'the bloody, the impious regicides.' The poet Cowley[54] is no longer preferred to the sublime genius of Milton,[55] in whose comprehensive powers were united the highest excellencies of poetry, the acuteness of rational logic, and the deep sagacity of politic science. The recovered sense and taste of the nation can see and acknowledge that the works of Nevil,[56] Sydney,[57] and Harrington,[58] are performances which excel even the antient classics on the science of policy. In the character of Andrew Marvel[59] are allowed to be united in an exalted degree the wit, the patriot, and the legislator; and the keen satire and judicious reflections of Marchemont Nedham[60] are read with pleasure and applause.

[54] Abraham Cowley (1618–67).   [55] John Milton (1608–74).
[56] Henry Neville (1620–94).   [57] Algernon Sidney (1623–83).
[58] James Harrington (1611–77).   [59] Andrew Marvell (1621–78).
[60] Marchamont Nedham, also spelled as Marchmont and Needham (1620–78).

[VOL. 6 (1781), PREFACE]

[v] The public advantages which must attend a disinterested principle in historians is acknowledged by all parties, and by all parties it is equally hated and equally persecuted. The man of genius, who is capable of writing a plausible tale to pamper the vanities of the great, to serve the purposes of power, or to humour the prejudices of a prevailing faction, is certain of meeting with all those emoluments and that popularity which forms the wish of the honest man, and is the sole object of the ambitious; but should an historian arise, whose abilities as a statesman, politician, legislator, moralist, and philosopher, rendered him capable of attaining the highest degree of perfection in the sublime and comprehensive walk of history; should he be capable of giving such animation to his representation of facts as to command attention; should his narrative be sufficiently elegant to gratify taste: should his sagacity be sufficiently profound to ascertain those leading and often opposite principles and inclinations, which form the different characters of men; should he be capable of making use of every opportunity which incidents and events afford to instruct the reader on the subject of morals, religion, policy, and good government; should his integrity and his resolution be sufficient to decide upon every fact, and every character, without regard even to the nearest tie of relationship, as equity should prompt and truth should authorise, instead of gaining admirers by the honest exercise of his talents, he would raise an innumerable host of enemies: he would never meet in the breast of his reader with that impartiality, of which he had set the illustrious example, and all the imperfect sons of earth among the living would clamour in behalf of the guilty dead. It is perhaps the difficulty of these circumstances, which must take place in all countries, and which are greatly aggravated in England by the venomous rancour of contending factions, which has occasioned the subject of history to have been so long neglected in this country: [vi] and whilst England has been renowned for producing the best authors in every other species of writing, she was obliged to a foreigner for the best and the most faithful narrative of the civil and military achievements of her gallant sons. Rapin[61] long maintained an unrivalled popularity in this country, but it was more from the circumstance of his having no competitor than from

---

[61] Paul de Rapin Thoyras (1661–1725), author of *Histoire d'Angleterre* (10 vols., The Hague, 1724–7), translated into English by Nicholas Tindal. Rapin's was the most popular

the intrinsic merit of his work: he is, indeed, infinitely less partial in his account of the civil wars in the reign of Charles the First than almost any other writer of that period of our annals, but he is very prolix, and his narrative is destitute of all those animating graces and just reflections which are necessary to form an agreeable and instructive history. Guthrie[62] and Ralph,[63] who wrote after Rapin, may be classed among the few faithful historians,[xlii] and their several narratives abound with very just remarks and pertinent reflections. Guthrie's style often rises even to the sublime, and Ralph's is not wanting in animation; but these authors are too careless writers to arrive at that elegance and correctness necessary to satisfy the nicety of modern taste; they are also very prolix to a degree of tediousness. In this state of general history Mr. Hume, blessed with that genius and profound sagacity necessary to form a complete historian, had reason to flatter himself with the prospect of enjoying, without a rival, all that extensive fame and popularity which is justly due to the instructors of mankind; but whether he conceived, from the reasons above mentioned, that a candid relation of our domestic broils, as it must necessarily displease all factions,[64] would deprive him of the reward of his abilities and his industry; or whether, as I am more inclined to believe, that he had entertained prejudices inimical to that candour which must have placed him at the head of all our historians, his history, whilst it serves as an elegant pastime for the hours of leisure or idleness, leaves the reader perfectly ignorant as to characters, motives, and often facts: but as Mr. Hume's prejudices have fallen in with the prejudices of the prevailing faction in this country,[65] and as his

---

[xlii] The author has confined her observations to the writers of general history.

history of England until it was supplanted by Hume's in the second half of the eighteenth century.

[62] William Guthrie (1708–70), author of *A General History of England* (4 vols., 1744–51).

[63] James Ralph (1705–62), author of *The History of England during the Reigns of K. William, Q. Anne and K. George I, with an Introductory Review of the Reigns of the Royal Brothers, Charles and James* (2 vols., London, 1744–6).

[64] This was Hume's self-presentation in his short autobiography, 'My Own Life' (1776), which Macaulay had clearly read.

[65] Macaulay refers to the alleged revival of 'Toryism' since the accession of George III. While this idea, promoted by Burke and the Rockingham Whigs, has rightly been refuted regarding parliamentary politics, it may have been more relevant for local politics in specific settings. In Bristol, for instance, the Tory Steadfast Society was revived during the American conflict and disseminated John Wesley's writings on passive obedience.

admirable genius is fully equal to the inspiring every unlearned, incurious and negligent reader with the prejudices of the author, he has for a long time maintained an unrivalled popularity in the walk of English history, and has been regarded by the few discerning friends of Revolution principles, and the admirers of those pa-[vii]triots who have spilt their blood in the public cause, as the having helped to forward, with other concurring circumstances, the declension of Whig sentiments, and the wonderful increase of those opinions and principles which were so justly decried by the nation towards the middle of this century.

Animated with the love of liberty, and an enthusiastic regard to English patriotism, I ventured to take the pen in hand, with the intention of vindicating the insulted memories of our illustrious ancestors, and of exposing to the public the evils which this country has suffered from the intrigues of faction and the rage of party; and I vainly hoped that the conviction of uncontrovertible argument, founded on fact, would, in a series of time, extinguish the baneful influence of party spirit; would gradually and almost imperceptibly incline the people to consider the objects of their proper interest, and that all ranks would unite in the laudable and generous attempt of 'fixing dominion's limits to its proper end'[66] of realizing all those advantages in our mixed form of government, which experience has found to be only theoretical; of restraining the oppressions of the great, by the cutting off a few noxious privileges, which are equally mischievous to themselves as to the community; and of curbing the licentiousness of the common people by the coercion of wholesome laws, and a well regulated police. This, without any unconstitutional design, or any wild enthusiastic hope of being able to influence the minds of a nation in favour of a democratic form of government, who from the beginning of time have been under the rule of regal sway, and whose laws, manners, customs, and prejudices are ill adapted to a republic, is the grand aim of my writings: and this I cannot help regarding as a patriotic and pious design, because, in my opinion, religious and moral turpitude, in a great measure, flow from political error; and that the miseries of natural evil are from the same cause highly aggravated.

---

[66] Macaulay is likely using these quotation marks for emphasis rather than in reference to a specific work.

As republican principles and notions have always been too unpopular in this country to found on them any rational scheme of interest or ambition, it was obvious to me, that, however erroneous might be the opinions of the few republicans whom opportunity enabled to take an active part in the af-[viii]fairs of England, that their conduct was founded on principle, because diametrically opposite to their interest, and even their safety; accordingly the fate of every one of this party, who did not change with the changing times, was banishment, an ignominious death, or the entire ruin of their fortunes: whilst, on the contrary, the men whose conduct was governed either by Whig or Tory principles, were, as the different factions prevailed, in their turn triumphant; and it is from the conviction only of the integrity of their motives that I appear in my history to be partial to the leaders of the republican party.

In Mr. Hume's very artful narration of facts, he represents Charles the First as a prince whose government had in no degree exceeded the arbitrary precedents which had been set by his predecessors; and as the English had formerly submitted, without a murmur, to the despotic sway of these monarchs, he argues, that the crown had acquired a kind of right by the peaceable possession of a long usurped tyranny; and that consequently Charles fell a victim to the malignancy of the times, rather than to any faults in his administration, which urged the necessity of taking up arms against him.[67] That the government of the greater number of our princes, particularly that of Henry the Eighth, and even many parts of Elizabeth's administration, was directly contrary to Magna Charta, and to the rule of all free governments, cannot be disputed with Mr. Hume; but as that servility and implicit obedience to the unjust commands of the sovereign, which accompanied the times of political ignorance in this country, after the power of the Barons was broken by Henry the Seventh, and the religious factions which took their rise in the reign of Henry the Eighth, occasioned the parliaments to acquiesce with the lawless pretensions of their monarchs, the form of a free government was in some measure preserved, and by that means a remedy yet remained in the constitution to correct those evils which time, ignorance, and opportunity had occasioned. The knowledge of ancient literature, and consequently the knowledge of Roman and Greek policy, had made no inconsiderable progress in this country during the reigns of Henry the Eighth, Edward,[68] Mary, and Elizabeth; and on the accession of

[67] *Hume's History*, v, esp. pp. 542–3.   [68] Edward VI, reigned from 1547 to 1553.

James, the more civilized part of the nation began to entertain very large
and very comprehensive notions on the subject of civil liberty: they
beheld with regret that large portion of undi-[ix]vided power which
the crown had acquired by the arbitrary courts of justice, which had
been erected during the administration of the Tudor race; and they
determined to seize the first favourable occasion to reduce the regal
prerogative to its ancient limits, left a long and undisputed possession,
with accidental circumstances favourable to the strengthening these
usurpations by a military force, should for ever put it out of the power
of the people to regain that authority which is necessary to the existence
of a free government. The ill policy of Charles the First in the wars with
Spain and France, which he entered into in the beginning of his reign,
afforded to the friends of liberty a full opportunity to make their own
terms with the court. The king's necessities were pressing, and the
constitution allowed of no impositions on the people which were not
authorised by the voice of their representatives. The question in dispute
between the king and the commons immediately became critical: it was
necessary for the sovereign to relinquish the encroachments of his
predecessors, or to assume the essential authority of a despotic monarch,
by levying arbitrary taxes on the people, without the consent of parliament.[69] The prejudices of Charles induced him to chuse the latter of
these expedients: taxes were levied by the king's authority only, the use
of parliaments was altogether laid aside, and the form and spirit of the
government became entirely despotic. By the corrupt decision of
the judges, in the case brought before them by the famous Hamden,[70]
the king, for twelve years,[71] enjoyed in tranquility the triumph he had
gained over the liberties of his country, and might, perhaps, have fixed
the constitution on the basis of despotism, had he been possessed of the
temporizing spirit of Elizabeth; or had he employed ministers equally
subtle and equally able to those consummate politicians who directed the
councils of this princess. It was indeed more owing to the furious and
bigotted conduct of Laud,[72] than to the spirit and resolution of the
people, that the smallest vestige of freedom at this time remains in

---

[69] Notably, the collection of 'tonnage and poundage' (two customs duties) and later ship
money.

[70] John Hampden (1595–1643).

[71] Macaulay refers to the period between 1628 and 1640.

[72] William Laud (1573–1645), appointed archbishop of Canterbury in 1633, and executed
in 1645 during the Wars of the Three Kingdoms.

England: his absurd and impolitic persecution of the Presbyterians, whose religious principles were somewhat more favourable to civil liberty than were those of the Church of England, threw that whole party into the scale of opposition; and when united to the partizans of civil liberty, the balance of popular opinion became greatly in disfavour of the king's pretensions and administration. However, though the large majority of the nation [x] felt very sensibly the yoke of tyranny, their discontent was expressed in unavailing murmurs, 'till the influence of Laud prevailed over the ill-fated Charles to excite the resentment of his Scotch subjects, by impositions and novelties in matters of religion.[73] The necessity which this produced of calling a parliament, and the union of the Scotch and English male contents, soon brought matters to that point of civil contention, in which the success of parties can only be decided by the sword. After a long and bloody contest, victory declared itself on the side of the male contents, and the power of disposing of the king, and forming the government, fell entirely into the hands of the English parliament.

In this situation of affairs it is certain that the popular leaders might have cut off all the dangerous prerogatives of the crown, without any innovation in the form of the government; and the natural good sense and virtue of the king might have inclined him to have kept within the limits of those narrow bounds, which the male-contents must have found necessary, for the security of public liberty and the preservation of the party, to have prescribed: but besides the danger which was to be expected from the king's matrimonial connection, and the rancour of his partizans, a very unfortunate difference subsisted between the king and the parliament on the subject of religious government; and the men who at this time had the prevailing influence in the councils of the nation, had a predilection for those popular governments which had raised the glory of Pagan societies to the acme of human greatness: they also recollected the tranquility with which Charles was suffered for twelve years to trample on the laws and liberties of the land; that England was at last indebted for her deliverance to the vigour of Scotch opposition, rather than to the determined spirit of her own sons; and they conceived that there was a malignity in this form of government productive of a servility which secured its permanence. They thought that victory gave them a right to inflict on the conquered party that

---

[73] The Bishops' Wars in 1639 and 1640.

punishment, which, on motives of policy and motives of revenge, themselves must have sustained in the same situation; and they regarded it as a duty incumbent on them to make use of the opportunity which the fortune of war, or a peculiar providence, had put in their hands, to bar every avenue thro' which tyranny could possibly again slide into the administration of the government. Thus reasoned [xi] every honest individual in that party, who were the chief instruments in the death of the king; and they reasoned as human beings blind to the events of futurity, events which often foil the wisdom of the deepest politician, and render the boasted sagacity of the intelligent a subject of derision to the vulgar and the ignorant. Could these generous patriots, who had ventured life and fortune in the vindication of the rights of nature, and the liberties of the land, have fathomed the depth of Cromwell's hypocrisy; could they possibly have foreseen that a nation who had undergone such hardships and dangers for the attainment of freedom, who had dethroned a sovereign, descended from a long line of princes, for having encroached on their native rights, would submit to a state of slavery to a private individual, no ways exalted above his brethren in any of those endowments which constitute the true greatness of character, or excelling in any quality, but in the measure of a vain and wicked ambition, and in a dissimulation calculated to deceive those who are too honest to suspect the concealed vices which lay hidden under a well acted hypocrisy; could they possibly have foreseen, that a party who had sacrificed a man of virtue to secure the permanence of freedom in their civil and religious government, should be so far instigated by the principles of envy and revenge, as to give up all their dear bought rights to a prince, whose character, in point of morals and probity, was at best very questionable, and sacrifice their religious security to the prejudices and rancour of an opposite faction; they would undoubtedly have taken the lead in all pacific counsels, and have closed with the subdued monarch on as safe and secure terms as the circumstances of the time and the nature of things would admit. Had the form of government intended by the popular leaders taken place, and had Englishmen at this day lived under the sway of a well regulated democracy, we should have looked up to these execrated characters with all that respectful veneration which was paid by the Greeks and Romans to the illustrious founders of their republics. It may be very agreeable to the barbarity of vulgar ignorance to entertain prejudices against men, whose conduct has not been attended with that success which grace endeavours of a similar nature in more fortunate individuals: but surely it is incompatible with the wisdom of an historian to judge of actions by consequences, and without any regard to motives; to deal out panegyric or invective accord-[xii]ing to the measure of success or ill fortune which attend those persons who figure in the walk of public life.

As the Jacobites[74] have carried their panegyric of the first Charles to a height which induced the utter condemnation of all those who opposed this monarch on public grounds, it was impossible to do justice to the patriotic characters which figured in this age, without examining into the conduct and administration of this prince with a degree of rigorous justice and vigilant enquiry which his unhappy fate would otherwise have rendered ungenerous and inhuman: but in this inquiry I was so far from feeling myself the bloody-minded Republican, as I have been termed by the butcherly writers of these days, and so far even from possessing the stoicism of the first Brutus, that I shed many tears whilst I was writing his catastrophe,[75] and I have endeavoured to do justice to that part of his conduct which I thought truly great, and worthy the imitation of posterity.

I have also been accused of the want of humanity and sympathy, because I have in my writings appeared insensible to the rigour of that fate which fell on some very culpable state delinquents, and in particular on the earl of Strafford: but in this case I shall appeal to the judgment of the candid, whether the sympathising, according to the fanciful distinctions of power, birth, office, or fortune, with a few individuals who possess these advantages, and the beholding without pain, and even with triumph, the happiness of the community at large sacrificed to the rapacious lusts of interested governors, is more rational than that generous and extensive sympathy which regards, with an equal eye of compassion, the infirmities and the afflictions of all men, and who censures in proportion to the magnitude and the extent of the mischiefs which attend the selfish conduct of the powerful; and whether there is either reason, good sense, or rational humanity, in exclaiming against all those who brought the earl of Strafford to justice for advising the king to levy arms against his subjects, and consequently, if victorious, of subduing

---

[74] The supporters of the Stuart royal family after the Glorious Revolution, named after James's Latin name, Jacobus.

[75] Hume had famously written that he had shed a generous tear for Charles I (and the Earl of Strafford); see Hume, 'My Own Life', in *Essays, Moral, Political, and Literary*, ed. Eugene F. Miller (Indianapolis, 1987), p. xxxvii.

the free principles of the constitution, and thus entail on present and future generations the misery of perpetual slavery; and at the same time acknowledging the justice of inflicting a similar punishment for crimes of a very inferior nature, which perhaps arise from motives of necessity, and which only militate against the peace of individuals.

[xiii] I well knew what personal disadvantage I set out with, from that impartiality which I had determined to observe on the conduct of the different factions, which have harassed the internal peace of this empire; and when I gave up the emoluments of favour, the countenance of the great, and the gratification of popular applause, on a principle of public utility, I had some reason to expect esteem for my integrity and industry, and especially as I have never thrown any personal abuse on any individual, in or out of power; nor have ever sullied my pen with those anonymous writings calculated to anguish the feeling heart, to fix an indelible stain on the manners of Englishmen, and to inflict the poignancy of mental sufferings not only on the defamed persons, but on all those who are attached to them, either by the ties of blood, or the yet stronger ties of affection. I have endeavoured, with the most indefatigable pains, to make my History useful to men of all conditions; and I am persuaded that no moderate churchman, or honest lawyer, can, on cool reflection be offended with the historian's free observations on the conduct of men who have been the authors of much public and private mischief, and whose violent counsels, and dishonest practices, have frequently disturbed the peace, and endangered the liberties of the empire. If I have been severe on misguided princes, and bad ministers, it is with a view only to the interests of the people; and if all historians would preserve the same honest rule, instead of varnishing, with false colours, the vices of the powerful, it would, from that general desire which all men have of preserving some degree of reputation after death, form a kind of literary tribunal, productive of a very useful reformation in the conduct of those favoured sons of fortune on whose good or bad qualities the happiness and welfare of societies depend. The candid and the generous will, undoubtedly, from these considerations, behold, without malice or resentment, the wicked or weak conduct of their ancestors represented in its proper light; and especially when they reflect that it would be very unbecoming the character, and contrary to the duty of an historian, to spare even the memory of a parent, if he was found defective in those patriotic virtues which eminently affect the welfare of society.

If the warmth of my temper has occasioned me to be guilty of any petulancies in my first productions, they arose from the inexperience of the historian, and the early period of life in which she began to write history; but though I have been pursued with virulent invectives, I have never yet been made ac-[xiv]quainted with my literary faults. Criticisms formed with judgment and temper command attention; but when personal invective supplies the place of argument, and the reputation of authors are attacked in order to decry their writings,[76] it is a very strong symptom in favour of those productions against which the battery of abuse is levelled; and in this case an individual, in the full enjoyment of that internal satisfaction which a faithful exertion of mental abilities affords the rational mind, must look down with contempt on the angry croud, nor suffer their fierce and loud clamours, in any respect, to divert him from pursuing the grand object of his honest ambition.

Jan. 1781,
Laurence-street, Chelsea,
Middlesex.

[VOL. 7 (1781), CH. VII]

[473] [...] Every necessary previous circumstance being thus laid, in a manner to ensure success, Algernon Sidney was, on the 7th of November,[77] brought up to the King's-Bench bar, and indicted for treason. The indictment produced on this occasion for confusion, verboseness, and invective, exceeded all the compositions of this kind; and Sidney, instead of pleading, offered to shew, that it was impossible to plead sensibly to such a jumble of things, distinct both in nature and in law. He made a tender of a special plea, but withdrew it on being told by the court that he must either plead or demur, and that his life depended on the validity of his plea, or rather on the sentence which should be passed upon it. Mr. Williams, the counsel for the prisoner,[78] prompted him to rely on the plea; but, on the complaint of the

---

[76] This was written after Macaulay had been harshly treated in relation to her marriage to 21-year-old William Graham in 1778. Within months of the marriage she was mocked in a flurry of publications, including *A Bridal Ode on the Marriage of Catharine and Petrucio*, *A Remarkable Moving Letter!*, *The Patriot Divine to the Female Historian* and *The Female Patriot*.

[77] In 1683. [78] One of Sidney's counsels.

attorney-general,[79] he received a severe reprimand from the chief-justice.[80] With this indecent partiality, or rather avowal of the design to defraud the prisoner of his life, closed the prelude to the trial, and Sidney, with a kind of protest against the constraint put upon him, pleaded not guilty. In justification of a demand the prisoner had made of a copy of his indictment, he produced the statute of the forty-sixth of Edward the Third, wherein it is expressed, that *tout partes & tout gentes*, should have a copy of every record as well against the king as others. In answer to this, the chief-justice quoted the rule of court in the case of Sir Henry Vane[81] and lord Russell;[82] and when Sidney replied with a question, Is this a good law, my lord? he was silenced with a rule of the court, and a command to arraign him on the indictment, accompanied with this remonstrance, we must not spend time in long discourses [474] to captivate people. When the prisoner excepted to several of the jury for not being freeholders, the exception was over-ruled by an arbitrary dictate of the court; for the trial being in Middlesex, it could not be alledged, as in lord Russell's case, that the want of freehold in the city was no challenge.[83] In ransacking the closet of the prisoner, some discourses on government had been found,[84] which, though written with a sagacity, a conspicuity, a spirit, and an energy which must endear the memory of the illustrious writer to all those who have any true taste for literature, or whose breasts are animated with any spark of public spirit, yet the principles it maintained, though favourable to liberty, are such as

---

79 Sir Robert Sawyer, of Highclere Castle (1633–92), Attorney-General for England and Wales in 1681–7.

80 George Jeffreys, 1st Baron Jeffreys (1645–89), known as 'the Hanging Judge'.

81 The Parliamentarian Sir Henry Vane the Younger (bap. 1613–62) was granted clemency by Charles II on his restoration but was indicted for high treason by a royalist grand jury in Middlesex. He was denied counsel in the court proceedings and was executed in 1662. Before the Treason Act 1695, people accused of treason were as a rule not allowed counsel.

82 William Russell (1639–83), leading member of the Whig opposition during the Exclusion Crisis. He attended meetings in relation to the Rye House Plot, but, unlike other conspirators, he did not flee to the Dutch Republic, and was tried and executed in July 1683.

83 Russell had complained that he was convicted by a jury without freehold in London. The chief justice had responded: 'we have very few Freeholders capable of being impannel'd, because the Estates of the City belong much to the Nobility and Gentlemen that live abroad, and to Corporations: therefore in the City of London the Challenge of Freeholders is excepted'. *The Tryals of Thomas Walcot, William Hone, William Lord Russell, John Rous & William Blagg for High-Treason for Conspiring the Death of the King, and Raising a Rebellion in This Kingdom* (London, 1683), p. 32.

84 Sidney's *Discourses concerning Government*, which was finally published in 1698.

the best and the wisest men under all governments have been known to embrace. The whole discourses contain three distinct books, or chapters, and were written in answer to Filmer's Patriarcha.[xliii] It was evident, that the work must have taken some years in composing, and the ink was so old that it might have been written half a century past;[85] yet some mangled passages of these discourses on government were made part of the indictment, and was delivered by the king's counsel as an overt-act of the treason with which the prisoner was charged. The attorney-general, after asserting, that there had been for several years past a design of raising a rebellion, proved by insinuations and public libels spread abroad, that the king was a Papist, and had endeavoured to subvert the rights of the people, entered in-[475]to the particular conspiracy of the assassination, enlarged on the design for an insurrection, and informed the court, that whilst Aaron Smith[86] was in Scotland, the prisoner was preparing a most seditious and traiterous libel, to persuade the people of England that it was lawful to rise in arms. When the attorney-general had finished this envenomed harangue, plainly calculated to deceive the jury, and give an improper bias to their minds, West,[87] Rumbold,[88] and Keyling,[89] were called upon to open the evidence, with an account of what they knew concerning a general insurrection. Sidney interposed with an interrogatory concerning the legality of the evidence; but the chief-justice, though he professed not to know whether he had received a pardon or not, ordered West to be sworn; and

[xliii] In this book the divine right of monarchy is asserted, and the position is grounded on the supposition, that the patriarchs exercised regal authority; and that such a right descended to all their posterity, according to the rule of primogeniture. The whole work is a jumble of gross absurdity, false assertions, and false conclusions; and if it proves any thing, it proves that every modern government is an usurpation: yet the mere attempt to ascertain a divine right to government, gave it some weight with the monarchical enthusiasts of these times, and on this reason was deemed worthy of the notice of Sidney and of Locke.

[85] It was in fact written during the Exclusion Crisis and probably begun in the second half of 1681; see Jonathan Scott, *Algernon Sidney and the Restoration Crisis, 1677–83* (Cambridge, 1991), p. 201.
[86] Aaron Smith (d. 1701), lawyer and conspirator.
[87] Robert West (bap. 1649, d. in or after 1712), London lawyer of the Middle Temple, who led a group that planned to assassinate the king in 1682–3.
[88] Richard Rumbold (1622–85), a Parliamentarian soldier in the civil war who was exiled for his role in the 1683 Rye House Plot and later executed for his part in Argyll's Rising in 1685.
[89] Josiah Keeling, a London oil merchant and Nonconformist, and a minor intriguer.

when Sidney asked again, whether it was ordinary that the witness should say any thing, unless it was to him and his indictment, he was silenced by a recrimination that this method of proceeding, however irregular, had been practised in the prosecutions of the popish conspirators.[90] These witnesses, which were brought out to prepossess the jury, all declared, that they had no personal knowledge of the prisoner; that what they heard of his being engaged in the plot was by hearsay only; that according to this hearsay evidence, the prisoner at the bar, and major Wildman,[91] had been very instrumental in breaking off the connection with the Scots, because they could not agree upon the declaration to be made on the insurrection; and, what is very particular, they plainly contradicted one another; Rumsey[92] swearing that he had his intelligence from West, and West that he had his from Rumsey.

[. . .]

[488] The chief-justice, who had with such singular courage overruled eight or ten very important points of law, and decided [489] them without hearing counsel, was the only man capable of conducting the proceedings against the prisoner to a happy issue; and contrary to what had been done in lord Russell's case, he attended on the ceremonial of passing sentence. Sidney, with a spirit and perseverance equal to that which he had displayed during the course of his trial, when summoned to speak on the occasion, declared, that he had not had a trial, for some of his jury were no freeholders, and no precedent could be shewn of any man's having been so tried when the indictment was laid in a county. He requested that a day of hearing might be appointed, and counsel assigned to argue the point. He shewed that there was a material defect in the indictment, which made it absolutely void, for the words *defensor fidei*,[93] had been left out: that the papers had no otherwise been proved upon him than by a similitude of hands, which, in a criminal case, ought not to have been permitted: that, however, there was no treason in them. He desired the nature of the thing might be examined, and said that he was willing to put his life upon that issue: that the duke of Monmouth[94] had now surrendered himself, and if he would say there had been any such

---

[90] i.e. the Popish Plot (1678), a fictitious but widely believed plot which framed Catholics as planning the assassination of Charles II to bring his Catholic brother, the Duke of York (afterward James II), to the throne.

[91] Sir John Wildman (*c.* 1621–93).   [92] John Rumsey (fl. 1660–86).

[93] i.e. Defender of the Faith.

[94] James Scott, 1st Duke of Monmouth, 1st Duke of Buccleuch (1649–85), Charles II's illegitimate son and rebel leader, who was executed in 1685.

confutations as had been deposed, he would acknowledge whatever the court pleased: that he had been brought up to be arraigned on the seventh, by Habeas Corpus granted the day before, when no bill had been exhibited against him, and when his prosecutors could not know it would be found, unless they had a correspondence with the grand-jury: that he was deterred by the court from putting in his plea: that he had been refused a copy of the indictment, which, by an express statute, is allowed to all men: that the jury had not been summoned as they ought to have been by the ordinary bailiff, but consisted of such only as had been selected by Burton and Graham.[95] All these objections were over-ruled by the chief-justice, with an insolence yet more brutal than his behaviour during the trial. Judge Withins,[96] who appeared to be drunk, told the prisoner [490] he asserted a falsehood; and immediately after Mr. Bampfield[97] had, with modesty, interposed, by saying, he hoped his lordship would not proceed to judgment when there was so material a defect in the indictment as had been pointed out by the prisoner, the chief-justice declared, that there remained nothing for the court to do but to pronounce sentence as the law required. Here the prisoner threw in his last remonstrance: 'I must appeal to God and the world,' said he, 'that I am not heard.' 'Appeal to whom you will,' replied the chief justice, in a passion; and then reproaching the prisoner with the grace he had received from the king in the general pardon, and also with lying under particular obligations to his bounty and mercy, he, with the usual affectation of tenderness and charity, proceeded to pronounce the sentence, which he had no sooner finished, than the prisoner, with a loud and firm voice, expressed himself as follows: 'Then, O God! O God! I beseech thee to sanctify these sufferings unto me, and impute not my blood to my country, nor the city through which I am to be drawn; let no inquisition for blood be made for it: but if any shall be made, and the shedding of innocent blood must be revenged, let the weight of it fall only on those who persecute me, for righteousness sake!' Jeffries, starting from his seat, declared that the prisoner's senses were affected, and Sidney in return calmly stretched out his arm, and desired him to feel if his pulse did not beat at its ordinary rate. Instead of applying for mercy

---

[95] Burton and Graham were sheriffs.
[96] Sir Francis Wythens or Withens (1634–1704).
[97] One of Sidney's counsels.

to the throne, he demanded justice; and set forth in a petition to the king, the injuries which had been done to the laws in his person, and desired to be carried to the royal presence, that he might have an opportunity of shewing the king how much his own interest and honour were concerned in giving that redress which his judges had refused. If any regard to common decency had remained with the court, this just request must undoubtedly have been granted; for every man who was capable of feeling for himself, or his country, was shocked at a precedent [491] destructive of all personal security: even the rancour of party underwent a momentary suspension, and gave way in the generality to sentiments of justice; and the court demurred for a fortnight before they ventured to sign the warrant for execution.

That elevation of sentiment, that dignity of soul which appears in every part of Sidney's conduct, and which age and infirmity had in no degree abated, shone forth with a singular lustre on the fatal day which put a period to his glorious life. He walked on foot to the place of execution; he asked no friend to attend him; he ascended the scaffold with the air of one who came to harangue, or to command, not to suffer; he told the sheriffs, who had returned a packed jury against him, that it was for their sakes only that he reminded them, that his blood lay on their heads; and when he was asked if he had any thing to say to the people, he answered, 'I have made my peace with God, and I have nothing to say to man: I am ready to die, and will give you no farther trouble.' Thus saying, he hastened to the block, and his head was severed from the body with one stroke of the axe.

Thus died the man, who had formed his life and manners after the brightest patterns of human virtue which the best ages of mankind afford. 'If I might live, and be employed,' wrote Sidney to one of his friends, who was importuning him to come over, and use the interest he had with Monk[98] for his personal security and advancement under the monarchy, 'can it be expected that I should serve a government which seeks such detestable ways of establishing itself? Ah! no, I have not learnt to make my own peace by persecuting and betraying my brethren more innocent and worthy than myself: I must live by just means, and serve to just ends, or not at all. After such a manifestation of the ways by which it is intended the king shall [492] govern, I should have renounced any place of favour into which the kindness and industry of my friends might

---

[98] George Monck, 1st Duke of Albemarle (1608–70).

have advanced me, when I found that those who were better than me were only fit to be destroyed. Whilst I live I will endeavour to preserve my liberty, or at least not consent to the destroying it; I hope I shall die in the same principles in which I have lived, and will live no longer than they can preserve me. I have in my life been guilty of many follies; but as I think of no meanness, I will not blot and defile that which is passed by, endeavouring to provide for the future. I have ever had in my mind, that when God should cast me into such a condition as that I cannot save my life but by doing an indecent thing, he shews me the time is come that I should resign it. My thoughts as to king and state depending on their actions, no man shall be a more faithful servant to him than myself, if he make the good and prosperity of his people his glory; none more his enemy, if he doth the contrary.'[99]

The administration of the government, from the first period of the restoration, was not of a complexion and tendency to conciliate the affections of a man, whose notions, in regard to the management of public affairs, were formed on the nicest principles of justice and honour; and, according to the resolution mentioned in the above letter, as long as the republican party had any existence in England, Sidney was active in every scheme which tended to promote their cause; and after his return to England, he joined the popular party,[100] in the hopes either of regulating the English monarchy on more correct principles, or of re-establishing that mode of government, which he conceived would more naturally produce the security of the subject, and the honour of the nation.

[493] Such sentiments carried into practice, and sealed with the blood of this illustrious Englishman, it is to have been imagined, would have rendered his memory sacred to that country on which his writings and heroic virtues have reflected lustre; but there is a spirit of bitterness, of rancour, of envy, and the worst species of levelling gone forth among us, which even the crown of martyrdom cannot escape. We are told, that when the Romans once beheld their Cato in a situation not quite agreeable to that consistent dignity which graced the public and the private virtues of this godlike man, they modestly stepped aside,

---

[99] This letter was frequently reprinted in the eighteenth century, including by Macaulay's friend Thomas Hollis in his edition of Sidney, *Discourses concerning Government: With His Letters, Trial, Apology and Some Memoirs of His Life* (London, 1763), pp. 15–30.
[100] i.e. the Whigs.

and instead of triumphing over humanity, by proclaiming aloud this small blemish in an exalted character, they turned their eyes from the wounding fight. This was the generosity of ancient manners; but what was the conduct of Englishmen on the assertion of the French minister, Barillon,[101] published near a hundred years after the martyrdom of their last eminent patriot, that he had received two several sums from the court of France?[102] Why, instead of turning their eyes from the scandalous page, or even of examining into the nature of an assertion which, inaccurately considered, carries the form of an act somewhat derogatory to the honour of their hero, they exulted in the weakness of humanity, and consequently in their own shame. In the fancied corruption of the most perfect pattern of human excellence they found an authority for enormous deviations from common honesty, and by inculcating the doctrine of an irresistible depravity, and levelling every human character, they imagined they had, in some measure, conciliated reputation with the mammon of unrighteousness; for if every man is a villain in his heart, there can surely be no infamy. Thus whilst England has been considered and respected by foreigners as the mother of heroes, legislators, patriots, and martyrs, her own sons take a satisfaction in convincing the admiring world, that they were under a gross mistake, and that England never produced any [494] character considerably above the stamp of vulgar life; but there is a glaring impolicy as well as meanness and wickedness in these attempts. Let the man who fattens on the spoils of corruption, who wantons in the parade of ill-gotten riches, who feasts on the bread of the deluded, let him suffer the honest man to reap that meagre harvest which he disdains; let him be suffered to enjoy his poverty and his honest fame; let him at least rest secure in the sanctuary of martyrdom, lest by persuading all mankind that virtue is a non-entity, the market should be over-stocked with villains; that the price of his commodity should be lowered; and that abler politicians should attain the object of his desires, for this he may be allured, that all those eminent talents which are necessary to constitute a truly great man, could never fail of meeting with an unlimited success in the ways of a corrupt advancement.

---

[101] Paul Barillon d'Amoncourt, Marquis de Branges (1630–91), the French ambassador to England in 1677–88.
[102] In the second edition of the second volume (1773) of John Dalrymple's *Memoirs of Great Britain and Ireland* (3 vols., 1771–90), II, pp. 285–92.

There is, undoubtedly, much of malice and of falshood in the party-writings of our ancestors; but that general spirit of levelling which pervades modern society, is a new circumstance of corruption among us, and takes its rise from an excess of vanity, which is indeed common to the human character, but which owes its luxuriant growth to circumstances which help to destroy that humility which must ever rationally attend on insignificance, and seduces every man into a false persuasion of self-importance. What with the opportunity of puffing in the public newspapers, a feather well adjusted, a title, a ribbon, unexpected riches acquired in the East, or a successful monopoly, every individual becomes of consequence; and when the mountains are levelled the mole-hills will appeal: but if with the breath of calumny and slander, if with the poisonous ink of detraction, we sully the characters of the illustrious dead, what hope can we reasonably entertain that the present degeneracy of manners [495] should not increase with a rapid course through all succeeding ages! The contemplation of a great character never fails to warm the young and generous student into the noble attempt of imitative virtue, and helps to guard the mind against the impulse of selfish passions, and the contagion of example. It is indeed only by dwelling on the sublime beauties of heroic character; that we can discover that amazing opposition of the hateful and the lovely in moral excellence and moral deformity, and that we can be animated into a passion for disinterested virtue; but what patterns shall we select for the model of youthful emulation, if we admit of modern scepticism in regard to the reality of that virtue which we have long adored in the sacred memories of our forefathers: besides, it must deaden all generous attempts to an exalted conduct, when one supposed error in the judgment, one failing of humanity brought to public view by accident, or private malice, shall obscure the lustre of a life of glory, and level a great character to the base standard of common humanity; for as no individual whilst he continues in a state of frailty, can be certain that he shall always enjoy his understanding free from any alloy of error, or any cloud of insanity; or that he shall every moment of his existence bear the sovereign rule over his temper, his passions, and his prejudices; he will never, with all the labour and the forbearance necessary to build up an eminent virtue, be induced to purchase that transitory fame which may only serve to render him a more conspicuous object of the contempt of the multitude.

That a man of Sidney's rank, acknowledged abilities, and unstained character, would have been received with open arms by the English government, had he been willing to render his talents subservient to his private interest, and the giving strength and permanence to the prerogatives of the crown, or to forward the criminal designs of the court, is, I think, a matter of so [496] self-evident a nature, that all arguments tending to prove the position would be useless and ridiculous. That Sidney had rejected the importunities of his family, and the invitations of his friends; that he had refused to avail himself of the advantage which attends great parts and endowments, to establish an interest with the present government equal to what he had enjoyed with the last, appears from the whole tenour of his conduct, and from his letters of correspondence; and can the rankest party-writer, who possesses any particle of common sense, or any degree of modesty, deny that the firmest principles of honour and integrity must regulate the desires and inclinations of that man who, from motives of conscience and opinion, could reject the opportunity of acquiring distinction and riches in his own country, and submit to a voluntary banishment and precarious subsidence from the favour of a foreign prince!

If I was addressing a public renowned for candour and for discernment, I should say, that such a life as that of Sidney's, supported by his writings, and sealed with his blood, was more than sufficient to counterbalance any assertion which could be made in his disfavour: I should observe, that the inflexibility of his temper in matters in which he believed himself to be in the right, would not differ him meanly to supplicate his own father for money, or in the smallest point to recede from principle, though reduced to great straits and difficulties in a foreign country: I should assert, that it was more probable that Barillon might charge his master with money which was never paid, than that a man of Sidney's high spirit and inflexibility of temper should be prevailed on to take money from the court of France for any mean and dishonest purpose: but, in the present state of manners and opinions, I shall exclude every supposition and every argument which might rationally be drawn from established character and an incorrupt and active integrity, manifested by a long succes-[497]sion of repeated acts of forbearance, self-denial, and personal danger. I shall allow in its fullest latitude Mr. Barillon's assertion, that Algernon Sidney, who had been some years supported in those extremities which his integrity had brought him into, by a pension from the French king, received two several sums of money from the same prince after his return to England, and 'I believe', says the minister, 'he may be gained to your majesty's service:' but what was this service? Was it betraying the liberties of his country to a foreign or domestic tyrant? was it to increase the power of France to the prejudice of his native country? No; it was to procure the dissolution of a base and venal Parliament; it was to disband an army raised on the design of establishing despotism in England; it was to pull down a minister who had been the principal agent in concluding the king's infamous money-negotiations with the court of France, and who had been the promoter of corruption in Parliament, and of arbitrary power in the state. 'The sieur Algernon Sidney,' writes Barillon to his master, 'is a man of very high designs, which tend to the re-establishment of a republic: he is in the party of the Independents and other sectaries, and this party were masters during the late troubles; they are not at present very powerful in Parliament, but they are strong in London; and it is through the intrigues of the sieur Algernon Sidney, that one of the two sheriffs, named Bethel, has been elected.'[103] Let that party, who inveigh against Sidney for his prejudices in favour of a republic, say if this conduct was a deviation from principle; and if not, what becomes of the assertion that Sidney was bribed by the court of France? Does not bribery consist in the engaging a man to do that for money which is not agreeable to his inclinations, his opinions, and his principles; and which he would not otherwise have done without it? If any part of lord Howard's[104] evidence is to be credited, he saw Sidney take sixty guineas out of his pocket for the purpose of [498] forwarding the designs of the popular party against Charles. It is highly probable that as the faction in England, on whom Sidney had any influence, were composed of Independents, the generality of whom were in mean cir-cumstances, that great part of the money which he at different times received from the court of France, might have been expended in useful donations to support his credit and his influence with his partizans: but suppose it was really pocketed for his own use and emolument, there is sufficient matter in the apology written by himself, and published after his death, to justify him fully on this point. After relating several attempts which had been made to assassinate him in his exile, Sidney

---

[103] Extract from a dispatch from Mr. Barillon to Louis XIV, 1680, cited in Dalrymple, *Memoirs of Great Britain and Ireland*, II, p. 287. A transcription of this material can be found in Baschet Correspondence PRO 31/3, no. 147, pp. 402–3, held by the National Archives, Kew, London.

[104] William Howard, 3rd Baron Howard of Escrick (*c.* 1626–94).

proceeds as follows: 'The asperity of this persecution obliged me to seek the protection of some foreign prince, and being then in the vigour of my age, I had reputation enough to have gained honourable employments; but all my designs were broken by messages and letters from this court, so as none durst entertain me; and when I could not comprehend the grounds of dealing with me in such a way, when I knew that many others who had been my companions, and given, as I thought, more just causes of hatred against them than I had done, were received into favour, or suffered to live quietly, a man of quality, who well knew the temper of the court, explained the mystery to me, by letting me know that I was distinguished from the rest because it was known that I could not be corrupted.'[105] If a Fabricius[106] should arise from the dead, and make any objection to Sidney's having condescended to accept, in these circumstances of persecution, a decent support from the bounty of a liberal monarch, we should attend with gravity to his scruples and endeavour to remove them by entering into the nature and exigencies of modern life: we should assert, that it was a just and competent knowledge of the value of external advantages, which gave the stamp of virtue to acts of forbearance: we should argue, that a total indifference to a state of poverty or affluence, as [499] it in a manner annihilates all temptations to every species of venal corruption, it in a great measure weakens the merit of public and private integrity; and that a man's rejecting, with a becoming contempt, every external advantage which would naturally follow a deviation from principle, did not lay him under any obligation to refuse advantages which were in no manner connected with any such derogatory circumstances; and that those noble sentiments which led great minds to despise the wages of iniquity, could be no rational bar to the receiving emoluments and favours from the liberality, the ostentation, or the personal affection of an individual, who did not require any sacrifice of the nicest rules of honour, or the strictest dictates of principle. Arguments like these might, in all probability, have convinced the Roman consul, that the regard which Sidney paid to the alleviating his necessities, when such an alleviation could be obtained without any deviation from principle or honour, rather heightens than decreases the merit of his acts of forbearance: but with what face of serious

---

[105] From 'The Apology of A. Sydney in the Day of His Death', *Discourses concerning Government*, pp. 170–1.

[106] Gaius Fabricius Luscinus Monocularis, elected Roman consul in 282 BC, and known for incorruptibility.

argument can we encounter the overstrained delicacy of an age, who, on all occasions where the detraction of an illustrious character is not in question, acknowledge such a necessity in the article of money as to authorise every species of venality, although attended with the most destructive consequences, and aggravated with the additional crimes of deception, treachery, and the breach of private and public trust.

This ridiculous charge of corruption, though it has been the loudest, has not been the only attack which has been made on the moral character of the illustrious patriot, whose persecutions and sufferings we have just narrated. Mr. Hume, whose partiality on the side of the court in this part of his history, is a greater disgrace to his admirable genius and profound sagacity than any other page of his historical writings, accuses Sidney of ingratitude, in having obtained a pardon of the king, and then [500] entering into measures to disturb his government.[107] In all my researches on this subject, I have not found this pardon to be ascertained; and as I have before observed, I cannot discern any occasion for such a particular pardon. The brutal Jeffries only reproached the prisoner with the grace he had received in the general act of indemnity, and in the letters of thanks which Sidney wrote to the French minister, who transacted this business of his return to England, there is only mention made of a passport from the king: but provided that Sidney's having received a pardon was a proved fact, whoever reads in his Apology the state of the case, will find that all the ingratitude and baseness lay on the side of the king, who, with the arm of injustice and oppression, persecuted to death the man from whom his family had received in their distress personal obligations, and to whose interposition he owed the preservation of his life.

During the period of Sidney's sentence and execution, he wrote a long vindication of himself, and delivered it to the sheriffs, but suspecting that it would be suppressed, he gave a copy of it to a friend. The event proved this, to be a necessary caution, for it was not till after it was known that written copies were dispersed in several hands, that it was suffered to be printed. In this vindication Sidney gives a general account of the persecution he had suffered from the court of England during his residence in foreign countries, and enters into a very minute detail of the hardships and injustice which he had met with during his

---

[107] *Hume's History*, VI, p. 317 (note).

trial, a detail which ought to be carefully perused by every Englishman, as a necessary caution against the sophistry of the bar, and the dishonesty of the bench; as a necessary caution to watch, even with a jealous vigilance, over the proper nomination and independence of juries, and as a necessary caution against that unlimited doctrine, which has of late years [501] prevailed, that juries are bound in all cases, and in all circumstances, to take the law from the mouth of the judge. The whole of Sidney's vindication is written with a spirit, in all respects, equal to what might have been expected from the illustrious author of the Discourses on Government: he confuted the testimonies on which he had been condemned, and asserted, that to reach him, the bench had been filled with men who were the blemishes of the bar; and he regretted death chiefly because it had been inflicted by mean hands. In his own injuries, he lamented those which his country had sustained; and he laid down those great and generous principles of policy which can alone give any permanent happiness to civil society. Instead of praying for the king, he prayed for his country; instead of drawing a veil over the cause for which he suffered, he addressed his Maker as engaged in it with himself. 'Bless thy people', concluded he, 'and save them: and though I fall by idols, suffer not idolatry to be established in this land: defend thy own cause, and defend those who defend it: stir up such as are faint, direct those who are willing, confirm those who are wavering, give wisdom and integrity to all. Grant that I may die glorifying thee for all thy mercies; and that at the last, thou hast permitted me to be singled out as a witness to thy truth, and, even by the confession of my opposers, for that good old cause in which I was, from my youth, engaged, and for which thou hast often and wonderfully declared thyself.'[108]

We are told by Burnet, that these last words furnished much matter for the scribblers of these times;[109] and by Echard, that Sidney's address to the Deity was thought so enthusiastical and shocking, that his death was much less pitied and lamented than that of lord Russell, though the hardships he met with were greater than any man had met with before him.[110] Of what kind were these people, and by what principles they were governed, who were so violently [502] shocked with an address,

---

[108] *The Very Copy of a Paper Delivered to the Sheriffs, Upon the Scaffold on Tower Hill ... Decemb. 7, 1683, by A. Sidney, Before his Execution there* (n.p., 1683), pp. 6–7.

[109] Burnet, *History of His Own Time*, II, p. 981.

[110] Laurence Echard, *The History of England* (3 vols., London, 1707–18), III, p. 701.

which plainly shewed the sincerity of those sentiments, by which the author had professed to direct his conduct, may easily be determined: but it is to be observed, that the address, upon the whole, met with the same unfair treatment as the Discourses on Government had met with from the lawyers; it was tortured into a confession of the conspiracy, although it plainly refers to that perfection, even unto death, with which the author had been pursued by the court, for the part he had taken during the civil wars, and the opposition of his principles to every mode of tyranny.

[VOL. 8 (1783)]

[Ch. VI, 275] ^Ann. 1688^ The enemies of James[111] did not fail to make the most of the advantages they had gained by their subtle manoeuvres. Some said that the king's flight was the effect of a disturbed conscience, labouring under the load of secret guilt; and those whose censures were more moderate, asserted that his incurable bigotry had led him even to sacrifice his crown to the interests of his priests; and that he chose rather to depend on the precarious support of a French force to subdue the refractory spirit of his people, than to abide the issue of events which threatened such legal limitations as should effectually prevent any farther abuse of power.

The whole tenour of the king's past conduct undoubtedly gave a countenance to insinuations which were in themselves sufficiently plaus-ible to answer all the purposes for which they were industriously circu-lated; but when the following circumstances are taken into consideration, viz. that timidity is natural to the human mind, when oppressed with an uninterrupted series of misfortunes; that the king's life was put entirely into the hands of a rival, whose ambitious views were altogether incom-patible with even the shadow of regal power in his person; that the means taken to increase the apprehensions which reflections of this nature must necessarily occasion, were of the most mortifying kind, it must be acknowledged that if the principles of heroic virtue might have produced a different conduct in some exalted individuals, yet that the generality of mankind would, in James's situation, have sought shelter in the proffered generosity of a trusted friend, from personal insult, personal danger, and

---

[111] i.e. James II.

from all the harassing suspence under which the mind of this imprudent and unfortunate monarch had long laboured.

[276] The opposition of James's religious principles to those of his subjects; his unpopular connection with the court of France; but, above all, the permanent establishment of a rival family on the throne of England, has formed in his disfavour such an union of prejudice and interest as to destroy in the minds of posterity all that sympathy which on similar occasions, and in similar misfortunes, has so wonderfully operated in favour of other princes; and whilst we pay the tribute of unavailing tears over the memory of Charles the First; whilst, with the church of England, we venerate him as a martyr to the power and office of prelates; whilst we see with regret, that he was stripped of his dignity and life at the very time when the chastening hand of affliction had in a great measure corrected the errors of a faulty education; the irresistible power of truth must oblige us to confess that the same adherence to religious principle which cost the father his life, deprived the son of his dominions; that the enormous abuse of power with which both sovereigns are justly accused, owed their origin to the same source, the errors arising from a bad education, aggravated and extended by the impious flattery of designing priests: we shall also be obliged to confess that the parliament itself, by an unprecedented servility, helped to confirm James in the exalted idea he had entertained of the royal office, and that the doctrines of an absolute and unconditional submission on the part of the subject, which, in the reign of his father, was in a great measure confined to the precepts of a Laud, a Sibthorpe,[112] and a Manwaring,[113] were now taught as the avowed doctrines of the church of England, were acknowledged by the two universities,[114] and implicitly avowed by the large majority of the nation. So great indeed was the change in the tem-[277]per, manners, and opinions of the people, from the commencement of the reign of Charles the First to the commencement of the reign of his son James, that at this shameful period, the people gloried in having laid all their privileges at the foot of the throne, and execrated every generous principle of freedom, as arising from a spirit totally incompatible with the

---

[112] Robert Sibthorpe or Sibthorp (d. 1662), English clergyman who defended the divine right of kings in the reign of Charles I, and was denounced by Locke and Shaftesbury.
[113] Roger Maynwaring (sometimes spelled Mainwaring or Manwaring), (*c.* 1589/1590–1653), Bishop of St Davids, and defender of the divine right of kings.
[114] i.e. Oxford and Cambridge.

peace of society, and altogether repugnant to the doctrines of Christianity.

This was the situation of affairs at the accession of the unfortunate James: and had he been equally unprincipled as his brother the deceased king; had he professed himself a protestant, whilst he was in his heart a papist; had he not regarded it as his duty to use his avowed omnipotent power for the restoring to some parts of its ancient dignity a church which he regarded as the only true church of Christ; or had he, instead of attacking the prerogatives of the prelacy, suffered them to share that regal despotism which they had fixed on the basis of conscience, the most flagrant abuses of civil power would never have been called in judgment against him; and parliaments themselves would have lent their constitutional authority to have rivetted the chains of the empire in a manner as should have put it out of the power of the most determined votaries of freedom to have re-established the government on its ancient foundation. From this irremediable evil England owes its deliverance alone to the bigotted sincerity of James; a circumstance which ought, in some measure, to conciliate our affections to the memory of the sufferer, and to treat those errors with lenity, which have led to the enjoyment of privileges which can never be entirely lost, but by a general corruption of principle and depravity of manners.

[278] It was said by the witty duke of Buckingham,[115] that 'Charles the Second might do well if he would,' and that 'James would do well if he could:'[116] an observation which says little for the understanding of James, but a great deal for his heart; and with all the blemishes with which his public character is stained, he was not deficient in several qualities necessary to compose a good sovereign. His industry to business was exemplary, he was frugal of the public money, he cherished and extended the maritime power of the empire, and his encouragement of trade was attended with such success, that, according to the observation of the impartial historian Ralph, as the frugality of his administration helped to increase the number of malecontents, so his extreme attention to trade was not less alarming to the whole body of the Dutch than his

---

[115] George Villiers, 2nd Duke of Buckingham (1628–87), courtier and poet.

[116] The origins of these quotations are untraced, but they were frequently quoted in the nineteenth century.

resolution not to rush into a war with France was mortifying to their stadtholder.[117]

In domestic life, the character of James, though not irreproachable, was comparatively good: it is true, he was in a great measure tainted with that licentiousness of manners, which, at this time, pervaded the whole society, and which reigned triumphant within the circle of the court; but he was never carried into any excesses which trenched deeply on the duties of social life; and if the qualities of his heart were only to be judged by his conduct in the different characters of husband, father, master, and friend, he might be pronounced a man of a very amiable disposition. But those who know not how to forgive injuries, and can never pardon the errors, the infirmities, the vices, or even the virtues of their fellow-creatures, when in any respect they affect personal interest or inclination, will arm against them the sensibility of every humane mind, and can never expect from [279] others that justice and commiseration which [they] themselves have never exercised. But whilst we execrate that rancorous cruelty with which James, in the short hour of triumph, persecuted all those who endeavoured to thwart his ambitious hopes, it is but justice to observe, that the rank vices of pride, malice, and revenge, which so deeply blacken his conduct, whilst he figured in the station of presumptive heir to the crown, and afterwards in the character of sovereign on the successful quelling the Monmouth rebellion,[118] were thoroughly corrected by the chastening hand of affliction; that the whole period of his life, from his return from Ireland to the day of his death, was spent in the exercise of the first Christian virtues, viz. patience, fortitude, humility, and resignation. ^Brettonneau's life of James the Second^[119] Brettonneau, his biographer, records, that he always spoke with an extreme moderation of the individuals who had acted the most successfully in his disfavour; that he reproved those who mentioned their conduct with severity; that he read, even with a Stoical apathy, the bitterest writings which were published against him; that he regarded the loss of empire as a necessary correction for the misdemeanors of his life,

---

[117] James Ralph, *The History of England: During the Reigns of K. William, Q. Anne, and K. George I. With an Introductory Review of the Reigns of the Royal Brothers, Charles and James* (2 vols., London, 1744–6), I, p. 1078.

[118] See note 94, above.

[119] François Bretonneau, *An Abridgment of the Life of James II. King of Great Britain, &c. Extracted from an English Manuscript of the Reverend Father Francis Sanders, of the Society of Jesus, and Confessor to His Late Majesty* (London, 1703).

and even rebuked those who expressed any concern for the issue of events which he respected as ordinations of the Divine will. According to the same biographer, James was exact in his devotion, moderate even to abstinence; in his life, full of sentiments of the highest contrition for past offences; and, according to the discipline of the Romish church, was very severe in the austerities which he inflicted on his person.[120] As this prince justly regarded himself as a martyr to the Catholic faith, as his warmest friends were all of this persuasion, as his conversation in his retirement at St. Germains,[121] was entirely in a great measure confined to priests and devotees, it is natural that his superstition should in-[280]crease with the increase of religious sentiment; and as he had made use of his power and authority, whilst in England, to enlarge the number of proselytes to popery, so in a private station he laboured incessantly by prayer, exhortation, and example, to confirm the piety of his popish adherents, and to effect a reformation in those who still continued firm to the doctrines of the church of England. He visited the monks of La Trappe once a year, the severest order of religionists in France; and his conformity to the discipline of the convent was so strict and exact, that he impressed those devotees with sentiments of admiration at his piety, humility, and constancy. Thus having spent twelve years with a higher degree of peace and tranquillity than he had ever experienced in the most triumphant part of his life, he was seized with a palsy in September 1701, and after languishing fifteen days, died in the sixty-eighth year of his age, having filled up the interval, between his first seizure and final exit, with the whole train of religious exercises enjoined on similar occasions by the church of Rome, with solemn and repeated professions of his faith, and earnest exhortations to his two children, the youngest of whom was born in the second year of his exile, to keep stedfast to the religion in which they had been educated. These precepts and commands have acted with a force superior to all the temptations of a crown, and have been adhered to with a firmness which obliges an historian to acknowledge the super-iority which James's descendants, in the nice points of honour and conscience, have gained over the character of Henry the Fourth,[122] who, at the period when he was looked up to as the great hero of the protestant cause, made no scruple to accept a crown on the disgraceful terms of abjuring the principles of the reformation, and embracing the

---

[120] Ibid., pp. 73–4, *passim.*   [121] The Jacobite court in France, until 1713.
[122] Henry (or Henri) (1553–1610), king of France from 1589 to 1610, who was raised as a Protestant but converted to Catholicism during his reign.

principles of a religion, which, [281] from his early infancy, he had been taught to regard as idolatrous and prophane.

The dominion of error over the minds of the generality of mankind is irresistible. James, to the last hour of his life, continued as great a bigot to his political as his religious errors: he could not help considering the strength and power of the crown as a circumstance necessary to the preservation and happiness of the people; and, in a letter of advice, which he wrote to his son, whilst he conjures him to pay a religious observance to all the duties of a good sovereign, he cautions him against suffering any entrenchment on royal prerogative. Among several heads, containing excellent instructions on the art of reigning happily and justly, he warns the young prince never to attempt to disquiet his subjects in their property or their religion; and, what is very remarkable, to his last breath he persisted in asserting, that he never intended to subvert the laws, or procure more than a toleration and an equality of privilege to his catholic subjects.[123] As there is great reason to believe this assertion to be true, it shews, that the delusion was incurable under which the king laboured, by the trust he had put in the knavish doctrines of lawyers and priests; and that neither himself, nor his protestant abettors, could fathom the consequences of that enlarged system of toleration which he endeavoured to establish.

[...]

[Ch. VII, 329] ^Ann. 1689^ The dethronement of king James, and the completion of the Revolution in the settlement of the crowns of England and Scotland on the prince and princess of Orange, &c.[124] has formed an epocha in the annals of our country, so universally celebrated by the voice of all factions, that a writer must be possessed of the enthusiasm of a martyr, whose regard for the strict letter of truth, leads to neglect or to contradict the opinion of his countrymen on this important subject, and who does not, like the humble petitioners to the throne, usher in a long list of grievances, with panegyrical compliments on the cause, and the source of those evils on which he animadverts. These are contradictions which are very easily swallowed in modern history, where a reader never looks for, or even desires instruction, and expects at the expence of the real and sound reputation of the unfortunate writer, and of every principle of truth on which useful instruction can be founded, to be

[123] Bretonneau, *An Abridgment of the Life of James II*, pp. 179–91.
[124] i.e. William III and Mary II.

indulged in all his vain, ridiculous, and destructive prejudices. Mr. Hume, who is assiduously careful not to offend in any point of popular recommendation, gives the prince of Orange great credit for the not using any undue influence, or the not putting any apparent constraint on the convention, from the authority of whose resolution he was admitted to sovereignty.[125] It is, however, certain, that the perverse prejudices of faction, the ticklish situation of affairs in Ireland,[126] and the fear of being left in the lurch by their deliverer, if he was not gratified to the utmost extent of his ambition, induced the Whigs to give way to the settlement of the crown, without adding any new trophies to the altar of liberty, or even of renovating those sound principles in the constitution, which, in the length of time, had fallen a sacrifice to the lusts and the opportunities [330] of power. A repeal of the disfranchising statute of Henry the Sixth; a revival of the statute of Edward the Third for annual parliaments, with a bill to prevent those from sitting in parliament who are interested in defending all measures of government, whether good or bad, and who find in the emoluments of office, advantages arising from the distress and burthens of the people, were so necessary to the rendering the British constitution, as explained in the Bill of Rights,[127] the best of all possible constitutions, that it opens a wider field for more corrupt abuses, than ever were produced by all the monarchical, oligarchical, and aristocratical tyrannies in the world; because, under the specious appearance of democratical privilege, the people are really and truly enslaved to a small part of the community, and in the first instance are sold by a set of wretches, whose paucity of numbers place them within the compass of bribery, whose dependant situations hardly allow them a freedom of choice, in what is called the right of election; whose ignorance, on a supposition of honesty, renders them very inadequate to the trust reposed in them by the constitution, and whose needy situations, and obscure conditions, cause a small pecuniary temptation to be of more balance in the scale of the mind, than every public mischief which it is possible to ensue from the most abandoned venality.[xliv]

[xliv] The method of destroying corruption in the first instance by cutting off the small boroughs, by which even one dependant elector sends as many members to parliament as a large county; the extending the right of election, and adding to the county members,

[125] *Hume's History*, p. 529.
[126] The civil war in Ireland between Jacobites and Williamites continued until 1691.
[127] Of 1689 (but sometimes referred to as 1688).

[331] These important grievances, and an endless variety of mischiefs, which from the same source, necessarily branch out into as endless a variety of successive ills all tending to the ruin of public virtue, to the discouragement and total disappointment of real merit, and to the reward of villainy and the worst species of corruption, did not escape the vigilant attention of patriotism at the period of the revolution: but whilst the friends of liberty in general exclaimed, that the Bill of Rights was very inadequate to what ought to have been insisted on in a period so favourable to the enlargement and security of liberty, as a crown bestowed by the free voice of the people, those members of the convention, who had been most active in indulging the wishes of William, in regard to an undivided sovereignty and undiminished prerogatives, hoped to obtain from his gratitude, his good sense, and their present state of power and consequence, all those advantages which they had for the present sacrificed to the exigence of the occasion, or rather to the earnest desire of shutting every door of hope to the restoration of the exiled family.

To the inexpressible grief of the Whigs they found, in the short space of a year, that they had been entirely mistaken in the notions they had formed of the character of William, and their own importance; they had the mortification of seeing those who had acted the most inimical to their party, and the free principles of the constitution, viz. the marquis of Halifax,[128] the earl of Danby,[129] and the lord Nottingham,[130] [332] taken into the bosom of their hero, resume their places in the cabinet,[xlv] and also the whole influence of government extended to the silencing all enquiries into the guilt of those persons who had been the chief

has been so ably set forth in several pamphlets, that I shall only add, that if this scheme should fail of preventing the abuses of corruption, the introducing the mode of election by ballot, a mode used in every wise government in all cases of election, would infallibly remedy the ruinous evil; an evil grown to such an enormous height, that many gentlemen who are in the possession of boroughs, by the situation of their landed property, bring them to market on every new parliament, and sell them to the minister, from the sums of five to ten thousand pounds.

[xlv] Even the cruel and profligate [Percy] Kirke [(*c.* 1646–91)] was taken into the service of the new government, and sent over to exercise those barbarities in Ireland, which he had formerly exercised on the subjects in England.

[128] George Savile, 1st Marquess of Halifax (1633–95).
[129] Thomas Osborne, (1632–1712), 1st Duke of Leeds (known as the Earl of Danby between 1673 and 1689).
[130] Daniel Finch, 2nd Earl of Nottingham (1647–1730).

instruments in the cruel persecutions in the late reign, and to the obtainment of such an act of indemnity as should effectually screen every delinquent, however notorious, from the just vengeance of injured patriotism.

A conduct thus calculated to inspire resentment, and raise suspicion, did not fail to rouse the indignation and jealousy of the Whig party to the highest pitch of opposition. So great was their present distrust of William, that they even joined with the church to disappoint the presbyterians of what had been promised them by all parties, namely, a comprehension;[131] because they apprehended, that William would acquire influence over a body who were at present the most inimical to his pretensions, by the addition of members who would look up to him as their patron, and who, from a similarity of religious principle,[132] would be naturally inclined to a personal attachment. They stood firm to the resolution they had formed of avoiding the errors made by the parliaments in the late reigns, of granting the crown an independent revenue; and they took measures to secure themselves from the opposition of the Tories, by adding to the bill for restoring corporations to their original rights, a clause, which, during the space of seven years, disabled [333] from the right of electors in corporations all persons who had been any wise accessary to the new modelling them.

The equity and moderation of this clause could not easily be disputed; and William finding himself on the point of falling into the hands of a party who were determined so effectually to circumscribe his power, as should give reality and permanence to that liberty which had been declared to be the only object of his views, desires, and undertakings, broke like an enraged lion from the toils of patriotism, flung off that party with whom he had been closely connected, with whom he had successfully intrigued during the preceding reigns, and by whole zeal and activity he had been elevated to the state of sovereignty, threw himself entirely into the hands of men against whom it was pretended his hostilities had been solely directed, dissolved the parliament, took upon himself the command of the forces in Ireland, and left the queen, and her friends the Tories, to confirm the victory gained over the Whigs.

---

[131] The Comprehension Bill intended to admit many Nonconformists to the Church of England, but the line between orthodox churchmen and Nonconformists had hardened, and the bill was dropped. Its replacement was the Toleration Act 1689.

[132] William was a Dutch Calvinist.

The neglect of not carrying the Scotch claim of rights into execution,[133] had raised such a flame of resentment in that nation, as actually to give rise to a conspiracy in favour of the abdicated king; who had he been at liberty to have pursued these advantages by the dictates of common policy, might have returned to the possession of his dominions with as large a majority of voices in his favour, as that by which he had been expelled: but William, happily delivered from the difficulties into which his ingratitude had plunged him by the unfavourable situation of his rival, viz. his state of absolute dependence on the popish interest in Ireland, and on the French [334] court, was, at length, enabled by the national antipathies of one party, the remembrance of past perfections in the other, and the fears of popery in all, to defeat every plan of reformation which had been formed in the generous warmth of patriotism by the Whigs; to carry every point of personal ambition; to secure an independent revenue on the crown; to burthen the nation with a standing debt, and a standing army; to involve it, contrary to the interest of a commercial maritime power, in expensive land armaments;[134] and, lastly, to entail on posterity a perpetuity of those internal divisions which had taken their rise from the civil contentions in the reign of Charles the First, and which, in the two last reigns, had brought the three kingdoms on the brink of slavery and perdition.

What fatal encroachments the new system introduced by William has made in the ancient constitution of England; what an unexampled mode of tyranny it has established; what an universal depravity of manners it has occasioned, must be left to the detail of history to describe; and as it is impossible for an historian not initiated in the sacred mysteries of ministerial craft to give any satisfactory account of that complicated system of corruption by which the affairs of this country has been conducted through the seventeenth century,[135] it is fully sufficient to observe that it has banished from the helm of government every species of abilities but those which belong to financiering; that is, a dexterity in devising new modes of pecuniary oppression, and a skilful use of the public money for the destruction of that independence in parliament on which the security and safety of the people necessarily depend. Under such cir-[335]cumstances of administration, it is no wonder that the

---

[133] Claim of Right Act 1689, passed by a Convention of the Scottish Estates.
[134] The Anglo-French War (1689–97), part of the Nine Years War, and the War of the Spanish Succession (1701–14).
[135] Now called the eighteenth century.

internal and external good of society should have been entirely neglected; that the natural resources of a great commercial state, though yearly declining in its vigour and strength, should have been mistaken for the highest point of prosperity; and that we should find ourselves at the brink of political mortality, at the time when we vainly imagined we were exalted above the reach of those calamities which have ever been found to attend the want of wisdom in counsel, and the loss of national virtue.

The late earl of Chatham,[136] whose splendid administration makes a capital figure in the annals of this country, is universally called the minister of the people; but whoever accurately traces the steps by which this great statesman acquired the necessary department in power to render his talents in any extent useful to his country, will find that Mr. Pitt, instead of having been forced on the crown by the voice of a free people, either in their collective or representative capacity, was, as a necessary prelude to his being appointed to the office of prime minister, obliged to sacrifice to the prejudices of the sovereign all those popular principles which had graced his parliamentary harangues for the series of many years, and which had raised him to the highest pitch of public favour and esteem.[137] I shall not pretend to criticize on the conduct of a war which was attended with such a brilliant success; and shall only observe, that our large armies on the continent, our numerous subsidies to German princes, and the corruptions which have prevailed through the whole system of administration, whilst they have filled the pockets of needy contractors, and swelled [336] to an enormous height the lucrative appendages to office, oppressed the nation with such an additional burthen of taxes and debt, as to forbid any hopes of salvation, but from a circumstance so out of the ordinary course of sublunary affairs as to render it a perfect miracle in political history, viz. a patriot king[138] and a patriot ministry[139] co-operating with the body of the people to throw off

---

[136] William Pitt the Elder, 1st Earl of Chatham (1708–78), was Secretary of State for the Southern Department and Leader of the House of Commons in 1756–61 – first in a brief coalition with the Duke of Devonshire and from 1757 more successfully with the Duke of Newcastle – and Lord Privy Seal and nominal leader of the government in 1766–8, though illness plagued his second term in government. Macaulay refers to Chatham's first period in government, during the Seven Years War.

[137] Despite having argued against continental land wars and in favour of a naval ('blue-water') strategy in opposition, once in government Pitt was willing to support continental warfare and the Protestant interest in Europe.

[138] Bolingbroke, *The Idea of a Patriot King* (1738), in *Works*, III, pp. 35–126.

[139] John Almon, *A Review of the Reign of George the Second* (London, 1762), p. 215.

the shackles of septennial parliaments,[140] to reinstate the people in their constitutional right of election, and, by this means, to introduce such a rigid plan of oeconomy, as may, in a process of time, in a great measure, restore the wasted finances of the country.

Mr. Pitt was so sensible of the corrupt and lavish manner in which the business of the nation was carried on, even when it was struggling under the difficulties of an expensive war,[141] that he always disavowed the having any other part in the management of affairs, but the conduct of the military operations: and so little independent consequence did this fortunate minister obtain from the brilliant successes which had attended his administration, that he was not suffered to crown the expectations of the public by a peace adequate to the expensive exertions of Great Britain, and the low state to which she had reduced her enemies; and instead of being able to carry any one point in favour of the popular interest, or the security of national prosperity, he found himself deserted by that septennial parliament who had lent him their support whilst the influence of the crown was used in his favour; and his successor, lord Bute,[142] as firmly supported in the concluding an inadequate destructive peace, as he had experienced in the conduct of a glorious war.

[337] The fatal consequences of the lavish profligacy of those ministers who declared that the finances of the nation were too far exhausted even to pursue the career of victory, or to take the proper advantage of enemies who were prostrate at our feet, this unhappy and deluded country has too severely experienced: but now that the increased corruption of administration, and the unhappy catastrophe of the American war,[143] has so greatly accelerated the downfall of this empire, as to bring on, in our own days, that ruin which we vainly hoped to escape, at the expence of our posterity; now that the feeling sense of our calamities has brought conviction home to the heart of every disinterested citizen, let us not, by throwing a veil over the defects of the revolution, mislead the judgement of the public in regard to those matters of which it is of the utmost importance that they should be well instructed; let us not, out of an illiberal partiality to the vices and errors of our progenitors, endeavour to continue those delusions, by which the vulgar part of society have been led to prefer empty sounds to substantial realities, and have been taught to consider the protestant succession in the illustrious house of

[140] The Septennial Act 1716.   [141] i.e. the Seven Years War.
[142] John Stuart, 3rd Earl of Bute (1713–92), First Lord of the Treasury in 1762–3.
[143] The American Revolutionary War, 1775–83.

Hanover[144] as an advantage adequate to all the blessings which flow from good government, and the enjoyment of a well regulated freedom.[xlvi] ^Second Address to the Public from the Society for Constitutional Information^ 'What repeated warning,' says a spirited writer, 'have we received of the increasing venality of our representatives; and how often have we neglected the opportunity of placing the public liberty upon a permanent basis; but so long as there [338] could be a doubt concerning the extent of the contagion, so long as our representatives condescended to spread the slighted veil over their infidelity, we acquiesced in the deceit, and chose to expect that relief from time which is only attainable by virtue; as if universal experience had not shewn, that the first infringement of national rights, which is permitted with impunity, is the introduction of every evil; that the attempts of ambition never finish but with the patience of mankind; and that there is no medium between opposing the least encroachment, and submitting to the greatest; but with our deluded country-men every pretext, however futile and ridiculous, has been alternately sufficient to quiet their fears, and lull their jealousies; sometimes their liberties have been invaded, to secure them the better against the attacks of tyranny; sometimes because a patriot king enjoyed the throne; sometimes they were persuaded to forego redress, because the minister was embarrassed with war; sometimes because he dared not interrupt the public peace; sometimes for fear of excluding the people's real friends from power; sometimes because the people's real friends had obtained the power they sought, and must not hazard its loss. Wretched nation, that has been induced to make the disease inveterate in expectation of a cure, and that did not understand that it was a matter of no consequence in what name, or by what party, they were enslaved.'[145]

As a close to this long narration of national evils and national follies, so conspicuous in the mournful annals of the two last centuries, I appeal to the ingenuous and un-[339]corrupted part of my countrymen, which

---

[xlvi] The author, in this observation, does not intend any disrespect to this illustrious house; but only to censure that ministerial craft, by which this universally acknowledged blessing has been used to give a kind of sanction to the worst of measures, and to the most alarming encroachments on constitutional freedom.

[144] In 1714, in accordance with the Act of Settlement 1701.
[145] [Capel Lofft,] *A Second Address to the Public from the Society for Constitutional Information* (London, 1782), p. 10.

class of historians have been the real friends of the constitution; those who, by humouring the prejudices of all factions, have left the judgment of the reader in such an embarrassed state as to be incapable of forming any just opinion of men, of measures, or of the true interest of their country; or those writers who, like myself, in an honest contempt of the ill-founded rage and resentment of all denominations of men and interests, have, through the whole course of my narrative, closely adhered to the purest principles of civil and religious freedom; have marked every deviation from constitutional rectitude; and have not only pointed out the destructive enormities of marked tyrants, but have endeavoured to direct the judgment of the public to the detection of those masked hypocrites, who, under the specious pretence of public good, have advanced their private interest and ambition on the ruin of all that is valuable to man.

FINIS

2

Loose Remarks on Certain Positions to be Found in Mr. Hobbes's 'Philosophical Rudiments of Government and Society', with a Short Sketch of a Democratical Form of Government, in a Letter to Signor Paoli (1767)

Introduction to the Text

Loose Remarks was Macaulay's earliest known pamphlet, first published anonymously in 1767 and two years later in a second edition under her name. This edition reproduces the first edition, with Macaulay's errata highlighted in square brackets. The pamphlet is divided into two separate parts, the first of which seeks to refute key positions in Thomas Hobbes's social and political thought, with the second providing a brief sketch of Macaulay's preferred form of government, what she called a 'democratical government'. The two parts are on the face of it distinct, but they are united by her defence of democracy. Using democracy in a positive sense was unusual at the time and thus a significant conceptual move by Macaulay. While she believed that representative democracy was superior to direct democracy, she was clear that the people should 'give directions' to their representatives, a topical issue to which she would return in *An Address to the People of England, Scotland and Ireland* (1775).

Macaulay's attention in the first part is fixed on the English translation of Hobbes's *De Cive* (1642/1647), published as *Philosophical Rudiments of Government and Society* in 1651, and more specifically his arguments against the natural sociability of human beings and in favour of absolute, monarchical government. According to Macaulay, since Hobbes argued that human beings were born with an aptitude for reason, he should also

85

have accepted that they were born for society itself, as reason will lead us to it. Politically, she departed from Hobbes in a similar way to Locke: legislative and executive power could be separated, and the social contract was formed between the people and the sovereign rather than among individuals in the state of nature. If sovereigns transgressed the terms of the contract, they must be resisted.

The second part is addressed to Pasquale Paoli (1725–1807), a military and political leader of the Corsican opposition to Genoese and later French rule over the island. The Corsican revolution attracted the interest of the likes of Jean-Jacques Rousseau and James Boswell. In Britain, enthusiasm for the Corsican cause ran high. Paoli went into exile in Britain in the 1760s, but his presence in London turned out to be a disappointment. Macaulay wrote to Benjamin Rush (1746–1813) in 1770: 'Ever since Paoli has resided in England he has been in the hands of the Ministry, receives a pension from them and has been seen by very few of the friends of Liberty and consequently is totally disregarded by the people.'[1]

Horace Walpole described the second part of the work as a 'printed advice for settling a republic'.[2] While republics could be aristocratic or democratic, Macaulay's preference for the latter was explicit, though her democracy would include separate interests and political orders. The purpose of a 'Democratical Form of Government' was 'to make all interests unite in the welfare of the state', she wrote to Rush in a correspondence published with the second edition of the *Loose Remarks* in 1769. She proposed a bicameral system, with a Senate made up of members who had previously served in the lower house. The Senate would not be vested with any coercive power and had only an advisory role; 'like the fathers of adults', as she described it to Rush.[3]

The second part of the pamphlet was clearly inspired by James Harrington (1611–77). In his *Oceana* (1656), Harrington had put forward constitutional mechanisms such as rotation in office and agrarian law because he largely agreed with Hobbes's pessimistic interpretation of human nature. Somewhat puzzlingly, Macaulay accepted these mechanisms in the same pamphlet in which she rejected Hobbes's anti-social

---

[1] *Correspondence*, p. 71.
[2] Horace Walpole, *Memoirs and Portraits*, ed. Matthew Hodgart (rev. ed., London, 1963), p. 213.
[3] *Correspondence*, p. 68.

view of humanity. Whereas Harrington's political thought was calculated to 'maketh evil men good',[4] Macaulay was confident that a rightly constituted government could nurture 'the innate generous principles of the soul' (p. [30]). For Macaulay, human beings were not naturally egotistical but became corrupted by power and wealth, or by servility in absolute monarchies. In other words, constitutional mechanisms were needed to keep human beings good rather than to make them good – a subtle but important difference. It should be noted, however, that she was more prepared to stress elsewhere that 'the want of power is the only limitation to the exertion of human selfishness'.[5]

Macaulay was confident about the theory of the tract, writing to Rush: 'I hope, if you take the trouble, with these comments, to read over again that little tract, you will find it what I pretended to make it, a perfect skeleton of a democratical form.'[6] Later in life, after the outbreak of the French Revolution, she became less optimistic about some of the constitutional mechanisms she had proposed. As she reflected in a letter to President George Washington in June 1790:

> I endeavoured to keep out corruption by enforcing a general
> Rotation; but I must acknowledge to you that the corruptions which
> have crept into our Legislature since the revolution, with the wise
> caution used by the french patriots in the rules to which they have
> subjected their National Assembly, have led me to alter my
> opinion ... I should have thought it safer to have made them
> incapable of holding at least any Civil Office whilst they were
> Members of the Legislature.

Macaulay came to prefer the French example of 'confining the Legislature to one equal Assembly' as opposed to the bicameral system she had recommended in the sketch, and which the Americans had adopted.[7] In the final pamphlet of her life, as we shall see, she expressed admiration of the French for extending 'the right of election to every man who is not a pauper'. Since paupers lived on the alms of society, she was convinced that they 'cannot reasonably have a right to enjoy its political privileges', underlining the limitations to her democratic vision,

---

[4] James Harrington, *Aphorisms Political* (2nd ed., London, 1659), p. 2.
[5] Macaulay, *An Address to the People of England, Scotland and Ireland* (London, 1775), pp. 27–8. See also p. 160, below.
[6] *Correspondence*, p. 69.　　[7] *Correspondence*, p. 277.

which chimed with that of the Levellers in the seventeenth century and most reformers in her own day.[8]

One of the controversial aspects of Macaulay's pamphlet is her proposal to eliminate England's common law rights of inheritance for women. This policy formed part of her onslaught on primogeniture and her conviction that aristocratic wealth needed to be diluted. The proposal has prompted suggestions that she was unconcerned with the situation of women.[9] Her later writings disprove such claims, and indeed this policy may have been intended to prevent men from marrying women for their wealth.

[8] Macaulay, *Observations on the Reflections of Edmund Burke* (London, 1790), pp. 77–9.
[9] Susan Staves, '"The Liberty of a She-Subject of England": Rights Rhetoric and the Female Thucydides', *Cardozo Studies in Law and Literature*, 1 (1989), pp. 161–83.

Loose Remarks on Certain Positions to be Found in Mr. Hobbes's 'Philosophical Rudiments of Government and Society', with a Short Sketch of a Democratical Form of Government, in a Letter to Signor Paoli (1767)

[1] Loose Remarks, &c.

Mr. Hobbes, in his Philosophical Elements of a True Citizen,[1] sets out with an intention to confute this received opinion, That man is a creature born fit for society. To do this, he enumerates the vicious affections inherent in human nature, which affections are confined to the innate quality of selfishness. From these premises he draws this inference, that man cannot desire society from love, but through hope of gain: therefore, says he,[i] the original of all great and lasting societies consisted, not in the mutual good will men had toward each other, but in the mutual fear they had of each other.

[2] The opinion that man is born fit for society cannot, we apprehend, be affected by Mr. Hobbes's position, is granted; since in his enumeration of the laws of nature, which he calls the dictate of right reason, he takes in all those virtues which render man not only fit for society, but amiable in it; and asserts,[ii] that reason, which is the law of nature, is given by God to every man for the rule of his actions. But Mr. Hobbes says,[iii] that infants are born incapable of reason, and all men are born infants; therefore man is not born a creature fit for society.

Mr. Hobbes's argument to prove that man is not born a creature fit for society, seems to be of the same nature with the following:

---

[i] Vide Hobbes's *Philosophical Rudiments concerning Government and Society*, 8vo. ed. 1751. [This almost certainly refers to the 1651 duodecimo edition since her page references match this edition and the second known edition of *De Cive* in English is part of Molesworth's collection of Hobbes's *English Works* (1839–45).]

[ii] Chap. iv. p. 58, art. 1.   [iii] Chap. i. p. 6, annot. 1.

[1] This is a translation of the original Latin title.

New-born infants are incapable of walking;

Therefore man, being born an infant, is not born a creature fit for walking.

But infants are born with two legs, and the power of motion, which are the [3] means for that action when it becomes necessary to their state;

Therefore man, by being born with the necessary means, cannot be said to be born unfit for walking.

– And infants, tho' born incapable of reason, by being born with human attributes, are born with the means necessary for attaining it;

Therefore man, by being born with the necessary means, is born a creature apt for reason; and a creature apt for reason is a creature apt for society.

We apprehend Mr. Hobbes's reasoning is mere quibbling; and this, because it is obvious that the meaning of the philosophers whom Mr. Hobbes attempts to confute is,[2] that man is born a creature fit for society, notwithstanding his reasoning faculties do not immediately arrive at maturity. In his infant state, society is the only means of preserving his being; this makes him love it. In his maturer age, what Mr. Hobbes calls the dictate of right reason makes him capable of it. This reason, according to the same author, is given by God to every man for the rule of his actions; therefore no man is exempt [4] from this capability. This amounts to what the philosophers have advanced, that man is born a creature fit for society.

Mr. Hobbes, in the enumeration of the rights of that man whom a society have trusted with the supreme command, inserts the following:[iv] *Meum et tuum*,[3] just and unjust, and the like, it belongs to this man to determine. These determinations are called the civil laws, and the civil laws are no other than the commands of him who hath the supreme authority; and[v] this supreme governor is not to be bound to the civil law, for that would be to be bound to himself. Now, says he,[vi] this same supreme command seems so harsh to the greatest part of men, that they hate the very naming of it, and will have a city well enough constituted, if

---

[iv] Vide Dominion, chap. vi. p. 90, et 99.   [v] Chap. vi. p. 98, et seq.
[vi] Chap. vi. p. 103 et [10]4.

[2] Perhaps chiefly Aristotle; see Hobbes, *Philosophical Rudiments concerning Government and Society*, p. 3; Aristotle, *Politics*, 1.2., 1253a3.
[3] i.e. mine and yours.

they who shall be the citizens convening do agree concerning certain articles propounded, and in that convent agitated and approved, and do command them to be observed, and punishments prescribed to be inflicted on the breakers of them. Who sees not that [5] the assembly who prescribed these things had an absolute power? If this assembly dissolves without appointing certain times of meeting, there is a power somewhere left to punish those who shall transgress the laws, which cannot possibly be without an absolute power.

It is evident from this jumble, that Mr. Hobbes, either wilfully or ignorantly, here confounds absolute with limited power. There is a power left to punish those who shall transgress the laws, says he. The very meaning of the word law in this case is a supposition of certain approved articles, to the transgression of which there is affixed certain penalties; therefore a power lodged in the hands of one or more magistrates to inflict fixed penalties on the transgressor of fixed laws, is merely executive. This power can only reach an offender of fixed laws; therefore the offender is punished by the words of the law; not by the will of the inflicter. If there are regal privileges annexed to this executive power, we call it a limited power, because restrained by the aforesaid laws; if without this power, merely executive; if with the [6] aforesaid privileges bound to no laws, absolute.

A monarchy,[vii] says Mr. Hobbes, is derived from the power of the people transferring its right to one man. The whole right of the people conveyed on him, he can then do whatsoever the people could do before he was elected; and the people is no longer one person, but a rude multitude, as being only one before by virtue of the supreme command, now conveyed from themselves on this one man. This elector monarch can do his subjects no injury, because they have subjected their right and will to defend themselves to him: neither doth he oblige himself to any for the command he receives; for he receives it from the people, who ceaseth to be a person as soon as that act is done; and the person vanishing, all obligations to the person vanisheth.

A contract made by two contracting parties must be equally binding; therefore Mr. Hobbes's figure of the dissolution of [7] the person does not serve his argument a whit; for if the person, viz. the people, dissolves, the obligation, if void of one side, is so of the other. If the

---

[vii] Vide Dominion, chap. vii. art. 11, p. 118, et seq.

person continues any breach of the contract, tho' it only affects an individual, disfranchises that person from the obligation of performing their part of the contract; and if a people, in transferring their right to the monarch, look upon themselves dissolved as a body, and return to so many individuals, yet if that monarch refuse to perform those stipulated articles previous to his being vested with that right, he by his non-performance forfeits that right: that right forfeited returns again to the people, and he himself is no more than one of the multitude. Farther, there can be no such contract without an obligation mentioned or supposed; for the will of the contractor is necessary to the making of a lawful contract, and no rational person can will so absurdly as to give up his natural right to another, without the proposing to himself more advantages than he could otherwise have enjoyed, had he not divested himself of that right.

We get a right over irrational creatures, [8] says Mr. Hobbes,[viii] in the same manner that we do over the persons of men, viz. by force and natural strength: our dominion, therefore, over beasts hath its original from the right of nature, not from divine positive right; for then no man might have killed a beast for his food but he to whom the Divine pleasure was made manifest by holy writ; a most hard condition for men indeed, whom the beasts might devour without injury, and yet they might not destroy them.

Yet this is, according to Mr. Hobbes's opinion, the same predicament in which a man stands who has given up his natural right to a monarch. If it is hard to be in the power of a beast to be destroyed without injury, (whose hunger alone compel him to blood-shed) is it not harder to be in the power of the creature man, whose appetites are more various and more capricious than a beast; and these appetites most commonly wax so wanton by power, that they create affections which seem to have no one principle in nature or reason, but all noxious to the safety of man: [9] therefore an absolute monarch is a beast of a more peculiar and a more hurtful nature than any other in the creation.

Parents can claim no dominion over their children from the act of generation, says Mr. Hobbes;[ix] that right belongs to the mother only, not from that act, but because she may rightly, and at her own will, breed

---

viii Vide Dominion, [Chap. viii.] art. 10, p. 132 et [13]3.
ix Vide Dominion, Chap. ix. p. 135 et 136, article I, et 2.

him up, or adventure him to fortune: if she breed him up, it is supposed to be on condition that he is her servant.

We know that the right of parents to expose their children has been the civil law of many countries; but that they have a natural right so to do is a bold assertion of Mr. Hobbes's [CM *err.*: Mr. Hobbes], which nature and reason contradict. The mother's care for the preservation of her young is an invariable dictate of nature through all her works. Different animals have many qualities opposite to each other, and peculiar to their different species; yet the tenderness of maternal feeling is common to all, and is a compelling force to obey [10] this dictate. The human species are more strongly bound to this obligation than brute animals: reason and morality strongly urges the care and preservation of an existence by themselves occasioned as a duty never to be omitted; by the law of justice, therefore, they, being thus bound to this act, cannot have it in their option whether they will do it or not: but Mr. Hobbes will rather advance any absurdity, than own that power has its rights from reasonable causes. We are of Mr. Hobbes's opinion, that it is very absurd to derive the right of parents over their children from the act of generation; their right proceeds only from the tender feelings which are inseparable from the quality of parents. This is the first natural obligation owed by children; this makes it more advantageous for them to be under the commands of their parents, than under any other government. The many benefits which a parent confers on a child in the helpless state of infancy, adds to the first natural obligation. In a maturer age, these obligations have force enough to make it the duty of a child to obey his parents in all things, if their commands are not op-[11]posite to the laws of his country, or the dictates of reason: but, as this authority has only its right from supposed benefits bestowed, it must be greater or less in proportion to the degree of those benefits. Parents that are enemies, instead of benefactors, forfeit that right, which alone has its foundation from the obligation of received benefits.

Mr. Hobbes, in his comparison of the state of nature with the civil, says,[x] that the grievance of subjects does not arise from the ill institution or ordination of the government, (because in all manner of governments subjects may be oppressed) but from the ill administration of a well-established government.

---

[x] Vide Dominion, Chap. x. p. 150, art. 2.

We agree with Mr. Hobbes, that the grievances and oppressions of subjects arise from the ill administration of government; but to this must add, that, if Mr. Hobbes was as well acquainted with the science of policy, as he is an adept in the art of confounding things, he would know that the peculiar excellence of a government, properly constituted, is to raise [12] those to the administration whose virtues and abilities render them capable of this arduous task; and to deprive those of that office, who upon trial are found at all defective: therefore, a well-constituted government can never be so long ill administered as to become a grievance to the subject.

Mr. Hobbes,[xi] in his praise of monarchy, says, that the following arguments, hold forth monarchy as more eminent than other governments: first, that the whole universe is governed by one God: secondly, that the ancients preferred the monarchical state beyond all others: thirdly, that the paternal government instituted by God himself, was monarchical: and, lastly, that other governments were compacted by men on the ruins of monarchy.

That the universe is governed by one God we will not dispute; and will also add, that God has an undoubted right to govern what he has himself created, and that it is beneficial to the creature to be governed by the Father of all things; but that this should be an argument for a man to govern [13] what he has not created, and with whom a nation can have no such paternal connexion, is a paradox which Mr. Hobbes has left unsolved.

The second argument, that the ancients preferred the monarchical state before all others, is an assertion contradicted by the only civilized societies in ancient history, viz. the Greeks, from whom alone we can learn ancient prudence. They disdained this government, and called all pretenders to it tyrants and usurpers.[4]

The third argument, that the paternal government instituted by God was monarchical, is an assertion which is contradicted by many examples in the only history through which we know of this institution. The

---

[xi] Vide Dominion, chap. x. p. 150, art. 3.

[4] This is a simplification, but in his refutation of Filmer, Sidney highlighted that Xenophon had preferred aristocracy rather than monarchy when condemning democratic disorder. *Discourses concerning Government*, ed. Thomas Hollis (London, 1763), pp. 138–9. See also Temple Stanyan, *The Grecian History* (1707; 2 vols., London, 1766), I, p. 194.

power Adam had over his children is not mentioned as of the monarchical kind. We find him no where exercising this power or claiming it as his due; and yet there could not have been a more equitable occasion for exercising it, than the perfidious murder of Abel presented.[5] But, if Mr. Hobbes could prove that the paternal power instituted by God was monarchical, he cannot from that conclude that the monarchical government is [14] preferable to all others, without falling into his usual absurdities, viz. that a man ought to have a right of governing creatures whom he has not generated, because God has given him a right of governing creatures whom he has generated.

The last argument, that other governments are compacted by the artifice of men on the ruins of monarchy, makes against the subject of his praise, viz. absolute monarchy. If absolute monarchies were instituted in the earliest times, before the invention of mankind was improved by experience, those other governments built on its ruins, which have both experience and invention for their founders, should be infinitely more excellent from these superior advantages.

Some there are, says Mr. Hobbes,[xii] who are discontented with the government under one, for no other reason, but because it is under one; as if it were an unreasonable thing, that one man should so far excel in power as to be able at his pleasure to dispose of all the rest. These men, sure, if they could, would withdraw their allegiance from under the dominion of [15] God: but this exception against one is suggested by envy, while they see one man in possession of what all desire. For the same reason, they would judge it to be as unreasonable if a few commanded, unless they themselves either were, or hoped to be, of the number; for if it be an unreasonable thing, that all men have not an equal right, surely an aristocracy must be unreasonable also.

The question of government is here artfully, or perhaps ignorantly, confined to two classes, which are equal usurpations on the rights of men, viz. absolute monarchy, and absolute aristocracy. Other comparisons would be too unfavorable to the author's system: but who but such dreamers as Mr. Hobbes does not see, that to be in the absolute power of one, or many men, is justly the object of aversion to any but to those who

---

[xii] Vide Dominion, chap. x. p. 151, art. 4.

[5] Adam and Eve's younger son, who was murdered by his brother Cain out of jealousy.

have fallen into that state of bestiality, to which Aristotle compares men who submit to absolute government.[6]

Because, says Mr. Hobbes, we have shewn, that the state of equality is the state of war, and that therefore inequality was introduced by a general consent; this inequality, whereby he, whom we have [16] voluntarily given more to, enjoys more, is no longer to be accounted an unreasonable thing.

By this dogmatic assertion, that the state of equality is the state of war, it is plain that the poor philosopher is entirely ignorant of the following truth, that political equality, and the laws of good government, are so far from incompatible, that one never can exist to perfection without the other.

But, as if Mr. Hobbes intended to shew, that there was no absurdity, however extreme, that he could not fall into, he farther observes, that sure those men who think it an unreasonable thing, that one man should so far excel in power, as to be able to dispose of all the rest, if they could, would withdraw their allegiance from God. As there are few men, but the ingenious author of this observation, [who] would be absurd and wicked enough to put such an equality between God and man, I think it no farther necessary to answer this blasphemy than the order of controversial argument requires. Sure, says the author, such men, if they could, would withdraw their allegiance from God: that is, because men will not [17] submit to be absolutely at the mercy of a weak brother, these men would, if they could, withdraw their allegiance from God. What is this but putting the creature upon an equality with the Creator? If not, where lies the comparison? for the same men, who would not be in the power of a creature, as weak, and perhaps weaker, than themselves, might bless the fate that only subjected them to the merciful, unerring jurisdiction of God. Mr. Hobbes, in his last observation, has given a strong reason against the government under one. But this exception against one, says he, is suggested by envy, whilst they see one man in possession of what all desire. Is it not a very unreasonable thing, that one man, without

---

[6] Sidney had written that '[Filmer] endeavours to take from us the use of reason, and, extinguishing the light of it, to make us live like the worst of beasts, that we may be fit subjects to absolute monarchy. This may perhaps be our author's intention, having learnt from Aristotle, that such government is only suitable to the nature of the most bestial men, who being uncapable of governing themselves'. *Discourses concerning Government*, p. 95.

pretension to superior virtue, should be alone in possession of what all men desire? and that every other individual in a whole nation, however fruitful that nation is of worthy eminent men, should be thus deprived of their share in the government? which must be esteemed the most consummate reward of virtue, if the possession of it is what all men desire.

I confess, says Mr. Hobbes,[xiii] that it is a [18] grievance when a monarch exacts, besides the honorable sustaining of his own household, and the necessary charges of the commonwealth, sums to satisfy his lusts, enrich his sons, kindred, favourites, and flatterers. This is indeed a grievance, but of the number of those that accompany all kinds of government, and are more tolerable under a monarchy than in a democracy; for, tho' the monarch would enrich them, they cannot be many, because belonging but to one.

This assertion is one of Mr. Hobbes's political axioms. They cannot be many, because belonging but to one. Now, if the sons, kindred, and favorites of a monarch, may not be many, because belonging but to one, (tho' we see that this is not an infallible consequence, by the train of kindred, wives, concubines, and favorites, which partake of the wealth of an Asiatic monarch[7]) yet his flatterers may be as numerous as are those of a number of men; for flatterers follow the power, not the person. The common pomp of a court is a heavy burthen to society; and a man who has but few kindred and favorites, may lavish on them few the spoils of a [19] whole nation. That this, in more or less degrees, has been the constant practice of every absolute monarch, the present situation of the greater number of inhabitants of France, Spain, and all countries where this detestable government has taken place, fully evinces. The constant expences of the Asiatic monarchs, without mentioning the examples of a Lewis the Fourteenth of France, a Harry the Eighth of England, or the more ancient ones of a Caligula, a Claudius, a Nero, a Vitellius,[8] are examples that the lusts of one man is sufficient to dissipate all the riches that the industry and frugality of a whole nation can collect.

[xiii] Vide Dominion, chap. x. p. 153, art. 6.

[7] This view of 'oriental despotism' came to the fore in Montesquieu's *Persian Letters* (1721) and was further accentuated in *The Spirit of the Laws* (1748).

[8] Nero and Caligula are traditionally considered to be among the most tyrannical and debauched of the Roman emperors. The ancient historian Suetonius portrayed Claudius as being a womaniser and controlled by women, and Vitellius as an obese gorger.

Mr. Hobbes goes farther on with his observation. In a democracy, says he, there are many powerful families to be rewarded.

Men that deserve reward have, indeed, ever been rewarded in popular governments; but then it has been with honors of little cost, tho' peculiarly adapted to please and reward generous minds; such as the various crowns given by the Romans to their most virtuous citizens, or statues erected of them in the public places, both to perpetuate the memory of their wor-[20]thiness, and also the well-conducted gratitude of their country. Few, if any, are the instances which Mr. Hobbes could have produced, where a democracy [CM *err*.: democracies] ever impoverished the commonwealth, to enrich their favorites, however worthy they esteemed them.

A monarch, says Mr. Hobbes, may promote unworthy persons; yet oft-times he will not do it: but, in a democracy, all the popular men are supposed to do it, because it is necessary. However necessary Mr. Hobbes may suppose this to be, it is, very certain, that all democracies have taken contrary courses. If by chance any unworthy persons were promoted to high offices, they were never continued long in them; and tho' monarchs may do other wise, it is almost always their practice to employ the most unworthy men they can find: and, indeed, the designs of a general assembly and an individual being commonly very different, the same sort of persons cannot be proper to execute both. The design of a general assembly must ever be the good of the commonwealth, as conducive to their own general and particular good: this leads them to pitch on those [21] people, whose virtues and abilities are most capable to serve the republic [CM *err*.: public]. Now, the designs of an individual being commonly to gratify his own lusts and private advantages, and those lusts and private advantages being ever incompatible with the good of the public, it leads him to employ those villains, whose abilities are equal only to cunning, and proper only to the destruction of the commonweal.

Another grievance which is complained of in monarchy, says Hobbes,[xiv] is that perpetual fear of death, which every man must be in, when he considers, that the ruler hath not only power to appoint what punishments he lists on any transgressions, but that he may also in his

---

[xiv] Vide Dominion, Chap. x. p. 154, art. 7.

wrath and sensuality slaughter his innocent subjects. This is the fault of the ruler, not of the government. All the acts of Nero are not essential to monarchy; and subjects are often less undeservedly condemned under one ruler, than under the people. Kings are only severe against those who either trouble them with impertinent counsel, or oppose their will: wherefore, some Nero [22] or Caligula reigning, no man can undeservedly suffer but such as are known to him, and such as are remarkable for some eminent charges; and not all neither, but they only who are possessed of what he desires to enjoy; for they that are offensive and contumelious are deservedly punished. Whosoever, therefore, in a monarchy, will lead a retired life, let him be what he will that reigns, he is out of danger.

I should be glad to find out what our author could mean by this absurd paradoxical distinction, that a tyrant's having it in his power to slaughter his innocent subjects, is the fault of the ruler, not of the government. Tho' a ruler be malicious or sensual enough to desire the slaughter of innocent people for the gratification of his vices, yet, if the nature of the government does not allow him that power, his inclinations alone will not give it him; therefore his capability of committing these injuries must proceed from the vicious nature of the government, and the sufferings of innocent subjects from the fault of the ruler is a consequence of that viciousness.

Mr. Hobbes's next nice distinction is, that [23] the acts of a Nero are not essential to monarchy. If Mr. Hobbes means that Nero, tho' in possession of monarchical power, was not under a necessity of doing all the evil that this power made him capable of doing, he is in the right: but I cannot see any advantage he can draw from this argument; for tho' the execrable villainies that Nero committed was not essential to the nature of his power, but proceeded from the profligacy of his disposition, yet that profligacy, which was much encreased, if not created, by abso- lute power, could not have been fatal to his subjects, had he not been vested with that power; therefore, these accidents, tho' not essential, are the natural consequences of that power.

Our author's next assertion is, that subjects are often less undeservedly condemned under one ruler than under the people. I could wish he had taken the pains to have given us one single instance to support this assertion: I really do not know one example in settled governments, where the power of the people ever, through malice, wantonness, or rapaciousness, tortured or put to death one fellow-citizen. If such accidents have ever happened, it has been through [24] mistake; and these examples are so rare, that, were he to produce them against the numbers of innocent and worthy people which [CM *err.*: who] have suffered under monarchical power, they would be found as light in the balance, as his own empty arguments against proofs positive.

One would think, by our author's following arguments, that he had thrown off his usual gravity, and intended to ridicule the subject of his declared veneration. Kings, says he, are only severe against those who trouble them with impertinent counsel, or oppose their will: therefore, some Nero or Caligula reigning, no man can undeservedly suffer, but such as are known to him, or are remarkable for some eminent charges; and not all neither, but such as are possessed of what he desires to enjoy; for they that are offensive and contumelious are deservedly punished. Whosoever, therefore, in a monarchy, will lead a retired life, be he what he will that reigns, is out of danger. – Could the most inveterate enemy to absolute monarchy urge stronger arguments against it, than this man has unwittingly done? whereby he allows, that there does subsist in this kind of government the [25] most irremediable inconveniences [CM *err.*: inconvenience]. 1st. Men cannot give advice to absolute monarchs in the most important affairs of a nation, even tho' inexperience, ignorance, or stupidity, should make them incapable of judging rightly themselves, without being offensive, contumelious, and justly liable to severe punishments. This is making it an impossible thing to mitigate, or in any manner to remedy, the evils that must happen to a nation from being governed by a bad, ignorant, or foolish prince. We are very much obliged to Mr. Hobbes for saving us the trouble of confuting that silly argument, urged by most favorers of kingly government, viz. that an ignorant prince may be helped by understanding counsellors. He is above such stale deceit, and plainly tells us, that it is foolish, and even unlawful, to attempt to oppose, or in any manner correct, an evil which must overwhelm a whole nation in confusion, shame, and misery. By this plain-dealing Mr. Hobbes does fairly acknowledge, that there is in this sort of government a malignity which cannot be avoided, or in any manner corrected. These are [CM *err.*: This is one of] the prevailing argu-[26]ments which Mr. Hobbes uses to make men in love with kingly power.

The second is, that no man can deservedly suffer, but such as are known to their monarch, and such as are remarkable for eminent charges; and not all these, but such as are possessed of what he desires to enjoy: therefore, they that will lead a retired life are out of danger, be he what he will that reigns. Worth and innocence, Mr. Hobbes says, will not in this situation protect a subject; but flight and obscurity are the only things which can preserve him: that for these reasons, the most eminent charges of the state must be abandoned by the wise and virtuous to those desperate people, whose mad desire of raising their fortunes, or their necessities, incites them to run the hazard which attend these stations; their principles being such, as does not prevent their complying with the most unjust commands, or the most absurd measures. Mr. Hobbes farther adds, that the only probable security there is for safety, is to dispossess yourself of every thing that is desirable. This is Mr. Hobbes's description of a regal government, which he has made more into-[27]lerable than his state of nature, viz. every man at war with every man; for in this state, strength, prudence, and fortitude, may support one; flight and obscurity is the last resource; but Mr. Hobbes cannot prove, that even flight and obscurity will save a whole society from the evils of his regal government. There are many objections to this assertion: 1st. Numbers of people may suffer before the disposition of a bad monarch can be known. 2dly, It is not to be supposed, that such a monarch would be left alone without society, and the privilege of making use of his subjects for his state, convenience and amusement. I think Mr. Hobbes cannot propose this as a means to be taken only by a few; for that would be as if he was to say, that plague and famine were not evils, because a small number might escape them.

[29] A Short Sketch, &c. Addressed to Signior Paoli

Warm wishes for the welfare of yourself and illustrious countrymen, renowned Paoli! are the motives that stimulate me to address you on the important subject of Corsican liberty. Free establishments are subjects I have studied with care; and the strong rumors which prevail, that the Corsicans are going to establish a republic, makes me address you, as if this was the determined point to which your views were turned.

Of all the various models of republics, which have been exhibited for the instruction of mankind, it is only the democratical system, rightly balanced, which can secure the virtue, liberty, and happiness of society. In such constructions [30] alone are to be found impassable bars to vicious pre-eminence; and the active ambition of man will stimulate him to attain excellence, where excellence can alone procure him distinction. The very nature of slavish dependance and proud superiority are equally baneful to the virtues inherent in mankind: the first, by sedulous attention and mean adulation to please its master, undermines, and at last subdues, the innate generous principles of the soul; and the fond delights of superiority extinguish all the virtues which ennoble human nature, such as self-denial, general benevolence, and the exalted passion of sacrificing private views to public happiness.

Having endeavored to specify the advantages accruing from a democratical republic, I shall enter, first, into those things essential to the proper form of this species of government; and, 2dly, into that part of the constitution which defends it from corruption.

It is necessary to the proper form of this republic, that there should be two orders in the state, viz. the senate and the people.

[31] The first order is necessary, because in a well-constituted senate there is wisdom; and, if this order is prevented by proper restraint from invading public liberty, they will be the surest guardians of it. The second order is necessary, because that, without the people have authority enough to be thus classed, there can be no liberty.

The form of the republic being thus established, let the debate be in the first order, viz. the senate; and the result in the second order, viz. the people, tho' with the power of debating likewise.

Let not the number of men that represent the first order be above fifty, to prevent the confusion which usually springs from assemblies too numerous. Let the order of the people be represented by a certain number of men, not under two hundred and fifty, elected out of this order by the several districts or cities into which this island may be divided.

Let the generals, admirals, civil magistrates, and officers of every important post, be taken out of the senatorial order, *i.e.* among those who have held the rank of senators, with the privilege of having a [32] vote in the senate during the time that they are in office, tho' not otherwise elected into that assembly. Let the power of electing these magistrates and officers be in the representative body.

Let the senate, or its committee, meet thrice every week, or occasionally, as the necessity of their office requires. Let the representatives of the people meet at stated times, or occasionally, as the necessity of their office requires.

Let there be the power of appeal from every court of justice to the senate, and then to the representatives of the people.

Let the affairs of commerce, and all matters relative to the state and executive powers of government, be determined by the representative body, after they have been first debated in the senate; but let not the representative assembly have the power of determining peace and war, imposing taxes, the making and altering laws, till these subjects have been first debated by the senate, and proposed by them to the collective body of the people. Let these proposals be promulged a fortnight [CM *err.*: one month] before the meeting of the representatives towards the passing them; that [33] the people may have time to deliberate on them, and give what directions they shall judge proper to their representatives.

Now, having settled what relates to the form and established powers of the republic, we must consider that part which defends it from corruption.

This must be considered under these two articles, viz. the rotation of all places of trust, and the fixing the Agrarian on a proper balance.

The rotation of all the places of trust is so strong a preservative against the decay of a republic, that the Roman constitution, tho' otherwise defective, might perhaps have stood to this day, had the Romans never dispensed with that salutary ordinance. This dispensation was one of the fatal wounds, which hurried on its dissolution in the very meridian of its glory. The prolongation of the commands of Marius, Sylla, Pompey, and Caesar,[9] were the means which its unnatural, and too much pampered citizens made use of to destroy it. The downfall of this glorious republic has been a notable argument, with shallow politicians, against every con-[34]stitution of this kind; but it serves wise legislators cautiously to avoid those faults which produced this fatal effect.

The examination of the defective part of the Roman constitution will shew the importance of the second article, viz. the fixing the Agrarian on a proper balance.

The Agrarian of the Roman republic was never fixed on a proper balance: Brutus and Publicola either did not foresee the evil that such a neglect would produce, or, content with the glory they had acquired, left this achievement to succeeding patriots.[10]

---

[9] Well-known Roman generals and statesmen who held high office multiple times and for unprecedentedly long periods in the final two centuries of the Roman Republic.

[10] Lucius Junius Brutus and Publicola were among the Roman aristocrats who overthrew the monarchy and became consuls in 509 BC, traditionally viewed as the first year of the Roman Republic.

But this was the capital defect which brought this excellent fabric to decay; this was the defect which the Gracchi made such generous efforts to amend.[11] Had they succeeded in their attempt, the Roman republic might have been as immortal as time itself; for, had the Agrarian been ever fixed on a proper balance, it must have prevented that extreme disproportion in the circumstances of her citizens, which gave such weight of power to the aristocratical party, that it enabled them to subvert the fundamental principles [35] of the government, and introduce those innovations which ended in anarchy. Anarchy produced its natural effect, viz. absolute monarchy. Thus ended a government, whose salutary influence raised her citizens to a degree of perfection beyond the powers of vulgar conception; and thus succeeded a government, whose baneful influence debased its subjects to as low a state of infamy, as that of the others had been great and glorious. A due consideration of these effects will, I hope, make manifest the necessity of the rotation and proper Agrarian. There remains now to shew the best method of fixing these regulations.

First, the rotation. Let the whole senate be changed once in three years, by a third part at a time yearly. Let the vacant posts be supplied from the body of the representatives, by the election of the people. Let that body undergo the same rotation, and be supplied from the people. If any of the representative members should be elected into the senate, that are not by the course of the rotation to go out of the representative council, their [36] places must be supplied from the people. Let no member of either the senatorial or representative body, be capable of re-election under the space of three years. Let the admirals, generals, civil magistrates, and all the officers of important posts, lay down their commission at the end of the year, nor be capable of re-election under the aforesaid time of probation. The rotation thus settled, we come to the second consideration, viz. the proper Agrarian.

Let the Agrarian be settled in such a manner, that the balance of land inclines in favor of the popular side. To prevent the alteration which time would make in this balance, let the landed and personal effects of

---

[11] The Gracchi brothers, Tiberius and Gaius, were tribunes of the plebs between 133 and 121 BC. They tried to redistribute public lands controlled mainly by aristocrats to the poor and veterans, but were both killed by the aristocrats in the senate who were opposed to agrarian reform.

every man be equally divided at his disease [*sic*, i.e. decease], between the males, heirs of his body; in default of such heirs, between his male heirs in the first and second degree of relationship.

If any man during his life-time, by gift, make a distribution of his estate or effects contrary to the meaning of this law; let his heirs, by suit in the proper courts of justice, obtain a lawful distribution, and [37] let the penalty incurred by the offender be an immediate dispossession of his estate and effects to his lawful heirs.

Let no females be capable of inheriting or bringing any dower in marriage.

The provision for every female, who, through any natural defect, is not capable of marriage, must be made by way of annuity by the male heirs nearest of kin. These, I think, are irresistible bars to the alteration which time would otherwise make in the balance.

If the exigencies of the republic should ever find it necessary to lodge the executive powers of government in the hands of one person, let there be a law made to limit it to one month.[12] Let the representative assembly have the power of nominating the person, and continuing this command from month to month, if the exigencies of the state demands it; but let not any one person be capable of holding this office above a year.

The remedy of a dictator should never be made use of, but in the most desperate cases; and, indeed, it is not probable that [38] such a government should ever be in a situation to want it.

This, renowned Paoli! is but the rough sketch of that only form of government which is capable of preserving dominion and freedom to the people. If a farther correspondence on the same subject should prove agreeable to you and your illustrious, countrymen, I shall in my next treat at large of the militia, the police, the education of youth, and other points necessary to good government, and the farther security of liberty.[13]

The necessity of having an unrestrained power lodged in some person, capable of the arduous task of settling such a government as the above described, is too visible to need any recommendation; nor is it less so, that there is no person so capable of this high employment as Signior

---

[12] The Roman dictator had to resign his office once his specific task had been accomplished, or alternatively after six months.

[13] A text matching this description never appeared, but she would write about these themes in her historical works, other pamphlets, and in *Letters on Education.*

Paoli, who, having long directed the councils of a brave people in the glorious struggle for liberty, should finish his career by making that liberty beneficial and permanent. This is an opportunity of immortalizing your name, renowned Paoli! which few [39] men have had within their power, and fewer have had wisdom enough to seize on, but rather through their folly have turned it to disgrace and infamy: but that you may be ranked among the foremost of mortals, with Timoleon, Lycurgus, Solon, and Brutus,[14] is the sincere wish of your great admirer and very humble servant.

FINIS.

[14] Ancient founders of states and lawgivers of Syracuse, Sparta, Athens and Rome, respectively.

Observations on a Pamphlet entitled 'Thoughts on the Cause of the Present Discontents' (1770)

Introduction to the Text

In 1770 Macaulay published a pamphlet against Edmund Burke's recent *Thoughts on the Cause of the Present Discontents*. The 'present discontents' refer to the Middlesex election dispute, discussed in the main introduction of this edition. Burke's pamphlet, a defence of the Rockingham Whig party connection, has become canonical for his analysis of British politics and especially his defence of party. Importantly, both Macaulay and Burke defended the right of voters to elect John Wilkes as their representative in the Middlesex election dispute. As Burke pointed out in his correspondence, however, the bitterest attacks on his pamphlet did not come from the court but from a section within the opposition: 'the republican faction' or 'the Bill of rights people'.[1] Burke called this segment 'a rotten subdivision of a Faction amongst ourselves', and remarked, probably tongue-in-cheek, of Macaulay's attack: 'the Amazon is the greatest champion among them ... You see I have been afraid to answer her'.[2] Macaulay argued that Burke's 'fine turned and polished periods carry with them a poison sufficient to destroy all the little virtue and understanding of sound policy which is left in the nation'. For her, what he promoted was nothing less than 'Aristocratic faction and party, founded on and supported by the corrupt principle of self-interest' (pp. [6–7]).

---

[1] Burke to O'Hara, 5 June 1770, and Burke to Shackleton, 15 August 1770, in *The Correspondence of Edmund Burke*, ed. Thomas W. Copeland et al. (10 vols., Chicago, 1958–78), II, pp. 140, 150.

[2] Burke to Shackleton, 15 August 1770, in *Correspondence of Burke*, II, p. 150.

The first Rockingham ministry in 1765–6 had indeed been taunted at the time for being unusually aristocratic, and Burke sought to pre-empt such criticisms in the *Present Discontents* by stating that he was 'no friend to aristocracy, in the sense at least in which that word is usually understood', that is to say, as 'austere and insolent domination'.[3] Nevertheless, he argued that the Whig aristocrats possessed property, rank and quality which gave them independence, thereby enabling them to stand up to the crown. Burke and his party were convinced that the accession of George III represented a watershed moment in British political history that destroyed the Whig system of government and ushered in royal corruption. By contrast, Macaulay believed that the canker had to be traced to the aftermath of the Glorious Revolution, in the wake of which the Whig party became a 'state faction' (p. [17]). Her pamphlet is thus noteworthy since it marks the beginning of her sustained critical commentary on the legacy of the Glorious Revolution. The new system favoured this state faction as long as the monarch was 'weak', but it gave '[h]is stronger and more confirmed successors [George III]' the opportunity 'to make use of the superior advantages of their situation, to throw off the fetters of former obligations' (p. [18]). Macaulay believed that the Commons needed to be purified to reclaim its proper function as a check on executive power. All the 'Country party' remedies, associated with Bolingbroke and rejected by Burke, were indeed necessary, especially the repeal of the Septennial Act, which her grandfather had voted against in 1716.

Macaulay's pamphlet went through five editions in one year, with the current edition being based on the third, corrected edition. It made a considerable impression on Horace Walpole, who believed that her short riposte exposed the Rockinghams' 'folly' of adhering to men rather than measures.[4] Her attacks on 'aristocratic Whiggism' were carried on by her friend Thomas Northcote and more famously by Thomas Paine.[5] Macaulay would later elaborate on her views about British politics after the Glorious Revolution in *History since the Revolution* (1778) and in the conclusion to the eighth and final volume of the *History of England*,

---

[3] Burke, *Thoughts on the Cause of the Present Discontents* (London, 1770), p. 15.
[4] Walpole, *Memoirs of the Reign of King George III* (4 vols., London, 1845), IV, p. 131.
[5] Northcote, *Observations on the Natural and Civil Rights of Mankind, the Prerogatives of Princes, and the Powers of Government* (London, 1781), pp. 44–5; Paine, *Rights of Man; Part the Second* (London, 1792), preface.

published in 1783. Before then, however, she would continue to argue for political reform and a broader franchise in *An Address to the People of England, Scotland and Ireland* (1775).

Observations on a Pamphlet entitled 'Thoughts on the Cause of the Present Discontents' (1770)

[5] Observations, &c.

It is an undertaking of the highest difficulty as well as delicacy to point out the corruptions or mistakings of men, whose disappointed ambition has led them to offer their services to an alarmed and inraged populace, and whose abilities of character and situation promise a successful exertion in the cause of opposition. In important parts of duty, every consequence which relates to self is to be hazarded; on this consideration, I will ever, notwithstanding the [6] long and malevolent persecution I have endured from the interested part of mankind for a work written on the general principles of honest policy, in all great points of national welfare, express my genuine opinions to my countrymen; and on this consideration alone I undertake the invidious task of making disagreeable observations on the baneful tendency of a pamphlet, entitled, 'Thoughts on the Cause of the present Discontents.'

To the disgrace of human nature, and the plague of society, an able head and an honest heart are but too often separated. The pamphlet in question is written with great eloquence, acuteness, and art; but its fine turned and polished periods carry with them a poison sufficient to destroy all the little virtue and under-[7]standing of sound policy which is left in the nation. Whilst the obvious intent of this pernicious work is to expose the dangerous designs of a profligate junto of courtiers, supported by the mere authority of the crown, against the liberties of the constitution,[1] it endeavours to mislead the people on the subject of the more complicated and specious, though no less dangerous,

---

[1] What Burke referred to as the 'king's men' or the 'court cabal'; see *Thoughts on the Cause of the Present Discontents* (London, 1770), pp. 12, 20, 38, 44.

manoeuvres of Aristocratic faction and party, founded on and supported by the corrupt principle of self-interest, and to guard against the possible consequence of an effectual reformation in the vitiated parts of our constitution and government; a circumstance much to be dreaded from the active exertion of a vigorous and enlightened zeal in the great body of the people.

[8] The multitude, whose judgments are, more especially in matters of government, directed by the warm impulse of present injury, are too apt, in the scale of comparison, to regard past evils with an eye of partial complacency. The offences of a present possessor of power throws a favourable shade over the equally atrocious crimes of his designing predecessors. The grievances attending his government, which are but the bitter consequences, or rather the fruits of seeds sown by his ancestors, are regarded as springing immediately from the particular policy of his administration; and thus the causes of political evils being never traced up to their sources, it is not surprizing that the generality of mankind are so unfortunately divided in their opinions concerning their cure.

[9] It is often retorted on speculative reasoners in policy, that not having been engaged in the practical parts of administration, they are apt to run into refinements incompatible with the gross and vicious nature of human affairs. Did these practical gentlemen ever attempt to prove that their speculative antagonists grounded their positions on a false mistaken notion of a non-existing virtue in mankind, there would be some weight in their assertions: but as all systematical writers on the side of freedom plan their forms and rules of government on the just grounds of the known corruption and wickedness of the human character, I shall be apt to suspect with the vulgar[i] (when on the authority merely of their experience, without argu-[10]ment or proof, statesmen thwart regulations drawn up on principles of public good, and to counteract particular interest) that their opinions are solely formed on sinister views.

That the modes of government which have ever been imposed on credulous man, have been all of them not only deficient in producing the just ends of government, *viz.* The full and impartial security of the

---

[i] Vide *Thoughts on the Cause of the present Discontents* p. 50. ['It is, besides, an effect of vulgar and puerile malignity to imagine, that every Statesman is of course corrupt; and that his opinion, upon every constitutional point, is solely formed upon some sinister interest.']

rights of nature; but that they have been rather formidable and dangerous cabals against the peace, happiness, and dignity of society, is not
owing to any moral impossibility in the forming a system which should
answer these just ends. The wisdom of man is fully adequate to the
subject. It would be unworthy the idea we ought to form of God, to
suppose him so capricious a [11] being as to bestow that high degree of
wisdom and ingenuity, which we often see displayed, in regulating the
more trifling concerns of life; which we often see displayed in the
support of tyrannic and destructive systems; and the not rendering
him adequate to regulations so necessary to his security, happiness,
and perfection; and without which, all the benevolent designs of
Providence in his creation appear to be almost totally frustrated.

To plan a form of government perfect in its nature, and consequently
answering all its just ends, is neither morally impossible in itself, nor
beyond the abilities of man, but it is the work of an individual. The
generality of mankind are too fond of accustomed establishments, however pernicious in their na-[12]ture, to adopt material alterations; and
this propensity has ever afforded full opportunity to the interested to
reject every part of reformation which tends effectually to establish
public good on the ruins of private interest.

In tracing the origin of all governments, we find them either the
produce of lawless power or accident, acted on by corrupt interest; the
same circumstance which attends the formation of government, attends
what is called their reformation; of this the history of our own country
affords a melancholy example. In all the great struggles for liberty, true
reformation was never by the ruling party either effected or even
intended; the flaws in the Revolution system left full opportunity for
private interest to exclude public good, and for a faction, who by their
struggles against former tyrannies[2] [13] had gained the confidence
of the people, to create, against the liberties and the virtue of their
trusting countrymen, the undermining and irresistible hydra, court
influence, in the room of the more terrifying, yet less formidable
monster, prerogative.

A system of corruption began at the very period of the Revolution,
and growing from its nature with increasing vigor, was the policy of
every succeeding administration. To share the plunder of a credulous

---

[2] James II.

117

people, cabals were formed between the representatives and the ministers. Parliament, the great barrier of our much boasted constitution, while it preferred its forms, annihilated its spirit;[3] and, from a controuling power over the executive parts of government, became a mere instrument of regal administration. It would be invidious and [14] even tedious to detail the moral and political evils which the system of administration which took place at the Revolution, and which has been regularly, and with little alteration systematically carried on from that period to the present times, has produced: the destructive grievance of a debt of one hundred and forty millions, a grievance which operates powerfully and variously against public freedom and independence; a strong military standing force, contrary to the very existence of real liberty; an army of placemen and pensioners, whose private interest is repugnant to the welfare of the public weal; septennial parliaments,[4] in violation of the firmest principle in the constitution; and heavy taxes imposed for the single advantage and emolument of individuals, a grievance never submitted to by any people, not essentially enslaved.

[15] Had any thing more than a mode of tyranny more agreeable to the interests of the Aristocratic faction, who took the lead in the opposition to the arbitrary administration of king James, been the probable consequence of the Revolution, that important circumstance in the annals of our country had never taken place.

The extension of popular powers has ever been regarded with a jealous eye by a misinformed and selfish nobility. To diminish the force of new acquired privileges, and as a bulwark to the party against the dreaded vengeance of a routed, though hardly subdued faction, the power of the reigning prince was to be strengthened by every diabolical engine which the subtle head and corrupt heart of a statesman could invent. The nation, instead of being the paymasters, [16] were to become the creditors of government. The larger the national debt, the stronger was supposed to be the operation of this state engine; the more the people were beggared, the more it diminished their constitutional independency; and the largeness of the revenue, necessary for the supply of so expensive a government, with the yearly interest to be paid to its creditors, it was foreseen would afford variety of excuses for levying exorbitant taxes on the public; and thus the management of the revenue

---

[3] See Bolingbroke, *Works*, II, p. 206, and III, pp. 18–19.   [4] The Septennial Act 1716.

would give so large an additional power to the crown, as to make ample amends for the loss of a few idle prerogatives.

The wicked system of policy set on foot by the leaders of the Revolutionists in the reign of king William, and which [17] proceeded perhaps more from fear of personal safety than from any very malicious intent against their country, was thoroughly completed under the administration of their sons; but whilst this state faction, who called themselves whigs, but who in reality were as much the destructive, though concealed enemies of public liberty, as were its more generous, because more avowed adversaries the tories, whilst they were erecting their batteries against those they termed inveterate Jacobites and prejudiced republicans, it never came into their heads, that they were ruining their own importance, and, consequently, rendering the crown strong enough to set all parties at defiance, to put them on their good behaviour, and to treat them with that contempt which is natural to a sovereign in the plenitude of independent power.

[18] A timid prince, in the new establishment of sovereignty, will subject his own interests and inclinations to the interests and inclinations of the faction by whose efforts he was raised to power, and by whose influence he is supported in it; his stronger and more confirmed successors will be apt to regard such a dependence in no more favourable a light than as a state of splendid vassalage, and be tempted to make use of the superior advantages of their situation to throw off the fetters of former obligations.[5]

That the loss of their power by his present majesty's having displayed the independent greatness of his situation, is the only grievance which a large faction in this country supposes to exist among us, and the only grievance they wish to see removed, has been generally surmised [19] by the jealous friends of liberty. That they should earnestly endeavour to conceal their sentiments from the eye of the public, it was natural to imagine; but that they should proclaim it to the world, and endeavour to argue mankind into hazardous exertions of opposition for their particular interests alone, is a consummate piece of indiscretion, which nothing could make us believe practical politicians to be guilty of, had we not been convinced to the contrary by the obvious tendency of the work intitled,

[5] George III is contrasted with George I and George II.

'Thoughts on the Cause of the present Discontents,' supposed to be written by a man whom we may justly esteem the mouth of the faction.[6]

In a work where all the fetters laid upon public liberty are not only regarded with indifference, but treated as [20] necessary evils, rather to be supported than abolished, we cannot help smiling to hear the author with all the power of eloquence pathetically lamenting, as a man who had remotely felt something of the humiliation, the dependent, invidious, and mortifying state of that very immediate slave to an absolute monarch, a minister of state: we cannot, I say, help smiling to hear a philosopher and a politician lament the natural consequence of those very circumstances which he esteems necessary in government.

We cannot help wondering at the corruptness of the heart, and the deception of the head of the same writer, who whilst he emphatically sets forth the tyranny growing from a trust too long [21] continued to parliaments,[ii] absolutely disclaiming against the quick return of [22]

[ii] 'A vigilant and jealous eye over executory and judicial magistracy, an anxious care of public money, an openness approaching towards facility to public complaint; these seem to be the true characteristicks of an house of commons; but an addressing house of commons and a petitioning nation; an house of commons full of confidence when the nation is plunged in despair; in the utmost harmony with ministers whom the people regard with the utmost abhorrence; who vote thanks, when the public call upon them for impeachments; who are eager to grant, when the general voice demands account; who in all disputes between the people and administration presume against the people; who punish their disorders, but refuse to inquire into the provocations to them: this is an unnatural, a monstrous state of things in this constitution; such an assembly may be a great, wise, and awful senate, but it is not to any popular purpose an house of commons.

This change from an immediate state of procuration and delegation to a course of acting as from original power, is the way in which all the popular magistracies in the world have been perverted from their purposes: it is indeed their greatest, and sometimes their incurable corruption; for there is a material distinction between that corruption by which particular points are carried against reason (this is a thing which cannot be prevented by human wisdom, and is of less consequence) and the corruption of the principle itself; for then the evil is not accidental, but settled; the distemper becomes the natural habit.

For my part, I shall be apt to conclude the principles of parliament to be totally corrupted, and therefore its ends entirely defeated, when I see two symptoms; first, a rule of indiscriminate support to all ministers, because this destroys their very end as a controul, and is a general previous sanction to misgovernment; and secondly, the setting up any claims adverse to the right of free election, for this tends to subvert the legal authority by which they sit.

They who will not conform their conduct to the public good, and cannot support it by the prerogative of the crown, have adopted a new plan; they have totally abandoned the shattered and old fashioned fortress of prerogative, and made a lodgment in the

---

[6] i.e. Burke.

power in the people's hands, on the shallow pretence of the horrible disorders at-[23]tending frequent elections, and the committing every three years the independent [24] gentlemen of the counties into a contest with the treasury. What was it which first gave rise to and increased these disorders to the present formidable pitch? but the lucrative prospect which a seat in parliament, in the present mode of corruption, gives for the enriching the representative, at the expence of his country and constituents; take away the cause and the effect will cease; take away from the representative, by a quick and thorough circulating round of rotation, every such lucrative and corrupt prospect [25] of private interest, and the warm contention for seats in parliament, both on the side of government and individuals, will sink into a coolness which will reduce such elections to the quiet calmness of a nomination for parish officers. If triennial parliaments will not serve the turn, change the half, or the whole of your parliament yearly, and deprive your representatives of a corrupt and standing interest in the legislature,[iii] by debarring every member of parliament of the capacity of re-election under a certain term of years.

[26] It certainly never ought to be regarded as a crime, to endeavour by every honest means to advance to superiority and power those of our own sentiments and opinions; but at a time when our expiring liberties, when the corruption of every salutary principle in the constitution calls instantly and loudly for a speedy and effectual reformation, should the contention be reduced to mere endeavours to advance party or friends to superiority and power, the people, whose interests seem entirely out of the question, would act wisely to suffer the contenders to fight their own battles, without in any sense engaging in the dispute.

---

strong-hold of parliament itself. If they have any evil designs to which there is no ordinary legal power commensurate, they bring it into parliament; in parliament the whole is executed from the beginning to the end; in parliament the power of obtaining their object is absolute, and the safety in proceeding perfect; no rules to confine, no after reckoning to terrify: parliament cannot with any great propriety punish others for things in which they themselves have been accomplices. Thus the controul of parliament upon the executory power is lost, because parliament is made to partake in every considerable act of government; impeachment, that great guardian of the purity of the constitution, is in danger of being lost, even to the idea of it.'

[Burke,] *Thoughts on the Cause of the present Discontents*, p. 35. *et seq.* [−37.]

iii The depriving every member of parliament of a corrupt and standing interest in the legislature, by rendering them incapable of serving any sinister views of the court, must effectually destroy the venom of that influence which the author of *The Cause of the Present Discontents* seems to think irremediable.

Equally averse is the author of the Cause of the present Discontents
against every other constitutional proposition for the remedying the
growing evils of our [27] government, as against the orthodox principle
of rotation; a place bill would set the executive power at variance with the
legislative, and hazard the forms of our excellent constitution.[7] The
forms of a constitution is sure of little advantage when its spirit is lost.
But an independent parliament, the true parliament of the people, is
intrusted with sufficient powers to keep the executive parts of the
government in a subordination, which must prevent any possible
infringement either of the form or the spirit of the constitution.

To correct evils which are allowed to be excessive, this mighty
champion of the whig faction, the author of the Thoughts of the Cause
of the present Discontents, proposes that the people, who are not to be
trusted with any additional [28] or original powers adequate to the
correcting the grievances arising from mistaken confidence, should meet
in counties and in corporations to scan the conduct of their representatives, and to send, I presume, disregarded petitions to the throne for the
dissolution of a body of men whom the very nature of their trust must
render corrupt, and whose successors in office, such a trust continuing,
must, from the very constitution of human characters, be equally treacherous and equally formidable.[8]

A more extended and equal power of election, a very important spring
in the machine of political liberty, is entirely disregarded by our author;
but he does not forget to flatter his sovereign with the hopes, that were
his party once taken into favour, the purse of [29] the people would be as
prodigally sacrificed to every lust of capricious grandeur and expence, as
it is at present supposed to be, to the venal machinations of state policy.[iv]

[iv] 'Suppose,' says the author of the Present discontents, 'we were to ask, whether the king
has been richer than his predecessors in accumulated wealth since the establishment of
the plan of favouritism, I believe it will be found that the picture of royal indigence which
our court has presented, until this year, has been truly humiliating; nor has it been
relieved from this unseemly distress but by means which have hazarded the affections of
the people, and shaken their confidence in parliament. If the public treasures had been
exhausted in magnificence and splendor, this distress would have been accounted for, and
in some measure justified. Nothing would be more unworthy of this nation, than with a

[7] Burke rejected constitutional reforms, including the shortening of the duration of
Parliament and place bills, designed to exclude 'placemen', i.e. office holders, from
Parliament; see *Present Discontents*, esp. pp. 49–52.

[8] Ibid., p. 52.

Such infamous flattery, could [30] it have any effect on a wise and just sovereign, was fitter for the royal ear than for public criticism. The public must consider moderation as the most useful virtue in a prince, and that a parliament fulfilling its duty will on no pretence whatsoever suffer more money to be raised on their constituents than is necessary for their defence, and the decent magnificence of their governors.

The disappointments produced by the treachery of leaders, after any sharp, obstinate, or dangerous opposition to government, is very pernicious to the freedom of society, by the languor which the want of confidence must necessarily introduce in popular exertions. It is for this reason [31] that I would warn my countrymen from entering into any dangerous or even vigorous measures against the conduct of their present governors, without exacting a political creed from leaders, who, under the specious pretensions of public zeal, are to all appearances only planning schemes of private emolument and private ambition. I would have them exact some particular promises of real public service; and be never persuaded out of this political truth, That as democratical power never can be preserved from anarchy without representation, so representation never can be kept free from tyrannical exertions on the rights of the people without rotation.

BERNER-STREET, OXFORD-ROAD, MAY 7, 1770.

FINIS

mean and mechanical rule to mete out the splendor of the crown. Indeed I have found very few persons disposed to so ungenerous a procedure.'
[Burke,] *Thoughts on the Cause of the present Discontents*, page 31.

4

A Modest Plea for the Property of Copy Right (1774)

Introduction to the Text

This pamphlet, printed in Bath in 1774 in its only known edition, weighs in on the landmark copyright case of *Donaldson* v. *Beckett* (1774). The Copyright Act 1710 allowed a copyright of twenty years, but British booksellers and their inheritors continued to presume a much longer right to literary property based on common law. The Scottish publisher Alexander Donaldson (1727–94) challenged the claim of a London bookseller to perpetual copyright to James Thomson's *The Seasons* (1730). After a trial in the House of Lords, the case was ruled in favour of limiting the term of copyright to fourteen years. Located in Bath at the time, Macaulay was hindered by her 100-mile distance from the capital, which made her reliant on reports in newspapers, though she may have also relied on her sources in Parliament for the debates, including her brother. Rather than becoming embroiled in legal details, Macaulay made a general case for why authors are entitled to benefit from their literary works. As usual, she preferred to argue from first principles rather than legal precedent, and thus challenged the common law tradition. The importance of literature for a country's fortunes could hardly be overstated, according to Macaulay. As she contended in a footnote, positive law must support literature for the sake of the 'freedom, virtue, religion, and morals of the people' (p. [25]). The pamphlet also reveals her rather low opinion of the 'multitude', who are repeatedly described as 'unthinking' and 'giddy', and, it is strongly implied, in need of intellectual guidance.

Karen Green has highlighted that Macaulay used 'fitness' for the first time in her published writings in this text, suggesting that she had become more immersed in philosophical studies at this time, nine years before her *Treatise on the Immutability of Moral Truth* (1783) was published.[1] Fitness was a crucial philosophical term for Macaulay, for whom immutable moral truths were revealed in the fitness of things discoverable through the use of reason. This had a political dimension for Macaulay, who believed that the law of the land should correspond to 'the moral fitness of things', associating herself at the beginning of *A Modest Plea* specifically with the natural law philosophy of Cicero.

---

[1] Karen Green, *Catharine Macaulay's Republican Enlightenment* (New York, 2020), p. 104.

A Modest Plea for the Property of Copy Right (1774)

[v] To The Public.

For the errors and improprieties which may be found in the following sheets, the Author's excuse is, that they were composed in a great hurry, under a heavy oppression of sickness, and languor of body, and at the distance of above a hundred miles [vi] from the capital, – a distance which deprived her of the advantage of seeing all the arguments urged by the council on both sides the question, or indeed any other argument but what she got from the news-writers.

These obstacles to the conducing with success a cause of such importance as literary property, where the welfare of many worthy members of society, and thousands yet unborn, are at stake, appeared so insurmountable, that she could not have had spirits and resolution to attempt it, had it not been for [vii] the encouragement given her by that generous benefactor to suffering merit, and patriotic citizen, her very good and worthy friend, Dr. WILSON,[1] who condescended to assist in the fatigue of correcting the press, and furnished her with the two interesting anecdotes, concerning the distressed circumstances in which Dr. WALTON died,[2] and the starving condition of MILTON'S posterity.

CATHARINE MACAULAY.

BATH, March 9, 1774.

[1] Rev. Thomas Wilson (1703–84), with whom Macaulay lodged in Bath at this time. See the general introduction for more details.
[2] See note xi, below.

[9] A Modest Plea for the Property of Copy Right.

I shall not enter on the subject of those precedents which a noble Lord, in his arguments on this important cause, so properly dismissed:[3] they were very injudiciously used: therefore, I shall only venture a few remarks on the pleas of equity, – of moral fitness, – and public convenience, – which it seems were urged by the council on the side of the respondent booksellers.

[10] Sir Edward Coke, that great oracle to well-meaning lawyers, says, I think, somewhat to the following purport, – 'That, the law of the land is the perfection of reason carried into practice in all matters of dispute between man and man.'[4] The good Chief Justice, when he made this eulogium on the law of England, undoubtedly agreed in sentiment with other old-fashioned philosophers, THAT THE PERFECTION OF REASON IS THE POWER OF JUDGING AGREEABLE TO THE ETERNAL RULE OF RIGHT, AND MORAL FITNESS OF THINGS.

It is a common observation, that the longer a wise man lives, the more he is confirmed in the opinion, that there is nothing in this terrestrial state worthy a wise man's regard and estimation: Indeed I am afraid there is too much truth in this observation, and that the world itself is grown too old and too wise. Oh, the happy days of ignorance!

[11] That worse than Goth, that infant in knowledge, the once-famed CICERO, amused himself with laying down excellent rules for government and law, to meet in one point of moral perfection for the protection, happiness, and virtue of mankind;[5] but we wiser moderns, have, I think, very unfortunately found out, that good government is too sublime a blessing for the frail state of human nature; and that the law

---

[3] Charles Pratt, 1st Earl Camden (1714–94); see *Cobbett's Parliamentary History of England* (36 vols., London, 1812–20), XVII, cols. 992–1001.

[4] 'reason is the life of the Law, nay the Common law itself is nothing else but reason, which is to be understood, of an Artificial perfection of reason, gotten by long study, observation, and experience, and not of every man's natural reason'. Coke, *The First Part of the Institutes of the Laws of England* (1628; 10th ed., London, 1703), book 2, ch. 6, sect. 138. Cited by many, including Hobbes in *A Dialogue between a Philosopher and a Student of the Common Laws of England*, first published in 1681; see *The Moral and Political Works of Thomas Hobbes of Malmesbury* (London, 1750), p. 589.

[5] Cicero (106–43 BC), Roman statesman, lawyer and philosopher, best known in the eighteenth century for *De officiis*, his speeches and letters, and *De finibus*. Macaulay is mainly alluding to the former here, as *De re publica* was not discovered until the nineteenth century.

of the land is so far from a rule of equity, that it is often incompatible with the moral fitness of things.[i]

Though I cannot agree with a very popular writer, that the common sense of mankind is an infallible rule for religion and morals;[6] yet surely it is very suf-[12]ficient to matters of common justice between man and man.

We are told, by the best authorities, that the common law is founded on common usage, and common usage on the common sense of the people. And if what one of the noble debaters,[7] on the side of the appellants,[8] advanced, be matter of fact, 'that for a succession of fourteen years no action was brought for the security of a property, on which great sums of money had been expended,' it is to be presumed, that, during this space of time, there were few or no invaders, and that this property, as in other cases of property, was for a long time effectually secured by the common sense of the people.[ii]

[13] Thus much in vindication of the pretensions of sordid booksellers, who, it seems, claim an equal privilege with the rest of their fellow citizens engaged in trade, to eat and drink; and if in the good graces of dame Fortune, to leave estates to their families. But authors, it seems, are beings of a very high order, and [14] infinitely above the low considerations of the useful, the convenient, and the necessary!

> Incessantly they toil, to instruct and please mankind,
> With studies pale, with midnight vigils blind;

---

[i] Though it may be right for Judges invariably to follow the rule of precedents, yet where precedents are wanting, if the common law is a law of equity, surely Judges have a right to set the first precedent according to equity.

[ii] If, according to what a noble Lord said in the Upper House, all literary works were at the time of the revolution in the hands of the Stationers' Company, the ravages which must have been made on this property by a number of invaders, were the property not secured by a supposed common law right, would have obliged them, before such a term as twenty years were expired, to have had recourse to the Legislature for a legal security. The proprietors of copy right assert, that the statute of the eighth of Queen ANNE [the Copyright Act 1710] was granted on the principle of facilitating legal redress: Had it been, taken in the sense of a full decision in the case, surely such a number of proprietors of old copies as now suffer by the present decision, would not have laid out their fortunes on such untenable property. But if it is so very obvious, that no common law right exists for securing copy right, surely the granting injunctions could only tend to deny to one party what the law entitled them to, and to amuse the other to their greater ruin.

[6] James Beattie, *An Essay on the Nature and Immutability of Truth* (Edinburgh, 1770).
[7] Lord Camden.   [8] Alexander Donaldson and his brother John.

Tho' thank'd by few, rewarded yet by none,
Content to appeal to Fame's superior throne;
Let but the Goddess the just prize bestow, –
For Fame is all that authors ask below![9]

These are undoubtedly fine sentiments; but, alas! the love of filthy lucre, or the cravings of nature, will sometimes prevail, even over the refinements of genius and science! There are some low-minded geniusses, who will be apt to think they may, with as little degradation to character, traffic with a bookseller[iii] [15] for the purchase of their mental harvest, as opulent landholders may traffic with monopolizers in grain and cattle for the sale of the more substantial product of their lands. They will be apt to consider, that literary merit will not purchase a shoulder of mutton, or prevail with sordid butchers and bakers to abate one farthing in the pound of the exorbitant price which meat and bread at this time bear; the brewer, the linen-draper, the hosier, &c. &c. will all think their ignorance in letters an excuse for extorting, for the mere necessaries of life, sums which the wretched author has not wherewithal to pay; and it is to be doubted, if a sheriff's officer, when a cast of his office is necessary to conduct the self-denying philosopher to the last scene of his glory, it is to be doubted, I say, whether he will abate one tittle of his accustomary extortions.

These are evils which the sublime flights of poetic fancy do not always soar above.

[16] Pope was so far from being ashamed of his oeconomical prudence, in the article of gain, that he boasted of the happy independence he had obtained by the sale of his literary publications; and represents the tantalizing state of an admired author with empty pockets, in the following forcible language:

'Is envied, wretched, and is flatter'd, poor.'[10]

This is the uncomfortable state of an admired author: for it is not every writer, who merits the approbation of the public, is sure of obtaining it,

---

[iii] Three members of the Upper House, the Bishops of GLOCESTER [William Warburton] and BRISTOL [Thomas Newton], and LORD [George] LYTTLETON, have not thought it beneath their station, as authors and nobles, to take large sums of booksellers for their literary publications.

[9] Alexander Pope, *The Temple of Fame: A Vision* (London, 1715), p. 28 (slightly altered).
[10] Pope, *Temple of Fame*, p. 20.

at least during his life-time. Such a disappointed being may possibly have gained a tolerable sum from a bookseller, on mistaken speculative grounds; and may be vulgar enough to be comforted with the prospect of a good dinner, for two or three years at least, for the chagrin which the want of judgment, or prejudice in the public, occasions him. An empty stomach is a bad at-[17]tendant on spleen and melancholy; and the best means of relieving a friend, oppressed with the two great evils of hunger and sorrow, is to refresh his spirits with proper nutriment for the body, before you attempt the administering that balsam of consolation intended for the relief of his mind.

To be more serious: with the intention of depriving authors of the honest, the dear-bought reward of their literary labours, they have been raised a little, higher instead of lower than the angels, and at the same time levelled with the inventors of a very inferior order: But supposing improvement of the human mind is not more worthy the attention of the Legislature, than the luxuries, or at least those conveniencies, which are not absolutely necessary to the ease of common life, were the inventor of inferior order and the author to stand upon the same footing, in regard to time and other circumstances, for the emoluments [18] arising from their different inventive faculties; the inventor of inferior order would find himself much better rewarded than the author, for his ingenuity. Every common capacity can find out the use of a machine; but it is a length of time before the value of a literary publication is discovered and acknow-ledged by the vulgar; and when the merits of a work of this kind, in regard to the honest intentions of the writer, and the execution of the composition is in general allowed, the malice of party prejudice, and that leaven of selfishness, which prevails in the characters of the greater number of individuals, may for a long term of years keep back the sale of a book, which teaches an offensive doctrine, or tells disagreeable truths to the public.

The names of BACON, NEWTON, MILTON, and LOCKE, have been brought into the arguments, as examples to prove that the first-rate geniusses have la-[19]boured in the literary way, on the single motive of delighting and instructing mankind:[11] Nay, the Player SHAKESPEARE, it is urged, made a generous bequest to the public, of every one of his almost inimitable dramatic productions.

---

[11] Lord Camden: 'It was not for gain, that Bacon, Newton, Milton, Locke, instructed and delighted the world'. *Cobbett's Parliamentary History of England*, XVII, col. 1000.

In the times in which this great Poet lived, genius and science were so little esteemed by the generality, that property in copy right was hardly thought worth securing: There were few individuals who would venture to print editions of any voluminous author; and if the player and the prompter, who published the first edition of SHAKESPEARE, were indemnified for paper and print, it is to be presumed, that they were indebted for the indemnification to those patrons of that poet to whom they dedicated his work: But be it otherwise, as SHAKESPEARE did not assign to any individual, or to the public at large, a right in his manuscripts, according to the most equitable idea of [20] obtaining property, they became the property of those persons, who first laid out money and labour on them.

That SHAKESPEARE is not one of those sublime characters who had no view of gain in their works, is obvious from a transitory view of his writings; the fame he has acquired he thought so far out of his reach, that he never took the pains of correcting a page; and if he had any view to instructing mankind, the view appears to be secondary to the view of gain, by that abundance of low ribaldry to please a barbarous audience, which load and disgrace the most excellent of his dramatic pieces.[iv]

[21]

> SHAKESPEARE, whom you and ev'ry play-house bill,
> Stile the divine, the matchless, – what you will,
> For gain, not glory, wing'd his roving flight,
> And grew immortal in his own despight.[12]

Disinterested principle had so little influence over the conduct of the Philosopher BACON, that the fortune and title he possessed were solely obtained, not as a reward for his virtue, genius, and science, but on the merits of his servile and corrupt compliance with the humours of the Sovereign, and his prostituting those glorious talents to the interests of

---

[iv] Shakespeare, when he first sought his fortune in London, took care of gentlemen's horses during their stay at the play-house; at length, by his industry, and the exertion of his great abilities, he became actor, author, and patentee: He wrote plays on the single motive of filling the house, and was so successful as to die with a fortune, which in the times he lived was called opulent. [See, e.g., Thomas Mortimer, *The British Plutarch; Or, Biographical Entertainer: Vol. 5* (London, 1762), pp. 1–28.]

[12] Alexander Pope, *The First Epistle of the Second Book of Horace, Imitated* (London, 1737), p. 5.

an arbitrary ill-designing Court.[13] Indeed, when this great Author published his Philosophical Ideas, they were so little understood that they were deemed literary lumber; [22] nay, the learned and royal JAMES, whom the EARL of SHAFTESBURY[14] terms the School-master of his people, compared it to the ways of GOD, past finding out.[15]

LOCKE was fortunate enough to live in times when the rights of nature, and the interest of the Sovereign who sat on the throne, were supposed to be inseparable; whatever therefore might be the generosity and disinterestedness of his character, he did not go without his reward.

NEWTON was gratified with a place and pension;[v] and MILTON, for his spirited and noble defence of [23] the people of England, had the honour of receiving thanks, accompanied with a present, from the most patriotic government that ever blessed the hopes and military exertions of a brave people. When indeed the times altered, and the matchless Author of Paradise Lost had fallen on evil days; when his prospects in regard to lucrative advantage was vanished; when he had lost his eyes in the attempt of fixing the ideas of good government and true virtue in the minds of a wavering people; when his fortunes were entirely ruined in the crush of his party; this excellent, this heroic, this god-like man, instead of flying, like TIMON of ATHENS,[16] from the haunts of the human species, amused his distressed imagination with forming, for the delight and the instruction of mankind, a Poem, whose merit is of such magnitude, that it is impossible for a genius inferior to his own to do it justice in the description.

[24] Such an example of love and charity, it is to be owned, does great honour to MILTON'S religious and moral principles, and to human nature; but yet I think it is an example, which may with much more

---

[v] So precarious is the respect which posterity pays to men of genius and science, that it was with some difficulty the admirers of this Great Philosopher could preserve to his statue the place of honour which the Royal Society had formerly assigned it.

[13] Francis Bacon was knighted and later ennobled by James I, whom he served as Attorney-General and Lord High Chancellor.

[14] Anthony Ashley Cooper, 3rd Earl of Shaftesbury (1671–1713), Whig Parliamentarian and man of letters, best known for *Characteristicks of Men, Manners, Opinions, Times* (3 vols., 1711).

[15] The exact quote from James I is untraced, but it echoes a phrasing in King James's Bible, Romans 11:33. Bacon himself quotes this line of Scripture in *The Advancement of Learning* (London, 1605), p. 484.

[16] Timon's reputation as a misanthrope was immortalised in Shakespeare's play, *Timon of Athens*, published in the *First Folio* in 1623.

propriety be brought on the other side of the question. Can any man, capable of feeling and tasting the compositions of MILTON, reflect without sorrow and anguish of heart, that a society of rational beings should be so void of every grateful sentiment, so dead to every moral instinct, as to suffer the posterity of this illustrious citizen, to be reduced to a state of poverty, which necessitated them, for the support of a miserable existence, to solicit a share in the distribution of public alms.[17]

In MILTON'S days, had literary property stood on the same footing it was supposed to stand on before [25] the fatal decision against it in the House of Lords,[vi] a bookseller, notwithstanding this worthy man was under the frowns of a Court; notwithstanding the virtue of his conduct had subjected him to a load of unpopularity, from the change of sentiment in his giddy countrymen; notwithstanding, I say, these difficulties, a bookseller, on speculative grounds, might possibly have given him such a sum for that incomparable Poem, as would in some measure have helped to support him comfortably under the cloud of his fortune, and enabled him to leave such a decent provision for his posterity, as to have prevented, to the indelible [26] disgrace of this country, the necessity of their asking alms.[vii]

For the propriety of the Lords' decision on literary property, it has been objected, that if there were no means of compelling the putting forth a second impression of a useful work, the impatient public must wait till a wife and children are provided for, by the sale of an edition: and that all learning would be locked up in the hands of the booksellers, who would set what price upon it their avarice chose to demand.

If the news-writers have been fair in their representation of the arguments urged by a noble and [27] learned debater[18] on the side of

---

[vi] If some positive law does not lend its aid to the support of the tottering state of literature in this country, this decision will be a more mortal stab to the freedom, virtue, religion, and morals of the people of England, than the unthinking multitude in general at present apprehend.

[vii] This will not appear an extravagant supposition, when we consider the price which the present BISHOP of BRISTOL got from the booksellers, for writing a few notes on this incomparable Poem. [Thomas Newton published an annotated edition of *Paradise Lost* in 1749, and in 1752 Milton's remaining poems. Eight editions had appeared by 1775 and Newton made £735 from his work. See also notes iii and 17.]

[17] Thomas Newton, 'The Life of Milton', in *Paradise Lost* (2 vols., London, 1749), I, pp. lvii–lviii. See also p. 129, above.
[18] Lord Camden.

the appellants, I protest, I do not understand the force of his objection. The public cannot want a second edition of a work before they have bought of the first; and surely neither that benevolent Lord, or the public, would wish to have it in their power to deprive the necessitous children of an ingenious man, with whose literary labours they had been delighted and instructed, of the just emoluments arising from those labours.

If the noble Lord supposes, that the proprietor of a copy would, through necessity or an inordinate desire of gain, keep up the price of an edition to an exorbitant height, it must be, because his high offices and occupations in the State have prevented him from being at all informed in the business of bookselling.

[28] It is the true interest of the proprietor of every copy, to sell off at the most moderate price, as many editions as with all his art and industry he can dispose of. Is the edition near sold? is the eager question of every author to his bookseller.[viii] And suppose the avarice of a proprietor of a valuable copy should, on mistaken grounds of interest, be led to keep up the price of his property, by giving none but expensive editions to the public; that public, according to what the noble Lord observed on another occasion, may have recourse to the unlimited power of printing editions of English authors, claimed by the Irish and the Americans.

It is the opinion of the noble Lord, that if there is any thing in the world common to all mankind, science [29] and learning are in their nature *publici juris*; and they ought to be as free and general as air and water:[19] Indeed, I am so far of this noble Lord's opinion, as to regard with horror those diabolical governments, who, by arbitrary decrees and punishments, have barred all the avenues of arriving at science and learning from a wretched people, who, to govern like beasts, they have endeavoured to deprive of the use of that reason, which was given by the benevolent Creator, for the preservation, the happiness, and the glory of the species. But sure if there is any thing which an individual can properly call his own, it is, acquired science, and those high gifts of genius and judgment, with which the Almighty has in a peculiar manner distinguished some of his creatures; gifts which, if they are properly

---

[viii] Besides lucrative advantage, every new edition is supposed to add to the reputation of a work.

[19] *Cobbett's Parliamentary History of England*, XVII, col. 999.

exerted for the service of mankind, deserve the respect, the care, and the attention of society.

[30] The council on the side of the appellants have made life of all those popular complaints, which, whether on true or false grounds, have at various times, by authors and the public, been made against the booksellers. The public do not sufficiently respect and love learning to be easily satisfied with the price of books, and it is impossible for a bookseller to satisfy the expectations of an unsuccessful author. But however avarice, (for avarice more or less governs all bodies of men) may formerly have occasioned booksellers to impose on the wants of a necessitous author, in the purchase of a copy, or on the public in the sale of a literary work, there are at present too many in the trade, for an author to be reduced to the necessity of disposing of a saleable copy for less than it is worth: Booksellers also, in these times, understand their interest better than to give very bad editions of authors. We have in general better paper, better print, and more elegant edi-[31]tions of English authors, than I believe were ever known, since literature flourished in England; and in regard to moderateness of price, books in these times, when every commodity, every material in the way of trade, pay such a high tax to the government; books, I say, are the cheapest articles sold.[ix] This is so notorious a truth to those enlightened, generous individuals, who understand the use of literature, and respect learned and ingenious persons, that they lament that frivolous taste, which is so generally prevailing, as to occasion both sexes to give with pleasure, to [32] see a farcical representation on the stage, or to revel at a masquerade, double, treble, and, in the last instance, often above ten times the sum, which they grudge to bestow on an instructive book.

These enlightened, generous individuals do, I say, lament that those debauchers of the good sense and morals of the people, those dealers in (not to give them a harsher name) trifling amusements, with dancers and singers, should be supported in all the high luxuries of pampered sense, and at the same time enabled to pocket thousands obtained from the

---

[ix] There are many who pretend they would not grudge the giving a reasonable price to an author for a book, but they are unwilling to comply with what they call the exorbitant demands of the bookseller: This is all fallacy and compliment; the author's and the bookseller's in this case are inseparable: If booksellers ask sufficient prices for their books, authors will insist on a sufficient price for copy right; but when books are sold as drugs, authors must lower their demands.

giddy, unthinking multitude;[x] whilst those who are fit to instruct and to delight the intellectual sense of man-[33]kind are driven to the greatest straits to obtain the necessaries and decencies of life.[xi]

The very few readers, among the public, are in so little danger of the want of mental food by the scarcity of editions, that, alas! the literary market is over-stocked, as those many warehouses which totter under the weight of immense piles of printed copies can very sufficiently evidence.[xii]

[34] Indeed there are so very few buyers of this kind of lumber, that though in general the authors of large and valuable works have been very very sparingly paid for the necessary expences attending [35] such compositions,[xiii] the consumption of time, and too often the loss of health, in these laborious undertakings, the booksellers have generally smarted for what they have given for copy right, especially in their dealings with some Scotch authors, who have tasted very largely of their generosity or credulity;[20] nay, according to common report, that mighty

---

[x] Not to mention more modern instances, FARINELLI [(1705–82), the stage name of Carlo Maria Michelangelo Nicola Broschi], and another famous Italian singer [possibly Senesino (1686–1758)], have built palaces in Italy, with the plentiful harvest which they reaped from the irrational taste of the English.

[xi] Dr. [Brian] WALTON [(1600–1)], the editor of the Polyglot Bible [*Biblia Sacra Polyglotta* (6 vols., London, 1653–7)], a work highly esteemed by all the literati in Europe, died in debt; nay, the great Archbishop [John] TILLOTSON [(1630–94)] died in mean circumstances; and if it had not been for a copy of his sermons, sold to the booksellers, his family might have been under the necessity of, perhaps, applying in vain for relief to their country.

[xii] There are many of our best authors, the poets excepted, who will not pay the re-publication; and works of merit sufficient to do the highest honor to the sense of the nation, are so little read, that they are scarce known, to any but the very learned. Thus we are daily losing somewhat of that vast stock, of useful ideas published by our ancestors; and the neglect of Englishmen to their best instructors, has been almost as fatal to knowledge, and to the fame of English authors, as accidental conflagrations, and those voluntary ones made by the GOTHS, the VANDALS, and the TURKS, on the manuscripts of the antient writers. This is an evil which would be greatly increased by rendering literary property common: In this case it will not be worth the while of individuals to make new editions of any works, which do not promise a quick return of money: And what kind of works must there be? They must be such trifling wretched compositions as please the vulgar; compositions which disgrace the press, yet are the best calculated for general sale.

[xiii] The purchasing a large number of books, with the expence of paying a variety of people, employed in searching and copying ancient records.

[20] Hume and William Robertson had become unusually wealthy by selling the copyright to their histories.

Colossus of literature, the great Dr. JOHNSON, before he happily experienced the munificence of a royal patron, used to acknowledge, that in this country booksellers were the best patrons to authors;[21] and for this last century they have by many people been considered as the sole support of learning.

It has, I am told, been urged by the council on [36] the side of the appellants, or by some one or other Member of the Upper House, in favour of the decision against the perpetuity of copy right, that it was possible a case might arise, where government should bribe a bookseller to suppress intirely the work of an author whose doctrine was contrary to the interests or ill designs of a corrupt court.

It would be a difficult task, even in this country, for a minister to divert out of the necessary channel of corruption, a sum sufficient to bribe an individual, who would always have it in his power to repeat his extortionate demands.

But supposing a minister should stand so much in awe of the doctrine and reflections of any particular author, as to expend large sums and emoluments to suppress them, and that he had the money at command, he would find it all thrown away in an impos-[37]sible attempt; for the public, as in the before mentioned case, might have recourse to the Irish and the Americans, who would furnish them with as many editions of the author as they pleased.[22]

But to come to the last and most important question agitated in the cause between the appellants Donaldson and the respondent booksellers, Is the rendering literary property common, advantageous or disadvantageous to the state of literature in this country? The question, I think, is easily answered, that it will not only be disadvantageous, but ruinous to the state of literature. If literary property becomes common, we can have but two kind of authors, men in opulence, and men in dependence.

The Romans, even in their degenerate days, had that high sense of merit in general, and of services [38] rendered the public; that, according to PLINY,[23] and other writers, in proportion to a man's character for literary abilities and virtues, in proportion to his power of rendering himself useful to his country and fellow citizens, and in proportion to his exertion of this power, he was sure of meeting from the generous hands of individuals an equal reward.

---

[21] Samuel Johnson (1709–84) received a royal pension in 1762.
[22] Dublin was a major market for reprints in the eighteenth century.   [23] The Younger.

PLINY, if I remember right, in speaking of his own success in life, and that of one of his cotemporaries, mentions the leaving legacies to learned and good men, as a practice common and familiar. We were of the same age, said he, we entered into life together, and we had the same number of legacies bequeathed us.[24] This being the custom among the Romans, with what ardor must it inspire every youthful breast, to deserve such grateful, such useful returns of bounty? But, alas! there never was any thing Roman [39] in the characters and conduct of the English people! When did ever an Englishman grow rich from the real, services he had rendered his country? No! Gothic institutions have, from the first establishment of our ancestors in these parts, tainted the minds of their posterity with such a leaven of the corrupted kind of selfishness, that an Englishman persuades himself he is acting with propriety, when he bequeaths the whole of his estate to a blockhead he despises in the fiftieth degree of relationship, tho' he leaves behind him many worthy ingenious friends, whom a small legacy would help out of very intricate circumstances.

If there ever is any money left in this country, out of the channel of relationship, the instances are rare; they are commonly returns for servile compliances with the will of the benefactor; or else the oeconomical bequester once for all pays for a seat among the [40] mansions of the blessed, those sums to hospitals and public charities, which he denied to the starving poor whilst he preserved any power of self-gratification.

That watchful guard, selfishness, is a never-failing check to any generous sally of the mind, or to any benevolent inclination in the human breast; and the means of obtaining wealth from the good opinion of his country or his friends being thus barred from a man whom fortune has denied to favour, yet of merit, of genius, and of virtue, sufficient to instruct and to enlighten mankind: If such a man is deprived of the necessary lucrative advantage by the right of property, in his own writings, is he to starve, or live in penury, whilst he is exerting, perhaps, vain endeavours to serve a people who do not desire his services? Supposing this man has a wife and children, ought he, for the mere whistling of a name, to exert those talents in li-[41]terary compositions,

---

[24] *The Letters of Pliny the Consul*, ed. William Melmoth (2 vols., London, 1747), II, pp. 407–9. Pliny's letter is to Tacitus.

which were much better employed in some mechanical business, or some trade, that would support his family? Will not such a man, if he has the tender feelings of a husband and a father, – if indeed he has the conscience of a religious or a moral man; will he not check every incentive arising from vanity, which would tempt him, for the purchase of an ill-bought fame, to expose to poverty and contempt those who, by the law of religion and nature, he is bound to cherish and protect?

Every independent man, not born to an estate, being thus, by a hard conjuncture of circumstances, prevented from exerting his talents for the delight and instruction of mankind, this important task can only be the lot of the opulent and the dependent; but, alas! genius and learning are, in our days, too humble and too modest to frequent the palaces of the [42] great; therefore, I am afraid, it is from dependent writers alone that we must expect all our future instruction; – but can that instruction be edifying which falls from a venal pen, exerted merely to earn the favour of a patron, by making that which is the worse appear the better reason, and by setting forth, in false colours, all the prejudices and corrupt views of the man from whose hard-earned bounty the author expects bread?

Thus much for the matter of those publications, which will succeed this great revolution in literary property. In regard to elegant editions, no proprietors of copy right, who hold such property on the life of an author, or for a small term of years, will find it worth their while to give very good editions of works, lest the public, who are fond of penny-worths in the article of books, should withhold their purchase 'till [43] the property became common; and in this case, the stile, if not the sentiments of the author, will be miserably mangled, and the shops full of those wretched editions of works, which would disgrace even an Irish press.

This will be the wretched state of literature, and editions of authors, if literary property continues to stand on the footing which the Lords' decision has put it; – a footing almost as bad as it stood on when, this country first emerged from a state of such Gothic barbarity and ignorance, that the mighty tyrants of the land could neither spell nor scribble their names and titles; – a footing so wretched, as, with the consideration of the ruin in which a set of useful members of society are at present involved, to induce me (not perceiving a more able advocate enter the lists), to write these arguments and observations in its defence, though

[44] oppressed with sickness, and in a very weak and languid state of health. But let not ministers and placemen[25] triumph, as if in a greater state of security from the reflections of their countrymen, by this mortal stab to the state of English literature: No; it will only affect those valuable works, built on more durable principles than the sandy foundations of temporary applause.

An author, dependent on a factious patron, will often write in more acrimonious terms, though not with the same patriotic view, as an independent man, on the conduct of government; and in proportion to the smallness of the time allotted for a writer to make his market of gain, the press will be employed with scandals, libels, acute reflections on public measures, and all those kind of compositions, calculated to please the generality, and to render government uneasy.

[45] But, whatever may be the malice, or the want of discernment in the minister, I am persuaded that Lord CAMDEN, to whose eloquence, and to that deference which is due to character, perhaps, we owe this decision; – I am persuaded, from the candour and humanity which that nobleman is known to possess, from that display of abilities and sagacity, that integrity, that strict adherence to justice so conspicuous in his conduct whilst he presided over the Courts of Common Pleas and Chancery;[26] – I am persuaded, from that patriotic spirit and love of country which has hitherto governed all his actions, and rendered his name dear to Englishmen; – I am persuaded, I say, that when this learned, this excellent Nobleman, considers this important subject in all its extensive view, he will be the first to move for a bill to relieve the holders of copy right from their present distress; to settle the lucrative advantage of authors for their writings on a permanent footing; [46] and thus to encourage useful literature, by rendering it convenient to the circumstances of men of independent tempers to employ their literary abilities in the service of their country.

---

[25] Placemen were members of parliament who held paid office, generally sinecures, and were expected to support the government with their votes.

[26] Camden was promoted to chief justice of Common Pleas in 1761. His most famous case involved Wilkes and the libellous *North Briton* in 1763, in which Camden ruled that general warrants were illegal. He gained great popularity as a result.

[47] Postscript.

By the arguments urged in the third page of this work, the Author does not presume to insinuate that copy right was not invaded before the statute of the eighth of Queen Anne: She is sensible that the statute itself mentions invasions, but thinks herself authorized in the opinion, that after the revolution literary property was for several years protected by the common notion, that the holder had an equitable, and consequently a legal right, by the words of the same statute, which calls the invasion 'a late invasion.'

FINIS.

5

An Address to the People of England, Scotland and Ireland on the Present Important Crisis of Affairs (1775)

Introduction to the Text

An Address to the People of England, Scotland and Ireland on the Present Important Crisis of Affairs (1775) was published in Bath, in two London editions and in New York. This edition reproduces the second London version of the text. The pamphlet's starting point is the aftermath of the general election in the autumn of 1774. Before the election, Macaulay's brother John Sawbridge had re-entered into a partnership with Wilkes, as the Society of the Gentlemen Supporters of the Bill of Rights launched an ambitious campaign, the pillar of which was the question of constituency instructions to members of parliament. The campaign was successful in the metropolitan region, and candidates were elected on Wilkeite platforms in Middlesex, the City of London – Sawbridge as one of them – and Southwark. In Bristol, Henry Cruger was elected on a similar platform, and in response to his fellow representative for the city, Burke condemned the doctrine of constituency instructions in a famous speech.[1] In the provinces, the Wilkeite campaign floundered and showed decisively the limitations of the movement for political reform outside of the cities and metropolitan areas. Surrey was the only county apart from Middlesex contested by a Wilkeite candidate, Sir Joseph Mawbey, who failed to become elected, though he was returned in a by-election the following year.

---

[1] *Burke's Speeches at His Arrival at Bristol, and at the Conclusion of the Poll* (London, 1775).

Macaulay voiced her frustration in this pamphlet in the year after the 1774 election. The provinces had 'reject[ed] the wise example set them by the city of London, in requiring a test from those they elected into the representative office', she wrote disappointedly (p. [6]). In her correspondence she described her aspiration for the *Address* as showing her 'unabated zeal for the prosperity and the liberties of the British Empire'. She cautioned, however, that she was pessimistic about the prospects of any change in policy direction, and that the pamphlet had been composed while she was ill. Yet, she hoped that 'the intention will be well accepted by the friends of Liberty', referring to political reformers on both sides of the Atlantic.[2]

The *Address* represents Macaulay's only direct intervention in the debate over the American colonies, whose constitutional right to no taxation without representation she believed had been violated by the British government. While the Rockingham ministry had repealed the Stamp Act of 1765, the Townshend Duties, introduced in 1767–8, placed indirect taxes in America on glass, lead, paints, paper and tea, imported from Britain. On taking office in 1770, Frederick (Lord) North (1732–92) repealed most of these duties, but fatally kept the tax on tea. American 'patriots' threw East India tea into Boston Harbour in 1773, and the British responded with the Intolerable Acts, or Coercive Acts, which ended local self-government in Massachusetts and closed Boston's trade.

Macaulay condemned Britain's hard-line response to the 'Boston Tea Party', and also denounced the Quebec Act of 1774, which had heightened anti-Catholic sentiments among New Englanders and English Nonconformists (and their allies). Under the terms of the Treaty of Paris of 1763, which concluded the Seven Years War, France had ceded New France (Canada) to Britain. The Quebec Act defined the structure of the provincial government and crucially altered the oath of allegiance to omit reference to the Protestant faith, as freedom to practise Catholicism was granted to the inhabitants of Quebec. This was anathema to Macaulay, who distinguished between 'toleration' and 'establishment' of Catholicism, which she as a historian of seventeenth-century England associated with absolute monarchy and intolerance, and which was thus 'altogether incompatible with the fundamental principles

---

[2] Macaulay to Mr and Mrs Northcote, 20 January 1775, *Correspondence*, p. 196.

of our constitution' (p. [17]). But the biggest problem was that Protestant Dissenters still laboured under civil disabilities. Between 1771 and 1774 the Feathers Tavern petitioners unsuccessfully sought relief from the obligation to subscribe to the Thirty-Nine Articles of the Church of England, which was required on nomination to a benefice, on matriculation at Oxford, and on graduation at Cambridge. Prioritising the rights of Catholics in Canada at a time when Protestant Dissenters were still treated as second-class citizens at home was a betrayal of Protestantism, according to Macaulay.

An Address to the People of England, Scotland and Ireland on the Present Important Crisis of Affairs (1775)

[5] An Address, &c.

The advantage of a second opportunity to correct a mistake, when the first has been neglected, is a happiness which few individuals, or bodies of men, experience; and a blessing which, if it oftener occurred in the affairs of life, would enable most of us to avoid the greater part of the misery which at present appears inseparable to the human state.

The Electors of this kingdom, however, have shewn themselves incorrigible, by re-[6]cently abusing what the author of *The Patriot* justly calls a high dignity, and an important trust;[1] and this after a ruinous experience of the effects of a former ill-placed confidence.

It is not to be supposed, that either the beauty of justice, the interests of liberty, or the welfare of individuals, as united to the common good, can have any avail with men, who, at this important crisis of British affairs, could reject the wise example set them by the city of London, and the county of Middlesex, in requiring a test from those they elected into the representative office; a test which, had it been generally taken, and religiously observed, would have dispersed the dark, cloud which hangs over the empire, restored the former splendor of the nation, and given a renewed strength, vigour, and purity, to the British constitution.[2]

Among the body of Electors, however, there are undoubtedly many who, by the most [7] cruel of undue influences, – that influence which

---

[1] Samuel Johnson, *The Patriot. Addressed to the Electors of Great Britain* (London, 1774), p. 2.
[2] Macaulay refers to the practice of candidates pledging themselves to the key points of the 'Bill of Rights' programme, including shorter parliaments, the exclusion of placemen, reform of the system of representation, a willingness to receive instructions and not to accept office or emolument from the crown.

the opulent exert over the needy, have in a manner been constrained to act contrary to judgment and inclination; while there are others who have been misled by their ignorance, and the sophistry of men of better understanding. – To these, and that large body of my countrymen who are unjustly debarred the privilege of election, and, except by petition and remonstrance, have no legal means of opposing the measures of government, I address myself on the present momentous occasion.

It can be no secret to any of you, my friends and fellow citizens, that the ministry, after having exhausted all those ample sources of corruption which your own tameness under oppressive taxes have afforded, either fearing the unbiassed judgment of the people, or impatient at the slow, but steady progress of despotism, have attempted to wrest from our American Colonists every privilege necessary to freemen; – privileges which they hold [8] from the authority of their charters, and the principles of the constitution.

With an entire supineness, England, Scotland, and Ireland, have seen the Americans, year by year, stripped of the most valuable of their rights; and, to the eternal shame of this country, the stamp act, by which they were to be taxed in an arbitrary manner, found no opposition, except from those who are particularly concerned, that the commercial intercourse between Great-Britain and her Colonies should meet with no interruption.[3]

With the same guilty acquiescence, my countrymen, you have seen the last Parliament finish their venal course, with passing two acts for shutting up the Port of Boston, for indemnifying the murderers of the inhabitants of Massachusets-Bay, and changing their chartered constitution of government:[4] And to shew that none of the fundamental principles of our boasted constitution are held [9] sacred by the government of the people, the same Parliament, without any interruption either by petition or remonstrance, passed another act for changing the government of Quebec;[5] in which the Popish religion, instead of being tolerated as stipulated by the treaty of peace, is established; in which

---

[3] The Stamp Act 1765 was repealed by the Rockingham ministry in 1766, supported by Britain's merchants.
[4] Macaulay refers to the Boston Massacre of 5 March 1770, in which British soldiers shot and killed several people 'mobbing' them, and the Intolerable Acts 1774.
[5] The Quebec Act 1774.

the Canadians are deprived of the right to an assembly, and of trial by jury; in which the English laws in civil cases are abolished, the French laws established, and the crown empowered to erect arbitrary courts of judicature; and in which, for the purpose of enlarging the bounds where despotism is to have its full sway, the limits of that province are extended so as to comprehend those vast regions that lie adjoining to the northerly and westerly bounds of our colonies.

The anxious desire of preserving that harmony which had so long and so happily subsisted between the Parent State and her Colonies, occasioned the Americans to bear, [10] with an almost blameable patience, the innovations which were continually made on their liberty, 'till the ministry, who imagined their moderation proceeded from ignorance and cowardice, by depriving them of almost every part of their rights which remained unviolated, have raised a spirit beyond the Atlantic, which may either recover the opportunities we have lost of restoring the breaches which for near a century have been making in our constitution, or of sinking us into the lowest abyss of national misery.

In these times of general discontent, when almost every act of our Governors excites a jealousy and apprehension in all those who make the interests of the community their care, there are several amongst us who, dazzled with the sun-shine of a court, and fattening on the spoils of the people, have used their utmost endeavours to darken your understandings on those subjects, which, at [11] this time, it is particularly your business to be acquainted with. There are others who, whilst they have the words Freedom, Constitution, and Privilege, continually in their mouths, are using every mean in their power to render those limitations useless, which have from time to time been erected by our ancestors, as mitigations of that barbarous system of despotism imposed by the Norman tyrant[6] on the inhabitants of this island.

These men attempt to persuade you, that those who appear the most anxious for the safety of their country are the least interested in its welfare. They have had the insolence to tell you, though in contradiction to the evidence of your feelings, that all goes well, that your Governors faithfully fulfil the duties of their office, and that there are no grievances worthy to be complained of but those which arise from that spirit of

---

[6] William I ('the Conqueror').

faction which, more or less, must ever exist in a limited monarchy. – These men have told [12] you, that you are no judges of the state of your political happiness; that you are made of too inflammable materials to be trusted with the knowledge of your injuries, even if you have suffered any and that those who appeal to you, do it only with the intention to betray you. – They have told you that Quebec, being on the other side of the Atlantic, it is of little consequence to you what religion is there established; that the Canada bill only secures to the inhabitants of that province privileges which were stipulated to them on the yielding the place to the English; and that those are as bad as Papists, who refuse to any people the enjoyment of their religion.

These men have attempted to divert you from the exacting a test as the rule of parliamentary conduct, and to bring into suspicion those who have been willing to enter into salutary engagements: They have told you, that such candidates, by promising more than they were able to [13] perform, only meant to delude you by an empty clamour of ineffectual zeal. – These men, in asserting that you are too profligate, too needy, and too ignorant to be adequate judges of your own business, endeavour to throw disgrace and contempt on those who have made an indefinite promise of obeying the mandates of their constituents.

These men have asserted, that unlimited obedience is stipulated in the acceptance of protection; and though such an assertion involves you and the subjects of every state in unlimited slavery, and unlimited slavery excludes every idea of right and power, yet they have also told you, that it is in vindication of your authority that your Governors have exerted an arbitrary power over your brethren in America.

In order to confound your ideas on the merits of the dispute, and to stifle your feelings of humanity, they have told you, that the Americans, though neither adequately or [14] inadequately represented in the case of taxation, stand on the same predicament with yourselves, and that there is no more injustice in inflicting a severe punishment on the whole town of Boston, for the supposed offence of a few of its inhabitants, than in the bombarding a town in the possession of an enemy, when, by such an act of hostility, a few of our own people dwelling in the town might accidentally be destroyed.

This, my friends and fellow citizens, is treating you, indeed, according to the appellations of ignorant and profligate, so freely given you; but as there are many of you who, I trust, deserve not these severe terms of reproach, I shall appeal to that measure of understanding which the

Almighty has given in common to man, and endeavour to convince you of the falshood of these assertions.

Men who are rid of the numerous ills which narrow circumstances occasion, and [15] this by pensions taken from the public treasure, may, from a selfishness inseparable to human nature, fancy that the times cannot be better; but that this is the mere delusion of those who rejoice at your expence, your own experience must, I think, fully shew you. Let the once-opulent trader, let the starving mechanic, bear witness to this truth, that our commerce has been declining with hasty steps for these last ten years: – Let the numerous half-famished poor which we meet at every turn in our streets; let the needy gentry, whose honest independent ancestors have handed down to them a moderate income, and who find that income yearly sinking from bare sufficiency to poverty, bear witness, that the high price of all the necessaries of life, with the oppressive burden of our taxes, are very weighty evils.

Though men of true virtue, my fellow citizens, (that is, men who have a just regard for the rights of nature, for the general happiness of the human species, and for the [16] happiness of their countrymen in particular) will not willingly associate with those of looser principles, yet they will undoubtedly endeavour to stop the career of that government, whose impolitic measures are every day adding numbers to the wretched mass of the ignorant, the needy, and the profligate.

To oppose government with success, such honest individuals must make use of the assistance of the multitude, and consequently, of good and bad citizens, of the rich and the poor, the learned and the unlearned, of the wise and the foolish, that is, of every man who will co-operate with them in their designs, whether he be led to such co-operation by the principle of justice, by interest, or by passion.[7]

Though Quebec is situated beyond the Atlantic, my fellow citizens, you are still to remember that it is part of the British empire; and that, though a toleration of all religions, where such indulgence can be used with safety to the welfare of the community, [17] is undoubtedly

---

[7] Macaulay's friend and political ally James Burgh had around this time politicised the notion of popular associations in his *Political Disquisitions* (3 vols., 1774–5), cited by Macaulay later in this pamphlet.

laudable, because agreeable to the principles of justice and the rights of nature, yet the establishment of Popery,[8] which is a very different thing from the toleration of it, is, for very just and wise reasons, altogether incompatible with the fundamental principles of our constitution.

I will, however, wave a subject which must ever be an invidious one while there are so many of us in communion with the Roman church, and which is perhaps impertinent, because it carries with it the appearance of a remote danger, while so many nearer mischiefs demand our present and our earnest attention.

It is not the establishment of the Popish religion in Quebec, even to the exclusion of a toleration to the Protestants except by favour of the crown, and this at a time when the test, and other arbitrary acts restraining the rights of conscience, hang over the heads of our own Dissenters,[9] of which we [18] now complain. – Our present objection is not to that which the Canadians enjoy, but to that of which they are deprived. – It is not the preservation, but the violation of the Royal Word, which stands the foremost in our list of grievances.[10]

In the act for the government of the province of Quebec, my friends and fellow citizens, we read despotism in every line. – The deluded Canadians, instead of being put in possession of all the privileges and immunities of English subjects, according to his Majesty's proclamation in 1763,[11] are indeed favoured with the full possession of their religion, as long as his Majesty, who is at the head of their church, is graciously inclined to continue to them such indulgence; yet in respect both to their civil and religious rights, they are in a more abject state of slavery than when they were under the French government.

The conquests of foreign nations are dan-[19]gerous triumphs, even to the liberty of republican states; but in limited monarchies, when on the conquered are imposed laws, opposite and hostile to the limitations of power in these governments, it never fails of subjecting the conquerors to the same measure of slavery which they have imposed on the conquered.

---

[8] i.e. Catholicism.
[9] The Test and Corporation Acts were a series of English penal laws that imposed civil disabilities on Catholics and Nonconformists. They remained in place until 1828.
[10] i.e. the coronation oath to maintain Protestantism.
[11] The royal proclamation issued by George III on 7 October 1763.

Had the government of Charles the Fifth[12] been confined to the sovereignty of Spain, the Spaniards might to this day have preserved a greater degree of freedom than any other of the European nations.

It was the Canada bill, and other transactions of the government, which equally threatened your security and welfare; that engaged the city of London, and the county of Middlesex, to exact from those they elected into the representative office, an engagement, by which their members were bound to endeavour, to the utmost of their abilities, the repeal of the unconstitutional [20] laws respecting America, which passed in the last session of the last parliament. And as septennial parliaments[13] are found to be the root from whence all our political grievances spring, they were also bound to endeavour the restoration of our ancient Privileges in respect to the duration of parliaments.

Surely, my friends and fellow citizens, this is a conduct which, at such a crisis of our affairs, was laudable and necessary; and a conduct which, if all the electors of Great-Britain had followed, we should not now have been at the eve of a civil war with America; nor such an interruption given to our commerce, as threatens the immediate ruin of thousands of families.

Surely, in such a state of our affairs, no honest and enlightened man could have refused binding himself to such endeavours; and though the obeying every mandate of con-[21]stituents may, in some very extraordinary conjuncture of opinions and circumstances, be wrong, yet at a time when the representatives had affected an entire independency on, or rather an absolute sovereignty over their constituents, this might be a sufficient reason for many worthy men, as a far lesser evil, to submit to an indefinite obligation of obedience.

Power is regarded by all men as the greatest of temporal advantages. The support given to Power, therefore, is an obligation; and, consequently, the protection given by governors to subjects, a positive duty. The subject can only be bound to obedience on the considerations of public good; but the Sovereign, on these considerations, and a thousand others equally binding, is tied to the exact observance of the laws of that constitution under which he holds his power.

---

[12] Charles V (1500–58), king of Spain from 1516 to 1556, Holy Roman Emperor and archduke of Austria from 1519 to 1556, and Lord of the Netherlands as duke of Burgundy from 1506 to 1555.

[13] The Septennial Act 1716.

The assertion that 'the Americans, tho' neither adequately or inadequately repre-[22]sented, stand on this same predicament with yourselves,' is too glaring a falshood to deceive you;[14] and I shall not affront your understanding so much as to fancy you can suppose that the positive punishment of the whole town of Boston for the offence of a few individuals, when those individuals might have been prosecuted according to law, can be a case similar to the running the hazard of hurting a few citizens in the attempt of re-taking one of our own towns from the enemy.

I have hitherto endeavoured to prevent your being misled by the sophistry of those who have an interest in deceiving you. I shall now give you some of the judicious observations of one of your best friends, in regard to the conduct of your government towards America. –

'Before the taxing of the unrepresented colonies of America was thought of (says Mr. Burgh[i]) the Ministry ought to have reduced exorbitant salaries, abated or abolished excessive perquisites, annihilated useless places, stopped iniquitous pensions, with-held electioneering expences, and bribes for votes in the House, reduced an odious and devouring army, and taxed vice, luxury, gaming, and public diversions: – This would have brought into the treasury ten times more than could have ever been expected from taxing, by force and authority, the unrepresented Colonies.

Even a conquered city has time given it to raise the contributions laid upon it, and may raise it in its own way. We have treated our Colonies worse than conquered countries. Neither Wales nor Ireland are taxed unheard and unrepresented in the British Parliament, as the [24] Colonies: – Wales sends members to parliament, and Ireland has done so; and as Ireland is not now represented in the British Parliament, neither is it taxed in the British Parliament.

It is frivolous to alledge, that because the Mother Country has been at expences for the Colonies, therefore the British Parliament may tax them, without allowing them any legal opportunity of remonstrating against the oppression. The Mother Country has spent her blood and her treasure in supporting, at different times, France against Spain, and

---

[i] [James Burgh,] *Political Disquisitions* [(3 vols., London, 1774–5), II,] page 313, et seq.

[14] Ministerialist pamphlets stressed this line of argument, notably Samuel Johnson, *Taxation No Tyranny* (London, 1775).

Spain against France, Prussia against Hungary, and Hungary against Prussia, and so on without end. Does this give our Parliament a right to tax all Europe?

What difference is there between the British Parliament's taxing America, and the French Court's laying England [25] under contribution? – The French Court could but do this if they had conquered England. – Have we conquered our Colonies?'

This excellent Author shews how the Americans, if there had been a necessity for such a measure, might have been taxed by our Parliament, without violating the right of representation; but, with the Bishop of St. Asaph, who speaks on this subject in a manner which must convince every man whose prejudices are only founded in ignorance, he is of opinion, that the most beneficial way of taxing the Colonies is the obliging them to an exclusive commerce with us.[15]

To all the restrictions laid on their trade, the Americans declare they will ever readily submit; and this on the generous consideration that they are supposed to be for the benefit and advantage of the whole empire.

[26] At the same time, my friends and fellow citizens, the Americans declare, that if you will not concur with your own, and their enemies, to oppress them, – that is, if you will not concur with men whose every act of administration are so many evidences of a formed design to enslave the whole empire, they will ever esteem an union with you their glory and their happiness.

That they will be ever ready to contribute all in their power towards the welfare of the empire; and that they will consider your enemies as their enemies, and hold your interests as dear to them as their own.

They exhort you for the sake of that honour and justice for which this nation was once renowned, – they intreat you by all those ties of common interest which are inseparable to the subjects of free states, not to suffer your enemies to effect your slavery in their ruin. They set before you in the strongest Colours, [27] all those disadvantages which must attend, that large independent power the sovereigns of Great-Britain will gain by the means of taxing, in an arbitrary manner, the Americans; – and they invite you, for these cogent reasons, to join with them in every legal method to disappoint the designs of our common foes.

---

[15] Jonathan Shipley, *A Speech, Intended to Have Been Spoken on the Bill, for Altering the Charters of the Colony of Massachusetts' Bay* (London, 1774).

It is not impossible, that after having tamely suffered the government, by a yearly increase of taxes, to beggar yourselves and your posterity, you may be led away with the delusive hope, that the Ministry, when they have the power to pick the pockets of your American brethren, will have the moderation to save those of their countrymen.

If these are your thoughts, my fellow citizens, little have you studied your own natures, and the experience of all ages; which must have convinced you, that the want of power is the only limitation to the exertion [28] of human selfishness; but should you be contented to bid defiance to the warnings of common policy, – should you be contented to be slaves on the hope that the Americans will bear the greater part of the burden of your enormous taxes, – be assured, that such an alternative will never be in your power: – No; – if a civil war commences between Great-Britain and her Colonies, either the Mother Country, by one great exertion, may ruin both herself and America, or the Americans, by a lingering contest, will gain an independency; and in this case, all those advantages which you for some time have enjoyed by your Colonies, and advantages which have hitherto preserved you from a national bankruptcy, must for ever have an end; and whilst a new, a flourishing, and an extensive empire of freemen is established on the other side the Atlantic, you, with the loss of all those blessings you have received by the unrivalled state of your commerce, will be left to the bare possession of your [29] foggy islands; and this under the imperious sway of a domestic despot, or you will become the provinces of some powerful European state.

If a long succession of abused prosperity should, my friends and fellow citizens, have entirely deprived you of that virtue, the renown of which makes you even at this day respectable among all the nations of the civilized world; – if neither the principles of justice or generosity have any weight with you, let me conjure you to take into consideration the interests of your safety and preservation: – Suffer me again to remind you of the imminent danger of your situation: – Your Ministers, by attacking the rights of all America, have effected that which the malicious policy of more judicious minds would have avoided. Your colonists, convinced that their safety depends on their harmony, are now united in one strong bond of union; nor will it be in the power of a [30] Machiavel[16] to take any advantage of those feuds and jealousies which

---

[16] i.e. a power-seeking and scheming politician, after Niccolò Machiavelli's *The Prince*.

formerly subsisted among them, and which exposed their liberties to more real danger than all the fleets and armies we are able to send against them. Your Ministers also, deceived by present appearances, vainly imagine, because our rivals in Europe are encouraging us to engage beyond the possibility of a retreat, that they will reject the opportunity when it offers of putting a final end to the greatness and the glory of our empire; but if, by the imprudent measures of the government, the public expences increase, or the public income decrease to such a degree that the public revenue fail, and you be rendered unable to pay the interest of your debt, then will no longer be delayed the day and the hour of your destruction; – then will you become an easy prey to the courts of France and Spain, who, you may depend upon it, will fall upon you as soon as they see you fairly engaged in a war with your Colonists;[17] and, according [31] to what is foretold you in a late publication, that conjuncture will prove the latest and the uttermost of your prosperity, your peace, and, in all probability, of your existence, as an independent state and nation.[18]

Rouse, my countrymen! rouse from that state of guilty dissipation in which you have too long remained, and in which, if you longer continue, you are lost for ever. Rouse! and unite in one general effort; 'till, by your unanimous and repeated Addresses to the Throne, and to both Houses of Parliament, you draw the attention of every part of the government to their own interests, and to the dangerous state of the British empire.

FINIS.

---

[17] France and Spain entered the war on the side of the Americans in 1778 and 1779, respectively.
[18] See the separately dated and paginated appendix in [Matthew Robinson-Morris, Baron Rokeby,] *Considerations on the Measures Carrying on with respect to the British Colonies in North America* (2nd ed., London, 1774), esp. pp. 5–6.

6

Selections from *The History of England from the Revolution to the Present Time in a Series of Letters to a Friend* (1778)

Introduction to the Text

This work of contemporary history, written and published in Bath in 1778, was intended as the first of two volumes, but the projected second volume never appeared. This edition reproduces the only London edition published, though there was also a Dublin reprint in 1779. The book covers the period from the Glorious Revolution to the Walpole era. It was written in epistolary form, and in a more conversational style than Macaulay's previous works. She drew on Country party pamphlet literature from the early eighteenth century, including Charles Davenant's *True Picture of a Modern Whig* (1701), to lambast the Whig party after the Revolution for abandoning its principles. She was scathing about William III, whom she regarded as exhibiting despotic characteristics in both England and the Dutch Republic.

The work became controversial thanks to the positions Macaulay took on the Whigs, Tories, and Jacobites. She offered a favourable opinion of Bolingbroke's project of a coalition of parties (p. [188]), while expressing sympathy for the Jacobite Francis Atterbury, sent into exile in 1722, and admiration for the speech of Lord Wharton – who also later went into exile as a Jacobite – in his defence. Many of her opinions expressed in this work resonated with early eighteenth-century Toryism, including her suspicion of the moneyed interest and foreign entanglements, including the Electorate of Hanover. She described the Tory-Jacobite MP William Shippen as 'a man justly celebrated for his steady and inflexible opposition to all the unconstitutional and ruinous measures which had been pursued through this reign' and 'the honest and deter-mined opposer of all continental connections' (pp. [335, 341]). Macaulay partially based her account on first-hand information from Alderman George Heathcote (1700–68), who seems to have been a friend of her father. Heathcote was a Jamaica-born West India merchant and London politician, who sat in the House of Commons between 1727 and 1747. He belonged to the opposition to Walpole, and turned to Jacobitism after the fall of Walpole, when the opposition Whigs abandoned their Tory allies. Macaulay herself came close to a Jacobite statement by suggesting that '[t]he wealth of the nation had been lavished upon, and its com-merce sacrificed to the interest and the security of Hanover' (p. [359]).

Wilkes was upset about Macaulay's modern history, as he believed it smacked of Toryism, and had himself a much rosier view of the Glorious Revolution.[1] Macaulay and Wilkes's friendship, which had never been warm to start with, declined further from this time. However, Capel Lofft, a founding member of the Society for Constitutional Information – which included her brother and many of her friends – published a positive response to her work, and the *Critical Review* wrote that it displayed 'the same spirit and elevation as in her *History [of England]*'.[2]

Unsurprisingly, *History since the Revolution* was highly critical of the Court Whig administration of Robert Walpole. This was problematic since she was on good terms with his son, Horace Walpole, who was infuriated, and wrote: 'whom does she approve but herself and her idolater – that dirty disappointed hunter of a mitre, Dr Wilson, and Alderman Heathcote, a paltry worthless Jacobite, whom I remember, and her own grandfather Sawbridge'.[3] The publication of *History since the Revolution* terminated their friendship. She regretted this, but was convinced that her reflections had been 'necessary', as she wrote to a joint acquaintance.[4] Robert Walpole was not in general highly regarded in Macaulay's circle, a position which distinguished them from the Rockingham Whigs, who celebrated his legacy. Burgh, for example,

---

[1] John Wilkes, *The History of England from the Revolution to the Accession of the Brunswick Line* (London, 1768).
[2] Capel Lofft, *Observations on Mrs Macaulay's History of England; (Lately Published) from the Revolution to the Resignation of Sir Robert Walpole, in a Letter Addressed to That Lady* (London, 1778); *Critical Review*, 45 (1778), p. 134.
[3] *The Letters of Horace Walpole*, ed. Peter Cunningham (9 vols., London, 1886), VII, p. 42.
[4] Macaulay to George Simon, 28 March 1778, in *Correspondence*, p. 85.

had earlier written to Macaulay of Walpole's 'villainous excise scheme', echoing Bolingbrokean complaints.[5]

Though Macaulay praises free trade and commerce in the book, one of its notable aspects is its thoroughgoing criticism of England's financial revolution in the 1690s. Her main sources for this critique were Country Tories such as Jonathan Swift, who believed that the creation of the national debt had generated a new 'moneyed interest'. This was allegedly a new class of moneylending parasites who lived off the state, lobbied for expensive wars on the Continent, and impoverished landowners and taxpayers, who bankrolled the payments of interest through taxes. This criticism of the politics of credit came to the fore in the reign of Queen Anne. It was exemplified by Swift's *Conduct of the Allies* (1711), and continued in the age of Walpole by his friend Bolingbroke. Much of what Macaulay writes about the national debt is borrowed from Swift's posthumously published *History of the Four Last Years of the Queen* (1758). Nevertheless, the selections below focus on this dimension of her text since this aspect of the work is essential for understanding her analysis of the legacy of the Glorious Revolution, her complaints against modern politics more broadly, and why she remained such a controversial figure.

[5] Burgh to Macaulay, 17 February 1769, in *Correspondence*, p. 89.

Selections from *The History of England from the Revolution to the Present Time in a Series of Letters to a Friend* (1778)

[78] LETTER III

The National Debt,[1] my friend, and the introduction of the funds in this country, has proved a wheel of such importance in the state-machine, and has so powerful an influence over the manners and liberties of the people of Great-Britain, that it will be necessary to enter into a detail of the rise, the progress, and the nature of this diabolical engine, which has long threatened to put a final end to the prosperity of our country, before I proceed in my narrative of the government of the next reign.

Though it is not probable that any pre-existing assembly should have foreseen all the inconveniencies which have arisen [79] from the practice of borrowing and funding, or that future parliaments would run such senseless lengths in practices which, from the beginning, threatened formidable consequences; yet the borrowing money on public credit, on the reason that it would introduce a prodigality in the management of the public concerns, was a measure too ruinous even for the corrupt parliaments in Charles the Second's time to comply with.

James the Second, my friend, with all his faults, was a frugal Prince: the revenue settled by parliament on his first coming to the throne was more than sufficient to defray the expences of his government; therefore, that bold stroke of policy, which delivered up the purse and the credit of the nation into the hands of the Prince, was reserved for the immortal William, and his whig partizans.

---

[1] The Bank of England was founded in 1694.

When the Prince of Orange, says a cotemporary writer,[2] was raised to the throne, and a general war began in these parts of Europe, the King, and his counsellors, thought it would be ill policy to commence his reign with heavy taxes on the people, who had lived long in ease and plenty, and might be apt to think their deliverance too dearly bought; and money being wanted to support the war, which even the [80] convention which put the crown on his head were very unwilling he should engage in, Burnet, Bishop of Salisbury,[3] is said to have proposed the expedient, which he had learned in Holland, of raising money on the security of taxes, which were only sufficient to pay a large interest.

Burnet, my friend, was not the only person whom the Dutch school of financing had rendered proficient in the certain way of ruining the independence of the people. As I observed before, the same expedient, on the same authority, was proposed to Charles the Second; but neither the art nor the influence of that Prince could carry the fatal point, even with a very venal and corrupt parliament; but, says our author, the motives which prevailed on the people at this time to fall in with the project were many and plausible; for supposing, as the ministers industriously gave out, that the war could not last above one or two campaigns at most, it might be carried on with very moderate taxes, and the debts accruing would, in process of time, be easily cleared after a peace; then the bait of large interest would draw in a great number of those whose money, by the dangers and difficulties of trade, lay dead upon their hands; and whoever were lenders to the government would by surest principle be obliged to support it; besides, the men of estates could not be persuaded, without time and difficulty, to have those taxes laid [81] on their lands, which custom hath since made so familiar; and it was the business of such as were then in power to cultivate a monied interest, because the gentry of the kingdom did not relish those notions in government to which the King, who had imbibed his politics in his own country, was thought to give too much way.[4]

---

[2] Jonathan Swift, *The History of the Four Last Years of the Queen* (London, 1758), pp. 157–8. The entire paragraph is transcribed from Swift's posthumous and controversial work.

[3] Gilbert Burnet (1643–1715), Scottish clergyman and historian, who together with other Whigs such as Locke had spent time in exile in the Dutch Republic before the Glorious Revolution.

[4] Swift, *History of the Four Last Years of the Queen*, pp. 158–9. Once again, the entire paragraph is reproduced from Swift, almost verbatim.

When this expedient of anticipations and mortgages was first put in practice, artful men in office and credit began to consider what uses it might be applied to, and soon found it was likely to prove the most fruitful seminary, not only to establish a faction they intended to set up for their own support, but likewise to raise vast wealth for themselves in particular, who were to be the managers and directors in it.

It was manifest that nothing could promote these two designs so much, as burthening the nation with debts, and giving encouragement to lenders; for as to the first, it was not to be doubted that monied men would be always firm to the party of those who advised the borrowing upon such good security, and with such exorbitant premiums and interest; and every new sum lent took away as much power from the landed men, as it added to their's: so that the deeper the kingdom was engaged, it was still the better for them. Thus a new estate and property sprung up in the hands of mort-[82]gagees, to whom every house and foot of land in the kingdom paid a rent charge free of all taxes and defalcations, and purchased at less than half the value; so that the gentlemen of estates in effect were but tenants to these new landlords, many of whom were able in time to force the election of boroughs out of the hands of those who had been the old proprietors and inhabitants: this was arrived to such a height, that a very few years more of war and funds would have clearly cast the balance on the monied side.[5]

As to the second, this project of borrowing on funds was of mighty advantage to those who were the managers of it, as well as to their friends and dependants; for funds proving often deficient, the government was obliged to strike tallies for making up the rest, which tallies were sometimes (to speak in the merchants' phrase) at about forty per cent discount; at this price those who were in the secret bought them up, and then took care to have that deficiency supplied in the next session of parliament, by which they doubled their principle in a few months; and for the encouragement of lenders, every new project of lotteries or annuities proposed some further advantage either as to interest or premium.

The pernicious practice of borrowing upon remote funds, my friend, necessarily produced a brood of usurers, brokers, [83] and stock-jobbers, who preyed upon the vitals of their country; and from this fruitful

---

[5] Ibid., pp. 161–2.

source, venality overspread the land; corruption, which under the government of bad Princes had maintained a partial influence in the administration of public affairs, from the period of the revolution, was gradually formed into a system, and instead of being regarded with abhorrence, and severely punished, as in former times, received the countenance of the whole legislature; and every individual began openly to buy and sell his interest in his country, without either the fear of shame or penalty.[6] In addition to this national evil, all the sources of justice were so grossly polluted by the partiality of party, that every misdemeanor of a public nature escaped both censure and punishment; whig and tory reciprocally lending their assistance to the cause, to protect the individuals of their party from the just resentment of their country, and the prosecution of the adverse faction.

[. . .]

LETTER IV

[. . .]

[198] From the period of the Revolution it had been the common practice of government to run the nation in debt, that is, for the parliament to grant more money to the crown than they could raise within the year. One debt, without an entire change in the system of oeconomy, naturally produces many; the necessities of the state increasing every year, every probable measure was pursued to facilitate the loan of money, and to introduce a credit founded on paper currency, which was to make up for the deficiency of real treasure, King William's wars having drained the kingdom of the greater part of its bullion.

[199] Pursuant to this scheme, in 1693 a bank was established on the principle of a transferable fund, and a circulation by bill, on the credit of a large capital. As there are never wanting in any society individuals ready to adopt any measure, or forward any scheme which promises even a temporary self-interest, five hundred thousand pounds was immediately subscribed, as a fund of ready money to circulate one million at eight per cent, which million was to be lent to the government, and the subscribers were incorporated by the name of the Governor and

---

[6] This interpretation of British politics was central to eighteenth-century reformist politics, but was shown to be highly exaggerated in Lewis Namier, *The Structure of Politics at the Accession of George III* (London, 1929), esp. ch. 4.

Company of the Bank of England, under a proviso, that at any time after the first day of August, 1711, upon a year's notice, and the repayment of the twelve hundred thousand pounds, the said corporation should cease.

Of all human errors, the errors of government are the seldomest corrected: instead of avoiding those measures which, during William's administration, had so evidently impoverished the nation, rage for war and conquest infected our councils the greater part of Queen Anne's reign; in proportion to the increasing expences of the war, the difficulty of raising supplies yearly increased; and the Commons, instead of paying off any part of the national debt, and getting rid of a swarm of stockjobbers and tax gatherers, which preyed on the vitals of the commonwealth, this session voted an enlargement of the bank almost to three millions, and pro-[200]longed the duration of the company to one and twenty years: the terms obtained for these advantages were, four hundred thousand pounds at six per cent and the circulation of two millions four hundred thousand pounds in exchequer bills.

Whilst the interest of England was thus sacrificed to the alternate triumph of party, and the cabals of jarring factions; whilst her blood and treasure were thus draining to establish the power and grandeur of the house of Austria, and the security of the States-General, France was reduced to extremities by the success of her arms the last campaign in Flanders, which to appearance had established the influence of the Marlborough junto over the councils of England, beyond the power even of the Queen to shake, and threatened the almost total extinction of the French monarchy. The taking of Lisle [i.e. Lille] exposed France to an invasion on the side of Flanders; on the side of Dauphine, the Duke of Savoy, by making himself master of the important fortresses of Exilles, La Perouse, the valley of St. Martin, and Fenestrelles, had secured a barrier to his own frontiers, and opened a way into the French provinces. The finances of the kingdom were reduced to the lowest ebb. In imitation of the English exchequer bills, Lewis[7] had issued mint bills; but all the various methods of raising money on credit failed.

[201] Unhappily for England, the great opinion which prevailed of the certainty of parliamentary security gave her the privilege of incurring a debt beyond the power of any other kingdom. In these circumstances of his finances, Lewis was neither able to pay, to cloath, or to feed his

[7] Louis XIV, king of France in 1643–1715.

troops; and, in aggravation of a scene of such accumulated distress, a
very inclement winter had produced a kind of famine in the land.
[. . .]

LETTER V

[. . .]

[309] The presbyterians, the dissenters of all denominations, and the
greater number of moralists, have dated the decline of virtue in England
to the licentious days of Charles the Second: certain it is, that decency of
manners, regard to public liberty and national good, received an irrecov-
erable check from the loose example of a profligate court, and from the
scoffs and revilings of all those who, in a vulgar sense, were called great
in the kingdom: and it is too true, my friend, that the æra of the
Revolution, instead of introducing a more correct and regular system
of manners, only added to the profligacy then prevailing, the meaner
vices of sordid rapacity and venal corruption.

It was now generally asserted, that every man had his price: the few
instances which the times exhibited of self-denial, on the principles of
honor and patriotism, were regarded as the effects of an enthusiastic
lunacy; the electors paid no regard to their privileges, but as it enabled
them to make a lucrative gain of their votes; the elected made the [310]
best market of their purchased seats; and opposition was now carried on
without other motive than the bringing obscure men into notice, and
enhancing the price of corruption: and yet, my friend, if ever the people
of this country had reason to be in a more particular manner watchful of
their political security and their national welfare, it was undoubtedly at
this period, when they had a foreign prince on the throne;[8] a prince, who
was a stranger to the laws and constitution of Great-Britain; a prince,
who, on all the principles which govern human affection, they had
reason to expect was strongly attached to the arbitrary system of government which prevails in every German principality, and whose predilection for his native country must naturally be increased by the implicit
obedience paid by all his hereditary subjects.

---

[8] George I, or Georg Ludwig of Hanover, king of Great Britain and Ireland between 1714
and 1727.

If any virtue had remained in England, these circumstances of well-grounded distrust would have awakened the attention and the caution of the people; but indeed it was so unfortunately the reverse, that for every law of the constitution, if there are any which yet remain unviolated, we are entirely indebted to the moderation or the timidity of our governors.

After the tame submission paid through the whole empire to the act for lengthening the duration of parliaments,[9] [311] an act, which in its obvious consequences took away every useful power from the people, and changed the constitution to the very worst species of government, namely, to that of a monarchy supported by aristocracy, you will not be surprized, my friend, that on the same shallow pretence of fears and apprehensions from the Pretender and his adherents,[10] that dangerous machine, a standing army, to the amount of above sixteen thousand men, was granted to the King by parliament, though in the time of profound peace, and acquiesced in by the people: and to render it yet more inimical to the safety of the subject and the freedom of the constitution, magna charta, and all the salutary statutes which guard the lives of individuals from arbitrary judgment, without any plea or pretence from any danger or inconvenience which had arisen from legal modes of trial, were set aside in all circumstances which respected martial offences: and this body of men, who from their particular situation are naturally too much dependent on the Sovereign, exposed to the lash of an arbitrary jurisdiction, nominated a court martial in all cases of corporal punishment, even to the touching their lives. In the year 1717–18 an act passed to this purpose, in which forty-six articles of war are enumerated, and where the punishment for the several offences committed against these articles are fines, imprisonment, whipping, and death.[11]

[312] In the act which settled the crown of Great-Britain in succession on the Hanover line,[12] among several wise limitations, were the following provisoes:

> That in case the crown and imperial dignity of the realm should hereafter come to any person not being a native of the kingdom of England, the nation should not be obliged to engage in any war for the defence of any dominions or territories which do not belong to the crown of England, without the consent of parliament:

---

[9] The Septennial Act 1716.   [10] The Jacobites.   [11] The Mutiny Act 1718.
[12] The Act of Settlement 1701.

That no person who should hereafter come to the possession of the crown should hereafter go out of the dominions of England, Scotland, or Ireland, without the consent of parliament.

The salutary limitations, my friend, which are to be found in this act were, to the eternal disgrace of whiggism, repealed by the whig faction;[13] and the provisoes were so ill kept, that a large sum of English money was given to enlarge the King's foreign territories, by the purchase of Bremen and Verden, territories taken from the King of Sweden by the assistance of England, and then sold to King George by the King of Denmark.[14]

[...]

[13] They were not officially repealed, but George I used the British navy in the Great Northern War in 1715–18 in defence of Hanover, which had been invited into the anti-Swedish alliance in the war thanks to Britain's naval strength. This was clearly against the letter and spirit of the Act of Settlement 1701, and it created tension between George I and his British ministers, who tried to limit Britain's involvement in the war.

[14] John Carteret, 2nd Earl Granville (1690–1763), Britain's ambassador to Sweden and later Secretary of State, negotiated a treaty with Sweden in 1719 which recognised Hanover's claim to the German territories of Bremen and Verden.

7

Selections from *Letters on Education, with Observations on Religious and Metaphysical Subjects* (1790)

Introduction to the Text

Macaulay's treatise on education takes the polite, epistolary form, addressed to the Roman matron Hortensia, who has been dubbed a 'suitable alter ego' for Macaulay on account of her advocacy for women, her eloquence, and her attention to the education of her daughter.[1] Macaulay worked on the book for several years.[2] Central to the *Letters on Education* is the contrast between civilisation and barbarity, which allowed her to criticise several aspects of modern civilisation, including chattel slavery, the condition of women, and animal cruelty. She also condemned haughty ideas of European superiority by highlighting that other parts of the world had outshone Europe in the past. Convinced that animals were included in God's plan for a future state, she deplored Hume for excluding animals from his utilitarian theory of justice (pp. [192–3]). The situation of animals is a recurring theme in the *Letters*, and perhaps their most notable aspect, along with their treatment of women, which has striking similarities with Mary Wollstonecraft, who reviewed the book. Wollstonecraft wrote in her *Vindication of the Rights of Woman* (1792): 'Coinciding with Mrs. Macaulay relative to many branches of education, I refer to her valuable work, instead of quoting her sentiments to support my own.'[3] Moreover, before Wollstonecraft, Macaulay

---

[1] Philip Hicks, 'The Roman Matron in Britain: Female Political Influence and Republican Response, ca. 1750–1800', *Journal of Modern History*, 77 (2005), pp. 35–69, at p. 62.

[2] *Correspondence*, p. 162.

[3] Wollstonecraft, *A Vindication of the Rights of Woman* (London, 1792), p. 236.

criticised prevalent but false ideas of 'female excellence', and the idea of female beauty as weakness propagated by Burke in *A Philosophical Enquiry into the Origin of Our Ideas of the Sublime and Beautiful* (1757).

The key difference between Macaulay and Wollstonecraft concerns the question of public versus domestic education. The *Letters* present strong arguments in favour of tax-funded instruction, as education is listed among 'the most important duties of government' (p. [274]). However, like Wollstonecraft's husband William Godwin, Macaulay did not ultimately trust modern, corrupt governments to provide a good education. Public education could never 'equal that which proceeds from the attentive zeal of an enlightened parent', who would be more prepared to make the self-sacrifice 'necessary to preserve the pupil from receiving any impression which may be mischievous to his future innocence and peace' (p. [20]). Unlike Wollstonecraft, Macaulay's *Letters* thus prescribe a private home education. She further argued that since the rich and powerful had the most influence, and could do the most harm, it made sense to focus on their domestic tuition.

Macaulay singles out Fénelon and Rousseau as the masters in the genre of educational treatises, but she also draws extensively on and frequently cites Locke. Like Locke, she finds corporal punishment ineffective, and like Rousseau, she writes that children should be allowed to develop natural strength rather than being swaddled. Despite her admiration for many aspects of Rousseau's *Émile*, she disagreed with his views on the differences between the sexes. The idea of innate mental differences between men and women was prejudiced, and moral excellence was the same for both. As creatures of God, men and women are endowed with the same capacities, and are obligated to cultivate them so as to live as God and virtue demand. Macaulay also made a forceful case for the co-education of boys and girls, which she was convinced would benefit everyone, as it would create better mothers for boys and girls. Moreover, friendship between brothers and sisters would nurture benevolent dispositions.

Macaulay's curriculum throws light on what she considered to be valuable literature, and thus on her own intellectual formation, although it does not exclude authors with whom she disagreed. In history, she recommended ancient Greco-Roman historians such as Plutarch, Livy and Tacitus along with modern ones, including Charles Rollin, Edward Gibbon and Adam Ferguson. She further proposed reading Epictetus, Cicero and Seneca in Latin; Shakespeare, Milton, Harrington, Hobbes,

Sidney, Locke, Addison, Steele, Pope, Johnson, James Harris, Lord Monboddo, Abraham Tucker and John Horne Tooke in English; and Boileau, Corneille, Racine, Molière and Voltaire in French. All these authors were to be read at different ages and for different purposes. She excluded novels from her curriculum, and the study of the Bible was saved for last, at the age of twenty-one, since she was concerned that reading it too early could lead to infidelity or fanaticism. Her purpose was 'to make a true Christian, that is, a Christian on conviction' (p. [137]).

The third part of the *Letters on Education*, not reproduced in this edition, is a revised version of *A Treatise on the Immutability of Moral Truth* (1783). As Karen Green has argued, the major difference between the original formulation of her philosophy in the *Treatise* (1783) and the *Letters on Education* is that the later work places more emphasis on sympathy as a key principle for binding human beings together.[4] As Macaulay put it in a letter to the *Monthly Review*, 'the quality of sympathy is the basis of all human virtue'.[5] This can be seen as a concession to the moral philosophy of Hume, for whom sympathy was a central philosophical concept, although her most important predecessor on this subject was Hume's friend Adam Smith, author of *The Theory of Moral Sentiments* (1759). There is no direct evidence that Macaulay had studied Smith, but it is likely that she did so considering how widely read she was in modern authors.

There has not been space to reproduce this remarkable work in its entirety; the present edition includes sections from the first and the second parts, in which she lays out her general views on education, religion, women, animals, ancient and modern civilisations, crime and punishment, hospitals and the maintenance of the poor, and the principle of sympathy and its political implications. The text is based on the original edition of *Letters on Education*, published in London in 1790 (there is also a Dublin edition from the same year).

---

[4] Karen Green, *Catharine Macaulay's Republican Enlightenment* (New York, 2020), pp. 153, 183.

[5] *Correspondence*, p. 292.

Selections from *Letters on Education, with Observations on Religious and Metaphysical Subjects* (1790)

[I] PREFACE

Of all the arts of life, that of giving useful instruction to the human mind, and of rendering it the master of its affections, is the most important. Several very distinguished persons in the rank of literature have acknowledged this truth, by exerting the power of genius in forming rules of discipline for taming the untractable mind of man, and bringing it into a proper subjection to the dictates of virtue. Indeed we have learned as much from our ancestors on this subject, as mere practical experience could suggest. But it is to the modern metaphysicians we owe those lights into the operations of the mind, which can alone afford us a reasonable prospect of success.

For without an adequate knowledge of the power of association, by which a single impression calls up a host of ideas, which arising in imperceptible succession, form a [ii] close and almost inseparable combination, it will be impracticable for a tutor to fashion the mind of his pupil according to any particular idea he may frame of excellence.[1] Nor can his instructions be adequate to any such management of the mental faculties as shall invariably produce volitions agreeable to the laws of virtue and prudence.

If the partizans of liberty and necessity would lay aside their subtle investigations,[2] which can never tend to real improvement, and would

---

[1] This philosophical empiricism was indebted to Locke's *Essay Concerning Human Understanding* (1689).

[2] Macaulay refers to the debate about whether the will is determined or free, which she addressed in *A Treatise on the Immutability of Moral Truth* (1783) and in the third part of *Letters on Education*. She positioned herself between extreme libertarianism and determinism, and shared Locke's position that human beings are free insofar as they follow rational principles. See Karen Green and Shannon Weekes, 'Catharine Macaulay on the Will', *History of European Ideas*, 39 (2013), pp. 409–25.

unite in acknowledging the power of those principles which govern the mind, we might then hope to see the education of youth assigned to men, whose learning, knowledge, and talents, place them at the head of the republic of letters. The culture of that artificial being, a social man, is in its nature so complex, there are so many evils to be avoided, so many important ends to be pursued; there is such a delicate machine to work upon, and so much to be apprehended from external causes, that the invention of the learned may be employed for ages, before such a system of education can be framed as will admit of no improvement.

[iii] Every work published on education that affords one new idea which may be found useful in practice, is worthy the attention of the public. Nor does the author of these letters aspire to any other merit than that of offering a few new hints on the subject, and throwing some illustration on those which have been already given. If the novelty of these should be made an objection to the work, let it be remembered that every thing new is alarming to the ignorant and the prejudiced; and that morals taught on immutable principles must carry a very different appearance from those founded on the discordant sentiments of selfish man.

A full persuasion of the equity and goodness of God, with a view to the purity and benevolence for which the precepts of our religion are so eminently distinguished, has been the author's sole guide in forming her instructions: on the full conviction, first, that it is on these attributes of the Deity we can alone build any such consistent system of morals as will render man generally innoxious and useful; or that will force con-[iv]viction on the repugnant mind. Secondly, that the precepts of the gospel are founded on the true interests of man, and have an equal respect to his temporal, and spiritual happiness.

In endeavouring to establish an opinion of the perfect equity and goodness of God, some censure must fall on those principles of religion, and those modes of faith, which represent him as partial in the distribution of reward and punishment.[3] But as the author has never gone out of her way to attack the religious opinions of others, nor has made use

---

[3] This seems to refer especially to Calvinist views on soteriology and predestination, which hold that God had elected those whom he will bring to heaven before the creation of the world. The main version of Calvinism in the British Isles is Presbyterianism, the national church of Scotland. A tenet of the kind of rational religion espoused by Macaulay – which was famously articulated by Locke's *Reasonableness of Christianity* (1695) – was that everyone can achieve salvation.

of any harsh expressions in her animadversions, she has a right to expect the same mildness and candour from those who may differ from her.

She is aware that the introducing sensible impressions in divine worship, with a view to induce religious sentiment, and raise the mind to the contemplation of Deity, has been productive of the greatest abuses in religion. But let it be remembered, that in a speculative theory of education, in which those principles are to be considered which have an uniform tendency to sublime, refine, [v] and soften the mind; the influence of such impressions could not be passed over. Their being adopted, and brought into practical use, must be left to the judgment of others, and that favorable period of time, when knowledge shall be too generally diffused through society, to give grounds for any such apprehension as the revival of a gross idolatry; and when the great and the luxurious, tired of their present modes of dissipation, may be willing to appropriate some of the ornamental arts to the service of religion.

Cavillers may raise objections to the author's rules of education on the following grounds. – That the plan can alone be carried into general practice by the opulent; and that the needy, and those of moderate fortune, are by their circumstances precluded from attempting it. To these objections the answer is plain and fair. – That it is men of opulence alone who can reap the choicest fruits of the industry and ingenuity of their species – That the education of the great, were it properly attended to, and pursued on the best rules, would be felt in the improved virtue of all the subordinate [vi] classes of citizens – That there would be no end of framing rules of education for all the different ranks and situations of men – And that general systems have only to do with general principles, which are to be carried into practice as far as private judgment and the particularities of situation may direct.

Having thus endeavoured to remove the principal objections which may be made to a work that has some small claim to original thinking, the author thinks it incumbent upon her to give to the public those reasons which induced her to reprint, in a new publication, what has already been given in another form.[4] First, the principles and rules of education now laid before the public, are founded on the metaphysical

---

[4] The third part of the *Letters on Education*, not reproduced in this edition, is a revised version of *A Treatise on the Immutability of Moral Truth*.

observations contained therein. Secondly, the candid criticism on these observations, by the critical and monthly reviewers,[5] gave her room to hope, that if some of the most important faults were corrected, they would be found worth the notice of all those who were deep thinkers enough to receive any pleasure from metaphysical disquisition. Thirdly, and lastly, the circumstance which [vii] corroborated the strength of these encouragements, was a letter, written without any intention of being published, which appeared in the Gentleman's Magazine for September 1789. It was found among the papers of a gentleman of uncommon celebrity in the literary world,[6] with whom she never had the happiness of being acquainted. A quotation from this letter respecting her immutability, will be seen in the note below.[i] She thinks the unbiassed judgment of Mr. Badcock a sufficient authority [viii] for reprinting the most important parts of the matter in another form: and shall only add, that she has endeavoured to correct the faults which he has candidly pointed out, as well as her abilities would admit.

[1] PART I

Introductory Letter

So you approve, Hortensia, of what I have advanced in favour of the future existence of brute animals; but you think that this novel doctrine

---

[i] 'I have at last seen Mrs. Macaulay Graham's metaphysical performance. Her work is really wonderful considering her sex; and in this I pay no ill compliment I hope to the ladies; for surely they themselves will generally acknowledge that their talents are not adapted to abstract speculations.'

'On a second perusal of Mrs. Macaulay Graham's book, I saw more, much more in it, than I did at the first hasty glance I took at it. I have read it through with attention, and was well repaid by the entertainment and satisfaction it afforded me. She is not only a bold and fervid writer, but a shrewd and acute reasoner. The language in some places is very animated, and flows in a strain of Ciceronian fullness.' – Original letters of Mr. Badcock, published in the *Gentleman's Magazine* for September, 1789.

[5] Macaulay refers to the *Critical Review* and the *Monthly Review*. Other journals had been less kind, however, including the *British Magazine and Review* and the *European Magazine and London Review*.

[6] Samuel Badcock (1747–88), Nonconformist minister and theologian, and a contributor to *Theological Repository* (1769–71), edited by Priestley.

supposes their lot to be better than that of the favoured creature, man; for instinct in them is sufficiently strong to prevent their falling into any evil which is not brought on them by external force, whilst reason is so impotent in man, as to render him the author of his own misery.

This acknowledgment in favor of the inferior part of the animal creation, so mortifying to the fond prejudices and pride of our species is [2] exceedingly flattering to me, because I believe, that I was the first person who led your atten[tion] to the sublimest of all speculations, viz. the agreement of God's providential government with our ideas of his infinite benevolence. Yes, I own with [CM *err.*: to] you, that it raises in me a mixed sentiment of contempt and anger, to hear the vain and contradictory creature, man, addressing the deity, as the god of all perfection, yet dealing out a severe and short mortality to the various tribes of his fellow animals, and assigning to himself an eternity of happiness, beyond even the reach of his imagination. What was man, before he was called into existence, but the dust of the earth? Can the meanest insect be less, and if man and brute were upon an equal footing before the almighty *fiat* went forth, what motive, worthy of divine wisdom, could influence the deity to draw the line of separation thus wide between his creatures?

The uniform voice of revelation every where proclaims God the universal parent of the creation. By this appellation, Hortensia, I would describe a relation more tender than what we commonly annex to our ideas of the author of nature. Almost every sect of Christians, in order to spur on the lazy virtue of their votaries, have represented the rigorous justice of God, in a light which confines his benevolence to a narrow sphere of action; and whilst he is represented as devoting to an eter-[3]nity of torments the far greater number of the human race, the gates of paradise are barred to all but the elect.[7] Tremendous thought! It is thus indeed that the gift of eternal life is a dangerous preeminence, and the balance becomes more than equal between us and the brute creation.

These are the melancholy visions of, perhaps, the greater part of the religious world, whilst to the eye of the modern philosopher, God is infinite only in his natural attributes; and because they [CM *err.*: he] cannot find a more satisfactory reason for the introduction of moral and natural evil, they limit [CM *err.*: he limits] the power and the benevo-lence of God, to a size which exactly squares with all the objects of sense.

---

[7] See note 3, above.

The philosopher contemplates the monster Nature, who is continually devouring and regorging itself, with rapture and delight. He views with a complacent sentiment, myriads of beings brought forth to animated and feeling life, merely to serve for the support of creatures, who in their turn must pay to the stern law of Nature, a tribute equally painful. If you will believe the philosopher, he contemplates the formidable strength of the lion, endued with powers destructive to every tribe of the terrestrial race, with pleasure; and whilst he is protected by circumstances from the devouring rage of this animal's hunger, the reflecting on his irresistible power, enlarges his ideas of the excellence of its maker.

[4] Such sentiments as these, Hortensia, you will find thickly sown through all the writings of the philosophers, both ancient and modern; for the ancients who were not assisted by gospel revelation, followed the simple course of metaphysical reasoning, and till the time of Socrates excluded every idea of morals out of their philosophy. Hence, though they allowed that there was in all animal beings an immaterial principle, yet they subjected this principle to an eternal round of degrading and afflicting unions with the forms of terrestrial existence. It was only the recompence of the virtuous to be again absorbed into the divine nature; and thus, by the loss of identity, the reward of the good man was a mere negative boon. The sound understanding and the benign mind of Socrates, rejected a system so degrading to the deity; he deeply considered the nature of moral virtue, and conceived it not only to be of divine origin, but worthy to be regarded as a part of the divine essence.[8]

The ray of hope which this view of the subject opened to the virtuous, became generally extensive in its influence, when it was confirmed by the Christian revelation; but the love of novelty, with the abuses of religion, have in these days recalled those errors which darkened the ages of the pagan world. It is in vain that the infidel endeavours to impose on our credulity, by a pretended admi-[5]ration of the most uncouth appearances in nature. No, we must either totally subdue in our mind its strongest and most natural desires, with that benign affection which chiefly dignifies the nature of man; or we must start with horror from the view of those deformities, which a wise Providence has thought proper to spread over the face of his works.

---

[8] This was not an unusual interpretation of Socrates in the eighteenth century; see, e.g., William Warburton, *The Principles of Natural and Revealed Religion Occasionally Opened and Explained* (London, 1753), p. 112.

Yes, Hortensia; I will not scruple to call the phenomenon of evil a deformity, as received in the doctrines of the infidel; but when we view it with the eye of a rational faith, when we consider it as a necessary prelude to future blessings, its ugliness changes into the properties of beauty, order, and harmony.

Bitterly should I regret a curiosity which had engaged me to outstep the limits of female education, and pry into the deepest recesses of science, was this more liberal view of things necessarily followed with a different idea of the character of the deity, than as he is represented in the books of our faith. Here, instead of that cold inexorable being, whose very perfections destroy the hope of the worshipper, we address a deity whose power is only equalled by his benevolence. A deity whom we are told regards us with the tenderness of an earthly parent, and who will not suffer one sparrow to fall to the ground without his notice.

This declaration must mean something more than the bare philosophical idea of the omnipre-[6]sence of the deity. For my part, I have always considered it as greatly in favour of the opinion, which the liberal and candid mind is apt to form on the fate of the brute creation, and have often wondered that the clergy have not from the authority of this text, laid more force on the necessity of extending our benevolence to the dumb animals, and that they have not in particular more strongly and more repeatedly reprobated every species of cruelty towards them, as opposite to the dictates both of natural and revealed religion. Especially as the presumptive proofs which can be collected from the reason of things, will lose their force, if not built on the perfect benevolence of God; an attribute which, when modified in human conception, answers to the purest ideas we can frame of beneficence, equity, and justice. I should have small hopes could I once suppose him so partially benevolent, as to make the final happiness of one part of the creation his care, whilst he sacrificed the rest to the devouring jaws of death, and to the rage of those relentless monsters, who, Proteus[9] like, assume an endless variety of forms to plague, to torture and destroy myriads of living beings, who, could they enjoy their existence in peace and security, would grace as well as beautify the face of Nature.

---

[9] A sea god in Greek mythology.

Don't be afraid, Hortensia, your friend is not going to take any poetic flight; excuse this one [7] figure made in order to avoid a tedious repetition; and I shall leave, as I have hitherto done, the regions of fancy to those favored mortals whom the more tuneful of the nine inspire.[10] Grave Urania[11] commonly delivers herself in humble prose; and if she deign but to patronize and favor my attempts, I will not envy the laurels which adorn the brows of our most illustrious bards.

But I think I hear you say, 'Whither are you going so fast; you have indeed said a good many things very well. But what have you done more than throw a few illustrations on a position, which I have acknowledged in the very letter to which this is an answer; what is all this to the solution of my difficulty, or rather, does not a correct idea of the equity of the deity give it greater weight? If the benevolence of God equally extends to all his creatures, why is instinct sufficiently strong in the brute to prevent his falling into any evil which is not brought upon him by external force; and why is reason so impotent in man as to render him almost on every occasion the author of his own misery?'

Be not in such a hurry my friend; you must indulge me a little while in the most delightful of all contemplations. I own to you that, hurried along with the train of ideas which this subject presents I had almost forgot your difficulty, which however I think does not gain force from the correctest [8] idea we can form of the equity of our maker. But in order to give the fullest satisfaction to your doubts, I must endeavour to explain in as comprehensive a manner as I am able, the ideas I have formed of infinite benevolence, and perfect equity. First, it is certainly inconsistent with these attributes to create any feeling being, without the intention and the power of conferring happiness; by which is meant the secure and uninterrupted enjoyment of those satisfactions which are naturally annexed to the boon of life. Had the powers of God been so limited as to render it impossible for him to have given life to that varied multitude of beings which exists [CM *err.*: exist] on this terrestrial globe, without its being attended with terror, endured with pain, and often ended with torture; the fatal gift would have been withheld, unless the short lived evil was a prelude to some ultimate good. It is perhaps the nature of all finite beings to know things only by comparison, and this

---

[10] The nine muses of Greek mythology.

[11] The muse of astronomy in Greek mythology, and later the muse of Christian poetry. Notably, Urania is the muse in book seven of Milton's *Paradise Lost*.

knowledge is well purchased, even with the expence of pain. It is on this reasoning, that I ground my opinion of the future state of brutes. Nor does this opinion limit within precise rules the divine will. For it is not necessary that infinite benevolence should confine itself to the bestowing only one mode of happiness, or that all the creatures of God should be equal in every kind of excellence. That there is a chain of subordination which gradually descends from [9] the highest possible excellence which can be enjoyed by a finite being, down to the lowest form of animated life, we have great cause to believe. It may be the intention of the deity to support, though with some variation, such a chain of subordination through the endless course of eternity; but this does not preclude the idea that a great share of happiness will be enjoyed, even by the lowest beings in the chain; for if their faculties for enjoyment are more confined in their number, their energy may be enlarged. I know it is natural to the pride and prejudices of man, to look down with contempt on the scanty portion of enjoyment which he supposes is the lot of his fellow animals; but a stricter attention to the nature of brutes than is given by the thoughtless to the varied works of creation, have convinced me, that the happiness of all the brute tribe, when unmolested by external evil, is very considerable; and that a dog who is well fed, and protected from insult and injury, is almost always happier than his master.

It must be acknowledged then, that the gift of reason and the powers of imagination have indeed made a fatal havoc on human happiness.[12] But these gifts are absolutely necessary to support man's state of pre-eminence on this globe, and to fit him for an exalted station in a future life. It is true, that from the creation, men have generally exercised their powers in such a manner as to occasion much [10] misery in this world to the far greater number of the species, and to cloud their hopes in futurity; but this phenomenon does not prove that reason and the enlarged powers of imagination will finally and absolutely produce more misery than good to any being who has possessed them. It is far from a necessary consequence, that these gifts should ever produce evil; and when misery attends them, it always proceeds from incidental causes. The human faculties rise, by practice and education, from mere capacity to an excellence and an energy which enables man to become the carver of his own happiness. It is the capital and distinguishing characteristic of our species, says lord Monboddo, that we can make ourselves as it were

---

[12] This is a central theme in Rousseau's *Discourse on Inequality* (1755).

over again, so that the original nature is so little obvious, that it is with great difficulty we can distinguish it from the acquired.[13]

The attention I have given to my own character, Hortensia, and to the means by which it has been formed, obliges me to subscribe, without reserve, to this opinion of the Scottish sage, viz. that man, in a state of society, is as artificial a being as his representation on the canvass of the painter. Nature indeed supplies the raw materials, and the capacity of the workman; but the effect is the mere production of art. I have often smiled, when I have heard persons talk of their natural propensities; for I am convinced, that these have under-[11]gone so great a change by domestic education, and the converse of the world, that their primitive modes are not in many beings even discernible. No; there is not a virtue or a vice that belongs to humanity, which we do not make ourselves; and if their qualities should be hostile to our happiness, we may ascribe their malignancy to human agency. There is not a wretch who ends his miserable being on a wheel, as the forfeit of his offences against society, who may not throw the whole blame of his misdemeanors on his education; who may not look up to the very government, by whose severe laws he is made to suffer, as the author of his misfortunes; and who may not with justice utter the hardest imprecations on those to whom the charge of his youth was entrusted, and to those with whom he associated in the early periods of his life. The very maniac, who languishes out his miserable existence in the phrenzy of distraction, and that more unfortunate madman, who retains a sufficient semblance of reason to colour his misfortune with the deformity of turpitude, might have found a cure, or a softening remedy to their maladies, from the sources of philosophy, had its balsam been administered before the passions had taken root in the mind.

To abate the pride of the lofty minded, let it be remembered, that our talents, our accomplishments, and our virtues, are chiefly owing to the care and [12] the wisdom of others; for when they are gained by the price of our own exertions, it is almost always at the expence of our innocence and our peace.

If this is the case, and that it certainly is so, the history of man sufficiently proves, why, though the magistrate should neglect his charge, does the parent consign to misery, the wretched offspring of whose fate he is entirely the master? Why does he not rear the moral

---

[13] James Burnett, Lord Monboddo, *Of the Origin and Progress of Language* (6 vols., Edinburgh, 1773–92), I, p. 25.

plant, committed to his care, to a vigorous maturity? and thus, by the powers of sympathy, partake of the good he bestows, and lay up a treasure in filial piety and virtue for the necessary wants of age.

It is a barbarous ignorance which has hitherto defrauded man of the means which he enjoys from his reasoning powers, to secure his happiness in the present and future state.

The ancients, to their honour be it spoken, had a much more anxious care for the morals of their offspring, than the moderns, and were consequently more elaborate in their plan of education. I have often read with pleasure, in the letters of the great men of Rome, at the time when the republic had almost touched the height of its depravity, the strongest sentiments of parental tenderness, and the most anxious care for the educational improvement of their children. In the dialogues of Plato, we may find, that no [13] expence was spared by the Athenians to bestow the benefits of learning on their sons;[14] and even the Europeans, after the revival of letters, made the education of their children the object of their most important concern. The slow progress of philosophical knowledge, retarded by foreign and domestic broils, by the continual wars which nation waged against nation, and family against family, the errors of paganism, and the superstitions which in general fastened on christianity, rendered it impossible that education in those times should be sufficiently correct to effect its best purposes.

But in these enlightened days, when we have gained some useful insights into the wondrous fabrick of the human mind, much might be done in the way of education towards the happiness of nations and individuals; but, good God! what use are we making of our advances in knowledge? a senseless course of dissipation, and an unwearied exertion to procure the means of luxury, diverts our attention from the objects of our true felicity, and renders us callous to the woes of others. We are always looking over the point within our reach, and attempting to lay hold of good, where it is impossible to be found. Generation still continues to impel generation to those abysses of misery which error prepares for her votaries.

Oh magistrates! Oh legislators! admit of some [14] variation in your views of interest; consider, that in attempting to teach others, you may gain truths of the utmost importance to yourselves. Consider what will be the solid satisfaction, which a benign temper must feel, in becoming

---

[14] *Dialogues of Plato*, trans. Floyer Sydenham (3 vols., London, 1767–79), *passim.*

the instrument of the present and future welfare of numberless beings. And you, parents, remember, that the misery or bliss of your posterity, in a great measure depends upon yourselves, and that an inattention to your duty, may draw on your head the guilt of many generations.

[15] [PART I] LETTER II

The Question of Public and Private Education considered.

The instruction of youth, Hortensia, was regarded by the ancients as an important part of the business of government, and many uniform plans of education have been given by Plato and other speculatists, for the forming the children of a state in such a manner as should best conduce to render them serviceable to its glory and prosperity.[15] To those who sacrifice the natural and feeling being, man, to a factitious and unfeeling being of their own creating; to those who regard him as the slave to the country which gave him birth, and would mould him to the fashion which is supposed best to suit its interests; to such legislators who would form man for the use of government, and not government for the use of man, the speculations of Plato and other moralists on this subject, must appear in a very advantageous light. For what can more conduce to the prosperity and permanent power of government, than to form in the earliest infancy the prejudices of its subject. Social man, as I have already observed, is a mere [16] artificial being, and when you have the power of moulding him, it is your own fault if his fashion does not suit your purposes. Why, says the legislator, give up to the caprice, and the ignorance of individuals an object of such importance? Why take out of the hands of the political father, that means of instruction by which the understanding of the people may be enlightened, and their morals preserved? And why subject the one to the tyrannical act of inflicting punishment for offences which, had he performed his duty, might have been avoided; and the other from falling continually a victim to his wants and his ignorance?

These arguments are so plausible, that in the present wretched state of domestic education, I have often thought them unanswerable. Yes; when

---

[15] Plato outlined his curriculum in *The Republic*.

I have beheld the small attention of the opulent to this first of social duties; when I have beheld a multitude of little wretches consigned to the care of penury and wickedness, and educated for the purposes of destruction; I own to you that I have turned my thoughts from the disgusting contemplation, and have endeavoured to amuse myself with speculative systems of public education. Yes, I have traced over, and with encreasing satisfaction, these airy works of the imagination. Here I have beheld with all that pleasure which benignity feels in viewing [17] objects of general utility and happiness, public nurseries for infants of all ranks, where a perfect equality was preserved in all the regulations which affect the health and well being of the race, than leaving these important cares to the nurses, and the physicians appointed by government to the office. I have shifted the scene, and pursued the various public institutions through all the progress of moral education, till I have produced multitudes of finished citizens fitted for those various occupations which are necessary to support the glory and the prosperity of society; all properly sorted, according to the allotments which best suit the rank or the genius of the subjects. These delightful reveries, however, did not so far intoxicate me, as to make me entirely pass over the difficulties which hang on my system.

No; I turned the other side of the telescope, and was frightened with the view of the enormous sums which it would annually take to support these useful institutions: but I was comforted with the recollection, that if the rules of oeconomy are preserved, numbers may be more easily provided for in the aggregate, than when they are separated into particulars; and therefore it would be lighter on the pockets of the people to pay a tax to government for the education of their offspring, than to take that charge on themselves, especially as such a tax might be regulated according to the [18] rank, the fortune, and consequently the expectations of the citizens. I will not expatiate here on all those various crimes which a public education if well planned, would prevent, nor on those enlargements of moral good, which it would effect. The subject is a fruitful one, and I could extend it to the size of a long letter, were I to explain to you the political advantages which might accrue from a wisely conceived, and a well administered plan of this kind, with the advancement which it must necessarily occasion in public and private happiness. But now I perceive a very formidable antagonist, who with a fierce and indignant aspect upbraids me with having deserted the cause of freedom, and of forging chains for the use of despotism.

He claims as his natural and unalienable right, the unmolested exercise of parental authority in the bringing up and tutoring his offspring; and he says, he shall regard himself as materially injured in this right, if he does not use his pleasure in the making his child either a Turk, an Infidel, or a Christian; a rogue, or an honest man, as best suits his views and purposes.

It is true, Hortensia, that I have put the claim of my adversary in a very disadvantageous light; but though there is a great deal to be said on both sides the question, I protest to you, that I never did hear any forcible argument urged against the [19] expediency of vesting government with the charge of education; for it is absurd to oppose natural rights to any scheme of policy which would probably tend to encrease the happiness of society, and the only political argument which we can admit on the subject, is that corrupt and narrow spirit which pervades all governments, which renders it [CM *err.*: them] faithless to every trust, and which consequently destroys every reasonable ground of confidence.

Yes, Hortensia, I do not know one European government who could be safely trusted with the care of education, nor that society, who would not by such a trust, endanger the eternal loss of their dearest rights; for what fetters can bind so strongly, or so fatally, as those which are fastened on the mind? but there are other reasons less obvious, yet as forcible, for the not taking the education of youth out of those hands to which it is at present entrusted.

First, if government were inclined to do their duty, they might, by the influence of wise laws, and a correspondent example, in a great measure obviate the evils which have in all ages arisen from the inattention, the ignorance, and the vices of parents: and should the ill-tutored youth have acquired, in the course of his domestic education, ill principles and habits, the converse of the world would meliorate his prejudices, would soften the inveteracy of his habits, and perhaps, in time, [20] would effect a total change in his opinions and sentiments.

2dly, A public education may be formed on the very best plan; may be conducted by the wisest rules; and yet, in many points, it may fall short of what may be effected by domestic instruction. The one cannot, in the nature of things, be so elaborate as the other; beside, what tutorage can equal that which proceeds from the attentive zeal of an enlightened parent? what affection less warm and intense will prescribe and follow such rules of self denial, as is necessary to preserve the pupil from receiving any impression which may be mischievous to his future innocence and peace? When the object is viewed in this light, it would be folly to give up the privilege of forming our offspring according to the brightest model of virtue which our imagination can conceive. Indeed, so forcible and so important appears in my eyes this last urged reason, for the preference of domestic education, that to those opulent idlers, who have neither the capacity nor the inclination to fulfil in their own persons, this most important of the parental duties, and who consign their children over to the care of school masters, I would recommend to them to be very liberal of their treasures to those enlightened persons who are every way qualified for the education of youth, and to insist on the limiting their pupils to a small number; for though the languages [21] may be very-well taught in large schools, yet the morals must necessarily be totally neglected.

I have in my former letter observed, that the ancients were more elaborate, and more correct in the education of their youth, than the moderns; but few treatises have been handed down to us on this important subject. The works of the stoics, are general principles of action, and rules of conduct; but they do not enter into the minutiae of things, nor give any precepts on the manner of forming the young mind, and rendering its powers ductile to the task of conforming to these rules.[16] I know indeed of no authors of repute who have touched on the subject, but Plutarch and Xenophon;[17] and generation succeeded generation, without adding one thought in the way of improvement to the ideas of these sages.

At length Fenelon took the pen in hand.[18] The penetration of this great man was only equalled by his genius. The human mind, which had puzzled every other examiner by the variety of its powers, did not entirely escape his search. His discoveries have been eminently useful to succeeding writers. Even in this day, the tutor of a prince would not be deficient in the duties of his high office, did he properly apply the rules for education which are to be found in the charming poem of Telemachus. His other work on education, though a little burthened with the [22] errors of superstition, is replete with judicious

---

[16] Macaulay refers to works such as Epictetus' *Discourses* and Marcus Aurelius' *Meditations*. She devotes several chapters to Stoic philosophy in Part III of the *Letters on Education*, not reproduced in this edition.

[17] i.e. Plutarch's *Parallel Lives* and Xenophon's *Cyropaedia*.

[18] François de Salignac de la Mothe-Fénelon (1651–1715), especially known for *The Adventures of Telemachus* (1699), and archbishop of Cambrai.

observations;[19] and without intending to diminish the merits of those excellent genius's[ii] who have illustrated the thoughts of Cambray, he has left them little more to do, than to amplify his hints to render them conspicuous to the vulgar reader, and to methodize them into practical use.

But to what a length has my ideas on one subject or another carried me? I intended that this letter should contain some general hints on the medical and moral education of infants. But I find that I have already exceeded the reasonable length of a letter; I will confine my next to this subject, and to this subject only.

[38] [PART I] LETTER IV

On the use of Animal Food – Sugar – Hardy Habits best acquired in Infancy – Great Attention unfavourable to the tender Organs of Children – Instruction to be communicated more as an Amusement than a Task – Amusement and Instruction of Boys and Gils to be the same.

When I recommended the use of gravy for sucking infants, Hortensia, it was merely on the notion of its being the best corrector of the acidities of human milk, and not with the view of bringing them up to be devourers of animal substances. No – the cruel necessity which our wants impose on us, to inflict that fate on other beings which would be terrible to ourselves, is an evil of sufficient weight, were the use of animal diet concerned within as moderate limits as the present state of things will admit. I can from my own experience affirm with Rousseau, that the taste of flesh is not natural to the human palate, when not vitiated by carnivorous habits.[20] Milk, fruit, eggs, and almost every kind of vegetable ailment, ought to be the principal part of the nourishment of children.

[39] I would not feed them with flesh above three times a week, and that well roasted and boiled. The swallowing blood almost in its natural state, fills a delicate mind with horror. It is a diet only fit for savages; and

---

[ii] [Jean-Jacques] Rousseau, [Caroline-Stéphanie-Félicité, Madame de] Genlis. [Genlis was the author of *Theatre of Education* (4 vols., 1779–80) and *Adelaide and Theodore; or, Letters on Education: Containing All the Principles relative to Three Different Plans of Education; to That of Princes, and to Those of Young Persons of Both Sexes* (3 vols., 1782).]

[19] In 1681 Fénelon published *Traité de l'éducation des filles*, published in English as *The Education of Young Gentlewomen* in 1699, and as *Instructions for the Education of a Daughter* in 1707.

[20] Rousseau, *Emilius and Sophia: Or, a New System of Education* (4 vols., London, 1762–3), I, p. 286.

must naturally tend to weaken that sympathy which Nature has given to man, as the best guard against the abuse of the extensive power with which she has entrusted him.

It is I believe generally agreed by all the medical profession, that the flesh of well grown animals, is easier of digestion than the flesh of young ones; and as it affords a more generous nourishment, a smaller quantity of the one will answer the same purposes as a larger quantity of the other. It will then be proper for the tutor to take especial care that the flesh of young animals be banished from the table of his pupils. Their constitution will receive advantage from it; and the taste they will thus acquire be more agreeable to the principles of benevolence, in forbearing to destroy life almost in the first moments of existence.

Sugar, from its acid qualities, and the oppression which any large quantity of it gives to a stomach not used by continual habit to his aliment, has lately been very generally banished out of the diet of children. Sugar plumbs, sweet cakes, and other enticing viands of the same kind with which we used to engage the affections of the little gluttons, are now prohibited, as injurious ways of [40] carrying our points with them; and a variety of other means are fallen upon to engage the infantine imagination. But though I am entirely of Mr. Locke's opinion, that we ought not to inflame the natural propensity of children to gluttony, into a habitual vice, by pleasing their palates as a reward to their obedience;[21] yet I am far from thinking that sugar should be entirely left out of the diet of children. Sugar has very valuable medical properties. It is antiputrescent in a high degree, and will agree with all stomachs when they are used to it. It has sufficient warmth to correct the coldness of raw fruit, and it has a sufficient stimulating quality to make up for the use of fermented liquors, which never ought to be given to children; besides, every taste is so general as the love which children have to sweet viands, should be attended to as the dictate of Nature for some useful end.

Let them be fed then once a day with fruit of some kind, dressed with sugar only; let care be taken that they eat a good deal of bread with this meal, and that their mouths are well washed after it with cold water; and thus the taste will be gratified, and every mischief avoided which can reasonably be expected from such an indulgence.

---

[21] Locke, *Some Thoughts concerning Education* (London, 1693), p. 51.

I cannot leave this subject, Hortensia, without making some remarks on a very capital neglect in the education of our ancestors in respect to the preservation of one of the most useful, as well as [41] ornamental of Nature's gifts. The material which compose the human frame, are more durable than perhaps is at present imagined. Nature, I am persuaded, never intended to deprive us of our teeth, whilst we had any use for them. It is absurd to suppose that she would take from us what is so necessary, both for the purpose of articulation, and chewing our food. No; it is warm liquors, warm beds, and warm night-caps, which deprive the mouth of its greatest ornament, and gives to age its highest deformity. Whilst every substantial corporal blessing is sacrificed to a vain and foolish idea of feminine beauty, our habits tend to deprive us of the reality. Formerly, when women had attained the age of thirty-five, they were obliged to give up every pretension to beauty; and vanity under the appearance of decency, sought to hide the injuries she had sustained from the joint operations of time and error. We are now more than verging on the other extreme; and old women greatly heighten all the defects of age, by ornaments so fantastic, as do in some measure even diminish the lustre of youth and beauty.

The medical treatment of infants is, I believe, very much the same in the nurseries of the opulent through the whole kingdom. But we should seldom or perhaps never hear of consumptions, if the custom was adopted of putting on the linen cold; and if the practice was continued of bathing [42] the whole body in cold water, from the period of infancy to a state of maturity. It is almost inconceivable to what a degree of hardiness children will attain, when their habits are all favourable to this end. Yes; if an absurd and senseless prudery did not interfere to taint the unspotted mind, by obtruding on it its own gross ideas, the little innocents, wholly taken up with their sports, would either not feel, or not regard, the action of the air on the naked bodies, and thus insure a robust constitution before that period when decency requires us to conform to the manners of society. Do not mistake me; I do not mean that children should not be cloathed, but let their cloathing be thin; never subject them to the trammels of stays; and when in health, suffer them to run about for at least an hour before you put on their ordinary dress.

It was formerly the practice to burthen the infant with shoes and stockings the moment its little body was emancipated from the restraint of swaddling clothes. It is now, I believe, the custom to let them go without shoes till they can walk, and to forbear for some time longer the use of stockings; but as the proper circulation of the blood must in a great measure depend on the firm texture of all the vessels in the extreme parts of the body, I am apt to think, that the luxury of shoes and stockings, not to make any mention of [43] carpets, has been of the most fatal kind. The whole train of nervous diseases, with the gout, and other chronic disorders, if they have not taken their rise from this indulgence, must be greatly aggravated by it; and for this reason, I would keep my pupils' feet unshackled, either by shoes or stockings, for the first half dozen years of their childhood; nor would I impose on them the latter, till they were of an age to be introduced in form into company, when a conformity to the manners becomes a very necessary part of conduct. What, says Hortensia, are we to give up the ornament of an elegant little foot, for schemes of advantage which are perhaps only visionary? What is health without beauty – that pleasing quality of the sex? And do not we know, that among our artificial perfections, that of a little foot is one of the most conspicuous? Why truly, Hortensia, I am sufficiently singular to regard health as one of the first human blessings; and even on the subject of beauty, I confess to you, that I differ so much with the crowd, as to believe, that if there is such a reality in nature as beauty, it must consist in symmetry and proportion.²² A foot too small for the size of the body, is, in my eye, rather a deformity than a beauty; it shows bad nursing almost as much as the rickets; it carries the imagination to all those disagreeable and painful inequalities which are the attendant on tight [44] shoes. And if littleness alone, independent of proportion, constitutes the beauty of feet, we can never pretend to vie with the Chinese, whilst we preserve the privilege of walking.ᶦᶦᶦ Nature, if you do not restrain her, or turn her out of her course, is equal to the task both of fashioning the beauty of the person, and conforming the strength of

---

ᶦᶦᶦ Mr. Locke, observes, that the women in China are very little, and short lived; and that these defects are by some imputed to the binding their feet, whereby the free circulation of the blood is hindered. If there is any truth in this observation, it shows, that it must be of no small importance to health, as well as beauty, to leave, whilst children are growing, every part of the body free, to be nourished as Nature designs. [Locke, *Some Thoughts concerning Education*, pp. 11–12.]

²² Cf. Burke, *A Philosophical Enquiry into the Origin of Our Ideas of the Sublime and Beautiful* (London, 1757), part III, sect. 4: 'Proportion not the cause of Beauty in the human species'.

the constitution; whilst every practice that counteracts her operations, will be found materially injurious in one or other, or in both of these interesting particulars.

Both Locke and Rousseau have very properly insisted on the not intrenching on the freedom of children, by taking up that time in the laborious task of learning, which Nature designed to be spent in those bodily exercises which are so necessary to corporal health and strength; and Fenelon observes, that you ought (with great care) to manage organs of young children, till they become strengthened by a more mature age.[23] Many ingenious devices have been proposed, and many more might undoubtedly be found, well adopted to the teaching children the rudiments of language [45] and science, under the pleasing guise of amusement. The state of a child's brain is so unfavourable to continued application, or to carry on a series of rational deduction, that it is no wonder the task of literature should be an object of terror; and to be dragged to it from some delightful sport, must render the mind particularly averse to such application.

It is observable, says Mr. Locke, that children will take a great deal of pains to learn several games, which, if they should be enjoined them, they would abhor as a task. As all unknown objects delight from their novelty, the curiosity of children is eager and insatiable; this, if properly called forth and directed, makes the business of instruction easy. The habit also of attention to all the objects which surround us, preserves the mind from the sollicitude of care, and the uneasiness of want; it secures our innocence and our peace; and it renders us active, useful, and agreeable. How many persons do we know, who go through life with so little of that knowledge which the larger volume of Nature amply discloses to the observing eye, that one would think they had some defect in their senses: yet these persons are not stupid; they are only ignorant; they have fallen into the hands of lazy of insufficient tutors, who have suffered the seed of time of knowledge to pass away without the enlargement of [46] the ideas, which by opening new views to our imagination, stimulates us to engage, with a chearful assiduity, both in the study of nature, and the production of art. The rules laid down by Rousseau, to pour instruction into the young mind, by using it to a close examination of sensible objects, and the methods which he

[23] Fénelon, *Instructions for the Education of a Daughter* (London, 1707), p. 37.

200

prescribes to excite the attention of children, and so set their reasoning faculties in motion, is, I think, one of the most useful parts of this entertaining performance; but though I heartily concur with the ideas he has given on this subject, and would advise every tutor to read his Emilius[24] with care; yet let him not be charmed with the eloquence and plausibility of the author, as to adopt altogether the rules laid down in this work on the subject of instruction. We were not born to play all our lives; industry, both corporal and mental, is necessary to our happiness and advancement, both in this, and a future state; and when the organs of the brain have attained a sufficient firmness for the task of literature, young pupils ought to be exercised in the study of books, or such inveterate habits of idleness will be acquired as will be impossible afterwards to subdue.

The moderns, in the education of their children, have too much followed the stiff and prudish manners of ancient days, in the separating the male and female children of a family. This is well [47] adapted to the absurd unsocial rigour of Grecian manners; but as it is not so agreeable to that mixture of the sexes in a more advanced age, which prevails in all European societies, it is not easy to be accounted for, but from the absurd notion, that the education of females should be of an opposite kind to that of males. How many nervous diseases have been contracted? How much feebleness of constitution has been acquired, by forming a false idea of female excellence, and endeavouring, by our art, to bring Nature to the ply of our imagination. Our sons are suffered to enjoy with freedom that time which is not devoted to study, and may follow, unmolested, those strong impulses which Nature has wisely given for the furtherance of her benevolent purposes; but if, before her natural vivacity is entirely subdued by habit, little Miss is inclined to show her locomotive tricks in a manner entirely agreeable to the trammels of custom, she is reproved with a sharpness which gives her a consciousness of having highly transgressed the laws of decorum; and what with the vigilance of those who are appointed to superintend her conduct, and the false bias they have imposed on her mind, every vigorous exertion is suppressed, the mind and body yield to the tyranny of error, and Nature is charged with all those imperfections which we alone owe to the blunders of art.

[24] i.e. *Émile*.

[48] I could say a great deal, Hortensia, on those personal advantages, which the strength of the mother gives to her offspring, and the ill effects which must accrue both to the male and female issue from her feebleness. I could expatiate on the mental advantages which accompany a firm constitution, and on the evenness and complacency of temper, which commonly attends the blessing of health. I could turn the other side of the argument, and show you, that most of the caprices, the teasing follies, and often the vices of women, proceeds from weakness, or some other defects in their corporal frame; but when I have sifted the subject to the bottom, and taken every necessary trouble to illustrate and enforce my opinion, I shall, perhaps, still continue singular in it. My arguments may serve only to strengthen my ideas, and my sex will continue to lisp with their tongues, to totter in their walk, and to counterfeit more weakness and sickness than they really have, in order to attract the notice of the male; for, says a very elegant author, perfection is not the proper object of love: we admire excellence, but we are more enclined to love those we despise.[iv]

There is another prejudice, Hortensia, which affects yet more deeply female happiness, and female importance; a prejudice, which ought ever to have been confined to the regions of the east, [49] [CM *err*.: because it accords with] the state of slavery which female nature in that part of the world has been ever subjected, and can only suit the notion of a positive inferiority in the intellectual powers of the female mind. You will soon perceive, that the prejudices which I mean, is that degrading difference in the culture of the understanding, which has prevailed for several centuries in all European societies. Our ancestors, on the first revival of letters, dispensed with an equal hand the advantages of a classical education to all their offspring; but as pedantry was the fault of that age, a female student might not at that time be a very agreeable character. True philosophy in those ages was rarely an attendant on learning, even in the male sex; but it must be obvious to all those who are not blinded

---

[iv] See Mr. Burke on the *Sublime and Beautiful*. ['love approaches much nearer to contempt than is commonly imagined; and accordingly, though we caress dogs, we borrow from them an appellation of the most despicable kind, when we employ terms of reproach'; 'There is a wide difference between admiration and love. The sublime, which is the cause of the former, always dwells on great objects, and terrible; the latter on small ones, and pleasing; we submit to what we admire; but we love what submits to us; in one case we are forced, in the other we are flattered into compliance.' See *Sublime and Beautiful* (1757; 2nd enlarged ed., London, 1759), pp. 116, 212.]

by the mist of prejudice, that there is no cultivation which yields so promising a harvest as the cultivation of the understanding; and that a mind, irradiated by the clear light of wisdom, must be equal to every task which reason imposes on it. The social duties in the interesting characters of daughter, wife, and mother, will be but ill performed by ignorance and levity; and in the domestic converse of husband and wife, the alternative of an enlightened, or an unenlightened companion, cannot be indifferent to any man of taste and true knowledge. Be no longer niggards, then, O ye parents, in bestowing on your offspring, every blessing [50] which nature and fortune renders them capable of enjoying! Confine not the education of your daughters to what is regarded as the ornamental parts of it, nor deny the graces to your sons. Suffer no prejudices to prevail on you to weaken Nature, in order to render her more beautiful; take measures for her virtue and the harmony of your family, by uniting their young minds early in the soft bonds of friendship. Let your children be brought up together; let their sports and studies be the same; let them enjoy, in the constant presence of those who are set over them, all that freedom which innocence renders harmless, and in which Nature rejoices. By uninterrupted intercourse which you will thus establish, both sexes will find, that friendship may be enjoyed between them without passion. The wisdom of your daughters will preserve them from the bane of coquetry, and even at the age of desire, objects of temptation will lose somewhat of their stimuli, by losing their novelty. Your sons will look for something more solid in women, than a mere outside; and be no longer the dupes to the meanest, the weakest, and the most profligate of the sex. They will become the constant benefactors of that part of their family who stand in need of their assistance; and in regard to all matters of domestic concerns, the unjust distinction of primogeniture will be deprived of its sting.

[189] [PART I] LETTER XX

Sympathy

Life should be a continued effort to banish our prejudices, and extinguish our vices, said the wise Alcander to his pupil Lysimachus, as they were sitting on the banks of a beautiful rivulet which commanded a large extent of the adjacent country.[25] Look at those sportsmen, who are so intent on running down an innocent animal, and who are cutting the thread of an existence which was given enjoyment, in such a manner, as to combine a high degree of mental with bodily pain. I know, my dear Lysimachus, that your sentiments are familiar to my own, and that by the power of sympathy, you actually partake of some of that misery which at this moment you see overwhelming a fellow creature. But these sportsmen are constituted of the same materials as ourselves; they have the same portion of sympathy given them by nature; and they, like us, are equally subject with the creature they are thus pursuing, to pain, to death, and to all the agonizing sensations which arise from excessive fear. They are, I dare say, honourable men too; they [190] believe that they would scorn to effect the destruction of a fellow man with such excessive odds; and if you were to tell them that it was possible for them in any given situation of power, and prejudice, to use the same cruel violence against one of their own species, they would regard you as an abusive defamer. But this, Lysimachus, is an error; there are no such partialities in nature existing between the species of animals. Beasts of prey do not devour one another, because, for wise purposes, they have an instinctive aversion to such food; but you see, when their appetites are in motion, they will destroy one another in contests for gratification. Where this instinct is weaker, there are some animals who actually eat their own young. Man, in the early ages of society, fed on man; and there is no violence which this being, who boasts that he is governed by reason, has not committed against his own species, whenever they have been found in opposition to his fancied interest. What atrocious cruelties has not pride, the lust of power, riches, beauty, and the dire passion of revenge, given birth to; and even where these keen excitements have been wanting, the mere insolence of superiority, and the force of habit, have given birth to injuries familiar to those now suffering by this hare. Not to mention the treatment given by some of [our] own countrymen to their African slaves; the [191] Spartans, a race of men not destitute of the qualities of the heart, actually hunted the Helotes in their sports. If men, Lysimachus, neglect to cultivate sympathy, which enables us to acquire notions of equity, and thus to trace the virtues of the sovereign mind, that quality in them, which carries the appearance of benevolence, is the mere power of habit. Not that I mean to insinuate that sportsmen are

---

[25] The dialogue between 'Alcander' and 'Lysimachus' in this letter is invented by Macaulay.

incapable of tender sentiment; no; when natural sympathy is not quite subdued, where habits are favorable to its exertion, it will rise and command attention. We boast much of modern refinements and civilisation; but I know of none that is worth the possessing except those which induce a more extensive benevolence than was formerly practiced among men. For if such appear to our advantage in the comparative line of reasoning, they never will amount to positive excellence till all our barbarous customs are abolished, and our sentiments change their heterogenous nature for a more consistent system of feeling. – Truly, says Lysimachus, I have often wondered that Plato, who was so deep a thinker, should have founded the rectitude of actions in human sentiment;[26] for these appear so liable to take their turn from the operation of causes under the controul of accident, that it is impossible to affix any idea of consistency or immutability to them. – You certainly are in the right, returned [192] Alcander, and Plato could never have deviated into this error, had not his attention been so much fixed on the contemplation of the governing mind, as to make him look over the confusion and contradiction which take place in human sentiment. But whilst one smiles at the rhapsodies of those who perhaps have carried Plato's ideas farther than it was carried by the philosopher, we cannot help feeling a little angry with systems, which confine rectitude to that mode of conduct which is the best adapted to support the happiness of man. Thus, when God subjected the far greater number of his creatures to this lord of the creation, he subjected them to a being, not bound by any tie in nature, or by the reason of things, to use equity and mercy in the exercise of his power; and to whose necessary wants are added all the excitements which arise from a whimsical, depraved, and luxuriant imagination. Absurd as is this opinion, Lysimachus, it has been supported by the great Mr. Hume, who says, he does not know by what principle the brutes can claim justice, which is another name for mercy, at our hands.[27] But the difficulties which confound these reasoners, lie in their founding rectitude on a principle of utility, and then in a confining utility to the benefit of their own species. But as utility, unless taken in a very general sense, is liable to mislead the judgment, every rule of human society, founded on partial, and even [193] mistaken views of interest,

---

[26] In book four of the *Republic*, Plato divided the soul into the rational, the spirited, and the appetitive parts. Plato's view of emotions is on the whole more negative than Macaulay seems to suggest.

[27] Hume, *An Enquiry Concerning the Principles of Morals* (London, 1751), pp. 44–5.

with the sentiments to which it gives rise, finds its justification on the plea of utility; and Mr. Hume's speculations on this subject are not free from the same errors. Thus inconsistency and mutability hang on his system, in the same proportion as they hang on every system of morals founded on human sentiment; but if we take utility in a general sense, and say that virtue consists in that conduct which is of general utility, we shall come to those essential differences which regulate the divine oeconomy, only with this distinction, that man must confine himself to what is general; it is omnipotence alone can extend to what is universal.

As the discerning the difference of human actions, (says Lysimachus,) as far as it respects rectitude and its contrary, is so necessary to virtue, I have often wondered that the reason of man, in the common proportion in which it is enjoyed, should be so unequal to the task.

Reason is not so unequal to this task as you think, Lysimachus, (replied Alcander;) she may indeed be confounded by sophistry, borne down by authority, or led into erroneous conclusions from false statements of facts, and false positions; but reason is always able to discern the moral difference of things, whenever they are fairly and plainly proposed; which, as I take it, establishes an immutable and abstract fitness in a more satis-[194]factory manner than what is called a moral consciousness from innate principles, which would create a jealousy in the mind of the deep thinker, that it has no grounds inseparable from power; but it is an arbitrary law imposed on our nature, for the purpose of a providential government.

Your observations (says Lysimachus) are too justly grounded, and too strongly enforced, not to carry persuasion to the unprejudiced mind. But, my dear tutor, how shall we account for the total silence on this interesting subject, which reigns through all the sacred writings. Had a benevolent conduct to the brute animals been so essential a part of moral duty as you seem to make it, ought we not to expect to have found it enforced either in the precepts of the old or the new law?[28]

What you say, (replied Alcander,) demands a very serious attention; and, to tell you the truth, I have myself been puzzled with this difficulty. However, we find that mercy is recommended, either directly, or by implication, in the tenor of scripture. Revealed religion does not under-take to teach a comprehensive system of ethicks to man;[29] much is left to the progress of enlightened reason; nor ought this oeconomy to surprize

---

[28] i.e. the Mosaic dispensation and the Gospel dispensation, respectively.

[29] A central theme in Locke's *Reasonableness of Christianity*.

us, when we consider that the long enumeration of cases, and distinctions which must have been used in order to give precision and clearness to the system, would rather have puzzled than improved the com-[195]mon sense of mankind. Religion would have been regarded as too complex a science for the vulgar class of men to understand; and that mystery has been flung by the crafty over the most simple propositions, and idolatry grown from distinctions founded on reason and truth, the history both of Paganism and Christianity bear ample testimony. Had any precise rules been given as to the subject on which we have been just discoursing, it would, above all others, have been liable to have been misunderstood; and either have occasioned an open violation of the divine commandment, or have given such a turn to principle and sentiment as might have interfered with such a use of the creatures, as religion, rectitude, and reason, allow. But I am persuaded, Lysimachus, of the advantage of an universal benevolence in every state of creation, and regard it as the best means to procure our happiness, both in the satisfaction which is naturally annexed to it, and in the rendering us acceptable to our maker. For, without presuming to set bounds to the goodness of God, or the measure in which he may deviate from the common course of things in favour of those who are deceived into error from the joint influence of authority and custom, we may venture to conclude, that those who are the most active in spreading happiness, and who abstain the most from all unnecessary acts of blood, as well as cruelty, bid [196] the fairest for rendering themselves fit for the enjoyments of a better state.

I have ever found too much indulgence from you, Alcander, to hesitate in giving you my thoughts freely on every subject; and I confess to you, that there is one objection to be made against your argument, which has great weight with me; that line of destruction which runs through all animal nature appears to militate strongly against the supposition, that the slaughter of the brute species by man is contrary to the intention of Providence, or repugnant to the divine mind.

Continue, Lysimachus, (returned Alcander) to use that freedom which I have ever encouraged in you; because it is favourable to the investigation of truth; nor am I surprised at the weight which this objection has on your mind. That line of destruction which regularly runs through all animal nature, is a phenomenon the most difficult to be accounted for of any which the divine oeconomy presents. But though the destruction of animal by animal is not only admitted by God, but is an universal principle in the mundane system, it does not follow that slaughter should be the delight and amusement of the human mind. A cat worries its [CM *err.*: his] prey, without considering whether she [CM *err.*: he] is doing evil, or the contrary; but man has sympathy in his nature, and his knowledge of the relation of things causes him to put himself in [197] the place of the sufferer, and thus to acquire ideas of equity, and the utility of benevolence, which, as far as it is improved, will carry us in an opposite line from cruelty, or unnecessary slaughter. And you see, Lysimachus, that my arguments do not tend to deprive men of a moderate use of the creatures; they only militate against unnecessary rigor, or making the death of our fellow animals part of our amusement. And this view of the question will appear to be warranted by the sanction of the divine mind, if we take into consideration the uninterrupted flow of gentle satisfactions which attend benevolence in its most liberal and extensive practice.

The dialogue between Alcander and his pupil, Hortensia, coincides exactly with my opinion on the subject of instruction; and, on these reasons, I have transcribed it for your use.

[198] [PART I] LETTER XXI

Morals must be taught on immutable Principles.

It is one thing, Hortensia, to educate a citizen, and another to educate a philosopher. The mere citizen will have learnt to obey the laws of his country, but he will never understand those principles on which all laws ought to be established; and without such an understanding, he can never be religious on rational principles, or truly moral; nor will he ever have any of that active wisdom which is necessary for co-operating in any plan of reformation. But to teach morals on an immutable fitness, has never been the practice in any system of education yet extant. Hence all our notions of right and wrong are loose, unconnected, and inconsistent. Hence the murderer, in one situation, is extolled to the skies; and, in another, is followed with reproach even beyond the grave. For it is not only the man of the world who idolises power, though in the garb of villainy, and persecutes dishonesty when united to weakness, but even those who bear the specious title of philosophers are apt to be dazzled with the

brilliancy of success, and to treat qualities [199] and characters differ-
ently, according to the smiles or frowns of fortune.

As an instance, to illustrate this observation, I will select out of the
huge mass of human inconsistencies, the praises bestowed by Xenophon
on Cyrus; who, whether a real or fictitious character, is set up by this
philosopher as a model of princely perfection.[30]

Cyrus, it is true, is represented as moderate in the gratification of his
appetites, liberal to his followers, and just, when he found justice
correspond with his interest; but, as [he] himself confesses, he never
practiced any virtue on other principles but those of personal utility; and
he animates his countrymen to exertions, which he dignifies with this
title, on motives of obtaining means, by the spoils of others, for future
enjoyment. In short, Cyrus was neither liberal from generosity, just from
honesty, nor merciful from benevolence; and the address he made use of
to enslave the minds of his subjects, is of the same kind as that used by a
courtezan to extend and preserve her influence over the hearts of those
she has trepanned into her snares. Cyrus was master of all those arts
which are necessary to obtain and preserve to himself and [his] successors an unjust measure of power; he enflamed with this lust all his
warlike followers, in order to eradicate from their minds the love of
freedom and independence. His [200] system of policy, of which many
parts are atrocious outrages on the rights of Nature, established the
firmest and the most extensive despotism that was ever established in
the East, and has, on these reasons, prevailed more or less in the Persian
dynasty, and in all the governments which have been built on its ruins;
yet Xenophon and Cicero, who were both republicans and philosophers,
extol Cyrus to the skies.[31] But had these men understood rectitude on
the principles of truth, they must have perceived, that power never can
be justly obtained but by conquest over those by whom we are first
unlawfully attacked, or by such a fair influence over the mind as shall
convince men that they will be safe and happy under our authority.

Cyrus is one of those plausible knaves who have been set up as models
for example; and, on these reasons, he imposes on all those who do not

---

[30] In the *Cyropaedia*, a partly fictional biography of Cyrus the Great, founder of the first
Persian Empire. It was written around 370 BC by Xenophon, and published in several
editions in English in the eighteenth century, translated by Maurice Ashley.

[31] Cicero, *Cato: Or, an Essay on Old Age*, trans. William Melmoth (London, 1773), p. 46.
See note 30 for Xenophon.

reflect deeply. But I am convinced, that a Caesar Borgia,[32] or a Cataline,[33] had their characters been united with a brilliant success, would have equally imposed on the vulgar; for as Helvetius very justly observes, it is only the weakness of the poor rogue which men despise; not his dishonesty.[34]

In order to take from public sentiment a reproach which leaves a deep stain on the human character, and to correct many irregularities, and even enormities, which arise from incorrect [201] systems of ethics, it ought to be the first care of education to teach virtue on immutable principles, and to avoid that confusion which must arise from confounding the laws and customs of society with those obligations which are founded on correct principles of equity. But as you have had patience to go through my whole plan of education, from infancy to manhood, it is but fair that I should attend to your objections, and examine whether my plan is founded on error, or on the principles of reason and truth. Know then, good Hortensia, that I have given similar rules for male and female education, on the following grounds of reasoning.

First, That there is but one rule of right for the conduct of all rational beings; consequently that true virtue in one sex must be equally so in the other, whenever a proper opportunity calls for its exertion; and, *vice versa*, what is vice in one sex, cannot have a different property when found in the other.

Secondly, That true wisdom, which is never found at variance with rectitude, is as useful to women as to men; because it is necessary to the highest degree of happiness, which can never exist with ignorance.

Lastly, That as on our first entrance into another world, our state of happiness may possibly depend on the degree of perfection we have at- [202]tained in this, we cannot justly lessen, in one sex or the other, the means by which perfection, that is another word for wisdom, is acquired.

It would be paying you a bad compliment, Hortensia, were I to answer all the frivolous objections which prejudice has framed against the giving a learned education to women; for I know of no learning, worth having, that does not tend to free the mind from error, and enlarge our stock of useful knowledge. Thus much it may be proper to observe, that those hours which are spent in studious retirement by learned women, will not

---

[32] Cesare Borgia (1475–1507) was an Italian cardinal, military leader, and a key figure in Machiavelli's *The Prince*.

[33] Lucius Sergius Catilina (108–62 BC) is notorious for the second Catilinarian conspiracy, an attempt to overthrow the Roman Republic.

[34] *A Treatise on Man, His Intellectual Faculties and His Education. A Posthumous Work of M. Helvetius* (2 vols., London, 1777), I, pp. 283, 302.

in all probability intrude so much on the time for useful avocation, as the wild and spreading dissipations of the present day; that levity and ignorance will always be found in opposition to what is useful and graceful in life; and that the contrary may be expected from a truly enlightened understanding. However, Hortensia, to throw some illustration on what I have advanced on this subject, it may be necessary to shew you, that all those vices and imperfections which have been generally regarded as inseparable from the female character, do not in any manner proceed from sexual causes, but are entirely the effects of situation and education. But these observations must be left to farther discussion.

[203] [PART I] LETTER XXII

No characteristic Difference in Sex.

The great difference that is observable in the characters of the sexes, Hortensia, as they display themselves in the scenes of social life, has given rise to much false speculation on the natural qualities of the female mind. – For though the doctrine of innate ideas, and innate affections, are in a great measure exploded by the learned, yet few persons reason so closely and so accurately on abstract subjects as, through a long chain of deductions, to bring forth a conclusion which in no respect militates with their premises.

It is a long time before the crowd give up opinions they have been taught to look upon with respect; and I know many persons who will follow you willingly through the course of your argument, till they perceive it tends to the overthrow of some fond prejudice; and then they will either sound a retreat, or begin a contest in which the contender for truth, though he cannot be overcome, is effectually silenced, from the mere weariness of answering positive assertions, reiterated without end. It is from such causes that the no-[204]tion of a sexual difference in the human character has, with a very few exceptions, universally prevailed from the earliest times, and the pride of one sex, and the ignorance and vanity of the other, have helped to support an opinion which a close observation of Nature, and a more accurate way of reasoning, would disprove.

It must be confessed, that the virtues of the males among the human species, though mixed and blended with a variety of vices and errors, have displayed a bolder and a more consistent picture of excellence than female nature has hitherto done. It is on these reasons that, when we compliment the appearance of a more than ordinary energy in the female mind, we call it masculine; and hence it is, that Pope has elegantly said *a perfect woman's but a softer man.*[35] And if we take in the consideration, that there can be but one rule of moral excellence for beings made of the same materials, organized after the same manner, and subjected to similar laws of Nature, we must either agree with Mr. Pope, or we must reverse the proposition, and say, that *a perfect man is a woman formed after a coarser mold.* The difference that actually does subsist between the sexes, is too flattering for men to be willingly imputed to accident; for what accident occasions, wisdom might correct; and it is better, says Pride, to give up the advantages we might derive from the per-[205]fection of our fellow associates, than to own that Nature has been just in the equal distribution of her favours. These are the senti-ments of the men; but mark how readily they are yielded to by the women; not from humility I assure you, but merely to preserve with character those fond vanities on which they set their hearts. No; suffer them to idolize their persons, to throw away their life in the pursuit of trifles, and to indulge in the gratification of the meaner passions, and they will heartily join in the sentence of their degradation.

Among the most strenuous asserters of a sexual difference in charac-ter, Rousseau is the most conspicuous, both on account of that warmth of sentiment which distinguishes all his writings, and the eloquence of his compositions: but never did enthusiasm and the love of paradox, those enemies to philosophical disquisition, appear in more strong opposition to plain sense than in Rousseau's definition of this difference. He sets out with a supposition, that Nature intended the subjection of the one sex to the other; that consequently there must be an inferiority of intellect in the subjected party; but as man is a very imperfect being, and apt to play the capricious tyrant, Nature, to bring things nearer to an equality, bestowed on the woman such attractive graces, and such an insinuating address, as to turn the balance on the other scale. Thus Nature, in a [206] giddy mood, recedes from her purposes, and subjects prerogative to an influence which must produce confusion and disorder in the system of human affairs. Rousseau saw this objection; and in order to obviate it, he has made up a moral person of the union of the two sexes, which, for

[35] Pope, *Of the Characters of Women: An Epistle to a Lady* (London, 1735), p. 14.

contradiction and absurdity, outdoes every metaphysical riddle that was ever formed in the schools. In short, it is not reason, it is not wit; it is pride and sensuality that speak in Rousseau, and, in this instance, has lowered the man of genius to the licentious pedant.[36]

But whatever might be the wise purpose intended by Providence in such a disposition of things, certain it is, that some degree of inferiority, in point of corporal strength, seems always to have existed between the two sexes; and this advantage, in the barbarous ages of mankind, was abused to such a degree, as to destroy all the natural rights of the female species, and reduce them to a state of abject slavery. What accidents have contributed in Europe to better their condition, would not be to my purpose to relate; for I do not intend to give you a history of women;[37] I mean only to trace the sources of their peculiar foibles and vices; and these I firmly believe to originate in situation and education only: for so little did a wise and just Providence intend to make the condition of slavery an unalterable law of female nature, that [207] in the same proportion as the male sex have consulted the interest of their own happiness, they have relaxed in their tyranny over women; and such is their use in the system of mundane creation, and such their natural influence over the male mind, that were these advantages properly exerted, they might carry every point of any importance to their honour and happiness. However, till that period arrives in which women will act wisely, we will amuse ourselves in talking of their follies.

The situation and education of women, Hortensia, is precisely that which must necessarily tend to corrupt and debilitate both the powers of mind and body. From a false notion of beauty and delicacy, their system of nerves is depraved before they come out of their nursery; and this kind of depravity has more influence over the mind, and consequently over morals, than is commonly apprehended. But it would be well if such causes only acted towards the debasement of the sex; their moral education is, if possible, more absurd than their physical. The principles and nature of virtue, which is never properly explained to boys, is kept quite a mystery to girls. They are told indeed, that they must abstain from those vices which are contrary to their personal happiness, or they will be regarded as criminals, both by God and man; but all the higher parts [208] of rectitude, every thing that ennobles our being, and that renders

---

[36] Rousseau, *Emilius and Sophia*, IV, pp. 35–6, *passim.*
[37] Perhaps an allusion to William Alexander, *The History of Women* (2 vols., 1779).

us both innoxious and useful, is either not taught, or is taught in such a manner as to leave no proper impression on the mind. This is so obvious a truth, that the defects of female education have ever been a fruitful topic of declamation for the moralist; but not one of this class of writers have laid down any judicious rules for amendment. Whilst we still retain the absurd notion of a sexual excellence, it will militate against the perfecting a plan of education for either sex. The judicious Addison animadverts on the absurdity of bringing a young lady up with no higher idea of the end of education than to make her agreeable to a husband, and confining the necessary excellence for this happy acquisition to the mere graces of person.[38]

Every parent and tutor may not express himself in the same manner as is marked out by Addison; yet certain it is, that the admiration of the other sex is held out to women as the highest honour they can attain; and whilst this is considered as their *summum bonum*, and the beauty of their persons the chief *desideratum* of men, Vanity, and its companion Envy, must taint, in their characters, every native and every acquired excellence. Nor can you, Hortensia, deny, that these qualities, when united to ignorance, are fully equal to the engendering and rivetting all those vices and foibles [209] which are peculiar to the female sex; vices and foibles which have caused them to be considered, in ancient times, as beneath cultivation, and in modern days have subjected them to the censure and ridicule of writers of all descriptions, from the deep thinking philosopher to the man of ton[39] and gallantry, who, by the bye, sometimes distinguishes himself by qualities which are not greatly superior to those he despises in women. Nor can I better illustrate the truth of this observation than by the following picture, to be found in the polite and gallant Chesterfield. 'Women,' says his Lordship, 'are only children of a larger growth. They have an entertaining tattle, sometimes wit; but for solid reasoning, and good sense, I never in my life knew one that had it, or who acted or reasoned in consequence of it for four and twenty hours together. A man of sense only trifles with them, plays with them,

---

[38] *The Works of the Late Right Honorable Joseph Addison* (4 vols., Birmingham, 1761), II, pp. 516–19, and IV, pp. 231–3.

[39] Short for 'le bon ton', and a reference to etiquette and fashion. 'The ton' referred to Britain's high society.

humours and flatters them, as he does an engaging child; but he neither consults them, nor trusts them in serious matters.'[40]

[211] [PART I] LETTER XXIII

Coquettry

Though the situation of women in modern Europe, Hortensia, when compared with that condition of abject slavery in which they have always been held in the east, may be considered as brilliant; yet if we withhold comparison, and take the matter in a positive sense, we shall have no great reason to boast of our privileges, or of the candour and indulgence of the men towards us. For with a total and absolute exclusion of every political right to sex in general, married women, whose situation demands a particular indulgence, have hardly a civil right to save them from the grossest injuries; and though the gallantry of some of the European societies have necessarily produced indulgence, yet in others the faults of women are treated with a severity and rancour which militates against every principle of religion and common sense. Faults, my friend, I hear you say; you take the matter in too general a sense; you know there is but one fault which a woman of honour may not commit with impunity; let her only take care that she is not caught in a love [211] intrigue, and she may lie, she may deceive, she may defame, she may ruin her own family with gaming, and the peace of twenty of others with her coquettry, and yet preserve both her reputation and her peace. These are glorious privileges indeed, Hortensia; but whilst plays and novels are the favourite study of the fair, whilst the admiration of men continues to be set forth as the chief honour of woman, whilst power is only acquired by personal charms, whilst continual dissipation banishes the hour of reflection, Nature and flattery will too often prevail; and when this is the case, self preservation will suggest to conscious weakness those methods which are the most likely to conceal the ruinous trespass, however base and criminal they may be in their nature. The crimes that women have committed, both to conceal and to indulge their natural failings, shock the feelings of moral sense; but indeed every love intrigue, though it does not terminate in such horrid catastrophes, must naturally

---

[40] *Letters Written by the Late Right Honourable Philip Dormer Stanhope, Earl of Chesterfield, to His Son, Philip Stanhope, Esq.* (2 vols., London, 1774), I, pp. 317–18.

tend to debase the female mind, from its violence to educational impressions, from the secrecy with which it must be conducted, and the debasing dependancy to which the intriguer, if she is a woman of reputation, is subjected. Lying, flattery, hypocrisy, bribery, and a long catalogue of the meanest of the human vices, must all be employed to preserve necessary appearances. Hence delicacy of sentiment gradually decreases; [212] the warnings of virtue are no longer felt; the mind becomes corrupted, and lies open to every solicitation which appetite or passion presents. This must be the natural course of things in every being formed after the human plan; but it gives rise to the trite and foolish observation, that the first fault against chastity in woman has a radical power to deprave the character. But no such frail beings come out of the hands of Nature. The human mind is built of nobler materials than to be so easily corrupted; and with all the disadvantages of situation and education, women seldom become entirely abandoned till they are thrown into a state of desperation by the venomous rancour of their own sex.

The superiority of address peculiar to the female sex, says Rousseau, is a very equitable indemnification for their inferiority in point of strength.[41] Without this, woman would not be the companion of man, but his slave; it is by her superior art and ingenuity that she preserves her equality, and governs him, whilst she affects to obey. Woman has every thing against her; as well our faults, as her own timidity and weakness. She has nothing in her favor but her subtlety and her beauty; is it not very reasonable therefore that she should cultivate both?

I am persuaded that Rousseau's understanding was too good to have led him into this error, had [213] he not been blinded by his pride and his sensuality. The first was soothed by the opinion of superiority, lulled into acquiescence by cajolement; and the second was attracted by the idea of women playing off all the arts of coquettry to raise the passions of the sex. Indeed the author fully avows his sentiments, by acknowledging that he would have a young French woman cultivate her agreeable talents, in order to please her future husband, with as much care and assiduity as a young Circassian[42] cultivates her's to fit her for the harem of an eastern bashaw.[43]

---

[41] Macaulay cites directly from Rousseau, *Emilius and Sophia*, IV, pp. 35–6.

[42] Circassia was a historical region along the north-eastern shore of the Black Sea. It was destroyed during the Russian–Circassian War (1763–1864) as the great majority of its native people, the Circassians, were either killed or exiled from the region, most of them to the Ottoman Empire.

[43] Rousseau, *Emilius and Sophia*, IV, p. 42.

These agreeable talents, as the author expresses it, are played off to a great advantage by women in all the courts of Europe; who, for the arts of female allurement, do not give place to the Circassian. But it is the practice of these very arts, directed to enthral the men, which act in a peculiar manner to corrupting the female mind. Envy, malice, jealousy, a cruel delight in inspiring sentiments which at first perhaps were never intended to be reciprocal, are leading features in the character of the coquet, whose aim is to subject the whole world to her own humour; but in this vain attempt she commonly sacrifices both her decency and her virtue.

By the intrigues of women, and their rage for personal power and importance, the whole world has been filled with violence and injury; and their [214] levity and influence have proved so hostile to the existence or permanence of rational manners, that it fully justifies the keenness of Mr. Pope's satire on the sex.[44]

But I hear my Hortensia say, whither will this fit of moral anger carry you? I expected an apology, instead of a libel, on women; according to your description of the sex, the philosopher has more reason to regret the indulgence, than what you have sometimes termed the injustice of the men; and to look with greater complacency on the surly manners of the ancient Greeks, and the selfishness of Asiatic luxury, than on the gallantry of modern Europe.[45]

Though you have often heard me express myself with warmth in the vindication of female nature, Hortensia, yet I never was an apologist for the conduct of women. But I cannot think the surliness of the Greek manners, or the selfishness of Asiatic luxury, a proper remedy to apply to the evil. If we would inspect narrowly into the domestic concerns of ancient and modern Asia, I dare say we should perceive that the first springs of the vast machine of society were set a going by women; and as to the Greeks, though it might be supposed that the peculiarity of their manners would have rendered them indifferent to the sex, yet they were

---

[44] Pope, *Of the Characters of Women.*

[45] The notion of 'Asiatic luxury' was a prevalent theme in the eighteenth century, especially in histories of Rome, in which it was frequently blamed for its decline. See, e.g., Montesquieu, *Considerations on the Causes of the Grandeur and Decadence of the Romans* (1734), and John Crevier, *The History of the Roman Emperors* (1749). The term occurs also in translations of *Plutarch's Lives* and in Fénelon's *Instructions for the Education of Daughters*, and a plethora of other books read by Macaulay.

avowedly governed by them. They only transferred that confidence which they ought [215] to have given their wives, to their courtezans, in the same manner as our English husbands do their tenderness and their complaisance. They will sacrifice a wife of fortune and family to resentment, or the love of change, provided she gives them opportunity, and bear with much Christian patience to be supplanted by their footman in the person of their mistress.

No; as Rousseau observes, it was ordained by Providence that women should govern some way or another;[46] and all that reformation can do, is to take power out of the hands of vice and folly, and place it where it will not be liable to be abused.

To do the sex justice, it must be confessed that history does not set forth more instances of positive power abused by women, than by men; and when the sex have been taught wisdom by education, they will be glad to give up indirect influence for rational privileges; and the precarious sovereignty of an hour enjoyed with the meanest and most infamous of the species, for those established rights which, independent of accidental circumstances, may afford protection to the whole sex.

[216] [PART I] LETTER XXIV

Flattery – Chastity – Male Rakes.

After all that has been advanced, Hortensia, the happiness and perfection of the two sexes are so reciprocally dependant on one another that, till both are reformed, there is no expecting excellence in either. The candid Addison has confessed, that in order to embellish the mistress, you must give a new education to the lover, and teach the men not to be any longer dazzled by false charms and unreal beauty.[47] Till this is the case, we must endeavour to palliate the evil we cannot remedy; and, in the education of our females, raise as many barriers to the corruptions of the world, as our understanding and sense of things will permit.

As I give no credit to the opinion of a sexual excellence, I have made no variation in the fundamental principles of the education of the two sexes; but it will be necessary to admit of such a difference in the plan as

---

[46] Rousseau, *Emilius and Sophia*, IV, pp. 35–6.

[47] This is a direct quotation from no. 53 of the *Spectator* (1 May 1711), which is likely to have been written by Addison's co-writer Richard Steele.

shall in some degree form the female mind to the particularity of its situation.

The fruits of true philosophy are modesty and [217] humility; for as we advance in knowledge, our deficiencies become more conspicuous; and by learning to set a just estimate on what we possess, we find little gratification for the passion of pride. This is so just an observation, that we may venture to pronounce, without any exception to the rule, that a vain or proud man is in a positive sense, an ignorant man. However if it should be our lot to have one of the fair sex, distinguished for any eminent degree of personal charms, committed to our care, we must not attempt by a premature cultivation to gather the fruits of philosophy before their season, nor expect to find the qualities of true modesty and humility make their appearance till the blaze of beauty has in some measure been subdued by time. For should we exhaust all the powers of oratory, and all the strength of sound argument, in the endeavour to convince our pupil that beauty is of small weight in the scale of real excellence, the enflamed praises she will continually hear bestowed on this quality will fix her in the opinion, that we *mean* to keep her in ignorance of her true worth. She will think herself deceived, and she will resent the injury by giving little credit to our precepts, and placing her confidence in those who tickle her ears with lavish panegyric on the captivating graces of her person.

Thus vanity steals on the minds, and thus a [218] daughter, kept under by the ill exerted power of parental authority, gives a full ear to the flattery of a coxcomb. Happy would it be for the sex did the mischief end here; but the soothings of flattery never fail to operate on the affections of the heart; and when love creeps into the bosom, the empire of reason is at an end. To prevent our fair pupils therefore from becoming the prey of coxcombs, and serving either to swell their triumph, or repair their ruined fortunes, it will be necessary to give them a full idea of the magnitude of their beauty, and the power this quality has over the frail mind of man. Nor have we in this case so much to fear from the intimations of a judicious friend, as from the insidious adulation of a designing admirer. The haughty beauty is too proud to regard the admiration of fops and triflers; she will never condescend to the base, the treacherous, the dangerous arts of coquettry; and by keeping her heart free from the snares of love, she will have time to cultivate that philosophy which, if well understood, is a never failing remedy to human pride.

219

But the most difficult part of female education, is to give girls such an idea of chastity, as shall arm their reason and their sentiments on the side of this useful virtue. For I believe that there are more women of understanding led into acts of imprudence by the ignorance, the prejudices, and the [219] false crafts of those by whom they are educated, than from any other cause founded either in nature or in chance. You may train up a docile idiot to any mode of thinking or acting, as may best suit the intended purpose; but a reasoning being will scan over your propositions, and if they find them grounded in falsehood, they will reject them with disdain. When you tell a girl of spirit and reflection that chastity is a sexual virtue, and the want of it a sexual vice, she will be apt to examine into the principles of religion, morals, and the reason of things, in order to satisfy herself on the truth of your proposition. And when, after the strictest enquiries, she finds nothing that will warrant the confining the proposition to a particular sense, she will entertain doubts either of your wisdom or your sincerity; and regarding you either as a deceiver or a fool, she will transfer her confidence to the companion of the easy vacant hour, whose compliance with her opinions can flatter her vanity. Thus left to Nature, with an unfortunate bias on her mind, she will fall a victim to the first plausible being who has formed a design on her person. Rousseau is so sensible of this truth, that he quarrels with human reason, and would put her out of question in all considerations of duty.[48] But this is being as great a fanatic in morals, as some in religion; and I should much doubt the reality of that duty which [220] would not stand the test of fair enquiry; beside, as I intend to breed my pupils up to act a rational part in the world, and not to fill up a niche in the seraglio of a sultan, I shall certainly give them leave to use their reason in all matters which concern their duty and happiness, and shall spare no pains in the cultivation of this only sure guide to virtue. I shall inform them of the great utility of chastity and continence; that the one preserves the body in health and vigor, and the other, the purity and independence of mind, without which it is impossible to possess virtue or happiness. I shall intimate, that the great difference now beheld in the external consequences which follows the deviations from chastity in the two sexes, did in all probability arise from women having been considered as the mere property of the men; and, on this account had no right to dispose of their

[48] Rousseau, *Emilius and Sophia*, IV, pp. 86–8.

own persons: that policy adopted this difference, when the plea of property had been given up; and it was still preserved in society from the unruly licentiousness of the men, who, finding no obstacles in the delicacy of the other sex, continue to set at defiance both divine and moral law, and by mutual support and general opinion to use their natural freedom with impunity. I shall observe, that this state of things renders the situation of females, in their individual capacity very precarious; for the strength which [221] Nature has given to the passion of love, in order to serve her purpose, has made it the most ungovernal propensity of any which attends us. The snares therefore, that are continually laid for women, by persons who run no risk in compassing their seduction, exposes them to continual danger; whilst the implacability of their own sex, who fear to give up any advantages which a superior prudence, or even its appearance, give them, renders one false step an irretrievable misfortune. That, for these reasons, coquettry in women is as dangerous as it is dishonorable. That a coquet commonly finds her own perdition, in the very flames which she raises to consume others; and that if any thing can excuse the baseness of female seduction, it is the baits which are flung out by women to entangle the affections, and excite the passions of men.

I know not what you may think of my method, Hortensia, which I must acknowledge to carry the stamp of singularity; but for my part, I am sanguine enough to expect to turn out of my hands a careless, modest beauty, grave, manly, noble, full of strength and majesty; and carrying about her an aegis sufficiently powerful to defend her against the sharpest arrow that ever was shot from Cupid's bow. A woman, whose virtue will not be of the kind to wrankle[49] into an inveterate malignity against her own sex for [222] faults which she even encourages in the men, but who, understanding the principles of true religion and morality, will regard chastity and truth as indispensable qualities in virtuous characters of either sex; whose justice will incline her to extend her benevolence to the frailties of the fair as circumstances invite, and to manifest her resentment against the underminers of female happiness; in short, a woman who will not take a male rake either for a husband or a friend. And let me tell you, Hortensia, if women had as much regard for the virtue of chastity as in some cases they pretend to have, a reformation would long since have taken place in the world; but whilst they continue

---

[49] i.e. rankle.

to cherish immodesty in the men, their bitter persecution of their own sex will not save them from imputation of those concealed propensities with which they are accused by Pope,[50] and other severe satirists on the sex.

[223] [PART I] LETTER XXV

Hints towards the Education of a Prince.

In all monarchies, Hortensia, the national prosperity, and the domestic felicity of a people, so entirely depend on the wisdom and goodness of the reigning prince, that it is a matter of some astonishment to a reflecting mind, how men should be first cajoled into placing such a trust in the infirm creature, man; and then should be so neglectful of their proper interest and safety, as to leave the education of the individual they have invested with sovereignty, to mere chance, or what is worse, to the care of weak or designing persons. For the histories of all nations demonstrate, that one feeble and wicked reign is often sufficient to mar the wisdom of ages.

I shall not trouble you with a dry and tedious discussion on modes of government; but it is certain, that all which can be alleged in favor of the monarchical form must, from the nature of things, depend on the personal virtues of the prince.

You will perhaps say, that no labour or cost is spared in the education of princes; that they are [224] put under the tuition of the most elevated men in the nation; that the arts and sciences court their attention; and that they have the advantage of selecting their servants out of the most respectable ranks in society.

If princes were placed under the tuition of men of the first worth and knowledge in the kingdom, Hortensia, instead of those of the most elevated rank, your observation might carry the appearance of weight: but it would be an appearance only; for what great effects can even a wise man produce by the most assiduous attention to the education of a being, surrounded from the instant of his birth by fawning courtiers? A being,

---

[50] Pope, *Of the Characters of Women.*

set up as a pageant for the idolatry of the public. A being, treated with ceremonies which from their nature must destroy every just idea of self, and of the relation in which he stands to the people whom he is to govern. A being, whose natural activity must be destroyed by the facility with which his every wish is indulged, and who becomes satiated even with variety, before other children are suffered to extend their pursuits beyond the most simple objects of enjoyment. And, to sum up all, a being, whose mind must be corrupted by the designing sycophants who crowd about him before his reason is sufficiently strong to perceive the difference between vice and virtue.

If a society would reap any advantage from the [225] personal virtues of their prince, they must educate him far from the precincts of a court[.] They must keep him a stranger to its vices, its servility, and its pageantry, till his understanding is sufficiently informed to despise its snares. They must select for his tutor a man of the first virtue, and of the most extensive learning; a man, who to the justest ideas of the rights of his species, unites a thorough knowledge of the domestic and foreign interests of the kingdom, its internal situation in regard to the state of the poor, the distribution of property, and other matters of intelligence, necessary to a just equality in the levying taxes, and in the encouragements to be given to national industry. He must understand morals on their true principles, not on mutable grounds, which bend to the temporary convenience of the moment, which adopt a partial for a general utility, which introduce a distinction between a state morality, and those obligations, which are allowed in private concerns to bind the species, and which confound in the vulgar, the plain ideas of right and wrong. He must be an adept in the knowledge of the human mind; he must be well versed in all the higher parts of philosophy; and his elevation of sentiment must be such as to direct his ambition to the sole object of bestowing on his country the blessing of a patriot king.[51] When such a man is found, it will be of no consequence whether he [226] is a nobleman or a commoner; whether he is rich or poor; his nobility of character will outweigh the nobility of birth; and it is always in the power of the public to grant him a pecuniary reward, which may bear some proportion to his eminent services.

A tutor thus judiciously selected from the body of the society, to the charge of this the most important office in the kingdom, ought to be

---

[51] This alludes to Bolingbroke's *Idea of a Patriot King* (1738).

trusted with the nomination of all the prince's domestics. If he does his duty, he will take care that the meanest of them be persons of worth, and good conduct; and that as they rise to importance by employments, which bring them nearer to the prince's person, and oftener in his presence, they be proportionably elevated in their talents, their understanding, their knowledge, and their philosophic virtues.

As courts, and every thing that carries the appearance of a court, should be avoided in the education of a prince; it ought to be a standing law of the realm, that no person go near the mansion in which the prince resides, without the especial leave of the council. Some few of the sons of the nobility and gentry, whose education has been particularly attended to, may be selected for his play fellows. For I would not have you think, that I intend to call a cloistered monk to the throne; on the contrary, my opinion is that [227] the prince, when he arrives at a proper age for useful reflection, ought to be introduced into all the various scenes of innocent life. But let care be taken, that the royal character be flung off; and should the *incognito* chance to be known, that every discouragement be given to an acknowledgment of the discovery. I am persuaded, that the want of sympathy with which princes are so often, and so justly reproached, proceeds as much from their never having beheld situations of distress, as from pride and arrogance of temper. Let my philosophic prince then, whose temper must have been rendered gentle and humane by a refined education, be often carried into those scenes of want and misery adapted to move even the obdurate heart to pity. Let him mingle his tears with those of the wretched, and let him enjoy the luxury of sympathy.

A prince, my friend, thus rendered benevolent by precepts, by practice, and by all those habits and customs which soften and excite sentiment, will never shut his ears to the just complaints of his people. He will on the contrary, regard them with all the tenderness of paternal fondness; he will regulate his government in such a manner as shall spread as much universal happiness among his people, as the nature of things will admit; he will encourage a spirit of benevolence among the opulent part of his subjects; he will discourage [228] that oppression which disfigures the face of a country with objects in the opposite extremes of the lordly palace, and the almost untenable hovel. He will not regard himself as seated on the throne of sovereignty for the gratification of self importance and indulgence, but will generously sacrifice even the repose of his life to the considerations of his duty.

To know the interests of humanity, says Marmontel, is the true study of a prince.[52] Whatever is just, whatever is useful, that is truth; and the truth, a king should investigate. This is the fit employment of a prince; to this he should dedicate his days; to know himself, and the nature of man, to develop the secret movements of the heart, the operations of habit, the specific qualities of character, the influence of opinion, the powers and the weaknesses of our frame; to study intensely the temper, the manners, and the resources of his people, together with the conduct of ministers; and in this noble enquiry to let in light to the judgment on every side, with a generous encouragement to those who have the spirit to call aloud for the redress of grievances committed in the prince's name.

This you will say, Hortensia, is requiring a great deal of princes, and is as far above what is set forth in real life, as the characters to be found in [229] the regions of romance. But history has furnished us with a few such sublime characters; and if all the frivolous ceremonies of a court, and its idle debauchery, were to give place to a close attention to the study of history, to systems of policy, to the various modes of government which have been carried into execution, or which have been projected by theorists, to all those works which treat on the rights of Nature, the social compact made or implied, and more especially the constitution of that state over which the royal pupil is destined to reign, it would enable him to form adequate ideas of the kingly office, and the importance of its duties. He would perceive the necessity of making the laws the sole rule of his conduct; he would perceive, that no sovereign can reign in freedom, who is under the necessity of intriguing with parties;[53] and that a prince, who closely unites himself to his people by mutual interest and mutual support, will have nothing to fear from the opposition of designing men.

But methinks, I hear some of the critics say, that all these good dispositions of mind, these wise determinations of a cool temper and a reflecting head, will disappear, and be no more, when the royal philosopher is brought from his retirement into the vortex of dissipation, and his virtue exposed to those temptations which irritate the passions, and stimulate to intemperance. It must [230] be confessed, Hortensia, that

---

[52] Jean-François Marmontel, *Belisarius* (London, 1767), p. 97.
[53] Bolingbroke, *The Idea of a Patriot King*, in *Works*, III, pp. 83–5.

the instances are so rare where wisdom has been found seated on the throne, that it may be regarded as a phenomenon of the most wonderful kind: but whilst history can boast of her Trajans, her Antoninus's, and her Julians,[54] they will serve as examples to prove, that precept, habit, and early impressions of the favourable kind, will do much to resist the tide of corrupting principles with which courts abound. And as these great examples are all to be found in men who have been raised from a private station to a throne, or who have been educated far from a court, it manifests the propriety of detaching the person of the prince from the seat of royalty.

Unfortunately for the reputation of women, or more candidly speaking, for the honour of *la belle passione*, these very extraordinary princes have been very little susceptible of its impression. The turbulent movements of love, and its enthralling power, is little adapted to the exertion of those active and passive virtues which are required in the conduct of a great Prince. Indeed every species of favoritism is hostile to the patriotism of a king, who is no sooner known to be under the influence of personal affection, than the ambition of all who surround him is fired with the view of gaining the ascendency over that affection. Adulation and treachery besiege the throne, and partiality con-[231]fers the recompence due to virtue upon elegant and polished vice.

Thus speaks Marmontel in his Belisarius, and his sentiments on the duties of the kingly character are very correct; but he gives the preference in this work to despotic forms of government, on the idea, that there is a more intimate union of interest between a prince and his people, than between the people and the individuals who form the component parts of popular governments.[55] Marmontel's idea in the abstract may be right, but it will never do in practice till mankind have sufficient sense to perceive their true interest, and a sufficient command over their passions to act in consequence of their perceptions. All therefore that can result from his fine spun reasoning, is what has been allowed by the greatest sticklers for democracy; namely, that could we be sure of a line of philosophic princes, the people might receive benefit, rather than injury, from the plenitude of their power. But now I hear a hundred voices raised against me for being so unreasonable as to wish to deprive princes of the joys of love and friendship, with many trite and

---

[54] The ones mentioned are often considered as among the best of the Roman emperors.
[55] Marmontel, *Belisarius*, pp. 72–3, 96.

foolish observations concerning the hardship of sovereignty on any terms, but that of making the interests of mankind bend to personal convenience, and personal pleasure. This is mere talking, without [232] once examining into self, or the nature of human ambition, which is such as to give an irresistable charm to sovereignty, on any terms. And if a vulgar feeling of ambition can annex the idea of such advantages to power, what must be the sentiments of a man inspired by education with the divine enthusiasm of general benevolence, and who has been taught to entertain adequate ideas of the privilege annexed to the royal station. The exalted privilege, that every act of virtue, every performance of duty, every instance of propriety in conduct, affect the public weal; of enjoying a power which extends even over the empire of folly and vice, and of being able to confer the most important obligations on successive generations.

These, Hortensia, are the glorious recompence which attend the giving up some private enjoyments, common in their kind, and calculated to relieve the tedium and the sorrows of private life, but not adapted to the artificial greatness of princes, who have so large a return of sincere panegyric for a conduct that bears any proportion to the elevation of their station, as to give them a stimulus in the article of reputation, which in the same extent can never attend men of inferior rank. How comes it then, that so few princes of all the long list who have reigned and tyrannized over [233] mankind, should have been inclined to give up satisfactions necessarily limited by the laws of Nature within the bounds of enjoyment which lies open to all men, to advantages peculiarly annexed to their situation.

It thus happens, because princes are corrupted by the allurements of pleasure in the earliest period of manhood. If they were kept from all temptation till the understanding was informed, and the mind had acquired sufficient strength to obey its dictates, the incitements to virtue, which royalty sets forth, would seldom fail of its effect. But as I mentioned enthusiasm, it will be necessary to observe, that the education of princes should in some respect differ from the education of their subjects. For let their natural vivacity and susceptibility be ever so great, you need not fear to drive them into a mischievous enthusiasm, because they have scope enough for the play of their virtues, without injuring their personal happiness; only whilst you endeavour to awaken their feelings to objects of public good, let not the virtue of frugality be forgotten; let it always be inculcated, that moderation is the most useful virtue in a prince; that regal dignity is not derived from the brilliant appearance which enlivens the palace; and that what is called the munificence of the sovereign, is squandering the substance of the people entrusted [234] to his care; the spoils of the poor and the indigent. In a word, that every shilling bestowed by a monarch on individuals whose services and talents have not been eminently useful to their country, is at the best a base abuse of confidence, unless it is taken from sums which might otherwise have been expended on personal gratifications.

[235] PART II, LETTER I

Influence of Domestic and National Education.

The modes of domestic education, Hortensia, as practised by the moderns, are not calculated to instil that wisdom into youth which is necessary to guard against the dangers that surround it. In a total ignorance of the nature of those things which constitute the happiness and the misery of the species, young persons are commonly initiated into the circles of conversation and the dissipated amusements of the age, at that period of life when the affections of childhood are by repeated impressions strengthened into passions, and when the passions of adults spring up in the mind.

[236] It is now, as Helvetius observes, that the youth finds himself attacked by a greater number of sensations; all that surrounds strikes him, and strikes him forcibly.[56] The imagination easily fascinated, both from its natural warmth, and the novelty of untried pleasures stamp on the ductile mind those various propensities which form its character through life. At this important period of existence, a public education, if it uniformly tends to instil the principles of equity and benevolence; if it uniformly tends to refine the mind and encrease its sympathy, will undoubtedly correct the intemperance of the gross and the malevolent affections. But though the education of the world will necessarily give a turn to the passions, yet it cannot teach the way to moderate and subdue them. It cannot teach us to be content with those limitations within which God has thought proper to confine human happiness; nor can it

---

[56] Helvetius, *Treatise on Man*, I, p. 25.

teach us to govern the imagination with such judgment as shall convert it from a source of perpetual evil, into a fountain of inexhaustible good.

It is indeed sufficient for the bulk of the people, if they are civilized in such a manner as to be innoxious in their conduct as citizens. That industry, which is necessary to their subsistence, will tame the turbulence of the imagination, and prevent it from being the source of mischief to themselves or others. But this is not the case [237] with the higher class of citizens whose circumstances and situation give them leisure, and opportunity, to indulge all the caprices of fancy. That wisdom which accompanies knowledge, is necessary to the great and opulent to prevent them from falling into those follies which blast in their bud the fairest fruits of fortune, and cloud the brightest prospects of human felicity.

If the higher classes of the people have not wisdom, who will be the framers of those laws which enlighten the understandings of the citizens in the essentials of right and wrong? Where shall we find those examples which are to direct the steps of the ignorant in the paths which lead to righteousness? Where that public instruction, which teaches to the multitude the relative duties of life? And where those decent and well regulated customs, which form the difference between civilized and uncivilized nations?

As the senses, Hortensia, are the only inlets to human knowledge, consequently human knowledge can only be gained by experience and observation.[57] Men as they gained ideas of good and evil, by experience, communicated their observations to their offspring. Domestic education therefore, must have begun with the beginning of the life of man; and when the species formed themselves into societies, their ideas were [238] necessarily extended from the variety of impressions and instructions which they received in such associations.

With the encrease of the flock of his ideas, man encreased his power of making comparisons, and consequently enlarged his knowledge of the relation of things. Some modes of conduct generally adopted, some rules and exercises fitted to a state of offence and defence, necessarily belong to all associations. Education then, in a state of the rudest society, must necessarily be more complex and more methodical than education in the natural, or more solitary state of man; who as he rises from this rude state of society, through all the degrees which form the difference between the

---

[57] This epistemological position is ultimately derived from Locke's *Essay* and was adopted by many of Macaulay's favourite authors in the eighteenth century, including Helvetius.

savage and the civilized nations, must receive impressions more numerous; his motives for action must grow more complex; his duties and his obligations must enlarge; the rules for his conduct must become more nice and various; his actions be more critically observed; his offences more certain-punished; and consequently his good or ill fate must depend in a more particular manner on his education, than when in a state of nature, or in a state of savage society. But when the manners of society refine, when standards of taste are established, when arts are practised, when sciences are studied, and when laws are numerous; it is then that the education of citizens, and more especially [239] of the better sort, becomes a matter of the highest importance and difficulty.

The first stages of the Roman republic present us with a set of military husbandmen. The fine arts were not practised among them; the sciences were not studied; nor commerce pursued. In this state of society, mankind exhibit rather a disgusting than a pleasing picture. The simplicity of their manners partakes rather of a savage rudeness, than a rational moderation; for the privation of those luxuries which equally tend to corrupt and improve the mind, allow them no means to acquire those graces and virtues which render the species objects of our admiration and esteem.

But the peculiar situation of the Romans, when they formed themselves into a distinct community, a spirit of heroism in their leaders, the patriotism and wisdom of several of their kings, gave a lustre to these republicans which never was acquired by any people in the same state of society. The love of glory, and the love of country, were passions pursued by the first Romans, with an enthusiasm which tinctured every part of their conduct and deportment. They became a nation of heroes; animated with these exalted affections, their manners were both simple and dignified. No assembly of men ever displayed such graceful virtues as the Roman senate, before the Romans were corrupted with power, and by the luxuries [240] it procures. They struck the ambassadors of Pyrrhus with awe and admiration. They suspended for a time the fierce rage of the barbarous Gaul; and they are now held forth by the virtuous literati, as models of all that is sublime in the human character.

At this period of the commonwealth, the public and domestic education of the Romans had only two objects in view. The one was, that of making illustrious citizens; and the other, of aggrandizing the society at the expence of the private interest of its members. Animated with a warm zeal for the prosperity of the republic, they lost sight of those advantages which men propose to themselves when they unite in society, viz. the acquiring and securing by an union of force, every enjoyment which is not found at variance with the peace and security of others. In a wild delirium of exalted passion, the Romans little attended to the useful precepts of philosophy; accordingly their virtues were often at enmity with their humanity, and their greatness with their rational happiness. The fondest admirers of the stern Brutus,[58] hardly envy him the glory of an obdurate justice, which with a steadiness that appeared to border on insensibility, triumphed over the urgent calls of parental affection, and thus buried the characters of the man and the father, in that of the inflexible judge. We respect the [241] filial piety of Manlius,[59] much more than that immoveable spirit of discipline, which, deaf to the mild dictates of equity, put a sudden period to the life of a hopeful and a virtuous son. And whilst we admire the incorruptible integrity of a Fabricius,[60] we can hardly determine whether the devotement of a Decius was an act of cool and resolute reason, or an act of glorious insanity.[61]

[257] [PART II] LETTER V

Observations on the State of the Romans after the Subversion of the Commonwealth.

The natural equality of man, Hortensia, is a truth which forces itself on candid attention, and dispels from the reluctant mind those prejudices, which national prosperity, or individual greatness, engrafts on human selfishness. We are fond of availing ourselves of situation, and of making comparisons which gratify our pride and conceit. Persons even of deep reflection have pretended to discover an apparent difference in the

---

[58] Lucius Junius Brutus ordered the execution of two of his sons for plotting to restore the monarchy in the early semi-mythical history of the Roman Republic.

[59] Titus Manlius Imperiosus Torquatus was a Roman consul and dictator who gained a reputation for his filial duty when defending his father against accusations by a plebeian tribune.

[60] Gaius Fabricius Luscinus, censor in Rome in 275 BC, and presented as unbribable by Plutarch, Cicero, and Dante.

[61] Decius was the Roman emperor from 249 to 251, and is known for reviving the office of the censor, and for persecuting Christians.

mental qualities of the inhabitants of the east and the north, and have given to the effect of climate those virtues which alone depend on moral causes.[62] Others, with an audacity more blameable, have dared to tax the Deity with partiality. They give to their own colour only, the quality of external beauty: and they persuade themselves, that the swarthy inhabitants of India and Africa, are a degree below them in the scale of intelligent Nature.

It is true, that most of the European states have at this day an apparent superiority in government, in arts, and in arms, to the inhabitants of Asia [258] and Africa. But if we reflect on the rise and fall of nations, we shall find, that accident alone, without the assistance of internal excellence, has produced this superiority, and that it has appeared and disappeared in the same society, as accident was favourable or unfavourable to its existence.

It is to the inhabitants of Asia that we owe the rudiments both of the sciences and the arts; and the savage barbarism which is now displayed on the sultry shores of Africa, has at some period or another been exceeded in every country of Europe.

The Romans themselves, Hortensia, are an incontestable example of the effect of accident, situation, and government, on national character and prosperity. In the history of this wonderful people we behold the extremes of virtue and vice, of greatness and meanness, of felicity and wretchedness, predominant according to the situation into which they were carried by the course of things. Cincinnatus returning from the conquest and sovereign rule to cultivate his little farm with his own hands, presents to the mind the sublimest image of national character that human society can afford.[63]

If you are amused with moral contrasts, Hortensia, compare the conduct of the consul Curius[64] and that of Caius Caesar,[65] under the obligation of similar trusts. The one, on being arraigned for diverting to his private use the spoils of the enemy, [259] substantially proved, that out of an immense treasure he had only detained a small wooden vessel, which he intended for the purposes of private devotion. The other, appropriated from Gallic spoils a treasure sufficient to repair his ruined

---

[62] Montesquieu, *The Spirit of the Laws* (1748), book 14.

[63] Lucius Quinctius Cincinnatus (*c.* 519 – *c.* 430 BC) was a Roman statesman and military leader of the early Roman Republic who later became a legendary symbol of virtue.

[64] Manius Curius Dentatus (d. 270 BC), consul and a plebeian hero of Rome.

[65] i.e. Julius Caius Caesar.

fortune, and to bribe over half his countrymen to his interest. Yet in the fairest days of Rome, the integrity of Curius was not more personally singular, than in its declension from virtue was the corruption of Caesar. The Romans of Caesar's days were derived from the same stock as were the Cincinnati; and if we may believe the tale of history, the stock which produced the race of demi-gods, were a handful of desperate adventurers, who had a settlement to seek, and who procured one by seizing and occupying a small spot of unappropriated land in Italy.

What then, will you say, were those important causes which, under the direction of Providence, laid the foundation of Roman greatness, and continued to operate with such an unexampled success? Those important causes, Hortensia, were all comprised in the warlike abilities of the first kings of Rome; in the well-timed prediction of the future greatness of the city; and the philosophic virtues and legislative abilities of Numa Pompilius.[66] It was the laws, the example, the precepts, and the active wisdom of this great man, which [260] gave to Roman manners and customs a superiority over all the states of Italy.

It has been already shewn in a preceding letter, that Rome owed the first steps of her aggrandizement, more to the rectitude of the counsels than to the prowess of her arms.[67] This aggrandizement however, by introducing an alteration in the state of things, introduced a change in the national character of the Romans. Their public counsels were corrupted by the lust of conquest; and their private manners, by the possession of riches and power. The spoils of conquered nations flowed in with a full tide on the commonwealth, and offered to individuals the most inviting opportunities for rapacity and plunder. The abuse of power and riches was carried by the Romans to its highest excess. Their slaves were innumerable; and they were treated with a cruel indignity. Their public shows, both from their expensive magnificence, and the nature of the exhibition, were adopted both to debauch their taste, and to render them callous to the feelings of humanity. The simplicity and frugality of primitive times were turned to every mode of luxury which invention could furnish, either to delight the sense, to sooth the caprice of taste, or gratify the pride of wealth. Poverty was no longer honourable; it was treated with scorn and insult. Moderation in the enjoyments of appetite, gave [261] way to the most vicious excess;

---

[66] The legendary second king of Rome, famous for founding religious institutions.
[67] Part II, Letter I, above.

and when the proscription of the last triumvirate had carried off all the leaders of the patriot band, there hardly remained a vestige either of public or private virtue in the whole empire.

From the imperfection of our nature, our virtues have their necessary limits. The down-hill road of vice and depravity presents a free and uninterrupted course. The Romans, in the days of Augustus,[68] when compared to the same people in the days of Cincinnatus, will fill a virtuous mind with disgust and contempt. Yet when we look forward from this stage of their corruption, to the period when Christianity gained a legal establishment under Constantine,[69] we shall find that the manners of the Augustan age were pure, in comparison with the succeeding periods of the empire. With a well acted hypocrisy, Augustus endeavoured to colour his trespass against decency and public opinion, and to provide for his reputation, by making an edict against lampoons and satires. At this period, Cornelius Sisenna was reproached in full senate with the licentious conduct of his wife;[70] but these lingering remains of old prejudices did not long continue to alarm or molest imperial voluptuousness; and those vices, which in the decline of the commonwealth could be attacked by the nice and delicate satire of Horace, grew to a height under the emperors, that [262] modern language cannot describe. In short, Hortensia, the gross luxury of the Romans under a Nero,[71] an Heliogabulus,[72] and other sovereigns of similar character, is neither fit for me to particularize, nor you to read. Nor can I give you a more adequate idea of it, than you will receive from the following description of the clearest and most lively historian that modern times have produced: 'Consigning ourselves to the public scenes displayed before the Roman people,' (says Mr. Gibbon) 'and attested by grave and contemporary historians, their inexpressible infamy surpasses that of any other age or country. The luxuries of an eastern monarch are secluded from the eye of curiosity by the walls of the seraglio. The sentiments of honour and gallantry have introduced a refinement of pleasure, a regard to decency, and a respect for the public opinion into the modern courts of Europe; but the corrupt and opulent nobles of

---

[68] The first Roman emperor, also known as Octavian.

[69] Constantine the Great was the first Roman emperor to convert to Christianity, in 312.

[70] See Elizabeth Rawson, 'L. Cornelius Sisenna and the Early First Century B.C.', *The Classical Quarterly*, 29 (1979), pp. 327–46.

[71] Roman emperor in 54–6.

[72] Elagabalus or Heliogabalus (204–22), officially known as Antoninus, was Roman emperor from 218 to 222.

Rome, gratified every vice that could be collected from the mighty conflux of nations and manners. Secure of impunity, careless of censure, they lived without restraint in the patient and humble society of their slaves and parasites. The emperor, in his turn, viewing every rank of his subjects with the same contemptuous indifference, asserted without controul his sovereign privilege of taste and luxury.'[73]

Enjoyment, whilst it relaxes the powers of the [263] mind, is supposed to soften the asperities of temper; and that in proportion as men become luxurious, they become tractable and open to the impressions of the softer passions. That point of moral depravity then, which unites the highest excess of self indulgence with a complacency for the misery of others, can never be described without raising sentiments of indignant horror; yet such is the representation of Roman manners, even at so early a period of despotism, as the reign of Nero. This frantic tyrant found it convenient for his reputation to lay the fire of Rome on the Christians,[v] who, from the novelty of their doctrines, and their opposition to paganism, were always obnoxious to popular clamour. A festival of the most extraordinary kind was prepared to reinstate the emperor in the good graces of his subjects. The gardens of Nero were decorated in the most sumptuous manner; booths were erected, where persons of all ranks were regaled with the most exquisite wine and viands; and where every kind of debauchery was pursued without disturbance or molestation. A horse race, which was honoured with the presence of the emperor, who mingled with the populace in the dress [264] of a charioteer, had a place in the innoxious part of the spectacle. But what will you say, Hortensia, to the exhibition of Christians nailed on crosses; of others sown up in the skins of wild beasts, and thus exposed to the fury of dogs; of others again, smeared over with combustible materials, set aloft on pillars, and made to serve as torches to illuminate the darkness of the night.

The faithful historian who relates these sufferings of the Christians, says, that their agonies were embittered with the scorn and derision of

---

[v] Mr. Gibbon is in doubt whether these Galileans, as Tacitus terms them, were Christians, who in the beginning were distinguished by that title, or some frantic zealots who followed the standard of Judas the Gaulonite, who had raised arms against the Roman power. [Edward Gibbon, *The History of the Decline and Fall of the Roman Empire* (6 vols., London, 1776–89), I, pp. 536–7.]

[73] Gibbon, *The History of the Decline and Fall of the Roman Empire*, I, pp. 210–11.

the spectators; but there wants not this addition to the picture, to complete either the horror of the scene, or the strength of your sentiments, which I dare say are replete with a scorn and indignation equal to what the good Pompilius[74] would have felt, could he have foreseen the infamy of that day.

[265] [PART II] LETTER VI

Causes which may have hitherto prevented Christianity from having its full Effect on the Manners of Society.

In the foregoing letters which I have written to you, Hortensia, I have noticed some of those leading customs in the republics of Sparta, Athens, and Rome, which stamped a national character on their citizens, and gave them a relative excellence over other societies.

Roman fortitude, patriotism, and simplicity, are virtues which have been but faintly copied by men bred under the light of gospel morality; and the Christian world would suffer much in a comparison with the Romans of the first four centuries after the building of the imperial city.

To account for so strange a phenomenon, it will be necessary to recall to our observation, that the period when the doctrine of Christianity was first propagated among men, though aptly fitted for the purpose of its extension, was very unfavourable to the purity of its votaries. The birth of the Messiah was in the very commencement of Roman slavery, when the Romans had lost [266] every primitive virtue both political and moral; and when Christianity became the established religion of the empire, the declension of Roman manners had touched the lowest point of moral depravity. Venality, insolence, servility, were vices that grew out of the very forms of the government, corrupted every part of society, and took deep root. Whilst Rome continued under the form of a republic, her citizens contenting themselves with substantial power, had left to the vanity of eastern slaves and despots, the forms of ostentatious greatness, and preserved to the very extinction of their liberty, a simplicity of manners well adapted to the practice of the Christian virtues. But when, for the distinction of personal merit and

[74] i.e. Numa Pompilius.

influence, an artificial subordination adapted to the support of family despotism was established; when those plain epithets which had been used to the greatest of the human race, became only the appellations annexed to vulgar life; when a menial office about the person of the prince exalted the citizen in the scale of rank above those who bore the first civil offices in the empire; when the fantastic titles of 'your honor, your excellency, your eminence, your illustrious highness,' &c. &c. were considered as rewards for personal service; it was then that the empire of corruption must have been universal, and must have stifled in the hearts of men those [267] sentiments of humanity and genuine integrity which had been acquired by the graces of the gospel.

When that persecution was withdrawn, which helped to curb the intemperance of the passions; when the episcopal order were freely admitted to the conversation of the sovereign, and made part of the corrupt court at Constantinople; when, to use the expression of an elegant writer, the Christians were advanced to those situations from which virtue either retires or is subdued, they began to doubt its necessary efficacy, and found it no difficult task to persuade themselves, that the ceremonies of religion were a convenient succedaneum for practical goodness, and that a saving faith was not altogether incompatible with a life of sin.[75]

Where the Barbarians had rendered themselves the masters of the Roman empire, they universally adopted the religion, the laws, and the customs of the conquered. Thus the morals of the Christians were not mended by their misfortunes. Some vices peculiar to a state of barbarism were added to the catalogue of Roman enormities; every thing mischievous in the policy of Constantine and his successors was engrafted in the Gothic constitutions. Europe is to this day swayed by the principles of their government; and all our prejudices, [268] manners, and ceremonies, owe their origin to the same corrupt source.

Much has been said of the progress of modern civilization, but it certainly has so little tended to bring us back to classic simplicity, that we are every day departing more and more from it; and vanity, with the extension of our ideas on the article of luxury, bids fair to extinguish some of the most useful of the moral virtues out of the human character.

---

[75] This does not seem to be a direct quotation, but possibly an allusion to Gibbon, *Decline and Fall*, I, p. 561.

It must be owned, that experimental philosophy has produced many discoveries in this age, which has greatly encreased the limits of human enjoyment. And if our improvement in the useful arts of life were properly adapted to the improvement of human sentiment, many of those vices which deform the present age might be reformed; for it is certain, that mind in man is so intimately connected with sense, that it is impossible to mortify the one without impoverishing the other. The manners of that people will be barbarous whose customs are gross; and virtue, by a wise disposition of things, will be found to be in union with a reasonable enjoyment. That human sentiment is yet in a low and barbarous state, the abuse of power which the brute creation suffer from our hands, bears a melancholy testimony. I mention this as a notorious instance of the state of modern barbarism, because the cruelties committed [269] on brutes are unprovoked. But even the wanton manner in which we spill the blood of our offending citizens, gives a dark complexion to the character of the times; and if after ages should produce societies refined to an exalted pitch of humanity, with what surprize and detestation will they regard their ancestors of the eighteenth century.

As several good men have, notwithstanding these untoward appearances, promised to themselves a return of the golden age, as depictured by the poets, it may not, Hortensia, be an un-entertaining speculation, to examine the utility of such means as shall appear to us the most likely to conduce to the highest degree, and the most universal extent of possible good.

[270] [PART II] LETTER VII

Duty of Governments towards Producing a General Civilization.

Before we enter into the examination of such means, Hortensia, as shall appear to us the most likely to conduce to the highest degree, and the most universal extent of possible good, we must enquire into the nature of those high and important obligations which, in the reason of things, must be annexed to the office of government.

What may be the nature and extent of those duties of government which, on a principle of equity, subjects have a right to demand for all the splendid gifts they bestow on their governors, is a question which so nearly concerns the interests of man, that it becomes a matter of wonder the accuracy of their reasoning should not, in this point, have produced an uniformity of opinion. But important as is this subject, there is no speculation on which a greater variety of opinions have been formed, on which the prejudices of the species have been more at war with their interests, or on which the feebleness or the inactivity of the [271] reasoning powers have been more exposed, or which more proves man to be the slave of custom and of precept.

It is well known, that a great part of the ancient, and even of the modern world, have made a deity of their government, in whose high prerogatives they have buried all their natural rights. The monstrous faith of millions made for one, has been at different times adopted by the greater part of civilized societies; and even those enlightened nations who have been the most famed for asserting and defending their liberties, ran into another species of idolatry, which is almost as much at war with the happiness of individuals. Instead of making a deity of the government, they made a deity of the society in its aggregate capacity; and to the real or imagined interests of this idol, they sacrificed the dearest interests of those individuals who formed the aggregate. Thus they reversed a very plain and reasonable proposition. Society with them was not formed for the happiness of its citizens, but the life and happiness of every citizen was to be devoted to the glory and welfare of the society.

When the happiness of an individual is properly considered, his interest will be found so intimately connected with the interests of the society of which he is a member, that he cannot act in conformity to the one, without having a proper [272] consideration for the other. But reason will revolt against a service for which it finds no adequate return; and when we admire the virtue of the ancients, we admire only that inflexible conduct which carried them to sacrifice every personal interest to principle.

The moderns are grown so lax in their devotions to the shrine of patriotism, as to bury in the ruins of public virtue all good faith and common honesty; a depravity in manners, which too plainly manifests that the change of conduct proceeds from the total want of principle, rather than from the having formed just ones. We have indeed made no accurate definitions either on the duties of government, or on the duties of a good citizen; and individuals, from the prevalent power of custom and precept, are content with privations which have no foundation in the common good.

Man is ever apt to run into extremes; no sooner do we discard one gross error, than we deviate into another of an opposite nature. It is said, that truth is always to be found in the mean;[76] if so, those must differ widely from her, who, to avoid the evil of such a power as is claimed by despots, of interfering with all private as well as public concerns, assert, that the true and only office of government, is to act the part of a good constable in preserving the public peace.

Thus, according to the opinion of the most [273] liberal of the moderns, governors have little else to do but to eat and drink, and to enjoy all the various emoluments annexed to the diadem and the purple,[77] without disturbing their repose by fulfilling any of those parental duties which subjects, in their political connexion, have a much greater right to expect from their sovereign, than children have to expect from their natural parent; for where much is given, much may with justice be required.

The marquis of Beccaria, in his excellent treatise on crimes and punishments asserts, that government has no right to punish delin-quency in its subjects, without having previously taken care to instruct them in the knowledge of the laws, and of those duties in public and private life which are agreeable to the dictates of moral rectitude.[78] This observation coincides with that strain of benevolence which runs through the whole of this excellent treatise. For not to dwell on the high injustice of assuming the power of punishment, without fulfilling the duties of instruction, it must be obvious to enlightened reason, that the sublime office of government consists in limiting, as far as the nature of things will allow, the bounds of evil, and extending the bounds of good. And thus much may be said, that whatever be the sanguine expectations formed from some useful discoveries made in the science of physics, the conveniences and the happiness enjoyed by the [274] generality of the world, will continue to be very moderate, unless the united force of society is steadily used to carry on the glorious work of improvement.

---

[76] Aristotle located moral virtue in the mean between two extremes in the *Nicomachean Ethics*.

[77] *OED*: of a person: wearing or entitled to wear this colour; of imperial or royal rank.

[78] Cesare Beccaria stressed that laws need to be clear, precise, and transparent in *An Essay on Crimes and Punishments* (1764; London, 1767), esp. ch. 5: 'Of the Obscurity of Laws', and ch. 45: 'Of Education'.

The education of the people, in the most extensive sense of this word, may be said to comprehend the most important duties of government. For as the education of individuals is for ever going on, and consists of all the impressions received through the organs of sense, from the hour of birth to the hour of death; public education, if well adapted to the improvement of man, must comprehend good laws, good examples, good customs, a proper use of the arts, and wise instructions conveyed to the mind, by the means of language, in the way of speech and writing.

[275] [PART II] LETTER VIII

Sympathy – Equity.

If we trace, Hortensia, the origin of those virtues in man, which render him fit for the benign offices of life, we shall find that they all center in sympathy. For had the mind of man been totally divested of this affection, it would not in all probability have ever attained any ideas of equity. Yes, it was the movements of sympathy which first inclined man to a forbearance of his own gratifications, in respect to the feelings of his fellow creatures; and his reason soon approved the dictates of his inclination. A strict adherence to the principles of equity, may be said to include the perfection of moral rectitude. This being granted, all human virtue will be found to proceed from equity; consequently, if the principle of equity itself owes its source in the human mind to the feelings of sympathy, all human virtue must derive its force from this useful affection.

When this benign affection holds a superiority in the mind to other affections, inclination will lead to the performance of the duties of humanity. But in those insensible minds where this [276] affection is originally weak, or where it is extinguished by the excess of hostile passions, equity, unsupported by benevolence, has either no place in the mind, or through the cold precept of tuition, bears a feeble sway.

We have reason to believe that all the passions which belong to humanity lie latent in every mind; but we find by experience that they continue inactive till put in motion by the influence of some corresponding impression; and that their growth and prevalence in a great measure depends on the repetition of those impressions which are in their nature adapted to affect them. Thus it will appear, that where we have power to direct the course of impression, we have power to command the state of the passions; and as laws, example, precept, and custom, are the prime sources of all our impressions, it must be greatly in the power of government to effect, by a proper use of these sources, that improvement on which true civilization depends.

It is known, that the power of custom over the mind arises from such a repetition of the same impression, as act to the weakening or destroying the source of every impression of contrary tendency. Could we therefore, by the spirit of our laws, exclude from society the operation of every impression which partook of the smallest tincture of cruelty, and did we encourage the operation of [277] every impression which had a benevolent tendency, it appears probable, that we should exalt the sympathizing feeling to a degree which might act more forcibly than the coercion of rigorous laws – to the restraining all acts of violence, and consequently all acts which militate against the public peace.

For example, were government to act on so liberal a sentiment of benevolence, as to take under the protection of law the happiness of the brute species, so far as to punish in offenders that rigorous, that barbarous treatment they meet with in the course of their useful services, would it not tend to encrease sympathy? would it not highly enlarge our notions of equity, by pointing out to public observation this moral truth, that tenderness is due to those creatures, without whose daily labour society would be bereaved of every enjoyment which renders existence comfortable?

When a large and gentle bullock, says Mandeville, after having resisted a ten times greater force of blows than would have killed his murderer, falls stunned at last, and his armed head is fastened to the ground with cords, as soon as the wide wound is made, and the jugulars are cut asunder, what mortal can, without compassion, hear the painful bellowing intercepted by his blood, the bitter sighs that speak the sharpness of his anguish, and the deep sounding groans with loud anxiety [278] fetched from the bottom of his strong and palpitating heart; or see the trembling and violent convulsions of his limbs, the reeking gore streaming from his wounds, and his struggling gasps, and last efforts for life, the certain signs of his approaching state.[79]

***

[79] Bernard Mandeville, *The Fable of the Bees: or, Private Vices, Publick Benefits* (3rd ed., London, 1724), p. 196.

Mandeville is mistaken; so forcible is the power of habit, that these dreadful sights are daily seen without exciting horror, or one soft tear or sigh of sympathy; and consequently habits such as these must tend to weaken and even to destroy this heavenly quality. Oh! Then let all slaughter houses be treated as nuisances; let them be sequestered from the haunts of men; let premiums be given to those who can find out the least painful manner of taking away the lives of those animals which are necessary for sustenance; let every other manner of depriving them of life be forbidden, under severe penalties; let the privation of life, by way of sport and amusement, be discouraged by example and precept; and it is more than probable, that such a spirit of benevolence will be diffused over the minds of the public, as may tend to the general practice of those virtues which reason approves, and which Christianity ordains.

It has been a question lately much agitated, whether any such necessity exists, as is pretended, of depriving those delinquents of their lives, who act against the public peace by treasonable of-[279]fences, and by injuring a fellow citizen's life or property. Those who take the benevolent side of the question, maintain, that the depriving a citizen of his life, is a breach of one of the fundamental obligations of government, and that there may be found a variety of punishments more fully adequate to the preservation of the public peace, than acts of violence which shock the sensibility of the feeling mind, and harden to a state of barbarism the unfeeling one.[80] Those who take the adverse side of the question, oppose these positions with many plausible arguments; but whether the necessity contended for really exists in the nature of things, or whether it exists only in the indolence of government, and their inattention to the happiness of the community in their individual capacity, certain it is, that the interests of humanity and the dictates of good policy, require that the examples of taking away life should be as few as the nature of things will admit. That all the ceremonies which attend this melancholy act, should be made as aweful as possible; and that to prevent the public from receiving any impression which may shock the compassionate part of the society, or contribute to steal the hearts of the more insensible, all executions should be performed in private.

---

[80] Notably, Beccaria.

The English, from the number of their charitable donations, from the heavy taxes they lay [280] on themselves to maintain their poor,[81] and above all, for the general diffusion of sentiment, which in a late attempt[vi] on the life of his Majesty, deterred the most servile courtier of the train to compliment their prince at the expence of justice and humanity, have proved themselves to be in a comparative sense, a benevolent people. Yet the long list of wretches who, on particular seasons of the year, are led out to execution without exciting a sufficient sympathy in the public to stop for an instant the career of trifling dissipation, proves too strongly that the English, like their neighbours, are yet in a state of barbarism. A moments attention to the melancholy situation into which a fellow creature is reduced, for errors from which we are preserved by a more happy destiny, is sufficient to spread the gloom of sorrow over a reflecting mind; and as every indulgence of sentiment tends to strengthen its force, such solemnities should be used at executions, as might serve to augment the compassion of the sympathizing, and raise the terror in the gay and the thoughtless.

Civilized Rome never saw scaffolds stained with the blood of their citizens; and she granted civic crowns to those who preserved their lives. The moderns have too widely departed from this line of policy, and in so doing have relaxed the ties of social life. Would it not be graceful, would it [281] not be setting a due estimation on the life of a citizen, were the supreme magistrate, in the tender character of a political parent, with the judge who is necessitated by the duties of his office to pass the fatal sentence, to put on black, and to continue this garb of mourning till after the execution of the criminal? Would it not be raising useful impressions in the minds of the public, were the following solemnities to be used at the execution? The prisoner to be conducted to the place of punishment with a long train of the officers of justice, and their proper attendants, in mourning. The train to be led by the officer of state, with the sword of justice elevated in his hand. The officer of state to be immediately

---

[vi] The case of Margaret Nicholson. [Nicholson (*c.* 1750–1828) assaulted George III in 1786.]

[81] Macaulay refers to the English system of Poor Laws, codified in the Elizabethan period, under which each parish collected a tax on property known as the poor rate.

followed by the officers of justice, and they by the executioner, with the instrument of his office; the executioner to be immediately followed by the criminal; the criminal to be followed by persons dressed in black, bearing his coffin; the procession to be closed by the inferior officers of justice and their assistants, and all the bells in the city to be made to toll during the passing of the procession.

To give strength to the impressions which these solemnities are calculated to make, the seat of execution, in the form of a large square, fenced in with high walls, should be placed at the further end of the city; the sword of justice, and other emblematical pieces of sculpture, may ornament its [282] gates, and over them may be written in large capitals, '*These are the gates which lead to death.*' At the entrance of this tremendous square the multitude ought to be dismissed, and none but the officers of justice with their attendants, the executioner, and the criminal with his relations or friends, be permitted to enter. After the execution, the body ought to be interred in a burying ground adjoining the square, and kept sacred for that purpose. The procession should return with the same solemnities with which it set out; and all public amusement or meetings, of a dissipated kind, should be prohibited on this day.

[283] [PART II] LETTER IX

Observations on Penal Laws – Houses of Correction – Charity.

After all that may with justice, Hortensia, be said on the sanguinary spirit of our penal laws, we shall be obliged to come to this melancholy conclusion; – that the obstacles to their reformation are so deeply rooted in the vices of society, as to allow of no hopes of amendment. For whilst artificial life sets forth, as in the present age, a variety of temptations adapted to captivate the imagination, and inflame to a maddening height the cupidity of our species – whilst even our clergy affect to fling off the restraints of religion; – whilst the contagion of example, and a participation in their vicious amusements, renders the poorer class of our citizens as luxurious as the rich; whilst the idle attendants on the great, more numerous than the industrious poor, contract all the wants and vices of opulence; our possessions, to use the words of an elegant writer, must be paled up with sanguinary edicts, and hung round with gibbets to scare every invader.[82]

Great hopes I know have been founded on the [284] new institution of sunday schools; but whilst a commerce with the world offers so many temptations and so many snares, the knowledge which can be gained by this method of instruction will hardly serve as an adequate means to protect the innocence of youth.

However, if these schools should save even a small number from the gallows, they ought not to be neglected. But as we are now examining that part of civil policy which tends to meliorate the state of the poor, and reform their manners, let us extend our enquiries to those defects in our laws, and those abuses in the exercise of power, which have been recommended to the consideration of the public, by the philanthropic Mr. Howard, now lost to society.[83]

It has been the custom of all Europe to punish the lesser offences against the peace and good order of society, by branding, whipping, pillory, and other such like modes of discipline. These were introduced no doubt with the design of strengthening the motives for good conduct, by awakening that sense of shame which education and the pride of nature impresses on every mind; but it is to be considered, that when such public circumstances of disgrace are once suffered, shame has no longer its influence over the mind, and those incentives can no longer exist which are the most likely to produce reformation. A citizen thus [285] marked with the indelible stain of infamy, has lost the means of providing for his wants in the way of an honest industry; and as it is natural that he should harbour in his bosom a resentment to that society by whom he is ruined, he will be strongly tempted to retaliate on the public by a course of violence and rapine.

Houses of correction where the minor offences are punished by employing the offenders in tasks of labor, have also made part of the police of all the European societies. But to the shame of Great-Britain it must be spoken, that we have considered the future happiness or amendment of our fellow citizens so little worth our notice, that these

---

[82] Oliver Goldsmith, *The Vicar of Wakefield* (2 vols., London, 1766), II, p. 101.

[83] The prison reformer John Howard (1726–90), author of *The State of the Prisons in England and Wales, with Preliminary Observations, and An Account of Some Foreign Prisons* (Warrington, 1777), and a series of local studies on prisons and hospitals published in 1789.

houses are better adapted to the eradicating out of the mind every principle of virtue, than to the correction of vice.

When delinquents are brought into one of these houses, they are under the necessity of associating with the most abandoned profligates in the whole society; thus their habits become totally depraved, and thus wretches, who are enclosed for the commission of one crime, are returned to society fitted for the perpetration of thousands.

In other societies, whose inhabitants are not so entirely taken up with their pleasures or with the business of a political and mercantile traffic, some care is taken to render such houses of confinement, houses of amendment. Every person enclosed is [286] kept by himself; solitude affords him time for reflection; and instead of receiving pernicious impressions by the conversation and actions of profligates, he is only visited by those whose office it is to lay before him every argument for reformation.

Such houses of confinement as have been used for the imprisonment of debtors, and for the security of those persons who are to stand a trial for public crimes, have been found more defective for every purpose that humanity or good policy would dictate, than even the houses of correction. Here the innocent and the guilty are equally involved in an abyss of misery, which often terminates in consequences as fatal to the life of the prisoner, as the most capital of our punishments. Here are to be seen imprudent spendthrifts, and prisoners only on suspicion, in want of every necessary of life: their lodging such as must produce in the most vigorous constitutions the slow disease which undermines the principles of health, and subjected to the contagion of those maladies which terminate existence by one of the most painful modes of bodily suffering.

Such monstrous abuses of power, and neglect of legislative duties, Hortensia, have been in too good hands for me to enter on any plans of reform. Mr. Howard's labors have already produced very good effects in many parts of this island, and if [287] you wish to be further acquainted with the subject, I recommend you to the perusal of a pamphlet published by Capel Lofft, Esq. of Suffolk, a gentleman, who has devoted very distinguished abilities to the cause of humanity, and who has written on almost every topic important to its interest. The title of the pamphlet is, 'Thoughts on the Construction and Polity of Prisons, &c. &c.'[84]

---

[84] *Thoughts on the Construction and Polity of Prisons, with Hints for their Improvement* (Bury St Edmunds, 1785) is attributed to Capel Lofft's fellow reformer John Jebb.

247

On leaving the subject of public prisons and houses of correction, let us enter on the more grateful task of examining those various establishments, formed on the principle of affording the relief of medicine to the sick. There are many abuses undoubtedly crept into all these institutions, which want the inspection of a Howard, and the attention of power; but however they may have deviated from the intention of the founders, they are all of them useful. And I wish the principle was extended to the building hospitals for incurables; for no incident can shock a feeling mind more than the seeing a forlorn wretch turned out of an hospital, to encounter all the horrors of want, under the heavy burthen of a lingering, painful, and fatal disease.

The great sums of money which are given away in this country in private and public acts of charity, with the ample provision the law has made for paupers, has reflected some lustre on the na-[288]tional character of the English; but it is very doubtful whether any great measure of good hath been obtained by these overflowings of opulence. The certainty even of so miserable a pittance as is sufficient to keep off the terrors of starving, must often draw the insensible and the idle into situations which might have been avoided by an active industry.

If our parish workhouses were upon a plan adapted to cherish and comfort life in its most helpless and decrepit state, they would be more expensive than the relieving the indigent; in modes more agreeable to that natural love of freedom impressed on every breast. At present, they are equally places of punishment, and liable to the exceptions which have been made to the houses of correction.

Without starting any invidious doubts as to the benevolent motives which may influence the authors and encouragers of acts of private and public charity, I must repeat my observation, that money is often a secondary good to the assistance which may be afforded the distressed in a variety of other ways; and that even where money is necessary for the relief of an object, a small degree of additional trouble in the manner of administering it, and the accompanying it with our advice and influence, in society, would render it more useful than if the sum given had [289] been trebled in value. Unfortunately we mistake the parting with what our opulence renders of little worth in our eyes, for that solid virtue, without which, as St. Paul says, the most dazzling modes of charity are of no account.[85] Of those who tread the giddy rounds of fashionable life, are

---

[85] For Paul on charity, see 1 Corinthians 13 in the King James Bible. In modern editions, ἀγάπη is translated as 'love' rather than 'charity'.

there any who regard it as a part of necessary goodness to give up a small portion of their time to the happiness of others? Hence it is that almost all charities, both private and public, are most shamefully abused, and rendered totally inadequate to the purposes intended. Whilst this idle spirit continues among us, we may accumulate tax upon tax, and never truly relieve the distresses of the poor. For no law can possibly answer the benevolent purposes of the legislature, but one that entirely takes the executive part out of the hands of those who have an interest in abusing the trust, and whose mean situations in life and low education render them deaf to the voice of sympathy, and callous to the stings of remorse.

But shall the fine gentleman and lady leave the pleasures that belong to opulence, and amuse themselves in the drudgery of business for the advantage of wretches fed by public charity? Shall the cares of the toilette, the pleasures of the chace,[86] the gaming table, and all the innumerable, &c. &c. which help to fill up the time of the sons and daughters of fortune, be laid aside for a [290] system of accounts and oeconomy, never used in the management of their own concerns – and this without any probability of gaining by it a title, or reaping the distinctions or emoluments of office? forbid it fashion – forbid it common sense!

I am aware, Hortensia, that the habits adopted by the gay and rich, and the common received notion, that a pleasurable life is the only way in which the advantages of fortune can be enjoyed, will raise insurmountable obstacles and objections to my opinion on the real duties of charity. To these objections, there is but one answer to be given, but that is a strong one, viz. That those who prize pleasure beyond satisfaction, have never experienced the superiority of the latter in the scale of happiness. That the virtues, like the vices, will by habit and indulgence grow into desires, and to the fruition of the virtuous desires, God in his wisdom and bounty has annexed an enjoyment unmixed with any alloy of disappointment and suffering. Benevolence is one of the most animating of the moral principles; and were it really felt and practised by the fashionable world, it would entirely subdue the daemon *Ennui*, who drives our nobility and opulent gentry from the terrestrial paradises they enjoy in this island, to hunt after happiness in every place of public resort both at home and on the continent.

---

[86] i.e. the chase, a reference to hunting.

[291] The sums that are yearly spent by our travelling gentry in Germany, Italy, and France, if laid out in judicious modes of charity and domestic hospitality, might be returned in a stock of enjoyment that would both invigorate and enliven the mind, and render it sensible to the soft and tranquil pleasures that an elegant retreat affords.[87]

---

[87] Macaulay refers to the Grand Tour.

8

Observations on the Reflections of the Right Hon. Edmund Burke on the Revolution in France (1790)

Introduction to the Text

When working on her *Letters on Education* in 1787, Macaulay said that she hoped to 'resume my pen on a political subject' once her treatise on education was finished.[1] The French Revolution, and more precisely her old antagonist Burke's reaction to it, furnished her with an opportunity to return to political pamphleteering. This resulted in her final publication and one of her most important political writings. When she opposed Burke's 'aristocratic Whiggism' in 1770, they had been on the same side on the Middlesex election dispute, even if they represented different factions of the broad opposition. They would later be on the same side again regarding the American crisis, at least in relation to Lord North's government. After the outbreak of the French Revolution, however, their positions could not have been further apart. In November 1790 Burke published his *Reflections on the Revolution in France* (1790) in response to the Unitarian minister Richard Price's *Discourse on the Love of Our Country*, which had connected the Glorious, American and French revolutions. Macaulay had not been present when Price delivered the address in November 1789, but her friends reported details of the event to her.[2] Macaulay addressed her pamphlet to the political reformer Charles Stanhope, 3rd Earl Stanhope (1753–1816), William Pitt the Younger's brother-in-law and chairman of the Revolution Society, to which Price belonged.

---

[1] Macaulay to Mercy Otis Warren, November 1787, in *Correspondence*, p. 165.
[2] Philip Mallet to Macaulay, 9 November 1789, in *Correspondence*, pp. 282–3.

Like Wollstonecraft's better-known and as quickly written riposte to
Burke, *A Vindication of the Rights of Men*, Macaulay accused Burke of
prioritising the art of composition at the expense of substance. She
believed that Burke had appealed to the passions instead of the reason
of humankind, and emphasised that her pamphlet was written to convince rather than to captivate. Macaulay agreed with Price that the
exclusion of James II and his son from the succession to the throne
and Parliament's legislation for an order of succession which prioritised
the closest Protestant relatives of the Stuarts, in the Act of Settlement
1701, sufficiently proved that the reigning Hanoverian royal family owed
their ascendency to the choice of the people. Burke, by contrast, inter-
preted the legislation as adhering to the hereditary principle as far as was
possible while excluding Catholic monarchs.

Drawing on her historical works, Macaulay wrote provocatively:
'without the prince of Orange, and the assistance of his Dutch army,
there could have been no Revolution' (p. [11]). Despite what Burke
seemed to think, the majority of people were little affected by James II's
alleged tyranny. The whole body of the people had long been seduced by
'the *poison* of church policy', and '*passive obedience* ... had so entirely
supplanted the *abstract notion* of the *rights of men*, which prevailed in the
opposition to Charles the first'. It was thus natural for the hereditary
principle to survive the Glorious Revolution. In this regard, Macaulay
invoked the authority of an old enemy: 'Mr. Hume justly supposes, that
if the revolution had happened one hundred years after it did, it would
have been *materially different* in all its circumstances.' Discarding the
hereditary principle entirely would have avoided the deliberate ambigu-
ity surrounding James's deposition and made party names and battles
unnecessary. Indeed, Walpole's entire '*system of corruption*', designed to
guard against Jacobitism, would never have come into existence (pp.
[12–13]).

According to Burke, the Act of Settlement 1701 had forever secured
the hereditary succession in Britain. For Macaulay, this resembled the
theory of 'the fanatic atheist Hobbes', according to whom the people,
after having chosen their government in the original state, 'for ever lose
their native privileges' (p. [14]). She castigated Burke for relying on
opinion, prejudice and the power of the imagination for political stability.
Prejudice was the source of both the foolish and the vicious in human
beings. Consistent with her philosophical and religious principles, she
wrote that the supreme being had enabled human beings to understand

and obey *truth*, which was the basis of happiness in this life and perfection in the next.

In opposition to Burke, Macaulay defended the principle of abstract right as opposed to prescription and historical right. She pointed out that Burke had been wrong to accuse Price of novelty when the Dissenting minister said that all legitimate power was based on the rights of nature, because that is what the English revolutionaries in the mid seventeenth century had argued. Against Burke, Macaulay returned to her critique of the politics of convention from her correspondence with Hume in the 1760s. If lawful governments are formed on the authority of conventions, it raises the question: who gave these conventions their authority? If they originated from the assent of the people, why were they allowed to give their assent to a new convention at one period of time and not another? If human beings were by *necessity* driven to recover their natural rights, who is to be the judge of this necessity? These questions will ultimately lead us to decide whether the one, the few, or the many have an inherent right to make laws for the community. According to Macaulay, this is the best line of argument in favour of the 'unalienable and indefeasible rights of man' to make and unmake laws via representation (p. [94]).

Macaulay viewed the French Revolution as something new in world history because the people manifested a complete unanimity of spirit. She even defended its violent dimension, at least partially. She argued that all revolutions contain evils, and it could hardly be otherwise for the French Revolution, since it was so complete and comprehensive. Considering the animosity between 'aristocratists' and 'democratists' on the eve of the revolution, it would have been impossible for it to take place without any violence. A degree of barbarity was also understandable, because the people were accustomed to such practices under the absolute monarchy. She stressed, however, that these evils had been greatly exaggerated in England.

This edition reproduces the only known London version of the work. However, excerpts from the *Observations* appeared in both volumes of *A Comparative Display of the Different Opinions of the Most Distinguished British Writers on the Subject of the French Revolution* (2 vols., 1793). Moreover, a Boston edition was also published in 1791, with a short preface justifying its appearance and connecting the French and the American revolutions in terms of which Macaulay was likely to have approved:

Priestley, Paine, and other observers on Mr. Burke's celebrated Philippick, have been read with avidity in America, while a pamphlet of equal merit has escaped the publick eye. It has happened to fall into very few hands on this side of the Atlantick, therefore a republication will doubtless gratify every American, who has not lost sight of those principles that actuated, and the perseverance that effected, the independence of America.

Observations on the Reflections of the Right Hon.
Edmund Burke on the Revolution in France (1790)

[5] Observations, &c.

My Lord,[1]

Your lordship's character as a patriot, a philosopher, and the firm friend of the general rights of man, encourages me to present to you the following Observations on Mr. Burke's famous Reflections on the Revolution in France. They claim no popular attention for the ornaments of stile in which they are delivered; they can attract no admiration from the fascinating charms of eloquence; they are directed, not to *captivate*, but to *convince*; and it is on the presumption that your lordship attends more to the *substance* and *end* of literary compositions, than to the *art* of their arrangement, which induces me to flatter myself with your approbation.

[6] It is not surprizing that an event, the most *important* to the dearest interests of mankind, the most *singular* in its nature, and the most *astonishing* in its means, should not only have attracted the curiosity of all civilized nations, but that it should have engaged the passions of all *reflecting* men.

Two parties are already formed in this country, who behold the French Revolution with a very opposite temper: to the one, it inspires the sentiments of *exultation* and *rapture*; and to the other, *indignation* and *scorn*. I shall not take upon me to consider what are the *secret* passions which have given birth to these last sentiments; and shall content myself with observing, that Mr. Burke has undertaken to be the oracle of this last party. The abilities of this gentleman have been fully acknowledged by the impatience with which the public have waited for his

---

[1] i.e. Stanhope.

observations; and when we consider that he has been in a manner educated in the great school of Parliament, that he has assisted in the public councils of the English nation for the greater part of his life,[2] we must suppose him fully competent to the task he has undertaken, of [7] censuring the politics of our neighbour kingdom, and entering into an exact definition of those native rights which equally attach themselves to every description of men.

Is there a rational observation, or argument, in moral existence, which this gentleman (so highly favoured by nature and circumstances for political debate) could possibly have passed over, on a subject in which he appears so greatly interested, and of which he has taken a full leisure to consider. When we find him then *obliged* to substitute a *warm* and *passionate declamation* to a *cool investigation,* and to address the *passions* instead of the *reason* of mankind, we shall be induced to give a fuller credit to our judgment and our feelings, in the view we have taken of this interesting object, and the pleasure it has given us.

Mr. Burke sets out with throwing a *great deal* of contemptuous censure on two club societies in London, for a very harmless exertion of natural and constitutional liberty.[3] They certainly had a right to compliment the French National Assembly on a matter of domestic government, and to express an *appro-*[8]*bation* of their conduct, with a freedom equal to that which Mr. Burke has taken in his letter to express his *abhorrence.*

The National Assembly of France have taken no such *supercilious state* upon them, as would render such a communication of sentiment ridiculous or presumptuous. As the patrons of *equal liberty*, they have not disdained the addresses of the *meanest* individual: consequently the Revolution Society then might rationally expect that their address would have met with a civil reception, though not clothed with the 'dignity of the whole representative majesty of the whole English nation.'[4]

But Mr. Burke thinks that these gentlemen have so strong a predilection in favour of the democratic arrangements which have taken place in

---

[2] Burke had been an MP since 1765.
[3] The full title of Burke's book is *Reflections on the Revolution in France, and on the Proceedings in Certain Societies in London Relative to That Event. In a Letter Intended to Have Been Sent to a Gentleman in Paris.* The two main societies that Burke had in mind were the Society for Constitutional Information (SCI) and the Revolution Society. See Burke, *Reflections*, pp. 3–4.
[4] Ibid., p. 6.

France, that they have been induced to wish, if not to indulge an hope, that some very important reformations may in the process of time also take place in this country; and these harmless operations of the mind in a *few obscure* individuals (for such are the members described who compose the offending clubs) have produced in Mr. Burke ap-[9]prehensions no ways consistent with the *high* opinion he has formed of the English constitution, or of the *strong* attachment which he supposes all that is *great* and *good* in the nation have to it.

Dr. Price, whose animated love for mankind and the spread of general happiness moved to express the effusion of his patriotic sentiment, in a sermon preached the 4th of Nov. 1789, at the dissenting meeting-house in the Old Jewry, is censured by Mr. Burke in *severe*, and even *acrimonious terms*. Among other parts of the very offensive matter with which he charges this sermon, the having asserted that the *King of Great Britain owes his right to the Crown by the choice of the people*,[5] is particularly selected, as worthy an historical and argumentative confutation.

The liberty that was taken in the year 1688, by a convention of Lords and Commons, to depose king James the reigning sovereign from the throne, and to vest the sovereignty of the realm in his daughter Mary, and her husband the prince of Orange; and afterwards by the legislature, to pass an act[6] to settle the succession in queen [10] Anne and her issue, and in default of these, in the heirs of king William's body, and in default of these, in the house of Hanover, (the Protestant descendants of the house of Stuart in the female line;) and this to the prejudice not only of king James, but of his son, who had been acknowledged as the lawful heir of his throne; and also to the prejudice of the house of Savoy, who by lineal descent were the next in regular succession;[7] are indeed facts, which *might warrant a plain thinking man* in the opinion, that the present reigning family owe their succession to the choice or assent of the people. But, in Mr. Burke's opinion, these facts are of no weight, 'because the whole family of the Stuarts were not entirely left out of the succession, and a native of England advanced to the throne; and because it was

---

[5] Richard Price, *A Discourse on the Love of Our Country, Delivered on Nov. 4, 1789, at the Meeting-House in the Old Jewry, to the Society for Commemorating the Revolution in Great Britain* (London, 1789), p. 25.

[6] The Act of Settlement 1701.

[7] The House of Savoy was excluded from the royal succession on account of its Catholicism.

declared in the act of succession, that the Protestant line drawn from James the first, was absolutely necessary for the security of the realm.'[8]

That those individuals of the family of the Stuarts, who had never committed any offence against the peace of the country, and whose mode of faith was not injurious to its [11] welfare, should not be set aside in favour of an absolute stranger to the blood, was certainly a *just measure*; and it was certainly *wise* to leave as *few* competitors to the crown as possible, whether on grounds founded in justice, or in mere plausibility. But there was a reason still more forcible for the conduct of the two Houses of Convention, and afterwards for the Parliament in their constitutional capacity; and the reason is this, that *without the prince of Orange, and the assistance of his Dutch army, there could have been no Revolution.* For the English nation at large was so little convinced of the *severe and grave necessity* which Mr. Burke talks of, that the people of themselves would never have been roused to have deposed king James; and they regarded all his innovations with such a *constitutional phlegm*, that had this unfortunate monarch possessed the qualities of *firmness, perseverance*, or *patience*, he must either have been killed by the dark means of *assassination*, or he would have *continued on the throne.*

That the friends of the Revolution knew they could not do without the assistance of [12] king William, is plain, by their laying aside the intention of vesting Mary *singly* with the sovereignty, on his declaring that if this event took place, he would return to Holland, and leave them to themselves.

However strongly the warm friends of freedom might wish that this abstract right of the people, of chusing their own magistrates, and deposing them for ill conduct, had been laid open to the public by a formal declaration of such a right in the acts of succession, this certainly was not a period of time for carrying these wishes into execution. The whole body of the people had swallowed deeply of the *poison* of church policy; *passive obedience*, by their means, had so entirely supplanted the *abstract notion* of the *rights of men*, which prevailed in the opposition to Charles the first; and so desirous were the triumphant party to prevent the revival of such a principle, by which their interests had been affected, that they took care to confound the *only just authority* they had for their conduct, in as great *a mist of words and terms as possible.* Besides, would

---

[8] Burke, *Reflections*, p. 22. Queen Anne (reigned 1702–14) was James II's daughter and a Stuart, but was Protestant.

William, who was the soul of the whole proceeding, have given way to a [13] claim, by which, in the plainest terms, he was bound to his good behaviour?

Mr. Hume justly supposes, that if the revolution had happened one hundred years after it did, it would have been *materially different* in all its circumstances.[9] Instead of thinking with Mr. Burke, that such a plain declaration of the rights of men would have tended to disturb the quiet of the nation, I firmly believe that it would have had a contrary effect; for, in this case, those endless disputes between the *Nonjurors, Tories,* and *Whigs,* would soon have had an end. For, the question not being involved in that *obscurity, contradiction,* and *absurdity,* in which it was enveloped by the revolutionists, *truth* and *reason* would have resumed their sway; *party jargon* would have been exploded; the people would have given a chearful obedience to the new government; and that dreadful *necessity* by which Sir Robert Walpole excused the introducing a settled *system of corruption* into the administration, would never have existed.[10]

When the succession to a crown in one family, or even the possession of private property, owes its origin to the people, most undoubtedly the authority from whence it's [14] derived, attaches itself to the gift as equally in every individual of the family through the whole line of succession, as in the first possessor. And I can hardly believe, that there was *one* enlightened member who composed part of that legislative body who settled the succession to the throne, could possibly think that body possessed of such a plenitude of power, as should give them a right, not only to *set aside* the regulations of their ancestors, but to *bind their posterity*, to all succeeding generations, in the permanent chains of an unalterable law. Should we once admit of *a power so incompatible with the conditions of humanity*, and only reserved for the dictates of *divine wisdom*, we have not, in these enlightened days, improved on the politics of the fanatic atheist Hobbes: *For he supposes an original right in the people to chuse their governors*; but, in exerting this right, the citizen and his

---

[9] This most likely refers to Hume's argument that 'Had men been in the same disposition at the *revolution*, as they are at present, monarchy would have run a great risque of being entirely lost in this island.' *Essays, Moral, Political and Literary,* ed. Eugene F. Miller (Indianapolis, 1987), p. 51.

[10] Macaulay had attacked Walpole's administration in a Bolingbrokean fashion in *History since the Revolution.* As a Whig, Burke defended it in *An Appeal from the New to the Old Whigs* (London, 1791), p. 63.

posterity for ever lose their native privileges, and become bound through the whole series of generations to the service of a master's will.[11]

We will now take into consideration the nature and tendency of the two different compliments which have been paid by Dr. Price and [15] Mr. Burke to his Majesty and his successors. Dr. Price, I think, puts their right to government on the *most dignified*, and perhaps, in the event of things, on the *most permanent* footing. But Mr. Burke would have done well to consider, whether such a compliment as he is willing to pay to royalty is at all *proper*, either for the subject to make, or the King to receive. To a weak prince, it would be apt to cancel in his mind *all the obligations* which he owes to the people, and, by flattering him in a *vain* conceit of a mere personal right, tempt him to break those sacred ties which ought to *bind* and *direct* his government. I am apt to believe, that almost *all the vices* of royal administration have principally been occasioned by a *slavish adulation* in the language of their subjects; and, to the *shame of the English people* it must be spoken, that none of the enslaved nations in the world address the throne in a more *fulsome* and *hyperbolical* stile of submissive flattery.

To a *wise* and a *good* prince, compliments of the same complexion, made and recommended by Mr. Burke, would be *offensive*. He would consider it as taking away the *noblest* and *safest title* by which he possesses his [16] power: he would consider it as acknowledging a kind of *latent* right in other families; and the liberality of his sentiment would incline him to triumph in the opinion, that he was *called* to government, and *continued* in it, by the *choice* and *confidence* of a free nation.

Mr. Burke seems to adopt *prejudice*, *opinion*, and the powers of the *imagination*, as the *safest grounds* on which *wise* and *good* statesmen can establish or continue the happiness of societies.[12] These have always been imputed by philosophers (a tribe of men whom indeed Mr. Burke affects much to despise) as causes which have produced all that is *vicious* and *foolish* in man, and consequently have been the fruitful source of human *misery*.

Mr. Burke has certainly a *fine* imagination; but I would not advise either *him*, or any of *his admirers*, to give *too much* way to such direction;

---

[11] See Macaulay's *Loose Remarks* (above pp. 91–103) for her criticisms of Hobbes.

[12] 'Prejudice renders a man's virtue his habit ... Through just prejudice, his duty becomes a part of his nature.' Burke, *Reflections*, p. 130.

for if from the virtue of our nature it does not lead us into *crimes*, it always involves us in *error*.

The being put into a situation clearly to understand and to obey the *principles of truth*, appears to be the basis of our happiness in this, [17] and our perfection in another world; and the *more* truth is followed and pursued in this dark vale of human ignorance and misery, the *more* we shall *encrease* our mundane felicity, and *secure* the blessings of a future existence. *Every opinion* which deviates from *truth*, must ever be a *treacherous* guide; and the more it deviates from it, it becomes the *more dangerous*.

Though a false opinion of the rights and powers of citizens may *enslave* the ductile mind into a state of passive obedience, and thus secure the peace of government; yet in the same degree does it inflate the *pride* and *arrogance* of princes, until all considerations of *rectitude* give way to *will*, the barriers of personal security are flung down, and thence arises that *tremendous necessity* which must be followed by a state of *violence* and *anarchy*, which Mr. Burke so *justly* dreads. That this is the case, the experience of all societies of men who acknowledge a *power* in their princes *paramount* to all resistance, fully evinces. These societies are obliged often to have recourse to violence and massacre; not indeed to establish any popular rights, but [18] in the way of force, to wreck their vengeance on their tyrants.

As to the right of *cashiering* or *deposing* monarchs for misgovernment, I cannot possibly agree with Mr. Burke, that in England it only existed in that Convention of the two Houses in 1688, which exercised this power over King James and his legal successors.[13] But I am clearly of opinion, that it is a right that ought *never* to be exercised by a people who are satisfied with their form of government, and have spirit enough to correct its abuses; and so far from *condemning* the French nation for not deposing or executing their king, even though the *strongest presumptions* of the *most atrocious guilt* should have appeared against him, I think, had they elected any other person to that high office, they would have thrown difficulties in the way of their liberty, instead of improving it. But it is the *wisdom*, and not the *folly* of the National Assembly, which gives *offence to* their *enemies*; and *forces even Mr. Burke* to contradict, in this instance, the rule which he has laid down, 'That monarchs should not be deposed for misconduct, but only when [19] its criminality is of a

---

[13] Ibid., pp. 21–2; Price, *Discourse on the Love of our Country*, pp. 28–9.

kind to render their government totally incompatible with the safety of the people.'[14]

But before we leave the subject of Dr. Price's patriotic effusions, we must take notice of a very heavy charge laid against him by Mr. Burke – no less than that of *prophaning* the beautiful and prophetic ejaculation, commonly called, *Nunc dimittis!*[15] made on the first proclamation of our Saviour in the Temple, and applying it, '*with an inhuman and unnatural rapture, to the most horrid, atrocious, and afflicting spectacle*, that perhaps was ever exhibited to the *pity* and *indignation* of mankind.'[16] That Mr. Burke's imagination was greatly affected by a scene, which he describes in the highest glow of colouring, I can well believe; but Dr. Price, who classes with that description of men stiled by Mr. Burke, *abstract philosophers*, has been used to carry his mind, in a long series of ideas, to the consequences of actions which arise in the passing scene. Dr. Price then, with *full as much sympathy* in him *as even Mr. Burke* can have, might not be greatly moved with the mortifications and sufferings of a *very* [20] *few persons*, however highly distinguished for the Splendour of their rank, when those mortifications led the way, or secured the *present and future happiness of twenty-four millions of people, with their posterity*, emancipated by their *manly* exertions, from all that is *degrading* and *afflicting* to the sensible mind; and let into the immediate blessings of *personal security*, and to the enjoyment of those advantages which above *all others* must be delightful to the feelings of an high-spirited people.

The *events* of human life, when *properly* considered, are but a series of *benevolent providences*: many of them, though very important in their consequences, are too much confounded with the common transactions of men, to be observed; but whenever the believer thinks he perceives the *omnipotent will* more immediately declaring itself in favour of the future *perfection* and *happiness* of the moral world, he is naturally led into the same extasies of *hope* and *gratitude*, with which Simeon was transported by the view of the infant Messiah.[17] Has Mr. Burke never heard of any millennium, but that fanciful one which [21] is supposed to exist

---

[14] This is a summary of Burke's position rather than a direct quotation.

[15] Nunc Dimittis, or the Song of Simeon, a canticle sung by the aged Simeon in the New Testament. Simeon had been promised by God that he would not die until he had seen the Messiah.

[16] Burke, *Reflections*, p. 99.   [17] Luke 2:25–35.

in the kingdom of the saints?[18] If this should be the case, I would recommend to him to read *Newton on the prophecies*.[19] He will find that this most respectable Bishop, *who was no ranter*, is of opinion, that *some passages* in the Revelations point out a period of time when the *iron* sceptre of *arbitrary* sway shall be broken; when *righteousness shall prevail* over the whole earth, and a *correct* system of equity take place in the conduct of man.[20] Every providence, therefore, by which any *insuperable object* to this transcendent blessing appears to be taken away, must rationally draw forth ejaculations of *gratitude* from the *benevolent* Christian. What ideas do more naturally associate in the human mind, than those of the first appearance of the infant Jesus, and his future universal reign in the hearts of his people?

But Mr. Burke thinks, that there was at least a great impropriety in expressing an approbation of the spirited conduct of the French nation, before time and circumstances had manifested that the freedom they had gained, had been used with *wisdom* in the [22] forming a new constitution of government, or in improving the old one. 'When I see,' says Mr. Burke, 'the spirit of liberty in action, I see a strong principle at work; and this for a while is all I can possibly know of it. The wild gas, the fixed air is plainly broke loose; but we ought to suspend our judgment until the first effervescence is a little subsided, till the liquor is cleared, and until we see something deeper than the agitation of a troubled and frothy surface.'[21]

The French Revolution was attended with something so *new* in the history of human affairs; there was something so *singular*, so *unique*, in that *perfect* unanimity in the people; in that *firm* spirit which baffled *every hope* in the *interested*, that they could possibly divide them into parties, and render them the instruments of a re-subjection to their old bondage; that it naturally excited the *surprize* and the *admiration* of all men.

---

[18] Millenarianism (or millennialism or chiliasm) is the belief that Christ will establish a 1,000-year reign of the saints before the Last Judgement. Burke associated Price with the Fifth Monarchists (*Reflections*, p. 108), a Puritan sect during the Commonwealth era. Their name was taken from the Book of Daniel, which prophesised that four ancient monarchies would precede the kingdom of Christ.

[19] Thomas Newton, *Dissertations on the Prophecies, Which Have Remarkably Been Fulfilled, and at This Time Are Fulfilling in the World* (3 vols., London, 1754–8).

[20] Macaulay is probably alluding to Newton, *Dissertations on the Prophecies*, III, pp. 396–7.

[21] Burke, *Reflections*, pp. 8–9.

It appeared as a *sudden spread of an enlightened spirit*, which promised to act as an effectual and permanent barrier to the inlet of those usurpations which from the very beginning of social life the *crafty* have imposed on *ignorance*.

[23] This was a triumph of *sufficient importance* to call forth the exultation of individuals, and the approbation of societies. But the two clubs who have the *misfortune* to fall under Mr. Burke's severe censure, did not testify a formal approbation of the conduct of their neighbours, till the deputies they had chosen for the transaction of their affairs, had manifested a virtue *equal* to so high a trust; for no sooner was the power of the court *sufficiently* subdued to enable them to act with *freedom* and *effect*, than they gave an example of *disinterested magnanimity*, that has *no parallel* in the conduct of *any* preceding assembly of men, and which was *never surpassed by any individual*. That memorable day in which the members of the National Assembly, with a *virtuous enthusiasm*, vied with each other in the alacrity with which they surrendered to the people all their feudal privileges, will for ever stand in the records of time as a monument of their *singular greatness*. Such an *instance of human virtue was surely a proper subject of applause and congratulation*.

Men who have suffered in their personal interests by the new order of things in [24] France, must naturally be inclined to *exaggerate* every blemish which appears in the conduct of a multitude, by whose spirit they have been deprived of many fond privileges. Their *petulant* observations, whilst their minds are *heated* by imaginary wrongs and injuries, is *excusable*; because it is a *weakness* almost inseparable from *human frailty*. It would, however, have become *Englishmen*, from whom might have been expected a *more sympathising* indulgence towards the *friends* and *promoters* of liberty, to have been more candid in their censures; but in no part of Europe perhaps, have the evils which must necessarily attend all Revolutions, and especially a Revolution so complete and comprehensive as that which has taken place in France, been more exaggerated, and more affectedly lamented.

Had this *great work* been effected without the shedding one drop of *innocent* or even *guilty* blood, without doubt it would have better pleased the *generous* and *benevolent* mind. But, was it *possible* that such a pleasing circumstance could ever have had an existence? If we take into consideration that [25] *animosity* which subsisted between the *aristocratists* and *democratists* on the eve of the Revolution, an animosity which was greatly heightened by the imprudent *insults* which the *Tier Etat*[22] had received, from the first mentioned body, we shall rather *wonder at the moderation* with which the people used their *complete* victory, than lament their cruelty. After the successful storming the king's camp,[23] and the flight or desertion of his Janizaries,[24] instead of that *order* and voluntary *subjection* to discipline which appeared in an armed mob, and which prevented *all* infringement on the rights of property, had the subdued party been delivered over to the *outrage* and the *pillage* of the rabble, the *horrid* scene might have been *parallelled* by examples drawn from the guilty violence of *civilized* nations, without calling our attention to *Theban* and *Thracian orgies*,[25] or a procession of American *savages* entering into *Onondaga*.[26] I do not indeed exactly know how much blood has been spilled in France, or how many individuals have fallen a sacrifice in the public commotions; but by all the general accounts which have been transmitted to us, the history of [26] monarchies will point out as many sufferers who have fallen in *one hour* to the *rage* and *outrageous pride* of kingly despots.

The punishment of the lamp-post, it must be owned, strikes terror to the mind, and calls forth an immediate effusion of *sympathy* to the sufferer.[27] But when *candid reflection* supersedes the *first emotions* of human tenderness, this truth will force itself on our consideration, that a people who had been used to such *barbarous* spectacles as that of beholding wretches, whose *destitute poverty* had in a manner *compelled* to the forlorn course of highway robbery, broken on a wheel, and *lingering* out the last hours of life under the *agonising* strokes of a stern executioner, would naturally regard hanging as a *mild* punishment on men whom they considered as the worst of criminals. Let us rejoice,

[22] The third estate. See esp. Emmanuel Joseph Sieyès, *What Is the Third Estate?* (1789).
[23] On 5 October 1789 an angry mob of Parisians marched on the Palace of Versailles, infiltrated the palace and tried to kill Queen Marie Antoinette. The situation was defused, and the royal family was brought to the Tuileries Palace in Paris.
[24] Janissaries were the Ottoman Sultan's household troops; Macaulay refers to the king's guards, and uses the same vocabulary as Burke.
[25] Burke, *Reflections*, p. 107. This is a reference to the goddess of Kotys (or Cotys), worshipped by certain ancient Greek tribes, and whose worship rituals were said to have included midnight orgies.
[26] Onondaga was the capital of the Iroquois League, an indigenous confederacy in northeast North America, and the main settlement of the Onondaga nation.
[27] Burke had referred to reports that mobs hung victims from lamp posts in Paris; see *Reflections*, pp. 101, 108.

then, that such *dreadful legal executions*, which must from their nature tend to *barbarize* men, are happily put an end to by the Revolution.

But Mr. Burke is now come to a scene which is calculated to draw forth *all* the energies of his imagination, and which conse-[27]quently he describes with the *highest possible* colouring. This is no other than the 6th of October 1789, when the king and queen were led in triumph to Paris.[28] I very much *honour the king of France* for that ease of temper which has enabled him to go through all his personal mortifications with a *manly dignity*; but it must be confessed that he brought them on himself, by a conduct, which, to say the best of it, was altogether imprudent.

The first involuntary visit which he made to the capital, was absolutely necessary, to appease the *fears* and the *resentment* which had been raised by his *ineffectual* attempt to *awe* the deliberations and the resolutions of the National Assembly by an *armed force*. In the second, he was carried to Paris to *prevent* the execution of *a design* formed by the court cabal, which, had it succeeded, might have *deluged* the nation in blood, and furnished the fuel of civil discord for years.

The Parisians shewed no intention, or even desire, to deprive in any respect their king of his personal liberty; till, by a very suspicious conduct, he appeared to have mani-[28]fested a design to corrupt the fidelity of his guards to their new government, and to set up the standard of arms in that quarter of the kingdom where the friends of despotism from every part of Europe might repair with safety. The *great* and *unabating* rage and indignation which the enemies to the new consti-tution have shewn for what they term the captivity of the king, plainly evinces the *necessity* that urged the measure.

Having endeavoured to shew the futility of Mr. Burke's observations and censures on the Revolution and Constitutional Societies; and likewise, that his severe pointed reflections on the conduct of the French nation, for having, as he says, committed on the vanquished party the most *unexam-pled* acts of atrocious violence, are not founded either in *truth* or *reason*; I shall proceed with my critical reflections on the animadversions of my author, who goes on in a very *free manner* to censure every part of the French constitution, to draw a comparison, between the British and the Gallic governments as they now exist, and to establish, in the way of [29] reasoning, a superiority in favour of the government of his own country.

---

[28] See note 23, above.

To shew that the National Assembly have committed a very *gross* and *ruinous* error, in the building a new structure, instead of improving an old one; Mr. Burke cites, in a triumphant manner, the conduct of the English nation. Our oldest reformation, he observes, is that of *Magna Charta.* 'You will see', says he, addressing his correspondent, 'that Sir Edward Coke, that great oracle of our law, and indeed all the great men who follow him to Blackstone, are industrious to prove the pedigree of our liberties. They endeavour to prove, that the ancient Charta, the Magna Charta of king John,[29] was connected with another positive Charta from Henry the first,[30] and that both the one and the other were nothing more than a re-affirmance of the still more ancient standing law of the kingdom.'[31] 'In the famous law of the third of Charles the first, called the Petition of Right,[32] the Parliament says to the king, Your subjects have inherited this freedom (claiming their franchises) not on abstract principles as the rights of men, but as the [30] rights of Englishmen, and as a patrimony derived from their forefathers.'[33]

This language of the parliament, when pleading for the freedom of their countrymen at the tribunal of a prince's throne, who was as little inclined to *admit*, and whose *prejudices* enabled him as little to *understand* the only reasonable grounds of the argument as any despot who ever swayed an eastern sceptre,[34] was well adapted to the *character* of the prince, and the *ignorance* of the multitude. But had the *circumstances* of Charles enabled him to *speak* and to *enforce* the sentiments of his mind, he would undoubtedly have made the following reply: You tell me upon your *own* authority, and the authority of *your lawyers*, that what you plead so strenuously for, is a patrimony derived from your forefathers, and grounded on the ancient law of the land. Be it so – Was not this ancient law *superseded by the authority of arms*, and the *entire* submission of the people to the Norman code established by William the Conqueror?[35] *Magna Charta*, then, and the other charters, must either

---

[29] John, reigned 1199–1216.
[30] Henry I, reigned 1100–35. In this quotation from the *Reflections*, Burke refers to Henry's Coronation Charter, also known as the Charter of Liberties or Statutes of the Realm, a written proclamation in which Henry made constitutional promises of good lordship.
[31] Burke, *Reflections*, p. 45.   [32] Of 1628.   [33] Burke, *Reflections*, p. 46.
[34] Macaulay alludes to 'oriental despotism'.
[35] Macaulay refers to the 'Norman Yoke', i.e. the idea that William I introduced oppressive feudalism in England in the wake of 1066. This historical argument was important for the Levellers in the seventeenth century as well as political reformers in Macaulay's day.

have been *extorted* from the *imbecillity* of the princes who granted [31] them, or they must have issued from the *voluntary donations of monarchs*; in either case, they only stand on a *resumable* right.

What the parliament could have answered to this plea, I know not, without calling in the aid of an *abstract right*; which they endeavoured to keep out of the view of the king, with as much care as Mr. Burke *endeavours* to keep it out of the view of all men. But certain it is, that the king, though he did not explicitly declare with all their force the above mentioned sentiments, yet he acted agreeable to their tenor the moment be got rid of this troublesome assembly: For, considering the articles of the petition of right as a *gift depending on his pleasure to fulfil or to resume*, he broke them whenever they thwarted his system of administration, and *imprisoned* those who on the strength of this statute withstood his authority.

I have myself always considered the boasted birthright of an Englishman, as an *arrogant* pretension, built on a *beggarly* foundation. It is an arrogant pretension, because it intimates a kind of exclusion to the rest of mankind from the same privileges; and it is [32] beggarly, because it rests our legitimate freedom on the *alms* of our princes.

I must own I was somewhat surprised to find a gentleman of polished manners, who has spent the best part of his life in the company of those who *affect* the nicest conformity to the rules of a refined civility, addressing the august representatives of the most *gallant* and *respectable* of the European nations, in terms which I should not use to a set of chimney-sweepers,[36] though acting the most ridiculously out of their sphere. Neither do I chuse to repeat all those expressions of ineffable contempt, which the strong glow of Mr. Burke's imagination has scattered through the whole of his reprehensions.

It is not my intention to make any formal comparison between the new constitution of France, and the present existing constitution of England; or to presume to censure a government, from which an industrious people receive protection, and with which the large majority of the nation are entirely satisfied. Yet it may not be inexpedient to observe, that we cannot with any grounds of *reason* or *propriety*, set up our own consti-[33]tution as the model which all other nations ought *implicitly* to follow, unless we are *certain* that it bestows the *greatest* possible

---

[36] Macaulay is turning Burke's vocabulary against him. Burke had said that the magistrates of France were 'learn[ing] their trade, like chimney-sweepers'; see *Reflections*, p. 272.

happiness on the people which in the nature of things any government can bestow. We ought to be *certain*, that this *model* will bear the most *nice* and *critical* examination. It ought to be void of any of those *obvious*, or more *concealed* causes, which produce *present evils*, and carry the mind to apprehensions of *future* mischiefs. We ought not at least to have had a *national debt*, swelled to a *magnitude* which *terrifies* even the *most sanguine* for its consequences.[37] Our parliaments ought to have been *eminently* distinguished for their *integrity*, and a *total* independence of any *corrupt influence*; and no *necessity ought to have existed in our affairs*, which have obliged us to *endure imposts*[38] which our ancestors would have *rejected with horror*, and *resisted*. If an Englishman sees any thing which is amiss in his own government, he ought not undoubtedly to look forward to any other remedy than those which the lenient hand of reformation will supply. But when the old vessel of a common-wealth is *torn to pieces* by the [34] *shocks* it has sustained from *contending parties*; when the people, disdaining and rejecting all those fond opinions by which they have been *enslaved to misery*, assert their native right of forming a government for themselves; surely in such a case the builders are bound by no law of *duty* or *reason* to make use of these old materials in the structure of their new constitution, which they suppose to have been of an injurious tendency. The leaders of the French Revolution, and their followers, see *none of those striking beauties* in the old laws and rules of the Gothic institutions of Europe, which Mr. Burke does. They do not profess to have any of the spirit of antiquarians among them; and they have not perceived, in the experience of old or ancient times, a *perfect harmony* arising from *opposition* of interests;[39] nor can they *understand* how such a combination can be formed as shall produce it. In such a view of things, they have chosen a simple rule for the model of their new structure, yet regulated with all that *art* and *design* which the experience of ages affords to the wisdom of man. They are accused of having entirely dismissed that useful guide *experience* [35] from their councils, but they think they have made *the best use* of it; whether this opinion of

---

[37] Macaulay had attacked the national debt and the financial revolution in *History since the Revolution* (above pp. 162–74) and elsewhere. Burke was also highly critical of debt financing in the *Reflections*; see esp. J. G. A. Pocock, 'The Political Economy of Burke's Analysis of the French Revolution', *Historical Journal*, 25 (1982), pp. 331–49.
[38] i.e. taxes.   [39] Burke, *Reflections*, pp. 50–1.

theirs is founded in truth, time, and the future history of man, must evince.

Mr. Burke, reasoning from what I regard as a groundless supposition, very pathetically laments, and very severely reprehends the conduct of those, who, holding out false and treacherous lures to the king, led him into concessions fatal to his personal power, and the constitution of the monarchy. That the parliaments of France never intended to make any *alteration* in the old government, I am thoroughly persuaded; and I am equally persuaded, that they fondly imagined the people would *freely* give their money for the redress of some of the most heavy of the grievances under which they laboured. They knew, by the experience of past times, that in voting by orders, the people had never gained any *solid* advantage from an assembly of the States General.[40] Neither the court, nor the parliament of Paris, who made the king so many splendid promises, were aware of the consequences which must arise from the general spread of knowledge among the people; [36] and in the event of things, they were *both disappointed* of their purposes; for the *Tier Etat*, reflecting on the *old practices* which the *crown*, the *clergy*, and the *nobility* had used against them, were determined to throw the whole weight of their natural scale into the balance, and to redress their own grievances, without waiting the effect of *humble* petitions and *discordant* councils. That neither the king, nor the parliaments of France, could long have prevented the *full* exertion of this power, (had they foreseen all the consequences which did arise from suffering the meeting of the States General), is to me very plain. A *regeneration* of the constitution would have been *equally* effected; but it would have been attended with a *tremendous* difference in its circumstances. It would have been ushered in by a general bankruptcy, and the waste of civil blood. 'Our enemies,' says a popular Leader in the National Assembly, 'may, by their machinations, make us buy our liberties dear, but they cannot deprive us of them.'[41] 'This breach of confidence,' as Mr. Burke terms it, 'to an easy and condescending king, will have a [37] dreadful effect on the interests of mankind, by sanctifying the dark suspicious maxims of tyrannous distrust; and will teach kings to tremble at what will be called the

---

[40] In the traditional composition of the Estates General, the third estate could be out-voted by the first estate (the clergy) and the second estate (the nobility).

[41] Possibly Mirabeau the Younger. Other candidates include Jérôme Pétion de Villeneuve and Gilbert du Motier, Marquis de Lafayette.

delusive plausibilities of *moral politicians*.'⁴² Be this as it may, the people of France had *certainly* a right to provide for their own *security* and *welfare* on those principles which *they* thought the most conducive to this *great end*, and to leave it to the wisdom of other nations to make suitable provision for theirs. It behoves them, however, to be careful to *cherish* and *preserve* the liberty they have *so nobly* gained; to suffer no intemperate spirit to produce that licentiousness which must bring anarchy in its train; nor to indulge a *capricious impatience*, by which their enemies, in working on their passions and *misguiding* their reason, may reduce them to their old state of bondage; in which case it is *certain*, power will reap *many* advantages from past transactions, by which it will be enabled to *tie fast* those *fetters* the giddy people will so well deserve.

Though I have hitherto spared my readers a detail of all the severe invectives which Mr. Burke has used against the leading mem-[38]bers who compose the National Assembly; yet, for the sake of those principles of *moral rectitude* which the torrent of his eloquence appears to *baffle* and *confound*, it will be necessary to notice his observations on the character and conduct of the nobles who have taken the lead in the French revolution, and who yet continue to support it. He accuses them with having assisted in the spoil and humiliation of their own order, to possess a sure fund for their new followers. 'To be attached to the subdivision, to love the little platoon we belong to in society (says Mr. Burke) is the first principle, the germ as it were, of public affections: it is the first link in the series by which we proceed towards a love of our country and mankind.'⁴³

What *splendid emoluments* and what *grand objects* of personal ambition those noblemen could have in view, who, whilst they *generously* sacrificed those privileges which are the most fondly coveted by human vanity, shut out their entrance to the public offices of the state, by resolutions which rendered such promotions incompatible with their legislative trust, I know not; but I hope we shall not [39] be so much *blinded* with the splendour of dazzling images, as to confound those *narrow affections* which bind small bodies together by the mutual ties of personal interest, to that *liberal benevolence*, which, disdaining the consideration of every

---

⁴² Burke, *Reflections*, p. 55. The quotation is not verbatim.   ⁴³ Ibid., pp. 68–9.

selfish good, chearfully sacrifices *a personal interest* to the *welfare* of the community.

Of the list of individuals whom Mr. Burke selects as examples of *true glory*, and as benefactors rather than destroyers of their country, some of them ought to have been for ever stampt with *infamy*, as the *pests* and *tyrants* of their species; and they are all of them of doubtful fame, as to any *honour* derived to their country by their ambitious projects, unless a *nation of slaves can receive glory* from *a capacity* of becoming the *scourge* of other societies.

Richelieu[44] was the grand instrument by which the court of France, in the reign of Louis the fourteenth, was enabled to massacre the greater part of the French Huguenots,[45] and to drive the remainder out of the kingdom.[46] Cromwell, indeed, who deprived his sovereign of life, *merely to usurp his power*, has, with many people, paid the debt of his crimes, by having, [40] through the general detestation which men conceived of his *treachery* and *tyranny*, rendered the Revolution and the Revolutionists odious, and thus paved the way for the restoration of the old government.

In the next argument presented to our attention, Mr. Burke has very strongly entrenched himself in the holds of the British constitution; and we will not attempt to pursue him into his fortress: For, though a natural vanity *might flatter us* with a *delusive hope* of victory, arising from the subtle objections which may be urged to every political proposition; yet the victory would cost *too dear*, if it subjected us to the reproach of any design against the peace and quiet of the community. But it will not, I think, be deviating from the highest point of decency and prudence, to make our objections to his general assertions. His proposition, 'that it is the great masses of property which form a natural rampart about the lesser properties in all their gradations,'[47] is not in our opinion founded in truth; for every citizen who possesses ever so *small* a share of property, is *equally* as tenacious of it as the most opulent [41] member of society;

[44] Armand-Jean du Plessis, Cardinal et Duc de Richelieu (1585–1642), chief minister to Louis XIII between 1624 and 1642.
[45] i.e. the French Protestants.
[46] Macaulay refers to the revocation of the Edict of Nantes in 1685 by Louis XIV, who declared Protestantism illegal. Burke had written that Louis XIII's 'support of that minister [Richelieu] against his rivals was the source of all the glory of his reign, and the solid foundation of his throne itself'. *Reflections*, p. 291.
[47] Macaulay is paraphrasing contents in *Reflections*, p. 78.

and this leads him to *respect* and to *support* all the laws by which property is protected. It is this sense of personal interest, which, running through every rank in society, and attaching itself to every one of its members who are not in the condition of a pauper, forms an impenetrable barrier to the security of wealth; for otherwise, as the numbers of the opulent must be *very* small in proportion to the number of those who form the great mass of the people, *envy* would operate so successfully against them as to destroy the force of artificial supports.

When the constitution of France is compleatly settled, and the commonwealth rests upon its basis, this disposition of the human mind, which operates so powerfully for the preservation of peace and order, will, as on former occasions, regain its natural force. For the operations of *power* on the property of the citizen, is not an *unexampled* event in the histories of civil societies.

The manner in which the National Assembly of France have endeavoured to secure and to defend the liberty of the different towns and provinces which compose that vast empire, come next under Mr. Burke's severe [42] criticism. But in his *endeavour* to bring *men* over to his sentiments on this subject, he is obliged to have recourse to all those *unfair* means which persons of genius think themselves entitled to use in the course of their argument; for what, indeed, but the *delusive* power of a subtle sophistry, can produce an apparent *concord* between propositions the most *opposite in their nature?* and what but an appeal to the passions of the reader, can prevent his assent to the *most obvious truths?*

The National Assembly of France are at one time accused by Mr. Burke of a scheme for *perpetuating* their power, at the expence of the rights of election; at another, of acting *weakly* and *meanly* in the having *limited* their sitting to the *short space of two years.*[48] In one view of things, they are accused of drawing to themselves, and to the city of Paris, *an exorbitance of power*, which, if not resisted, must end in the total subjection of the provinces, whose natural productions and acquired wealth are to be exhausted to pamper the luxury and gratify the avarice of the capital. In another, their politics are arraigned, for having left no leading *controuling power* in the empire, of *sufficient energy* to support a neces-[43]sary subordination of its parts. Such *palpable contradictions*, such *little arts* of *misrepresentation* we have seen daily thrown out in the public

---

[48] Ibid., p. 272.

papers by the *hostile faction*, who naturally endeavour to *mislead* the people into a *distrust* of their deputies, because they have guarded their liberties with too nice and too jealous a care. But we did not expect to see them collected together and set off with all the powers of literary composition, by one of the greatest orators of the age; and this in a work which the author holds out as an *exact standard*, by which the limits of *power* and of *freedom* are from henceforth *to receive their bounds*. Neither did we expect to find that the *humane* writer would have so far entered into the passions of the discontented party, as to *envy* the people of Paris that bread which is so necessary for their subsistence, and which cannot be otherwise supplied but by the produce of the provinces.

We were also greatly surprized to find Mr. Burke entering into such contradictions, as at *one time* to represent the excellencies of the English constitution as *obvious* to every observer, and so sensibly felt by its subjects as *unanimously* to bind their affections to its [44] principles, its rules, and its dictates; to the exception only of a few *idle, insignificant, speculative individuals*: and *at another, trembling* lest if the question of the abstract rights of men were brought before the eyes of the people, the most *dreadful* confusions might follow, and be attended with the *utter downfall* of every order in the church and state, of *every exclusive* privilege existing in its bodies corporate, and with the *general* pillage of the rich.

Such representations are certainly well adapted to *rouse* the selfish passions of the *timid* mind, and may serve the present purpose of the *hour*; but they will not stand the more *candid* and *cool* decisions which attend on *time*.

The *legitimate* power by which governments are made or altered, must either stand on the *native rights* of the species, or it must stand on an authority vested in an individual, or in a limited number of individuals, exalted to this authority, either by the positive law of a *revealed will*, or by some native superiority *evidently* attached to their persons. That this sacred trust has never been so for-[45]mally vested in *any* individual, or in *any given number* of individuals, is in a manner acknowledged by the most strenuous advocates for *passive obedience*; for all their arguments are built on presumptive grounds.

The contrary proposition to this, *viz. that native right in the social body to choose its own government*, which Mr. Burke *condemns* under the description of a *metaphysical foolery*, is allowed with all its weight of authority by the greatest part of the English Revolutionists; nor can any other *reasonable* ground of persuasion be made use of, to bring the people to concur in any plan of salutary or necessary reformation. With what pretence then, can Mr. Burke charge Dr. Price, or any of his adherents or admirers, with advancing a *novel* or a *mischievous* doctrine, when they assert that all legitimate power is founded on the rights of nature? 'But government (says Mr. Burke) is not made in virtue of natural rights, which may and do exist in total independence of it; and exist in much greater clearness, and in a much greater degree of abstract perfection; but their abstract perfection is their practical de-[46]fect. By having a right to every thing, they want every thing. Government is a contrivance of human wisdom, to provide for human wants. Men have a right that these wants should be provided for by this wisdom. Among these wants is to be reckoned the want out of a civil society, of a sufficient restraint upon their passions. Society requires not only that the passions of individuals should be subjected, but even in the mass and body, as well as in the individuals; the inclinations of men should frequently be thwarted, their will controuled, and their passions brought into subjection. This can only be done by a power out of themselves, and not in the exercise of its functions, subject to that will, and to those passions, which it is in its office to bridle and subdue. In this sense, the restraints of men, as well as their liberties, are to be reckoned among their rights.'[49]

To this very *ingenious* reasoning, and these *refined* distinctions between natural and social rights, the people may possibly object, that in delivering themselves *passively* over to the *unrestrained rule of others*, on the plea of control-[47]ing *their inordinate inclinations* and *passions*, they deliver themselves over to *men*, who, as *men*, and partaking of the *same* nature as themselves, are as liable to be governed by the same *principles* and *errors*; and to men who, by the great superiority of their station, having no *common* interest with themselves which might lead them to preserve a salutary check over their vices, must be inclined to *abuse* in the *grossest manner* their trust. To proceed with Mr. Burke's argument, should the rich and opulent in the nation plead their right to the predominant sway in society, from its being a necessary circumstance to guard their wealth from the gripe of poverty, the men in an inferior

---

[49] Burke's continuation further underlines his differences with Macaulay: 'But as the liberties and the restrictions vary with times and circumstances, and admit of infinite modifications, they cannot be settled upon any abstract rule; and nothing is so foolish as to discuss them upon that principle.' Ibid., pp. 88–9.

state of fortune might argue, that should they give way *to this plea in all its extent*, their moderate possessions would be exposed to the burden of *unequal* taxes; for the rich, when possessed of the *whole* authority of the state, would be sure to take the *first care* of themselves, if they should not be tempted to secure an exoneration of *all* burthens, by dividing the spoils of the public; and that the *abuse* of such high trusts must *necessarily* arise, be-[48]cause to act by selfish considerations, is in the very constitution of our nature.

To such pleas, so plausibly urged on all sides, I know of no *rational* objection; nor can I think of any expedient to remove the well-grounded apprehensions of the different interests which compose a commonwealth, than a *fair* and *equal* representation of the *whole* people;[50] – a circumstance which appears very peculiarly necessary in a mixed form of government, where the democratic part of the constitution will ever be in danger of being overborne by the energy attending on its higher constituent parts.

On such grounds of reasoning, there will be found no insuperable objections to those propositions of Dr. Price, which are so highly censured by Mr. Burke, as containing principles of the most *seditious* and *dangerous* nature; even though we should allow that every government which accords with the opinions and the inclinations of the large majority of the people, is, in an high sense of the term, a legitimate government.

We shall now proceed with that course of the argument in which Mr. Burke endea-[49]vours to shew, that the *unequal* representation which he allows to have taken place in *our government*, is a *perfection* rather than a *defect*. 'With us, when we elect popular representatives, (says Mr. Burke, still addressing his French correspondent), we send them to a council in which each man individually is a subject, and submitted to a government complete in all its ordinary functions. With you the elective assembly is the sovereign, and the sole sovereign; all the members therefore are integral parts of this sole sovereignty. But with us, it is totally different. With us, the representatives separated from the other parts, can have no action, and no existence. The government is the point of reference of the several members and districts of our representation. This is the centre of

---

[50] This was a long-standing aspiration of Macaulay's political circle. Her daughter referred to parliamentary reform as 'our grand object' in a letter to her mother in 1784; see *Correspondence*, p. 237.

our unity. This government of reference is a trustee for the whole, and not for the parts. So is the other branch of our public council; I mean the House of Lords. With us, the King and the Lords are several and joint securities for the equality of each district, each province, each city. When did you hear in Great Britain, of any province suffering from [50] the inequality of representation? what district from having no representation at all? Not only our monarchy and our peerage secure the equality on which our unity depends, but it is the spirit of the House of Commons itself. The very inequality of representation, which is so *foolishly* complained of, is perhaps the very thing which prevents us from thinking or acting as members for districts. Cornwall elects as many members as all Scotland; but is Cornwall better taken care of than Scotland?'[51]

If your Lordship sees the result of this argument in the same light as I do, you will consider it as equally recommendatory to an election of the *Lower House* in the *King* and the *Lords*, as of an inadequate representation made by the election of the Commons. For if the *King* and the *Lords* are several and joint securities for the equality of each district, each province, and each city; why should we throw the country into a state of *riot* and *confusion* every seven years? Why should we put ourselves to electioneering *expences?* Would it not be a *more convenient* [51] method to suffer the *King* and the House of *Lords to chuse* our representatives?

But this is not the point of view in which the friends of equal representation see the necessity of a reform: they do not alledge that Cornwall is better taken care of than any other district in Great Britain. The subject of their complaint is, that the important interests of the great body of the Commons is, by our *present inadequate state of representation*, sacrificed to the ambition of *private* individuals, who, by their *command* over boroughs, may make their *market* with government at the *expence* of the public. The *strong* and *firm* opposition which the *ruling powers* have given to *every* step towards this *reasonable* reformation, is not *one* of the *happiest* effects which arise from that continual war of *interests* so much admired by Mr. Burke and others. The jealousy it manifests of the people, is without *all* bounds of moderation; for the organ by which the democratic influence is exerted, has no very formidable energy. Its power is circumscribed and shut in by the immoveable barrier of laws, usages, positive rules of doctrine [52] and practice, counterpoised by the

---

[51] Burke, *Reflections*, pp. 269–70.

House of Lords, and in a manner *subjected to the Crown* by the prerogative of calling and dissolving parliaments.[52]

To proceed with the observations of my author – After a torrent of the
most pointed invective, Mr. Burke takes upon him to censure every part
of the conduct of the French Revolutionists; and among other acts, *one*
which I have always considered as founded in *truth, religion,* and the
purest morality; it is that of annihilating, by the force of a bright example,
those notions founded on *false* principles of honour, which fell so *severely*
and so *cruelly* on every family who had the misfortune to have produced
one *real* or *pretended* culprit. The infamy which families sustained for the
misconduct of any of its individual members, was one of the *strongest*
reasons which have been urged for *personal* imprisonment at pleasure;
and when this dreadful engine of despotism was removed, it surely
became expedient to *emancipate* the people from the *terror* of this
impending evil. But when the *most laudable transactions* of men are
represented as *crimes*, we ought to be *cautious* [53] how we give ear to
the suggestions of their *accuser*.

In the personal mortifications of the Queen of France, Mr. Burke
finds great reason to lament that the age of chivalry is no more; for, had
the same spirit existed in this, that existed in past ages, 'ten thousand
swords might have leaped from their scabbards, to *avenge even a look* that
threatened her with insult.'[53] The high colouring given by Mr. Burke to
those scenes of regal distress, will, I doubt not, captivate the imagination
of the greater number of his readers, in a degree equal to the effects
produced on the author by the *charms* of the Queen of France. But the
delusions of fancy are apt to subside in men of *cool* minds, when any *great*
object of public concern is held up to their view, to the prejudice even of
beauty and dignity, and all those external objects, adapted rather to
enslave our affections, than to *lead* our judgment.

The bringing the king and queen to Paris, and thus, by preventing
their escape, to disable them from forming new troubles in the kingdom,
was certainly regarded as a [54] measure of the *highest necessity*; and in
this view, must have been approved by the true friends of the revolution,
although it was attended with tumult and disorder.[54]

---

[52] As recently as 1784, the king had dissolved Parliament after only half of its term to give a
parliamentary majority to his new minister, William Pitt the Younger.
[53] Burke, *Reflections*, pp. 112–13.   [54] See note 23, above.

The age in which the spirit of chivalry was triumphantly prevalent, would indeed have been a very *improper* time to have attempted a regeneration of constitutions on a *popular* principle; but I have always regarded the necessity which gave birth to the orders of chivalry, as a mark of *disgrace* to the times in which they were formed. They were indeed a proper remedy to the evils arising from *ferocity, slavery, barbarism,* and *ignorance*; but now, when the causes no longer exist which rendered them useful, we should rather think of *freeing* society of all the evils inherent in those *false* notions of honour which they have given rise to, than endeavour to call back their spirit in its full force. That enthusiastic military fire, that *methodized sentimental barbarism,* which instigates men to deprive their fellow-citizens of life for *supposed* personal affronts, in *defiance* of the laws of *religion* and *society,* are the offsprings of chivalry, and unknown, to *all* [55] the nations of the *ancient civilized* world. But it is the *simplicity* of all *abstract principles,* against which Mr. Burke makes an *eternal* war; all the *devices* of pride, all the *fond conceits* of vanity, all the train of *pompous* ostentation, by which *naked* virtue is put *out* of her *rank,* to give way to the more imposing glare of external magnificence, are represented as useful ideas, 'furnished from the wardrobe of a *moral* imagination, which the heart owns, and the understanding ratifies, as necessary to cover the defects of our naked shivering nature, and to raise it to dignity in our own estimation.'[55]

It is not, according to *these* ideas, recommended by Mr. Burke, that the Scripture teaches us to *respect ourselves*; and although the maxims of the sacred writings are exploded by all politicians as *incompatible* with their views, yet certainly the *excellency* of their precepts consists in their being *exactly* fitted to a *temporal* as well as to a *spiritual* happiness. Neither in a *moral* view of things, can I perceive how the *ornaments* of artificial greatness, which is found to answer [56] all the purposes of *human pride,* should assist us in acquiring that *true* dignity of character which *alone* ought to constitute distinction; nor how we can truly respect ourselves, by *idolizing* the *mere phantom* of greatness, whether it be attached to our own persons, or the persons of others.

As every act of the French National Assembly is to be *condemned,* not only in the *gross,* but in the *detail,* the address of congratulation to the

---

[55] Burke, *Reflections,* p. 114.

king on the commencement of the present year, comes, among others, under Mr. Burke's severe animadversion.[56]

I have not indeed got this address by me; but if my memory does not deceive me, it contained a language the *best* adapted to sooth the personal afflictions of the king. Not the *smallest* hint was given, that any ill conduct in his Majesty had provoked the people to emancipate themselves from his power; it *thanked* him for his concurrence with their wishes; it represented their liberty, as the *necessary* consequence of their *enlightened* spirit, not of their sufferings under his administration; and it promised as loyal an attachment to his person, and to the distinction [57] he held as the first magistrate of the commonwealth, as could have been exacted by the authority of which he was dispossessed.

Whatever might have been held out as the ostensible object of the people in their demand for the meeting of their representatives, it certainly was intended by them to use their power, when thus vested with a legitimate form, and endued with a capability of legislation, not only to the *reformation* of abuses, but to the *regeneration* of their constitution; and thus the National Assembly became vested with the trust of legislation, in the *highest* sense of the word: nor could this trust be *limited* or *governed* by any of those rules and practices, which, for *reasons* drawn from *experience*, the people *condemned*, and were *determined to abolish*.

Thus the preserving the state from the ruin of an impending bankruptcy, *brought on* by the *prodigality* of courts, and the *regeneration* of the constitution, were the important services which the National Assembly were expected to perform for their constituents. And when we consider that these *important* and *difficult* services were to be per-[58]formed without that ready and effectual instrument of power, a *standing* army, (in whom *implicit* obedience is the *only* rule of action), we shall be obliged to confess, either that the men who undertook this *great* work were infected with a *daring insanity*, or that they were seconded by an *unanimity* in the sentiments of the people, which is *unparalleled* in the history of large empires, and which evidently destroys the force of *every* accusation which can be brought against them, as having rendered themselves the *instrument* of a faction, rather than the *faithful* deputies of the people.

A total reformation in the ecclesiastical system, and the new modelling the system of jurisprudence, were the *two leading points* in which *every*

---

[56] Ibid., pp. 103–4.

member of the empire agreed, excepting those individuals whose interests were personally affected by a change. It was a point of union in
which both the nobility and the people met; and several of those persons
who have been the *loudest* in their exclamations against the conduct of
the National Assembly, for having *disappointed* their body of the largest
share of the *spoils of the* [59] *crown*, and who have since united themselves
to the *mal-contents* among the lawyers and the clergy, were the most
active in the first movements of these grand points of reformation.

To begin with the reformation of the ecclesiastical system – It was
thought by the French nation, that *one hundred and four score* millions of
property, principally confined to the use of the *higher* orders of the
clergy, and thus prevented from entering into the common circulation
of other parts of property, was a *nuisance* in a treble sense.⁵⁷ It was a
nuisance, in the first instance, as a monopoly; in the second, it was a
nuisance, as giving a dangerous power to those who possessed that
monopoly; and in the third instance, as it tended, by the *natural course*
of moral causes in this *its excess*, to *corrupt* rather than to *encrease* and
invigorate those *qualities of the mind*, and those *spiritual endowments*,
which are to be desired in the teachers of religion. What real grounds
there were for this opinion, so generally conceived by the French nation
in the conduct of the clergy, I know not; neither shall I en-[60]quire, for
I am as little inclined as Mr. Burke can be to insult the unfortunate:
I shall only say, that as their temptations were *great*, and that their *nature*
was not *superior* to human infirmity, it was *probable* they produced their
due effects. But there is *one* sentiment in which I in some measure accord
with Mr. Burke. I do most sincerely lament that the *exigencies* of the
times would *not suffer* the National Assembly to indulge their clergy in a
life-enjoyment of their possessions. But this sentiment of mine is not of
so forcible a kind as to destroy *all other* sympathies. It would not lead me,
even if I possessed a similar portion of abilities with Mr. Burke, like him,
to *endeavour*, by the animating power of declamation, so to condole with
the sufferers as to combine all the energies of the *worst* passions of men
in favour of my opinion. I should not attempt to *rouse* and *inflame* the
resentment of the French clergy to a *repetition* of acts which have

---

⁵⁷ On 2 November 1789 the National Assembly passed a decree that classified all ecclesiastical property as *biens nationaux*, i.e. national goods. According to Burke, the confiscation of church property was motivated by a desire to secure national credit and protect
the moneyed interest. See esp. Pocock, 'Political Economy'.

renewed scenes of violence, and by which, after the *manner of old times*, they have set up the standard of Christ crucified, *to arm bigotry* in favour of *their* pretensions. Neither should I, among the more [61] peaceable members of that body, by representations the most touchingly affecting, open afresh those wounds on which it is to be hoped *religion has poured her healing balm.*

In the *attempt* to make the French National Assembly *singularly odious*, for the confiscations they have made of the church-lands, Mr. Burke asserts, that in many instances they have more violently outraged the principle, as well as the forms of public justice, than has been done by any other preceding power. The examples, he brings in proof, are the confiscations made by the fury of triumphant factions in the Roman commonwealth; and an example more in point in the person of Henry the Eighth, for Mr. Burke does *not chuse* to extend his observations to the conduct of Denmark, Sweden, and other states, on their profession of the reformed religion. Mr. Burke considers the *violences* of Marius and Sylla to be *much graced* in the formalities of *false accusations of treason* against the *most virtuous persons* in the commonwealth; and that the tyrant Henry the Eighth, who seized the property of the clergy for his own private use, and the emoluments of his favourites, [62] *dignified these acts of violence*, by assuming the character of the judge, and condemning the victims on *false pretences*.[58] Surely the French clergy would not have thought themselves *better used*, if the National Assembly had set on foot a commission to examine into the crimes and abuses which prevailed among them, and then to have governed their proceedings by reported truths, mixed with exaggeration and falsehood; surely this *mockery* of justice, *so much used* in old times, and this *covering* to the *deeds* of power, by *spoils torn* from the only consolatory remains of the sufferer, *his good fame*, will not be thought an example *proper* to have been followed, rather than the *plain* dealing of the French legislature.

But Mr. Burke has as great a dislike to the reform of the church police, as to the confiscations of the property of the more dignified part of the order. He is quite in a *rage*, that the *poor curates* should be taken out of the *hopeless poverty* into which they were plunged; and he *cannot endure* those regulations which took place in the *best* times of Christian societies. That bishops *should be confined* to [63] their dioceses, and the *care* of their

---

[58] Burke, *Reflections*, p. 172.

spiritual administration, instead of attending courts, and lavishing their incomes in the pleasures of the capital; and that the people should assume their rights of election; 'are solecisms in policy, which none but *barbarous, ignorant, atheistical minds* could dictate, and which no man of *enlarged* capacity and *generous* passions can obey.'[59]

On that article of the French ecclesiastical policy which confines bishops to their episcopal administration, it may not be improper to observe, that Bishop Leighton,[60] the *most eminent* of the Scotch prelates for his *piety* and his *zeal* for that order, *ardently wished* that such a regulation should take place on their re-establishment in Scotland under Charles the Second. I am far from saying that such a regulation is compatible with the state of things among us; and I think so well of the moderation of the clergy, and their regard to the constitution of the country, that I wish they were as *independent* a body as Mr. Burke *represents them to be.* But surely if *gratitude* for *past favours*, the *hopes* held out to *ambition* for the acquiring *further pre-*[64]*ferments*, and a very considerable number of church-livings in the *disposal* of the crown, *can in any respect* influence the minds of the clergy, they cannot be said to be *totally* independent.

I shall now take into consideration the second grand point of reformation, in which the nobles and people appear at first to have been in union, *viz.* the *new* modelling the system of jurisprudence;[61] but that a system of jurisprudence formed by *ignorant barbarians*, from codes of law adapted to support the *despotic tyranny* of the *Roman Emperors*, could not be in unison with the sentiments of an enlightened people, or capable of supporting the principles of a *free* government, was apparent to all parties: but personal interest, for reasons as apparent, at length produced an union between the lawyers and nobles. The National Assembly *justly* thought, that laws dictated by the *humane* spirit of an enlightened age, would be but *ill* administered by a tribunal formed under the influence of the *rankest* prejudices; and they conceived it as a *solecism* in politics, that Parliaments, who had been especially appointed to see that the laws and regulations framed by the As-[65]semblies of the States General, should

---

[59] This is not a direct quote.

[60] Robert Leighton (bap. 1612, d. 1684), archbishop of Glasgow.

[61] On 10 September 1789, the Assembly instructed a commission, with Jacques Guillaume Thouret (1746–94) as chairman, to submit a proposal for the immediate reform of the criminal law. Its report became law on 10 October 1789, and increased protection for accused people.

receive no injury from the edicts of the monarch, should be kept as a controul over the standing authority of the nation. It was on this reason that the old independent Parliaments, with all their merits, and all their faults, were abolished. Nor is it a wonder that in the change of the *prospect*, a change in the sentiments of the nobles should have taken place: for when they perceived that the system of the ancient tyranny was *better* adapted to their *personal* greatness than the *new order* of things, they, with Mr. Burke, looked on the Parliaments as a *convenient* power, under which they might rally. What a *ready convenience* for the play of a *delusive* policy would it have afforded, if the Parliaments, exerting their *old* authority under the crown, had pertinaciously refused to register the edicts of the Assembly! What a display of eloquence *in favour* of the *privileges* of the *nobles* and the *clergy*, might have been seen in their *remonstrances* to the Assembly! and what *useful* delays would it have afforded for the president of the National Assembly, in the name of the Majesty of the people, to have been obliged to [66] mount the Bed of *Justice*, after the example of the late monarchs of the realm; and in case of an *incurable* obstinacy, for the Assembly, through the means of the executive power, to have recourse to the *tedious* remedy of an imprisonment. With such advantages on their side, the *faction* in opposition would have had *reasonable* grounds of hope, that *centuries* might have elapsed before the constitution could have been in any sense of the word regenerated.

Before I leave this subject, it will be necessary to notice, that Mr. Burke *condemns the* conduct of the National Assembly for the distinction they have made in their treatment of the lawyers and their clergy, a distinction which I think every unprejudiced person will agree to be founded in justice, *viz.* the preference afforded the former by making them a suitable provision during life, in consideration that the civil offices, of which they were deprived, had been purchased with private property (as Mr. Burke observes) 'at an high rate.'[62]

The prevention of a national bankruptcy was thought an object of the most *momentous* [67] concern to the whole French nation. It was in order to avert this *impending* evil, that the States General were permitted to assemble;[63] and it was an object *principally* recommended to the deputies

---

[62] Burke, *Reflections*, p. 181. In fact, he wrote 'at a very high rate'.
[63] As a response to France's dire financial situation, the Estates General was summoned in 1789 for the first time since 1614.

of the people, by their united voice. In this state of public opinion, the arguments so plausibly, and indeed so forcibly urged by Mr. Burke *against the right* of the monarch to mortgage the public revenue, will not render the Assembly culpable for *endeavouring* to *keep faith* with the creditors of the crown. For though I never could perceive why on any *good grounds of reason*, the people should *quarrel* with their new constitution, because the *prodigality* of the *old government* had involved them in *distresses* which were in their nature irremoveable, which did not proceed from any *fraud* or *corruption* in their *new* servants, and which could not be mended by subjecting themselves to the *old* domination; yet certain it is, that the *enemies* of the new constitution have beheld the arrival of a moment big with that temporary distress and confusion which must ever attend a national bankruptcy, with the *utmost impatience*, as of bringing with it, [68] a *sure* prospect of *victory*. What an *opportunity* indeed, would it present, of setting forth *exaggerated* descriptions of public distresses, and of arraigning the members of the National Assembly as the *sole* authors of the nation's wrongs! The *anxious* and *provident* care which this Assembly has taken to ward off this disaster, and also to avoid, in the present irritable state of the public feelings, the imposing very heavy burthens on the people, is certainly a mark of political *sagacity*, and, *being such*, is treated with the *utmost bitterness of disappointed rage* by their opponents.

On the subject of the difficulties which the French Legislature have encountered in the talk of regenerating the constitution, it is natural to turn our minds on the *paper-currency* they have established,[64] and especially as it is a subject on which Mr. Burke has displayed the *whole force* of his ingenuity, to alarm the fears of the French nation, and to depreciate, and to render odious in their eyes, the conduct of their representatives.

On this subject I do profess a total ignorance: I have no financiering abilities; and I [69] wish with all my heart, that this art which Mr. Burke represents as a talent the *most highly* necessary in those who conduct the affairs of state, and which I consider as deriving its practical use from its *deceptious* address in *picking the pockets* of the people, was not so necessary an engine in the present modes of administration. A few observations however, which must occur to every thinking mind, I shall venture

---

[64] i.e. the *assignat* introduced on 19 December 1789. It was a form of currency not based on silver, but on the value of the confiscated church property.

to make. They are as follows: That the difference which Mr. Burke makes between the paper-currency of this country, and that which now subsists in France, is not *so much* in favour of England as Mr. Burke represents; for, as the French legislature have *not* issued more paper than they appear to have a *solid fund to support*, and a fund that is *obvious* to every man's eyes and understanding, its credit *ought not in reason* to have less stability than a paper currency founded on *confidence*. For, though every man believes, and on good grounds believes, that the bank of England has a sufficient property to answer for the payment of its notes; yet still although *this belief* should arise to a *moral certainty*, it cannot be *superior* [70] to a credit founded on an *obvious* fact. And should the French legislature continue this *wise* caution, of not issuing more paper than the state revenue can obviously support whilst the revolution stands on its *present* bottom, this paper, *whatever may be* the exigencies of the times, must *always* be of *some value*; whereas a failure of our national credit would, it is generally thought, render the paper money of this country of *no more worth than the intrinsic value of the paper*.

The diffusion of a general spirit of gaming, and the destructive practice of stock-jobbing,[65] *are evils* which I am afraid in a more or less degree must ever exist with national debts; and the *larger* the debt, the *greater* will be *the degree* of evil. That this spirit prevails in our capital to a very alarming height, the history of the *Bulls* and *Bears*[66] in the alley will *abundantly* testify: That it has been the *ruin* of many a fair fortune, *thousands of sufferers* can also testify:[67] That it has *enabled* and *tempted several* of those who are in the *secret* of affairs, to *pillage* the public unmercifully, same represents; and that the stocks have a *great* influence over the landed pro-[71]perty of this country, which rises or falls

---

[65] In his *Dictionary* (1755), Samuel Johnson defined a stockjobber as 'A low wretch who gets money by buying and selling shares in the funds', and illustrates this meaning with a quotation from Swift: 'The *stockjobber* thus from' Change-alley goes down, / And tips you the freeman a wink; / Let me have but your vote to serve for the town, / And here is a guinea to drink'. See Swift, *Miscellanies, in Prose and Verse. Volume the Fifth* (London, 1735), p. 225.

[66] Bulls and bears refer to market conditions, with the former indicating rising and the latter falling prices. The terms are believed to have derived from traders in animal skins, or alternatively from the way in which animals attack each other. Early usages of this terminology can be traced to Richard Steele's *Tatler* (1709) and Daniel Defoe's *Political History of the Devil* (1726).

[67] Including the fortune of her grandfather, Jacob Sawbridge.

according to their various fluctuations, the experience of the last American war *evinces beyond a doubt.*

All these evils, if evils they are, were *prognosticated* by those who stiled themselves the patriots of their country, from the *first* establishment of a funded debt, to almost the present period of time; and the reasons they urged to enforce the arguments they used against the measure, appear to me sufficiently convincing to have induced a *cautious moderation* in our councils. But they were not attended to; they were represented as the *chimeras of discontented speculative men*; the *encrease* of the national debt was set forth as both the *cause* and the *effects* of public *prosperity*; it was described as the *enlivening* principle of commerce, the *grand panacea* that was to keep us in an *eternal vigour*, the *steady hold* by which all the members of the community were to be *bound* in the bands of loyalty; and that there was *no excess* in the amount of the debt, that could be attended with *any ruinous* consequences.

[72] If such representations, so repeatedly made by a large party in the kingdom, and at present so generally adopted, are founded in truth, I cannot see how *causes* which have a *salutary effect* among us, should operate as *poison* to our neighbours; and I have a *better* opinion of the policy of the National Assembly in issuing their *assignats*, from the *strong* and *violent opposition* which was made to the measure by their *enemies*.

It must not be forgot, that, among the other œconomical regulations of the National Assembly, that which has taken place in their *list* of *pensioners*, fall equally with other of their acts, under the severity of Mr. Burke's pen. The amount of the public money given to this description of people by the court, was indeed *enormous*; and if we may give credit to the *Red Book*,[68] published by authority, there was *little* of the principles of *reason* or *justice* in the admeasurement of rewards to individuals, unless the *state* and the *country* are considered as *separate interests* in the account; and that the pleasing or gratifying the *prince* and his *favourites* should be reckoned in the value of an *hundred*

---

[68] Jean-Baptiste-Marie-Louis La Reynie de La Bruyère, *Le livre rouge, or, Red book: Being a List of Secret Pensions, Paid Out of the Public Treasure of France; and Containing Characters of the Persons Pensioned, Anecdotes of Their Lives, An Account of Their Services and Observations Tending to Shew the Reasons for which the Pensions Were Granted*, published in London and Paris in 1790.

[73] *pounds* to a *penny*, when set in the balance of *blood shed* in *defence* of the *nation*.

What indeed can escape Mr. Burke's censure, or what act of the French legislature can please him, (but the dissolving themselves, and leaving the king and the nobles to form their own rules of power), when he finds subject for *reproach* even in their acts of *sympathy* to the *indigent* part of the *citizens*? That Paris was always crowded with a numerous herd of mendicants, even more numerous, if possible, than those who infest and disgrace our capital, is certain; and should their numbers have encreased by the desertion of those opulent citizens who are out of temper with the government, it would neither be a *surprizing* nor an *alarming* circumstance: But it is an evil that time alone can cure, when the shock of so important a revolution has spent its force, and when the *ill humour* which at present rages in the breasts of the discontented shall sub-side, and lead them to return into the bosom of their country, and under the protecting laws of a regular government.

[74] In a very elaborate defence of all the artificial modes of greatness which have taken place in society, Mr. Burke has used all the powers of eloquence and subtlety to prove, that the crimes which have been committed by our species, have not arisen from the imperfection of institutions, but from the vices of individuals. In *one sense*, his argument will be found to be *just*; in *another, nugatory*: For though it must be acknowledged, that the crimes committed by Nero proceeded from the depravity of his character, yet the *opportunity* of committing those crimes, and perhaps that very *depravity* of sentiment from whence they proceeded, lay in the *vice* of the *imperial institution*.

With the same flow of eloquence, and the same subtlety, Mr. Burke recommends in all legislators, that *tardy* caution which suffers the *spirit of reform to evaporate* before their work is half-finished; 'for the evils latent in the most promising contrivances,' says Mr. Burke, 'should be provided for as they arise; one advantage is as little as possible to be sacrificed to another; for thus we compensate, we reconcile, we balance, we are [75] enabled to unite in a consistent whole, the various anomalies and contending principles that are found in the minds and affairs of men.'[69]

---

[69] Burke, *Reflections*, p. 249.

This *finely* imagined theory would undoubtedly be adopted by all wise and good legislators, did it in any manner suit with the *nature* of mankind, and that *leaven* of *selfishness* which taints *every principle* of human conduct. That perfect knowledge of human affairs, which Mr. Burke conceives, and justly conceives, ought to be inseparable from the office of legislation, will convince men, that when new constitutions are to be formed, it is necessary they should, in their formation, be regulated in all their circumstances by those principles which the legislators conceive to be *the best*; for if any thing which may be thought *defective* is left for the wisdom of future legislators to *correct*, the constitution must *remain defective*, as future reformers will find their *difficulties encrease*, instead of being *diminished*, by time. The reason is plain; for that which constitutes the *defects* in all governments, are those principles in them which support a *partial interest*, [76] to the injury of a *public one*; and the *prescription of time* with the *politic use of power*, has been found an *irresistible barrier* to every important part *of reformation* in the ordinary course of things.

The French legislature, in order to extinguish those local prejudices and provincial jealousies which formerly existed in the kingdom of France, arising from the different laws and customs which took place when the independent principalities were annexed to the crown; and also to regulate the rights of election in such a manner, as whilst it secured to the citizens at large this invaluable blessing, it should provide for the public tranquillity; conceived and executed a plan of dividing the kingdom into eighty-one departments.[70] Each of these departments are divided into smaller districts, called *Communes*; and these again into smaller districts, called *Cantons*. The primary assemblies of the *cantons* elect deputies to the *communes*, one for every two hundred qualified inhabitants. The *communes* chosen by the *cantons* chuse to the *departments*, and the deputies of the *departments* chuse the deputies to the *National Assembly*.

[77] A qualification to the right of election in the first instance, is placed at the low rate of the price of three days labour; the qualification of being elected into the *Commune*, is the amount of ten days labour; and

---

[70] This plan was presented to the National Assembly by Thouret from Rouen. Simon Schama, *Citizens: A Chronicle of the French Revolution* (New York, 1989), p. 475.

that of being elected a deputy to the *National Assembly*, is only *one* mark of silver.[71]

This plan, in theory at least, promises to unite the highest degree of *freedom* with the highest degree of *order*: it extends the right of election *to every man who is not a pauper*, and as such, by living on the *alms* of society, cannot reasonably have a *right* to enjoy its political privileges; and whilst it thus encourages industry, by rendering it a necessary quality to enjoy these privileges, it opens the door to every man of ability to obtain the highest honours of his country. But this plan, so plausible at least in its appearance, and so exactly agreeing with the rights of the citizens in the *strictest sense* of the word, is criticised by Mr. Burke in a manner *highly unworthy* of his great abilities, because he descends to the *arts* of a quibbling sophistry. He accuses the legislature of not attending to their avowed principles of the equal rights of [78] men, in *refusing* their *paupers* a vote. He asserts that the right of election granted in the first instance, is no privilege at all; and he foresees, that the most *fatal dissensions* will arise from regulations which seemingly tend to *harmonise every* jarring principle in the state, to subdue every prejudice of the mind hostile to the public welfare, and to combine all its affections in the character of a loyal citizen.[72]

In opposition to Mr. Burke's accusation, that the legislature, in the qualifications they have annexed to the rights of election, have acted in contradiction to their avowed principles of the equal rights of men, I shall, without sheltering myself under the cover of a practical use, (which may be used to justify every mode of tyranny), assert, that the French legislature have, in those qualifications, adhered to the rights of men in the *strictest sense*, even as they exist in their *abstract* perfection in a state of nature: for, who ever conceived, that, in a state of nature, a man who was either not inclined, or by bodily infirmity not able, to till the ground, had a right to the fruits produced by the labour of [79] others?[73] In this case, either in a state of nature, or in a state of society, the *right* of maintenance depends alone on the *laws of humanity*, proceeding from that sympathy which the benevolent Author of our being has for the *best purposes* woven into the mental constitution of all his *moral* creatures. But these laws of humanity do not oblige men to yield rights with the *donation of alms*, and to put those whom their charity has relieved, into

---

[71] Ibid., p. 498.   [72] Burke, *Reflections*, pp. 258–62.
[73] Locke, *Two Treatises of Government* (London, 1764), pp. 216–21.

a situation of *forcing* from them the fruits of their industry. It is on the basis of *industry* alone, the *only* principle which exactly squares with a native right, and *not on rent-rolls*, that the legislature has formed the rights of representation; and this on such liberal principles, that every man who has activity and industry, may qualify himself as to the matter of property, for a seat in the legislative assembly. As to the nature and operation of the privileges annexed to the first and second steps in the gradation, I conceive that the regular degrees, which directly point to the grand privilege of chusing the representatives, whilst they totally prevent *confusion*, and the errors of a *blind* choice, [80] do not, in *any* respect, render *nugatory* the right of its more *abstract* principle. For every man, in the Canton makes *his choice* of a deputy whom he thinks qualified by merit to represent him in the Commune, and *every* voter in the Commune has also *his choice* of a deputy to represent him in the department, who have a right to the choice of representatives.

As Mr. Burke has made it a point to object to *every* part of the French constitution as it now stands, and to every act of the legislature which respects this constitution, I must follow him through all his objections, and state those reasons which appear to me to have regulated their conduct. It is true that a senate, or an assembly of men who have had some controul over the voice of the people, some power of mitigating, regulating, or carrying into execution their laws, has always had a place in the ancient republics: But Mr. Burke himself seems to allow that they are not *absolutely* necessary in monarchies, or rather in any government which admits of a *standing permanent* executive power. It is true they appear to have been a necessary in-[81]stitution in the ancient republics; yet history will shew us, that their tendency has ever been *hostile* to the principles of democracy, and often ended in the *ruin* of freedom. To the *pride*, the *avarice*, and *corruption* of the Roman Senate, was undoubtedly owing the subversion of the republic. It is, I think, very little to the purpose of enlightening men's minds on the subject of modern government, to quote the reflections of ancient authors, or draw comparisons from ancient times, which were totally unacquainted with that *excellent* policy, by which the people's power is represented, and brought into regular action through the means of deputation. An assembly of men *thus appointed*, seems to unite in it all the energy and fitness to the affairs of government of the Roman Senate, in its most brilliant and perfect state, without the *latent* principles of *corruption* and *destruction* which lurked in this institution.

What Lord Bolingbroke could mean I know not, when he says, that he prefers a monarchy to other governments; because every description of a republic can be better engrafted on it, than any thing of a monarchy [82] upon the republican forms;[74] unless he refers to such a *qualified* monarchy as is confined to the *mere* office of an executive governor, with the *stability* that is annexed to *hereditary descent*; for sure it is *impossible* to engraft a democracy on any other description of monarchy. If this is his Lordship's meaning, the French monarchy, as it now stands, will be found to agree *perfectly* with it; and should experience prove it to be defective for the want of such a member as a senate, the defect must be supplied with all those *cautious* preventatives which experience can alone afford.

The *limitations* of power, in which the executive magistrate is confined, affords Mr. Burke a subject for the exertion of *all* the powers of his oratory. He *deplores* the mortified state of the fallen monarch; he sees nothing but *weakness* in the government, and *confusion* in the affairs of the empire; from the want of a *proper influencing power in the executive, and that cordiality which ought to subsist between it and the legislative.* He conceives, that without such a *controuling* influence, the executive office is a state of *degrada-*[83]*tion*, to which *no man of spirit* would submit. And if the present King and his successors respect their *true* glory, they will take *every* opportunity which time may present, of shaking off the yoke of their imperious masters, and resuming their former independence.

To these animadversions of Mr. Burke, it may be observed, that most of the limitations of which he complains, are either *inseparable* to the security of the democracy; or they have their grounds in a *just policy*, suiting itself to the present state of things. It is necessary that a popular legislature should be informed through *other channels* than the *executive power*, of such matters as may import that body to know: it is necessary that all the means by which *a personal influence* may be established by the *grant of lands* and *large pensions*, should be taken away; and for the same reasons of policy, it is necessary that the executive power *should not* be capable of *deluding the imaginations* of men, by creating *artificial distinctions* among them.

---

[74] Bolingbroke, *Works*, III, pp. 51–2; Burke, *Reflections*, p. 187.

According to Mr. Burke's political creed, Kings are only to *respect those* who serve their [84] *personal greatness*; and it is his opinion, that the successors to the throne of France in the Bourbon line, *must*, unless they are *illiterate men*, act on a principle *hostile* to the constitution which *they are sworn* to preserve. It is true, as Mr. Burke observes, this is *nature*; but are not those very *inclinations*, so inherent in man, the grounds for that *jealousy* which reflecting patriots entertain *of all persons* vested with the dangerous gift of *permanent* authority? And unless the present monarch of France, and his successors, shall conceive *very different ideas of glory* than they will *learn* from Mr. Burke; unless they shall conceive that the executing an office *faithfully*, reflects *more honour* upon them than any encrease of *personal greatness* they can gain by *treachery*; there is very little probability that they will obtain from a popular legislature, that enlargement of power[i] which may reasonably be given, when circumstances shall *convince* the public mind that there are no grounds for jealousy.

Mr. Burke extends his *commiseration not only* to the person of the King and his royal [85] issue, but *even* to the ministers of the crown in their civil capacity. In this commiseration, he *reprobates* a principle which is held out to the people of Great Britain as the grand *palladium* of their liberties, I mean the principle of responsibility; though the reprobation is indeed qualified by a distinction of *active* and *zealous* service, and the restraint of crimes. But it is a distinction which I cannot well understand; for if responsibility does not go to every part of a minister's conduct, in which he acts without due authority, it is indeed a *very* slight constitutional barrier against the *vices* of administration, especially when it is allowed among the prerogatives of our Kings, that they may chuse their own servants, and retain them in their office at pleasure: but will any minister who serves such a King (says Mr. Burke, when speaking of the present King of France) with but a decent appearance of respect, *cordially* obey the orders of those whom but the other day in his name they had committed to the Bastille? Will they obey the orders of those whom, whilst they were exercising *despotic justice* upon them, they conceived they were treating with [86] *lenity*, and for whom, in a *prison*, they thought they had provided an *asylum*.[75]

---

[i] Such as the full exercise of the *Veto*.

[75] Burke, *Reflections*, p. 292.

This is saying *very little*, either for the disposition of the ministers, or for the *spirit* and *principles* of the ancient government. Nor can I see that these gentlemen have any *reasonable* complaints to make against the conduct of the French legislature. It is true they are denied a seat amongst them; but this exception is not made on any *personal* ground: they do not except against the abilities of these gentlemen, or their honesty as individuals; but they will *not* permit either a *real*, or a *supposed influence*, to controul their own actions. They will not permit that the sanctuary, in which the Majesty of the people of France resides, should be *polluted* or *impeached* by any *suspicion of corruption*; and they will not endanger the liberties of their country, by giving *absolute power any motive*, which, in the event of things, may possibly tend to an *abuse* of *trust*.

The opinion which Mr. Burke endeavours to establish in his elaborate Reflections on the French Revolution, is the *incompatibility* of a truly popular government with the human [87] constitution: And the subject which affords him the most ample scope for the display of his argumentative powers, is found in the investment of that military force which is necessary to the support of all governments; for if that force is trusted to the people at large, they may be tempted to act in their natural capacity, and, by destroying or weakening the energy of those organs by which regular councils are held and enforced, induce a state of anarchy. And if the support of the government is made to subsist in a regular standing disciplined body, under the controul of an individual, that individual will become the *master of the people*, and *violate* the government he was appointed to defend.[76]

Either the establishment or the overthrow of an opinion so fatal to the proud hopes of man, must be left to time and experience; for I am sorry to say, that we have no notices on which we can attempt the construction of an opposite argument. We cannot venture to establish an opinion on the state of a country not yet recovered from the convulsive struggles which every important revolution must occasion. We can gain no light from history; for history furnishes *no example* of [88] any government in a large empire, which, in the strictest sense of the word, has secured to the citizen the *full* enjoyment of his rights. Some attempts indeed have been made of this kind; but they have hitherto failed, through the

[76] Ibid., p. 318.

treachery of leaders, or by the *rash folly* of the multitude. But though these circumstances will prevent cautious persons from giving a *decided* opinion on what may be the event of things, yet they do not so *benight* the understanding as to deprive the mind of hope. They do not prevent it from seeing that the present complexion of things in France has something of a different aspect from what history, or the state of other countries, presents to our view: Instead of that *barbarous ignorance*, or that *depravity* of *principle*, which are to be seen in other European States, and which might reasonably prevent the patriot from bestowing (if it were in his power) the full boon of liberty, we see a people *firm* and *united* in their efforts to *support* their rights, yet obedient[ii] to the dictates of that government [89] which they have appointed to defend them.

From what can this difference which subsists between the French nation and other societies arise, but in a more *general* diffusion of *knowledge*, and in a principle of action which consults the *public* good, as well as the gratifications of *self?* It is the business of *knowledge* to teach men their *real interests*; and it is to be hoped it will so far prevail over that *mist* which *inordinate* affections cast over the mind, as to enable the French municipalities to see, that if they so far *abuse* the power with which they have been invested for the defence of their rights, as to gratify a *private* passion at the expence of the *public* peace, they will induce a *necessity* which will lead to their *utter* destruction. It is to be hoped also, that a *true* sense of interest will enable the army to perceive, that the *moment they fling off the character of the citizen, and assume a controuling power over their country*, from that moment they become *individually slaves*; for the very circumstance in their condition by which this power must subsist, is a discipline inseparable to the [90] *strictest subordination*, and which in *all* respects must militate against their civil rights. When the Roman army was in the very height of their power; when it was enabled to depose and murder emperors, and raise private men to the imperial throne; when they were enabled to ravage the empire at their pleasure, and exact largesses from its spoils; they were, in an *individual* capacity, the *greatest* of slaves.

The patriot Frenchman has a prospect of hope which *never* yet offered itself to the view of society, and that is in the *disinterestedness* of those

---

[ii] Mr. Burke acknowledges this obedience, and calls it fanaticism.

councils to which he has confided his right. The republican parliament of England, by their *inordinate* thirst after public offices, and by using their power to their *own emolument*, gave *too much room* for the suspicions of a divided people to act in their disfavour; and it must be acknowledged, that the interests of self have been observed to act as much in popular councils as in courts. But the French legislature have set in this point, an example *unparellelled* in the history of man. To a *bold* and *enterprising* spirit, they have united a *disinterestedness* [91] of principle which has deprived their enemies of *every* means of opposition, but *vain* declamation, *groundless* accusation, and *impotent* hope. Long may they continue the *admiration* of the world in these important particulars! Long may they thus continue to *aggrandize* the character of man! And long may they continue to deserve a *monument of esteem* on the minds of their species, which neither *time*, nor *accident*, nor *adverse fortune, shall be able to efface!*

It cannot be denied that Mr. Burke has made a display of very *uncommon* abilities in his attack on the French Revolution; but why has he deigned to make use of the *mean arts* of abuse as an *auxiliary* in the contest? Why has he, by the most *invidious* comparisons, and *groundless* accusations, endeavoured to rouse all nations and all descriptions of men against them, and thus to *crush in their ruin all the rights of man?* Is the tendency of his publication a *recommendation* to the British government, to dragoon their neighbours into an adoption of their own system of policy? Would he re-[92]commend to the potentates of Europe, a renewal of that *wicked conspiracy* against the rights of men, which was planned by Henry the Fourth and his minister Sully,[77] and which was only prevented from taking place by the timely death of that monarch? – a plan, by which, through the *combination* of power, modes of government were to be *arbitrarily* imposed and supported, and the rights of conscience *abolished.* If such *violent* councils were indeed to take place of that *moderation* and *equity* which has hitherto been shewn, it would *prove* that the *forming treaties* and directing the *force of nations* were but *ill* trusted to the *secrecy* of cabinets. When we reflect that such dreadful purposes can never be effected without the effusion of *oceans* of blood, of such an invidious intention we must certainly exculpate Mr. Burke;

---

[77] Macaulay may have read the popular Pierre Mathurin de L'Écluse des Loges, *Sully's Memoirs*, trans. Charlotte Lennox (2 vols., London, 1751). Maximilien de Béthune, Duke of Sully (1559–1641), was chief minister under Henry IV and Louis XIII.

unless, by a *strange* modification of *sympathy*, the lives of plebeians, and those vulgar characters which compose the '*swinish multitude*,'[78] is held at *no value* in his account. Some of Mr. Burke's expressions, indeed, seem to warrant us in making such a supposition, though we *must acknowledge*, that, in [93] others, he appears to have a *concern* for the *spiritual*, if not for the *temporal* happiness of those he despises: 'Whilst', says he, 'the wealth and pride of individuals at every moment makes the man of humble rank and fortune sensible of his inferiority, and *degrades* and *vilifies* his condition;[iii] it is for the man in humble life, and to raise his nature, and to put him in mind of a state in which the privileges of opulence will cease, when he will be equal by nature, and may be more than equal by virtue, that this portion of the general wealth of his country is employed, and sanctified.'[79]

If Mr. Burke, in the management of his argument, could have descended from the *lofty* strain of a *poetic* imagination, to the *drudgery* of close reasoning, he would have perceived the *error* of deviating from the line of *expediency* into the question of *right*; for [94] when we once *give up* the point, that there is an *inherent* right attached to privileged persons to make laws for the community, we cannot fix on any other principle that will stand the test of argument, but the *native* and *unalienable* rights of man. For if we say that *lawful* governments are formed on the authority of conventions, it will be asked, *who gave these conventions their authority?* If we grant that they derived their authority from the *assent of the people*, how came the people, it will be said, to exert such an authority at *one* period of society, and not at *another?* If we say it was *necessity* that recovered to the social man the full rights of his nature, it will be asked, *who is to be the judge* of this necessity? why *certainly* the people.[80]

Thus, in *every* light in which we can place the argument, in every possible mode of reasoning, we shall be driven back to elect either the

---

[iii] This is a sad condition, indeed, for '*naked shivering nature:*' But what is the remedy? why, let them respect property, and seek 'their consolation in the final proportions of eternal justice.' Vide *Reflections*, page 147 and 351.

[78] Burke, *Reflections*, p. 117. This phrase became notorious; see, e.g., *A Rod for the Burkites ... By one of the 'Swinish Multitude'* (London, 1790).
[79] Burke, *Reflections*, p. 147.
[80] 'the common question will be made, *Who shall be judge,* whether the prince or legislative act contrary to their trust? ... To this I reply, *The people shall be judge*'. Locke, *Two Treatises of Government*, p. 414. See also note xxix in the section on Macaulay's *History of England* (above p. 34).

first or the second of these propositions; either that an individual, or some privileged persons, have an inherent and indefeasible right to make laws for the community, or that this authority rests in the unalienable and indefeasible rights of man.

[95] That the people have often abused their power, it must be granted; for they have often *sacrificed* themselves and their posterity to the *wanton will* of an individual, and *this* is the foundation of all the regal tyrannies which have subsisted in society; but *no abuse* of their power can *take away their right* because their right *exists in the very constitution of things*. If the French people therefore should be so *capricious* as to fling off their new constitution, and subject themselves to more *unequal* forms of government, or even to *tyranny*, it will be agreeable to the course of past experience: but such an exertion of power *cannot injure their right*; and whatever form or complexion any future government in France may bear, it can have no *legitimate* source, *but in the will of the people*.

I am,
My Lord,
With great esteem and respect,
Your Lordship's
Most obedient
Humble Servant,

The AUTHOR.

Index

Abel, 97

absolutism, xx, 11, 32, 34, 72, 85–7, 92–103, 106, 120, 146, 157, 253, 296

Acts of Parliament
Act of Settlement (1701), 83, 173–4, 252, 259
Act of Supremacy (1534), 14
Bill of Rights (1689), 77–8
Copyright Act (1710), 124, 131
Corporation Act (1661), xviii, 156
Habeas Corpus Act (1679), xxx, 61
Intolerable Acts (1774), 146
Mutiny Act (1718), 173
Occasional Conformity Act (1711), xiii
Quebec Act (1774), 146, 152, 156–7
Schism Act (1714), xiii
Septennial Act (1716), xiii, xviii, 82, 110, 118, 157, 173
Stamp Act (1765), xxviii, xxxiii, 146, 152
Test Act (1673), xviii, 156
Toleration Act (1689), xviii, xxiv, 79
Townshend Acts (1767-68), 146
Treason Act (1695), 58

Adam, 32, 97

Adams, John, xi, xviii, xxix, 2

Adams, Samuel, xxxi

Addison, Joseph, 177, 214, 218

Africa, 204, 232

afterlife, xii, xxii–xxiii, 182, 253, 263, 299

agriculture, xxix, 19

Albemarle, 1st Duke of. *See* Monck, George

Alexander, William, 213

Almon, John, xxviii, 81

ambition, 10, 46–8, 51, 54, 57, 74, 80, 83–4, 103, 115, 123, 227, 273, 279, 285

America, xvi, xviii, xxviii–xxxii, xxxiv–xxxix, 2, 19, 87, 146, 152, 154, 157–61, 254, 267, 289

American Revolution, xi, xvii, xxix, xxxi, xxxiv–xxxix, 2, 49, 82, 146–7, 157–61, 251, 253, 289

American War of Independence. *See* American Revolution

anarchy, 106, 123, 263, 273, 296

ancient constitutionalism, xxii–xxiii, 16, 73, 80

animals, xii, xxvi, xxxii, 43, 94–5, 175, 177, 184–9, 196–7, 203–8, 238, 242–3

Anne, queen of Great Britain, 32, 93, 131, 164, 171, 260

Antoninus, 226

arbitrary power, 9, 11, 14–15, 18–20, 39, 41, 51–2, 58, 67, 118, 153–6, 159, 172–3, 265

Arendt, Hannah, xxv

Argyll, Archibald Campbell, 9th Earl of, 59

Argyll's Rising, 59

aristocracy, xii, xvii, xxvi–xxvii, xxxii, 2, 77, 86–8, 96–7, 106, 109–16, 118, 173, 251, 253, 266

Aristotle, 92, 98, 240

Arnall, William, 12

Ashley, Maurice, 209

Asia, 99, 217, 232

Asiatic despotism. *See* oriental despotism

Asiatic luxury, 65, 99–100, 217, 234

Index

Astell, Mary, xv
atheism, xxiii, 252, 261, 285
Athens, 108, 191, 236
Atterbury, Francis, 162
Augustus, 234
Aurelius, Marcus, 195
Austria, 171
avarice, 136–8, 275, 293

Bacon, Francis, 133–5
Badcock, Samuel, 184
Bank of England, 167, 170–1, 288
Barillon d'Amoncourt, Paul,
    64, 66–7, 69
Barker, Hannah, xxxviii
barons, 14, 41–2, 51
Barron, Richard, 43
Beattie, James, 131
beauty, xxvii, 176, 187, 198–200, 203–4,
    212–22, 232, 280
Beccaria, Cesare, 240, 243
benevolence, xxiii, xxvi, 104, 141, 176, 182,
    184–9, 197, 201, 204–5, 207–9, 221, 224,
    227–9, 240–4, 249, 265–6, 273
Bible, 22, 31–4, 97, 135, 139, 177, 182, 206,
    248, 264–5, 281
bicameralism, 86, 104–5
Binckes, William, 31
Birch, Thomas, 27
Bishops' Wars, 53
Blackstone, William, 11, 269
Boileau-Despréaux, Nicolas, 177
Bolingbroke, Henry St. John, 1st Viscount,
    xvi, xxiii, xxxi, xl, 3, 9, 12, 81, 110, 118,
    162–4, 223, 225, 261, 294
Bond, W. H., xxxviii
Bongie, Laurence, xxxvii
Bonwick, Colin, xxxix
Book of Common Prayer, 24, 30
booksellers, 124, 130–3, 136–40
Borgia, Cesare, 210
Boston Tea Party, 146
Boswell, James, 86
Bourke, Richard, xl
Branges, marquis de. *See* Barillon
    d'Amoncourt, Paul
Bretonneau, François, 74–6
Brewer, John, xxxix
bribery, 13, 45, 67, 77, 80, 140, 158, 216, 233

Brissot de Warville, Jacques Pierre, xi, xx, xxx,
    xxxii
British constitution, xxii, xxx–xxxi, 11–13,
    76–84, 115–23, 147, 151–8, 172–4,
    258–61, 270–1, 274, 276
British Empire, xxix, xxxi, 82, 146, 151, 155,
    159–61, 173
Brown, John, xxxi
Brutus, Lucius Junius, 55, 105, 108, 231
Bucer, Martin, 34
Buckingham, George Villiers, 2nd Duke of, 73
Burgh, James, xi, xxiv, 2–3, 155, 158–9, 163–4
Burke, Edmund, xvi–xviii, xxiii–xxv, xxxii,
    xxxiv, xl, 49, 88, 109–23, 145, 176, 199,
    202, 251–300
Burnet, Gilbert, 11, 30–1, 70, 168
Bute ministry, xix
Bute, John Stuart, 3rd Earl of, xix, 82

Caesar, Julius, xxii, 105, 232–3
Cain, 97
Caligula, 99–102
Calvin, John, 34
Calvinism, 17, 34, 37, 79, 182
Cambridge, University of, 72, 147
Camden, Charles Pratt, 1st Earl of, 88,
    129–31, 133, 136, 143
Canada, 146–7, 152–6
cannibalism, 204
Carte, Thomas, 29, 32
Carter, Elizabeth, xiv
Cartwright, John, xx
Catholicism, xxiv–xxv, 15, 17, 27, 31, 42, 60,
    72–6, 80, 146–7, 152–6, 252, 260
Catilina, Lucius Sergius, 210
Cavaliers, 36, 38, 44–6
Chalus, Elaine, xxxviii
Chambers, Robert, xi
Champion, Justin, xxxix
charity, 61, 135, 141, 248–50, 292
Charles I, xi, xxii, 1, 20–38, 42–3, 49, 51–5,
    72–3, 80, 252, 260, 269
Charles II, xxv, 30–1, 46, 58, 60–2, 67–9, 73,
    167–8, 172, 285
Charles V (of Spain), 156
chastity, 18, 26, 28, 216, 220–2
Chatham, William Pitt, 1st Earl of, xix, 81–2
Chesterfield, Philip Dormer Stanhope, 4th
    Earl of, 214–15

Index

Echard, Laurence, 70
education, xii, xiv, xvi, xxiii, xxxvii, 10–12, 29,
	72, 107, 175–84, 187, 189–203, 208–11,
	213–31, 241, 246, 249
Edward III, 58, 77
Edward VI, 51
effeminacy, xviii, xxv–xxvi, 18
Elagabalus. *See* Heliogabalus
elections, xix, 38, 41, 77–8, 82, 87, 106, 120–3,
	145–6, 151–2, 158, 169, 172, 275, 279,
	285, 291–2
Elizabeth I, xxi, 14–19, 29–30, 40–2, 51–2, 244
eloquence, 115, 120, 143, 175, 201, 212, 257,
	273, 286, 290
empire, xxxi, 43, 45, 56, 73, 151–61, 282, 296
English Civil War. *See* Wars of the Three
	Kingdoms
English people, 12, 14, 17–19, 21, 39, 42, 45,
	59, 85, 103, 145, 262
English revolution, xi–xiii, xv, xxii, 2, 20–40,
	42–7, 253, 276
enthusiasm, xxii, 76, 86, 212, 227–8,
	230, 266
Epictetus, 176, 195
equality, xiii–xiv, xxii, xxvi–xxvii, 2, 9, 20,
	29–31, 35–40, 44, 76, 87, 97–9, 122, 193,
	212, 216, 223, 231, 258, 278–9, 292,
	299–300
equity, 15, 26–7, 37, 46, 48, 79, 129–31, 182,
	187–8, 204–5, 208, 210, 228, 231, 238,
	241–5, 265, 298
Erskine, David Steuart, xxi–xxii, xxiv, xxx
Estates General (France), 272, 285–6
Eve, 97
evil, xxiii, 87, 185–9, 208, 218, 229, 240
Exclusion Crisis, 58–9
executive power, 12, 39, 86, 93, 104, 107, 110,
	118, 122, 249, 286, 293–5

Fabricius Luscinus Monocularis, Gaius, 68,
	231
faction, 9, 13, 26, 37, 42, 44, 48–9, 51, 54–6,
	67, 77, 84, 109, 116–20, 122, 170–1, 251,
	276, 282, 286
Fairfax, Thomas, 29, 38, 40
fame, 7–10, 49, 64–5, 130–4, 139, 142, 274,
	284, 288
fanaticism, xxii, 45–6, 177, 220, 252, 261, 297
Farinelli, 139

Fénelon, François, 176, 195–6, 200, 217
Ferguson, Adam, 176
feudalism, 14, 41, 266, 269
Fifth Monarchists, 265
Filmer, Robert, 35, 59, 96, 98
financial revolution, xxxix–xl, 80, 164–72, 271,
	287–9
fitness, 124–45, 130–1, 206, 208
Forbes, Duncan, xl
Fox, John 'Tinker', 21
France, xvi, xix, xxi, xxix–xxxi, xxxiv, 2, 12,
	19, 23, 27, 52, 64, 66–7, 71–5, 80, 86, 99,
	146, 153, 156, 158, 161, 171–2, 250,
	257–9, 263–76
franchise, 38, 77, 79, 82, 87–8, 111, 291–2
Franklin, Benjamin, xxx
Frazer, Elizabeth, xxxvii
free trade, xxvii, 164
freedom. *See* liberty
French Revolution, xi–xii, xvii, xx, xxx–xxxii,
	87–8, 251–300

Gattey, François-Charles, xxxii
Gaul, 230, 232
Geneva, xxvii
Genlis, Caroline-Stéphanie-Félicité, Madame
	de, 196
Genoa, 86
gentry, xiii, 27, 29, 155, 168, 224, 249
George I, 119, 172, 174
George II, 119
George III, xviii, 3, 49, 110, 119, 156, 244
Germany, 81, 172, 249
Gibbon, Edward, 176, 234–5, 237
Gilby, Anthony, 34
Girondins, xx
Glorious Revolution, xxxi–xxxii, 1, 3, 13, 50,
	55, 71–84, 110, 117–19, 131, 162–72,
	251–2, 259–61
glory, xviii, 17, 31, 40, 43, 45, 53, 62–3, 65, 82,
	105–8, 132–4, 137, 159–61, 192–3,
	230–3, 239–41, 266, 274, 294–5
God, xxiii, xxv–xxvi, xxxii, 7, 9, 20–2, 24,
	31–5, 46, 61–3, 70, 91–2, 96–8, 117, 135,
	155, 175–6, 182–3, 185–9, 205–8, 213,
	228, 232, 249, 264, 292
Godwin, William, 176
Goldsmith, Oliver, 246
Goode, Henry, 22

304

CAMBRIDGE TEXTS IN THE HISTORY OF POLITICAL THOUGHT

Titles published in the series thus far

Aquinas *Political Writings* (edited and translated by R. W. Dyson)
Aristotle *The Politics and The Constitution of Athens* (edited and translated by Stephen Everson)
Arnold *Culture and Anarchy and Other Writings* (edited by Stefan Collini)
Astell *Political Writings* (edited by Patricia Springborg)
Augustine *The City of God against the Pagans* (edited and translated by R. W. Dyson)
Augustine *Political Writings* (edited by E. M. Atkins and R. J. Dodaro)
Austin *The Province of Jurisprudence Determined* (edited by Wilfrid E. Rumble)
Bacon *The History of the Reign of King Henry VII* (edited by Brian Vickers)
Bagehot *The English Constitution* (edited by Paul Smith)
Bakunin *Statism and Anarchy* (edited and translated by Marshall Shatz)
Baxter *Holy Commonwealth* (edited by William Lamont)
Bayle *Political Writings* (edited by Sally L. Jenkinson)
Beccaria *On Crimes and Punishments and Other Writings* (edited by Richard Bellamy; translated by Richard Davies)
Bentham *A Fragment on Government* (edited by Ross Harrison)
Bernstein *The Preconditions of Socialism* (edited and translated by Henry Tudor)
Bodin *On Sovereignty* (edited and translated by Julian H. Franklin)
Bolingbroke *Political Writings* (edited by David Armitage)
Bossuet *Politics Drawn from the Very Words of Holy Scripture* (edited and translated by Patrick Riley)
Botero *The Reason of State* (edited and translated by Robert Bireley)
The British Idealists (edited by David Boucher)
Burke *Pre-Revolutionary Writings* (edited by Ian Harris)
Burke *Revolutionary Writings* (edited by Iain Hampsher-Monk)
Cavendish *Political Writings* (edited by Susan James)
Christine de Pizan *The Book of the Body Politic* (edited by Kate Langdon Forhan)
Cicero *On Duties* (edited by E. M. Atkins; edited and translated by M. T. Griffin)
Cicero *On the Commonwealth and On the Laws* (edited and translated by James E. G. Zetzel)
Comte *Early Political Writings* (edited and translated by H. S. Jones)
Comte *Conciliarism and Papalism* (edited by J. H. Burns and Thomas M. Izbicki)
Condorcet *Political Writings* (edited by Steven Lukes and Nadia Urbinati)
Constant *Political Writings* (edited and translated by Biancamaria Fontana)
Dante *Monarchy* (edited and translated by Prue Shaw)
Albert Venn Dicey *Writings on Democracy and the Referendum* (edited by Gregory Conti)
The Dutch Revolt (edited and translated by Martin van Gelderen)

For EU product safety concerns, contact us at Calle de José Abascal, 56–1°,
28003 Madrid, Spain or eugpsr@cambridge.org.

www.ingramcontent.com/pod-product-compliance
Ingram Content Group UK Ltd.
Pitfield, Milton Keynes, MK11 3LW, UK
UKHW020350140625

459647UK00020B/2375